Foundations of Python Network Programming

Third Edition

Brandon Rhodes

John Goerzen

Apress®

Foundations of Python Network Programming, Third Edition

ISBN-13 (pbk): 978-1-4302-5854-4

ISBN-13 (electronic): 978-1-4302-5855-1

Managing Director: Welmoed Spahr
Lead Editor: Michelle Lowman
Technical Reviewers: Alexandre Beaulne and Peter Membrey
Editorial Board: Steve Anglin, Mark Beckner, Ewan Buckingham, Gary Cornell, Louise Corrigan, Jim DeWolf, Jonathan Gennick, Robert Hutchinson, Michelle Lowman, James Markham, Matthew Moodie, Jeff Olson, Jeffrey Pepper, Douglas Pundick, Ben Renow-Clarke, Dominic Shakeshaft, Gwenan Spearing, Matt Wade, Steve Weiss
Coordinating Editor: Kevin Walter
Developmental Editor: Gary Schwartz
Copy Editor: Kim Wimpsett
Compositor: SPi Global
Indexer: SPi Global
Artist: SPi Global
Cover Designer: Anna Ishchenko

Distributed to the book trade worldwide by Springer Science+Business Media New York, 233 Spring Street, 6th Floor, New York, NY 10013. Phone 1-800-SPRINGER, fax (201) 348-4505, e-mail orders-ny@springer-sbm.com, or visit www.springeronline.com. Apress Media, LLC is a California LLC and the sole member (owner) is Springer Science + Business Media Finance Inc (SSBM Finance Inc). SSBM Finance Inc is a Delaware corporation.

For information on translations, please e-mail rights@apress.com, or visit www.apress.com.

Apress and friends of ED books may be purchased in bulk for academic, corporate, or promotional use. eBook versions and licenses are also available for most titles. For more information, reference our Special Bulk Sales–eBook Licensing web page at www.apress.com/bulk-sales.

Any source code or other supplementary material referenced by the author in this text is available to readers at www.apress.com. For detailed information about how to locate your book's source code, go to www.apress.com/source-code/.

*To my wonderful nieces, Avery, Savannah, and Aila,
remembering our bicycle ride and the wild abandon with
which they always round the corner and plunge downhill.*

*I hope that they always approach life with such fearlessness,
whether they wind up doing any network programming or not.*

Contents at a Glance

Contents

About the Authors

Brandon Rhodes is a consulting programmer who also teaches the Python language professionally for organizations that are adding the language to their tool set. He has spoken at PyOhio; at PyGotham; at national PyCon conferences in Canada, Ireland, and Poland; and at Django conferences in Portland, Wales, and Warsaw, where he was delighted at the creativity of the organizers, who rented a circus tent for the occasion. He will chair the flagship PyCon North America conference in Portland in 2016–2017. Brandon is interested in how ideas like the Clean Architecture can help programmers organize code more effectively and in what we can learn from writers in other fields about offering kind and actionable critiques of each other's work. He currently lives in tiny Bluffton, Ohio, with his wife Jackie and their two cats.

John Goerzen is an accomplished author, system administrator, and Python programmer. He has been a Debian developer since 1996 and is currently president of Software in the Public Interest, Inc. His previously published books include the Linux Programming Bible, Debian Unleashed, and Linux Unleashed.

About the Technical Reviewers

Originally from Canada's great north, **Alexandre Beaulne** pursued a bachelor's degree in systems neuroscience at McGill University in Montreal, followed by a master's degree in financial engineering at HEC Montreal. His studies, however, culminated in his attendance at Hacker School in New York City. He has repeatedly made the unsupported claim that he "gets" Haskell's monads.

Peter Membrey is a Chartered IT Fellow with over 15 years of experience using Linux and Open Source solutions to solve problems in the real world. An RHCE since the age of 17, he has also had the honour of working for Red Hat and writing several books covering open source solutions. He holds a Masters degree in IT (Information Security) from the University of Liverpool, and he is currently a PhD candidate at the Hong Kong Polytechnic University, where his research interests include cloud computing, big data science, and security. He lives in Hong Kong with his wonderful wife Sarah and their son Kaydyn. His Cantonese continues to regress, though his Esperanto is coming along nicely.

Acknowledgments

Five years ago, as I was revising and rewriting to prepare a second edition of this book, I was deeply impressed by how much had changed in the half-decade since its debut in 2004. New web frameworks like CherryPy and Django were creating a revolution in how programmers wrote for the Web, while libraries such as mechanize and lxml were making it easier than ever to fetch information from HTTP servers.

As I wrap up this third edition, it is clear that the Python community has done it again! Improvements large and small have required changes to the text and, in some cases, a complete rewrite of entire chapters. From the core developers who produced the new Python 3 version of the language, to the authors of new web frameworks such as Flask and Tornado who continue to make the task of writing HTTP services both more convenient and much safer, to the programmers who maintain modules both inside and outside of the Standard Library, this new edition is first and foremost a reflection of the hard work that an entire programming language community—really, an entire ecosystem—has poured into the tools and libraries that help us write programs for the Internet.

A number of readers have contacted me since the second edition came out with questions, with ideas, or to point out where a program listing now failed or was no longer valid. I hope they know that their feedback was important to the process of creating this new edition, and I think a few of them will recognize where their ideas have wound up making noticeable improvements to the book.

Many thanks to the editors and reviewers at Apress who read my (at some moments, appalling) first drafts, who caught bugs and outright errors in my program listings, and who helped shepherd this rewrite through to completion. I want to give particular credit to the copy editors, through whom I have slowly learned not to say the word *very* or *actually* in every other sentence and thanks to whom I continue to make progress in my lifelong journey toward being able to tell when to use *that* and when to use *which* when connecting clauses.

Thanks, finally, to everyone who had to wait on an e-mail, bug fix, or meeting as I have been writing, and especially to my wife Jackie for all of her encouragement.

Introduction

It is an exciting moment for the Python community. After two decades of careful innovation that saw the language gain features such as context managers, generators, and comprehensions in a careful balance with its focus on remaining simple in both its syntax and its concepts, Python is finally taking off.

Instead of being seen as a boutique language that can be risked only by top-notch programming shops such as Google and NASA, Python is now experiencing rapid adoption, both in traditional programming roles, such as web application design, and in the vast world of "reluctant programmers," such as scientists, data specialists, and engineers—people who learn to program not for its own sake but because they must write programs if they are to make progress in their field. The benefits that a simple programming language offers for the occasional or nonexpert programmer cannot, I think, be overstated.

Python 3

After its debut in 2008, Python 3 went through a couple of years of reworking and streamlining before it was ready to step into the role of its predecessor. But as it now enters its second half-decade, it has emerged as the preferred platform for innovation in the Python community.

Whether one looks at fundamental improvements, like the fact that true Unicode text is now the default string type in Python 3, or at individual improvements, like correct support for SSL, a built-in `asyncio` framework for asynchronous programming, and tweaks to Standard Library modules large and small, the platform that Python 3 offers the network programmer is in nearly every way improved. This is a significant achievement. Python 2 was already one of the best languages for making programmers quickly and effectively productive on the modern Internet.

This book is not a comprehensive guide to switching from Python 2 to Python 3. It will not tell you how to add parentheses to your old `print` statements, rename Standard Library module imports to their new names, or debug deeply flawed network code that relied on Python 2's dangerous automatic conversion between byte strings and Unicode strings—conversions that were always based on rough guesswork. There are already excellent resources to help you with that transition or even to help you write libraries carefully enough so that their code will work under both Python 2 and Python 3, in case you need to support both audiences.

Instead, this book focuses on network programming, using Python 3 for every example script and snippet of code at the Python prompt. These examples are intended to build a comprehensive picture of how network clients, network servers, and network tools can best be constructed from the tools provided by the language. Readers can study the transition from Python 2 to Python 3 by comparing the scripts used in each chapter of the second edition of this book with the listings here in the third edition—both of which are available at `https://github.com/brandon-rhodes/fopnp/tree/m/` thanks to the excellent Apress policy of making source code available online. The goal in each of the following chapters is simply to show you how Python 3 can best be used to solve modern network programming problems.

By focusing squarely on how to accomplish things the right way with Python 3, this book hopes to prepare both the programmer who is getting ready to write a new application from the ground up and the programmer preparing to transition an old code base to the new conventions. Both programmers should come away knowing what correct networking code looks like in Python 3 and therefore knowing the look and flavor of the kind of code that ought to be their goal.

Improvements in This Edition

There are several improvements by which this book attempts to update the previous edition, beyond the move to Python 3 as its target language and the many updates to both Standard Library and third-party Python modules that have occurred in the past half-decade.

- Every Python program listing is now written as a module. That is, each one performs its imports and defines its functions or classes but then carefully guards any import-time actions inside an `if` statement that fires only if the module `__name__` has the special string value `'__main__'` indicating that the module is being run as the main program. This is a Python best practice that was almost entirely neglected in the previous edition of this book and whose absence made it more difficult for the sample listings to be pulled into real codebases and used to solve reader problems. By putting their executable logic at the left margin instead of inside an `if` statement, the older program listings may have saved a line or two of code, but they gave novice Python programmers far less practice in how to lay out real code.

- Instead of making ad hoc use of the raw `sys.argv` list of strings in a bid to interpret the command line, most of the scripts in this book now use the Standard Library `argparse` module to interpret options and arguments. This not only clarifies and documents the semantics that each script expects during invocation but also lets the user of each script use the `-h` or `--help` query option to receive interactive assistance when launching the script from the Windows or Unix command line.

- Program listings now make an effort to perform proper resource control by opening files within a controlling `with` statement that will close the files automatically when it completes. In the previous edition, most listings relied instead on the fact that the C Python runtime from the main Python web site usually assures that files are closed immediately thanks to its aggressive reference counting.

- The listings, for the most part, have transitioned to the modern `format()` method for performing string interpolation and away from the old modulo operator hack `string % tuple` that made sense in the 1990s, when most programmers knew the C language, but that is less readable today for new programmers entering the field—and less powerful since individual Python classes cannot override percent formatting like they can with the new kind.

- The three chapters on HTTP and the World Wide Web (Chapters 9 through 11) have been rewritten from the ground up with an emphasis on better explaining the protocol and on introducing the most modern tools that Python offers the programmer writing for the Web. Explanations of the HTTP protocol now use the Requests library as their go-to API for performing client operations, and Chapter 11 has examples in both Flask and Django.

- The material on SSL/TLS (Chapter 6) has been completely rewritten to match the vast improvement in support that Python 3 delivers for secure applications. While the `ssl` module in Python 2 is a weak half-measure that does not even verify that the server's certificate matches the hostname to which Python is connecting, the same module in Python 3 presents a much more carefully designed and extensive API that provides generous control over its features.

This edition of the book is therefore a better resource for the learning programmer simply in terms of how the listings and examples are constructed, even apart from the improvements that Python 3 has made over previous versions of the language.

The Network Playground

The source code to the program listings in this book is available online so that both current owners of this book and potential readers can study them. There is a directory for each chapter of this edition of the book. You can find the chapter directories here:

https://github.com/brandon-rhodes/fopnp/tree/m/py3

But program listings can go only so far toward supporting the curious student of network programming. There are many features of network programming that are difficult to explore from a single host machine. Thus, the source code repository for the book provides a sample network of 12 machines, each implemented as a Docker container. A setup script is provided that builds the images, launches them, and networks them. You can find the script and the images in the source code repository here:

https://github.com/brandon-rhodes/fopnp/tree/m/playground

You can see the 12 machines and their interconnections in Figure 1. The network is designed to resemble a tiny version of the Internet.

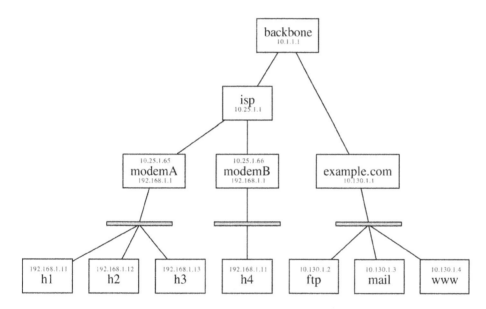

Figure 1. *The network playground's topology*

- Representing the typical situation of a client in a home or coffee shop are the client machines behind modemA and modemB that not only offer no services to the Internet but that are in fact not visible on the wider Internet at all. They possess merely local IP addresses, which are meaningful only on the subnet that they share with any other hosts in the same home or coffee shop. When they make connections to the outside world, those connections will appear to originate from the IP addresses of the modems themselves.

- Direct connections allow the modems to connect to an isp gateway out on the wider Internet, which is represented by a single backbone router that forwards packets between the networks to which it is connected.

- example.com and its associated machines represent the configuration of a simple service-oriented machine room. Here, no network translation or masquerading is taking place. The three servers behind example.com have service ports that are fully exposed to client traffic from the Internet.

- Each of the service machines ftp, mail, and www has correctly configured daemons up and running so that Python scripts from this book can be run on the other machines in the playground to connect successfully to representative examples of each service.

- All of the service machines have correctly installed TLS certificates (see Chapter 6), and the client machines all have the example.com signing certificate installed as a trusted certificate. This means Python scripts demanding true TLS authentication will be able to achieve it.

The network playground will continue to be maintained as both Python and Docker continue to evolve. Instructions will be maintained in the repository for how to download and run the network locally on your own machine, and they will be tweaked based on user reports to make sure that a virtual machine, which offers the playground, can be run by readers on Linux, Mac OS X, and Windows machines.

With the ability to connect and run commands within any of the playground machines, you will be able to set up packet tracing at whichever point on the network you want to see traffic passing between clients and servers. The example code demonstrated in its documentation, combined with the examples and instruction in this book, should help you reach a solid and vivid understanding of how networks help clients and servers communicate.

CHAPTER 1

Introduction to Client-Server Networking

This book explores network programming in the Python language. It covers the basic concepts, modules, and third-party libraries that you are likely to use when communicating with remote machines using the most popular Internet communication protocols.

The book lacks the space to teach you how to program in Python if you have never seen the language before or if you have never even written a computer program at all; it presumes that you have already learned something about Python programming from the many excellent tutorials and books on the subject. I hope that the Python examples in the book give you ideas about how to structure and write your own code. But I will be using all sorts of advanced Python features without explanation or apology—though, occasionally, I might point out how I am using a particular technique or construction when I think it is particularly interesting or clever.

On the other hand, this book does *not* start by assuming you know any networking! As long as you have ever used a web browser or sent an e-mail, you should know enough to start reading this book at the beginning and learn about computer networking along the way. I will approach networking from the point of view of an application programmer who is either implementing a network-connected service—such as a web site, an e-mail server, or a networked computer game—or writing a client program that is designed to use such a service.

Note that you will not, however, learn how to set up or configure networks from this book. The disciplines of network design, server room management, and automated provisioning are full topics all on their own, which tend not to overlap with the discipline of computer programming as covered in this particular book. While Python is indeed becoming a big part of the provisioning landscape thanks to projects such as OpenStack, SaltStack, and Ansible, you will want to search for books and documentation that are specifically about provisioning and its many technologies if you want to learn more about them.

The Building Blocks: Stacks and Libraries

As you begin to explore Python network programming, there are two concepts that will appear over and over again.

- The idea of a *protocol stack*, in which simpler network services are used as the foundation on which to build more sophisticated services.

- The fact that you will often be using Python *libraries* of previously written code—whether modules from the built-in standard library that ships with Python or packages from third-party distributions that you download and install—that already know how to speak the network protocol that you want to use.

In many cases, network programming simply involves selecting and using a library that already supports the network operations that you need to perform. The major purposes of this book are to introduce you to several key networking libraries available for Python while also teaching you about the lower-level network services on which those libraries are built. Knowing the lower-level material is useful, both so that you understand how the libraries work and so that you will understand what is happening when something at a lower level goes wrong.

Let's begin with a simple example. Here is a mailing address:

```
207 N. Defiance St
Archbold, OH
```

I am interested in knowing the latitude and longitude of this physical address. It just so happens that Google provides a Geocoding API that can perform such a conversion. What would you have to do to take advantage of this network service from Python?

When looking at a new network service that you want to use, it is always worthwhile to start by finding out whether someone has already implemented the protocol—in this case, the Google Geocoding protocol—which your program will need to speak. Start by scrolling through the Python Standard Library documentation, looking for anything having to do with geocoding.

```
http://docs.python.org/3/library/
```

Do you see anything about geocoding? No, neither do I. But it is important for a Python programmer to look through the Standard Library's table of contents pretty frequently, even if you usually do not find what you are looking for, because each read-through will make you more familiar with the services that are included with Python. Doug Hellmann's "Python Module of the Week" blog is another great reference from which you can learn about the capabilities that come with Python thanks to its Standard Library.

Since in this case the Standard Library does not have a package to help, you can turn to the Python Package Index, an excellent resource for finding all sorts of general-purpose Python packages contributed by other programmers and organizations from across the world. You can also, of course, check the web site of the vendor whose service you will be using to see whether it provides a Python library to access it. Or, you can do a general Google search for *Python* plus the name of whatever web service you want to use and see whether any of the first few results link to a package that you might want to try.

In this case, I searched the Python Package Index, which lives at this URL:

```
https://pypi.python.org/
```

There I entered *geocoding*, and I immediately found a package that is named pygeocoder, which provides a clean interface to Google's geocoding features (though, you will note from its description, it is *not* vendor-provided but was instead written by someone besides Google).

```
http://pypi.python.org/pypi/pygeocoder/
```

This is such a common situation—finding a Python package that sounds like it might already do exactly what you want and that you want to try it on your system—that I should pause for a moment and introduce you to the best Python technology for quickly trying a new library: virtualenv!

In the old days, installing a Python package was a gruesome and irreversible act that required administrative privileges on your machine and that left your system Python install permanently altered. After several months of heavy Python development, your system Python install could become a wasteland of dozens of packages, all installed by hand, and you could even find that new packages you tried to install would break because they were incompatible with the old packages sitting on your hard drive from a project that ended months ago.

Careful Python programmers do not suffer from this situation any longer. Many of us install only one Python package systemwide—ever—and that is `virtualenv`! Once `virtualenv` is installed, you have the power to create any number of small, self-contained "virtual Python environments" where packages can be installed and un-installed and with which you can experiment, all without contaminating your systemwide Python. When a particular project or experiment is over, you simply remove its virtual environment directory, and your system is clean.

In this case, you want to create a virtual environment in which to test the pygeocoder package. If you have never installed `virtualenv` on your system before, visit this URL to download and install it:

```
http://pypi.python.org/pypi/virtualenv
```

Once you have `virtualenv` installed, you can create a new environment using the following commands. (On Windows, the directory containing the Python binary in the virtual environment will be named `Scripts` instead of `bin`.)

```
$ virtualenv -p python3 geo_env
$ cd geo_env
$ ls
bin/  include/  lib/
$ . bin/activate
$ python -c 'import pygeocoder'
Traceback (most recent call last):
  File "<string>", line 1, in <module>
ImportError: No module named 'pygeocoder'
```

As you can see, the pygeocoder package is not yet available. To install it, use the `pip` command that is inside your virtual environment that is now on your path thanks to your having run the `activate` command.

```
$ pip install pygeocoder
Downloading/unpacking pygeocoder
  Downloading pygeocoder-1.2.1.1.tar.gz
  Running setup.py egg_info for package pygeocoder

Downloading/unpacking requests>=1.0 (from pygeocoder)
  Downloading requests-2.0.1.tar.gz (412kB): 412kB downloaded
  Running setup.py egg_info for package requests

Installing collected packages: pygeocoder, requests
  Running setup.py install for pygeocoder

  Running setup.py install for requests

Successfully installed pygeocoder requests
Cleaning up...
```

The python binary inside the `virtualenv` will now have the pygeocoder package available.

```
$ python -c 'import pygeocoder'
```

Now that you have the pygeocoder package installed, you should be able to run the simple program named `search1.py`, as shown in Listing 1-1.

Listing 1-1. Fetching a Longitude and Latitude

```
#!/usr/bin/env python3
# Foundations of Python Network Programming, Third Edition
# https://github.com/brandon-rhodes/fopnp/blob/m/py3/chapter01/search1.py

from pygeocoder import Geocoder

if __name__ == '__main__':
    address = '207 N. Defiance St, Archbold, OH'
    print(Geocoder.geocode(address)[0].coordinates)
```

By running it at the command line, you should see a result like this:

```
$ python3 search1.py
(41.521954, -84.306691)
```

And there, right on your computer screen is the answer to our question about the address's latitude and longitude! The answer has been pulled directly from Google's web service. The first example program is a rousing success.

Are you annoyed to have opened a book on Python network programming only to have found yourself immediately directed to download and install a third-party package that turned what might have been an interesting networking problem into a boring three-line Python script? Be at peace! Ninety percent of the time, you will find that this is exactly how programming challenges are solved—by finding other programmers in the Python community who have already tackled the problem you are facing and then building intelligently and briefly upon their solutions.

You are not yet done exploring this example, however. You have seen that a complex network service can often be accessed quite trivially. But what is behind the pretty pygeocoder interface? How does the service actually work? You will now explore, in detail, how this sophisticated service is actually just the top layer of a network stack that involves at least a half-dozen different levels.

Application Layers

The first program listing used a third-party Python library, downloaded from the Python Package Index, to solve a problem. It knew all about the Google Geocoding API and the rules for using it. But what if that library had not already existed? What if you had to build a client for Google's Maps API on your own?

For the answer, take a look at search2.py, as shown in Listing 1-2. Instead of using a geocoding-aware third-party library, it drops down one level and uses the popular requests library that lies behind pygeocoding and that, as you can see from the pip install command earlier, has also been installed in your virtual environment.

Listing 1-2. Fetching a JSON Document from the Google Geocoding API

```
#!/usr/bin/env python3
# Foundations of Python Network Programming, Third Edition
# https://github.com/brandon-rhodes/fopnp/blob/m/py3/chapter01/search2.py

import requests

def geocode(address):
    parameters = {'address': address, 'sensor': 'false'}
    base = 'http://maps.googleapis.com/maps/api/geocode/json'
    response = requests.get(base, params=parameters)
```

```
    answer = response.json()
    print(answer['results'][0]['geometry']['location'])

if __name__ == '__main__':
    geocode('207 N. Defiance St, Archbold, OH')
```

Running this Python program returns an answer quite similar to that of the first script.

```
$ python3 search2.py
{'lat': 41.521954, 'lng': -84.306691}
```

The output is not *exactly* the same—you can see, for example, that the JSON data encoded the result as an "object" that requests has handed to you as a Python dictionary. But it is clear that this script has accomplished much the same thing as the first one.

The first thing that you will notice about this code is that the semantics offered by the higher-level pygeocoder module are absent. Unless you look closely at this code, you might not even see that it's asking about a mailing address at all! Whereas search1.py asked directly for an address to be turned into a latitude and longitude, the second listing painstakingly builds both a base URL and a set of query parameters whose purpose might not even be clear to you unless you have already read the Google documentation. If you want to read the documentation, by the way, you can find the API described here:

```
http://code.google.com/apis/maps/documentation/geocoding/
```

If you look closely at the dictionary of query parameters in search2.py, you will see that the address parameter provides the particular mailing address about which you are asking. The other parameter informs Google that you are not issuing this location query because of data pulled live from a mobile device location sensor.

When you receive a document back as a result of looking up this URL, you manually call the response.json() method to interpret it as JSON and then dive into the multilayered resulting data structure to find the correct element inside that holds the latitude and longitude.

The search2.py script then does the same thing as search1.py—but instead of doing so in the language of addresses and latitudes, it talks about the gritty details of constructing a URL, fetching a response, and parsing it as JSON. This is a common difference when you step down a level from one layer of a network stack to the layer beneath it: whereas the high-level code talked about what a request *meant*, the lower-level code can see only the details of how the request is *constructed*.

Speaking a Protocol

So, the second example script creates a URL and fetches the document that corresponds to it. That operation sounds quite simple, and, of course, your web browser works hard to make it look quite elementary. But the real reason that a URL can be used to fetch a document, of course, is that the URL is a kind of recipe that describes where to find—and how to fetch—a given document on the Web. The URL consists of the name of a protocol, followed by the name of the machine where the document lives, and finishes with the path that names a particular document on that machine. The reason then that the search2.py Python program is able to resolve the URL and fetch the document at all is that the URL provides instructions that tell a lower-level protocol how to find the document.

The lower-level protocol that the URL uses, in fact, is the famous Hypertext Transfer Protocol (HTTP), which is the basis of nearly all modern web communications. You will learn more about it in Chapters 9, 10, and 11 of this book. It is HTTP that provides the mechanism by which the Requests library is able to fetch the result from Google. What do you think it would look like if you were to strip that layer of magic off—what if you wanted to use HTTP to fetch the result directly? The result is search3.py, as shown in Listing 1-3.

Listing 1-3. Making a Raw HTTP Connection to Google Maps

```
#!/usr/bin/env python3
# Foundations of Python Network Programming, Third Edition
# https://github.com/brandon-rhodes/fopnp/blob/m/py3/chapter01/search3.py

import http.client
import json
from urllib.parse import quote_plus

base = '/maps/api/geocode/json'

def geocode(address):
    path = '{}?address={}&sensor=false'.format(base, quote_plus(address))
    connection = http.client.HTTPConnection('maps.google.com')
    connection.request('GET', path)
    rawreply = connection.getresponse().read()
    reply = json.loads(rawreply.decode('utf-8'))
    print(reply['results'][0]['geometry']['location'])

if __name__ == '__main__':
    geocode('207 N. Defiance St, Archbold, OH')
```

In this listing, you are directly manipulating the HTTP protocol: asking it to connect to a specific machine, to issue a GET request with a path that you have constructed by hand, and finally to read the reply directly from the HTTP connection. Instead of being able conveniently to provide your query parameters as separate keys and values in a dictionary, you are having to embed them directly, by hand, in the path that you are requesting by first writing a question mark (?) followed by the parameters in the format name=value separated by & characters.

The result of running the program, however, is much the same as for the programs shown previously.

```
$ python3 search3.py
{'lat': 41.521954, 'lng': -84.306691}
```

As you will see throughout this book, HTTP is just one of many protocols for which the Python Standard Library provides a built-in implementation. In search3.py, instead of having to worry about all of the details of how HTTP works, your code can simply ask for a request to be sent and then take a look at the resulting response. The protocol details that the script has to deal with are, of course, more primitive than those of search2.py, because you have stepped down another level in the protocol stack, but at least you are still able to rely on the Standard Library to handle the actual network data and make sure that you get it right.

A Raw Network Conversation

HTTP cannot simply send data between two machines using thin air, of course. Instead, the HTTP protocol must operate by using some even simpler abstraction. In fact, it uses the capacity of modern operating systems to support a plain-text network conversation between two different programs across an IP network by using the TCP protocol. The HTTP protocol, in other words, operates by dictating *exactly* what the text of the messages will look like that pass back and forth between two hosts that can speak TCP.

When you move beneath HTTP to look at what happens below it, you are dropping down to the lowest level of the network stack that you can still access easily from Python. Take a careful look at search4.py, as shown in Listing 1-4. It makes exactly the same networking request to Google Maps as the previous three programs, but it does so by sending a raw text message across the Internet and receiving a bundle of text in return.

Listing 1-4. Talking to Google Maps Through a Bare Socket

```python
#!/usr/bin/env python3
# Foundations of Python Network Programming, Third Edition
# https://github.com/brandon-rhodes/fopnp/blob/m/py3/chapter01/search4.py

import socket
from urllib.parse import quote_plus

request_text = """\
GET /maps/api/geocode/json?address={}&sensor=false HTTP/1.1\r\n\
Host: maps.google.com:80\r\n\
User-Agent: search4.py (Foundations of Python Network Programming)\r\n\
Connection: close\r\n\
\r\n\
"""

def geocode(address):
    sock = socket.socket()
    sock.connect(('maps.google.com', 80))
    request = request_text.format(quote_plus(address))
    sock.sendall(request.encode('ascii'))
    raw_reply = b''
    while True:
        more = sock.recv(4096)
        if not more:
            break
        raw_reply += more
    print(raw_reply.decode('utf-8'))

if __name__ == '__main__':
    geocode('207 N. Defiance St, Archbold, OH')
```

In moving from search3.py to search4.py, you have passed an important threshold. In every previous program listing, you were using a Python library—written in Python itself—that knew how to speak a complicated network protocol on your behalf. But here you have reached the bottom: you are calling the raw socket() function that is provided by the host operating system to support basic network communications on an IP network. You are, in other words, using the same mechanisms that a low-level system programmer would use in the C language when writing this same network operation.

You will learn more about sockets over the next few chapters. For now, you can notice in search4.py that raw network communication is a matter of sending and receiving *byte strings*. The request that you send is one byte string, and the reply—that, in this case, you simply print to the screen so that you can experience it in all of its low-level glory—is another large byte string. (See the section "Encoding and Decoding," later in this chapter for the details of why you decode the string before printing it.) The HTTP request, whose text you can see inside the sendall() function, consists of the word *GET*—the name of the operation you want performed—followed by the path of the document you want fetched and the version of HTTP you support.

```
GET /maps/api/geocode/json?address=207+N.+Defiance+St%2C+Archbold%2C+OH&sensor=false HTTP/1.1
```

Then there are a series of headers that each consist of a name, a colon, and a value, and finally a carriage-return/newline pair that ends the request.

The reply, which will print as the script's output if you run search4.py, is shown as Listing 1-5. I chose simply to print the reply to the screen in this example, rather than write the complex text-manipulation code that would be able to interpret the response. I did so because I thought that simply reading the HTTP reply on your screen would give you a much better idea of what it looks like than if you had to decipher code designed to interpret it.

Listing 1-5. The Output of Running search4.py

```
HTTP/1.1 200 OK
Content-Type: application/json; charset=UTF-8
Date: Sat, 23 Nov 2013 18:34:30 GMT
Expires: Sun, 24 Nov 2013 18:34:30 GMT
Cache-Control: public, max-age=86400
Vary: Accept-Language
Access-Control-Allow-Origin: *
Server: mafe
X-XSS-Protection: 1; mode=block
X-Frame-Options: SAMEORIGIN
Alternate-Protocol: 80:quic
Connection: close

{
   "results" : [
      {
         ...
         "formatted_address" : "207 North Defiance Street, Archbold, OH 43502, USA",
         "geometry" : {
            "location" : {
               "lat" : 41.521954,
               "lng" : -84.306691
            },
            ...
         },
         "types" : [ "street_address" ]
      }
   ],
   "status" : "OK"
}
```

You can see that the HTTP reply is quite similar in structure to the HTTP request. It begins with a status line, which is followed by a number of headers. After a blank line, the response content itself is shown: a JavaScript data structure, in a simple format known as JSON, that answers your query by describing the geographic location that the Google Geocoding API search has returned.

All of these status lines and headers, of course, are exactly the sort of low-level details that Python's httplib was taking care of in the earlier listings. Here, you see what the communication looks like if that layer of software is stripped away.

Turtles All the Way Down

I hope you have enjoyed these initial examples of what Python network programming can look like. Stepping back, I can use this series of examples to make several points about network programming in Python.

First, you can perhaps now see more clearly what is meant by the term *protocol stack*: it means building a high-level, semantically sophisticated conversation ("I want the geographic location of this mailing address") on top of simpler, and more rudimentary, conversations that ultimately are just text strings sent back and forth between two computers using their network hardware.

The particular protocol stack that you have just explored is four protocols high.

- On top is the Google Geocoding API, which tells you how to express your geographic queries as URLs that fetch JSON data containing coordinates.

- URLs name documents that can be retrieved using HTTP.

- HTTP supports document-oriented commands such as GET using raw TCP/IP sockets.

- TCP/IP sockets know only how to send and receive byte strings.

Each layer of the stack, you see, uses the tools provided by the layer beneath it and in turn offers capabilities to the next higher layer.

A second point made clear through these examples is how very complete the Python support is for every one of the network levels at which you have just operated. Only when using a vendor-specific protocol, and needing to format requests so that Google would understand them, was it necessary to resort to using a third-party library; I chose requests for the second listing not because the Standard Library lacks the urllib.request module but because its API is overly clunky. Every single one of the other protocol levels you encountered already had strong support inside the Python Standard Library. Whether you wanted to fetch the document at a particular URL or send and receive strings on a raw network socket, Python was ready with functions and classes that you could use to get the job done.

Third, note that my programs decreased considerably in quality as I forced myself to use increasingly lower-level protocols. The search2.py and search3.py listings, for example, started to hard-code things such as the form structure and hostnames in a way that is inflexible and that might be hard to maintain later. The code in search4.py is even worse: it includes a handwritten, unparameterized HTTP request whose structure is completely opaque to Python. And, of course, it contains none of the actual logic that would be necessary to parse and interpret the HTTP response and understand any network error conditions that might occur.

This illustrates a lesson that you should remember throughout every subsequent chapter of this book: that implementing network protocols correctly is difficult and that you should use the Standard Library or third-party libraries whenever possible. Especially when you are writing a network client, you will always be tempted to oversimplify your code; you will tend to ignore many error conditions that might arise, to prepare for only the most likely responses, to avoid properly escaping parameters because you fondly believe that your query strings will only ever include simple alphabetic characters, and, in general, to write very brittle code that knows as little about the service it is talking to as is technically possible. By instead using a third-party library that has developed a thorough implementation of a protocol, which has had to support many different Python developers who are using the library for a variety of tasks, you will benefit from all of the edge cases and awkward corners that the library implementer has already discovered and learned how to handle properly.

Fourth, it needs to be emphasized that higher-level network protocols—such as the Google Geocoding API for resolving a street address—generally work by *hiding* the network layers beneath them. If you only ever used the pygeocoder library, you might not even be aware that URLs and HTTP are the lower-level mechanisms that are being used to construct and answer your queries!

An interesting question, whose answer varies depending on how carefully a Python library has been written, is whether the library correctly hides errors at those lower levels. Could a network error that makes Google temporarily unreachable from your location raise a raw, low-level networking exception in the middle of code that's just trying to find the coordinates of a street address? Or will all errors be changed into a higher-level exception specific to geocoding? Pay careful attention to the topic of catching network errors as you go forward throughout this book, especially in the chapters of this first part with their emphasis on low-level networking.

Finally, we have reached the topic that will occupy you for the rest of this first part of the book: the socket() interface used in search4.py is *not*, in fact, the lowest protocol level in play when you make this request to Google! Just as the example has network protocols operating above the level above raw sockets, so also there are protocols down *beneath* the sockets abstraction that Python cannot see because your operating system manages them instead.

The layers operating below the socket() API are the following:

- The Transmission Control Protocol (TCP) supports two-way conversations made of streams of bytes by sending (or perhaps re-sending), receiving, and re-ordering small network messages called *packets*.

- The Internet Protocol (IP) knows how to send packets between different computers.

- The "link layer," at the very bottom, consists of network hardware devices such as Ethernet ports and wireless cards, which can send physical messages between directly linked computers.

Throughout the rest of this chapter, and in the two chapters that follow, you will explore these lowest protocol levels. You will start in this chapter by examining the IP level and then proceed in the following chapters to see how two quite different protocols—UDP and TCP—support the two basic kinds of conversation that are possible between applications on a pair of Internet-connected hosts.

But first, a few words about bytes and characters.

Encoding and Decoding

The Python 3 language makes a strong distinction between strings of characters and low-level sequences of bytes. *Bytes* are the actual binary numbers that computers transmit back and forth during network communication, each consisting of eight binary digits and ranging from the binary value 00000000 to 11111111 and thus from the decimal integer 0 to 255. Strings of *characters* in Python can contain Unicode symbols like *a* ("Latin small letter A," the Unicode standard calls it) or } ("right curly bracket") or ∅ (empty set). While each Unicode character does indeed each have a numeric identifier associated with it, called its *code point*, you can treat this as an internal implementation detail— Python 3 is careful to make characters always behave like characters, and only when you ask will Python convert the characters to and from actual externally visible bytes.

These two operations have formal names.

Decoding is what happens when bytes are on their way *into* your application and you need to figure out what they mean. Think of your application, as it receives bytes from a file or across the network, as a classic Cold War spy whose task is to decipher the transmission of raw bytes arriving from across a communications channel.

Encoding is the process of taking character strings that you are ready to present to the outside world and turning them into bytes using one of the many encodings that digital computers use when they need to transmit or store symbols using the bytes that are their only real currency. Think of your spy as having to turn their message back into numbers for transmission, as turning the symbols into a code that can be sent across the network.

These two operations are exposed quite simply and obviously in Python 3 as a decode() method that you can apply to byte strings after reading them in and as an encode() method that you can call on character strings when you are ready to write them back out. The techniques are illustrated in Listing 1-6.

Listing 1-6. Decoding Input Bytes and Encoding Characters for Output

```
#!/usr/bin/env python3
# Foundations of Python Network Programming, Third Edition
# https://github.com/brandon-rhodes/fopnp/blob/m/py3/chapter01/stringcodes.py

if __name__ == '__main__':
    # Translating from the outside world of bytes to Unicode characters.
    input_bytes = b'\xff\xfe4\x001\x003\x00 \x00i\x00s\x00 \x00i\x00n\x00.\x00'
```

```
input_characters = input_bytes.decode('utf-16')
print(repr(input_characters))

# Translating characters back into bytes before sending them.
output_characters = 'We copy you down, Eagle.\n'
output_bytes = output_characters.encode('utf-8')
with open('eagle.txt', 'wb') as f:
    f.write(output_bytes)
```

The examples in this book attempt to differentiate carefully between bytes and characters. Note that the two have different appearances when you display their repr(): byte strings start with the letter *b* and look like b'Hello', while real full-fledged character strings take no initial character and simply look like 'world'. To try to discourage confusion between byte strings and character strings, Python 3 offers most string methods only on the character string type.

The Internet Protocol

Both *networking*, which occurs when you connect several computers with a physical link so that they can communicate, and *internetworking*, which links adjacent physical networks to form a much larger system like the Internet, are essentially just elaborate schemes to allow resource sharing.

All sorts of things in a computer, of course, need to be shared: disk drives, memory, and the CPU are all carefully guarded by the operating system so that the individual programs running on your computer can access those resources without stepping on each other's toes. The network is yet another resource that the operating system needs to protect so that programs can communicate with one another without interfering with other conversations that happen to be occurring on the same network.

The physical networking devices that your computer uses to communicate—like Ethernet cards, wireless transmitters, and USB ports—are themselves each designed with an elaborate ability to share a single physical medium among many different devices that want to communicate. A dozen Ethernet cards might be plugged into the same hub; 30 wireless cards might be sharing the same radio channel; and a DSL modem uses frequency-domain multiplexing, a fundamental concept in electrical engineering, to keep its own digital signals from interfering with the analog signals sent down the line when you talk on the telephone.

The fundamental unit of sharing among network devices—the currency, if you will, in which they trade—is the packet. A *packet* is a byte string whose length might range from a few bytes to a few thousand bytes, which is transmitted as a single unit between network devices. Although specialized networks do exist, especially in realms such as telecommunications, where each individual byte coming down a transmission line might be separately routed to a different destination, the more general-purpose technologies used to build digital networks for modern computers are all based on the larger unit of the packet.

A packet often has only two properties at the physical level: the byte-string data it carries and an address to which it is to be delivered. The address of a physical packet is usually a unique identifier that names one of the other network cards attached to the same Ethernet segment or wireless channel as the computer transmitting the packet. The job of a network card is to send and receive such packets without making the computer's operating system care about the details of how the network uses wires, voltages, and signals to operate.

What, then, is the Internet Protocol?

The *Internet Protocol* is a scheme for imposing a uniform system of addresses on all of the Internet-connected computers in the entire world and to make it possible for packets to travel from one end of the Internet to the other. Ideally, an application like your web browser should be able to connect to a host anywhere without ever knowing which maze of network devices each packet is traversing on its journey.

It is rare for a Python program to operate at such a low level that it sees the Internet Protocol itself in action, but it is helpful, at least, to know how it works.

IP Addresses

The original version of the Internet Protocol assigns a 4-byte address to every computer connected to the worldwide network. Such addresses are usually written as four decimal numbers, separated by periods, which each represent a single byte of the address. Each number can therefore range from 0 to 255. So, a traditional four-byte IP address looks like this:

130.207.244.244

Because purely numeric addresses can be difficult for humans to remember, the people using the Internet are generally shown *hostnames* rather than IP addresses. The user can simply type google.com and forget that behind the scene this resolves to an address like 74.125.67.103, to which their computer can actually address packets for transmission over the Internet.

In the getname.py script, shown in Listing 1-7, you can see a simple Python program that asks the operating system—Linux, Mac OS, Windows, or on whatever system the program is running—to resolve the hostname www.python.org. The particular network service, called the Domain Name System, which springs into action to answer hostname queries is fairly complex, and I will discuss it in greater detail in Chapter 4.

Listing 1-7. Turning a Hostname into an IP Address

```
#!/usr/bin/env python3
# Foundations of Python Network Programming, Third Edition
# https://github.com/brandon-rhodes/fopnp/blob/m/py3/chapter01/getname.py

import socket

if __name__ == '__main__':
    hostname = 'www.python.org'
    addr = socket.gethostbyname(hostname)
    print('The IP address of {} is {}'.format(hostname, addr))
```

For now, you just need to remember two things.

- First, however fancy an Internet application might look, the actual Internet Protocol always uses numeric IP addresses to direct packets toward their destination.

- Second, the complicated details of how hostnames are resolved to IP addresses are usually handled by the operating system.

Like most details of the operation of the Internet Protocol, your operating system prefers to take care of them itself, hiding the details both from you and from your Python code.

Actually, the addressing situation can be a bit more complex these days than the simple 4-byte scheme just described. Because the world is beginning to run out of 4-byte IP addresses, an extended address scheme, called IPv6, is being deployed that allows absolutely gargantuan 16-byte addresses that should serve humanity's needs for a long time to come. They are written differently from 4-byte IP addresses and look like this:

fe80::fcfd:4aff:fecf:ea4e

But as long as your code accepts IP addresses or hostnames from the user and passes them directly to a networking library for processing, you will probably never need to worry about the distinction between IPv4 and IPv6. The operating system on which your Python code is running will know which IP version it is using and should interpret addresses accordingly.

Generally, traditional IP addresses can be read from left to right: the first one or two bytes specify an organization, and then the next byte often specifies the particular subnet on which the target machine resides. The last byte narrows down the address to that specific machine or service. There are also a few special ranges of IP address that have a special meaning.

- *127.*.*.**: IP addresses that begin with the byte 127 are in a special, reserved range that is local to the machine on which an application is running. When your web browser or FTP client or Python program connects to an address in this range, it is asking to speak to some other service or program that is running on the same machine. Most machines make use of only one address in this entire range: the IP address 127.0.0.1 is used universally to mean "this machine itself that this program is running on" and can often be accessed through the hostname localhost.

- *10.*.*.*, 172.16–31.*.*, 192.168.*.**: These IP ranges are reserved for what are called *private subnets*. The authorities who run the Internet have made an absolute promise: they will never hand out IP addresses in any of these three ranges to real companies setting up servers or services. Out on the Internet at large, therefore, these addresses are guaranteed to have no meaning; they name no host to which you could want to connect. Therefore, these addresses are free for you to use on any of your organization's internal networks where you want to be free to assign IP addresses internally, without choosing to make those hosts accessible from other places on the Internet.

You are even likely to see some of these private addresses in your own home: your wireless router or DSL modem will often assign IP addresses from one of these private ranges to your home computers and laptops and hide all of your Internet traffic behind the single "real" IP address that your Internet service provider has allocated for your use.

Routing

Once an application has asked the operating system to send data to a particular IP address, the operating system has to decide how to transmit that data using one of the physical networks to which the machine is connected. This decision (that is, the choice of where to send each Internet Protocol packet based on the IP address that it names as its destination) is called *routing*.

Most, or perhaps all, of the Python code you write during your career will be running on hosts out at the edge of the Internet, with a single network interface that connects them to the rest of the world. For such machines, routing becomes a quite simple decision.

- If the IP address looks like 127.*.*.*, then the operating system knows that the packet is destined for another application running on the same machine. It will not even be submitted to a physical network device for transmission but handed directly to another application via an internal data copy by the operating system.

- If the IP address is in the same subnet as the machine itself, then the destination host can be found by simply checking the local Ethernet segment, wireless channel, or whatever the local network happens to be, and sending the packet to a locally connected machine.

- Otherwise, your machine forwards the packet to a *gateway machine* that connects your local subnet to the rest of the Internet. It will then be up to the gateway machine to decide where to send the packet after that.

Of course, routing is only this simple at the edge of the Internet, where the only decisions are whether to keep the packet on the local network or to send it winging its way across the rest of the Internet. You can imagine that routing decisions are much more complex for the dedicated network devices that form the Internet's backbone! There, on the switches that connect entire continents, elaborate routing tables have to be constructed, consulted, and constantly updated in order to know that packets destined for Google go in one direction, packets directed to an Amazon IP address go in another, and packets directed to your machine go in yet another. But it is rare for Python applications to run on Internet backbone routers, so the simpler routing situation just outlined is nearly always the one you will see in action.

I have been a bit vague in the previous paragraphs about how your computer decides whether an IP address belongs to a local subnet or whether it should instead be forwarded through a gateway to the rest of the Internet. To illustrate the idea of a subnet, all of whose hosts share the same IP address prefix, I have been writing the prefix followed by asterisks for the parts of the address that could vary. Of course, the binary logic that runs your operating system's network stack does not actually insert little ASCII asterisks into its routing table! Instead, subnets are specified by combining an IP address with a mask that indicates how many of its most significant bits have to match to make a host belong to that subnet. If you keep in mind that every byte in an IP address represents eight bits of binary data, then you will be able to read subnet numbers easily. They look like this:

- *127.0.0.0/8*: This pattern, which describes the IP address range discussed previously and is reserved for the local host, specifies that the first 8 bits (1 byte) must match the number 127 and that the remaining 24 bits (3 bytes) can have any value they want.

- *192.168.0.0/16*: This pattern will match any IP address that belongs in the private 192.168 range because the first 16 bits must match perfectly. The last 16 bits of the 32-bit address are allowed to have whatever value they want.

- *192.168.5.0/24*: Here you have a specification for one particular individual subnet. This is probably the most common subnet mask on the entire Internet. The first three bytes of the address are completely specified, and they have to match for an IP address to fall into this range. Only the last byte (the last eight bits) is allowed to vary between machines in this range. This leaves 256 unique addresses. Typically, the .0 address is used as the name of the subnet, and the .255 address is used as the destination for a "broadcast packet" that addresses all of the hosts on the subnet (as you will see in the next chapter), which leaves 254 addresses free to be assigned to computers. The address .1 is often used for the gateway that connects the subnet to the rest of the Internet, but some companies and schools choose to use another number for their gateways instead.

In nearly all cases, your Python code will simply rely on its host operating system to make packet routing choices correctly—just as it relies upon the operating system to resolve hostnames to IP addresses in the first place.

Packet Fragmentation

One last Internet Protocol concept that deserves mention is packet fragmentation. While it is supposed to be an obscure detail that is successfully hidden from your program by the cleverness of your operating system's network stack, it has caused enough problems over the Internet's history that it deserves at least a brief mention here.

Fragmentation is necessary because the Internet Protocol supports very large packets—they can be up to 64KB in length—but the actual network devices from which IP networks are built usually support much smaller packet sizes. Ethernet networks, for example, support only 1,500-byte packets. Internet packets therefore include a "don't fragment" (DF) flag with which the sender can choose what they want to happen if the packet proves too big to fit across one of the physical networks that lies between the source computer and the destination:

- If the DF flag is unset, then fragmentation is permitted, and when the packet reaches the threshold of the network onto which it cannot fit, the gateway can split it into smaller packets and mark them to be reassembled at the other end.

- If the DF flag is set, then fragmentation is prohibited, and if the packet cannot fit, then it will be discarded and an error message will be sent back—in a special signaling packet called an Internet Control Message Protocol (ICMP) packet—to the machine that sent the packet so that it can try splitting the message into smaller pieces and re-sending it.

Your Python programs will usually have no control over the DF flag; instead, it is set by the operating system. Roughly, the logic that the system will usually use is this: If you are having a UDP conversation (see Chapter 2) that consists of individual datagrams winging their way across the Internet, then the operating system will leave DF unset so that each datagram reaches the destination in however many pieces are needed; but if you are having a TCP conversation (see Chapter 3) whose long stream of data might be hundreds or thousands of packets long, then the operating system will set the DF flag so that it can choose exactly the right packet size to let the conversation flow smoothly, without its packets constantly being fragmented *en route*, which would make the conversation slightly less efficient.

The biggest packet that an Internet subnet can accept is called its *maximum transmission unit (MTU)*, and there used to be a big problem with MTU processing that caused problems for lots of Internet users. In the 1990s, Internet service providers (most notably phone companies offering DSL links) started using PPPoE, a protocol that puts IP packets inside a capsule that leaves them room for only 1,492 bytes instead of the full 1,500 bytes usually permitted across Ethernet. Many Internet sites were unprepared for this because they used 1,500-byte packets by default and had blocked all ICMP packets as a misguided security measure. As a consequence, their servers could never receive the ICMP errors telling them that their large, 1,500-byte "don't fragment" packets were reaching customers' DSL links and were unable to fit across them.

The maddening symptom of this situation was that small files or web pages could be viewed without a problem, and interactive protocols such as Telnet and SSH would work since both of these activities tend to send small packets that are less than 1,492 bytes long anyway. But once the customer tried downloading a large file or once a Telnet or SSH command disgorged several screens full of output at once, the connection would freeze and become unresponsive.

Today this problem is rarely encountered, but it illustrates how a low-level IP feature can generate user-visible symptoms and, therefore, why it is good to keep all of the features of IP in mind when writing and debugging network programs.

Learning More About IP

In the next chapters, you will step up to the protocol layers above IP and see how your Python programs can have different kinds of network conversations by using the different services built on top of the Internet Protocol. But what if you have been intrigued by the preceding outline of how IP works and want to learn more?

The official resources that describe the Internet Protocol are the requests for comment (RFCs) published by the IETF that describe exactly how the protocol works. They are carefully written and, when combined with a strong cup of coffee and a few hours of free reading time, will let you in on every single detail of how the Internet Protocols operate. Here, for example, is the RFC that defines the Internet Protocol itself:

```
http://tools.ietf.org/html/rfc791
```

You can also find RFCs referenced on general resources such as Wikipedia, and RFCs will often cite other RFCs that describe further details of a protocol or addressing scheme.

If you want to learn everything about the Internet Protocol and the other protocols that run on top of it, you might be interested in acquiring the venerable text, *TCP/IP Illustrated, Volume 1: The Protocols (2nd Edition)* by Kevin R. Fall and W. Richard Stevens (Addison-Wesley Professional, 2011). It covers, in fine detail, all of the protocol operations at which this book will only have the space to gesture. There are also other good books on networking in general, and that might help with network configuration in particular if setting up IP networks and routing is something you do either at work or even just at home to get your computers on the Internet.

Summary

All network services except the most rudimentary ones are implemented atop some other, more basic network function.

You explored such a "stack" in the opening sections of this chapter. The TCP/IP protocol (to be covered in Chapter 3) supports the mere transmission of byte strings between a client and server. The HTTP protocol (see Chapter 9) describes how such a connection can be used for a client to request a particular document and for the server to respond by providing it. The World Wide Web (Chapter 11) encodes the instructions for retrieving an HTTP-hosted document into a special address called a URL, and the standard JSON data format is popular for when the document returned by the server needs to present structured data to the client. And atop this entire edifice, Google offers a geocoding service that lets programmers build a URL to which Google replies with a JSON document describing a geographic location.

Whenever textual information is to be transmitted on the network—or, for that matter, saved to persistent byte-oriented storage such as a disk—the characters need to be encoded as bytes. There are several widely used schemes for representing characters as bytes. The most common on the modern Internet are the simple and limited ASCII encoding and the powerful and general Unicode system, especially its particular encoding known as UTF-8. Python byte strings can be converted to real characters using their decode() method, and normal character strings can be changed back through their encode() method. Python 3 tries never to convert bytes to strings automatically—an operation that would require it simply to guess at the encoding you intend—and so Python 3 code will often feature more calls to decode() and encode() than might have been your practice under Python 2.

For the IP network to transmit packets on an application's behalf, it is necessary that network administrators, appliance vendors, and operating system programmers have conspired together to assign IP addresses to individual machines, establish routing tables at both the machine and the router level, and configure the Domain Name System (Chapter 4) to associate IP addresses with user-visible names. Python programmers should know that each IP packet winds its own way across the network toward the destination and that a packet might be fragmented if it is too large to fit across one of the "hops" between routers along its path.

There are two basic ways to use IP from most applications. They are either to use each packet as a stand-alone message or to ask for a stream of data that gets split into packets automatically. These protocols are named UDP and TCP, and they are the subjects to which this book turns in Chapter 2 and Chapter 3.

CHAPTER 2

UDP

The previous chapter described modern network hardware as supporting the transmission of short messages called *packets*, which are usually no larger than a few thousand bytes. How can these tiny individual messages be combined to form the conversations that take place between a web browser and server or between an e-mail client and your ISP's mail server?

The IP protocol is responsible only for attempting to deliver each packet to the correct machine. Two additional features are usually necessary if separate applications are to maintain conversations, and it is the job of the protocols built atop IP to provide these features.

- The many packets traveling between two hosts need to be labeled so that the web packets can be distinguished from e-mail packets and so that both can be separated from any other network conversations in which the machine is engaged. This is called *multiplexing*.

- All of the damage that can occur to a stream of packets traveling separately from one host to another needs to be repaired. Missing packets need to be retransmitted until they arrive. Packets that arrive out of order need to be reassembled into the correct order. Finally, duplicate packets need to be discarded so that no information in the data stream gets repeated. This is known as providing a *reliable transport*.

This book dedicates a chapter to each of the two major protocols used atop IP.

The first, the *User Datagram Protocol* (UDP), is documented in this chapter. It solves only the first of the two problems outlined previously. It provides port numbers, as described in the next section, so that the packets destined for different services on a single machine can be properly demultiplexed. Nevertheless, network programs using UDP must still fend for themselves when it comes to packet loss, duplication, and ordering.

The second, the *Transmission Control Protocol* (TCP), solves both problems. It both incorporates port numbers using the same rules as UDP and offers ordered and reliable data streams that hide from applications the fact that the continuous stream of data has in fact been chopped into packets and then reassembled at the other end. You will learn about using TCP in Chapter 3.

Note that a few rare and specialized applications, such as multimedia being shared among all hosts on a LAN, opt for neither protocol and choose instead to create an entirely new IP-based protocol that sits alongside TCP and UDP as a new way of having conversations across an IP network. This not only is unusual but, being a low-level operation, is unlikely to be written in Python, so you will not explore protocol engineering in this book. The closest approach made to raw packet construction atop IP in this book is the "Building and Examining Packets" section near the end of Chapter 1, which builds raw ICMP packets and receives an ICMP reply.

I should admit up front that you are unlikely to use UDP in any of your own applications. If you think UDP is a great fit for your application, you might want to look into message queues (see Chapter 8). Nonetheless, the exposure that UDP gives you to raw packet multiplexing is an important step to take before you can be ready to learn about TCP in Chapter 3.

Port Numbers

The problem of distinguishing among many signals that are sharing the same channel is a general one, in both computer networking and electromagnetic signal theory. A solution that allows several conversations to share a medium or mechanism is known as a *multiplexing* scheme. It was famously discovered that radio signals can be separated from one another by using distinct frequencies. In the digital realm of packets, the designers of UDP chose to distinguish different conversations using the rough-and-ready technique of labeling each and every UDP packet with a pair of unsigned 16-bit *port numbers* in the range of 0 to 65,536. The *source port* identifies the particular process or program that sent the packet from the source machine, while the *destination port* specifies the application at the destination IP address to which the communication should be delivered.

At the IP network layer, all that is visible are packets winging their way toward a particular host.

```
Source IP → Destination IP
```

But the network stacks of the two communicating machines—which must, after all, corral and wrangle so many separate applications that might be talking—see the conversation as much more specifically being between an IP address and port number *pair* on each machine.

```
Source (IP : port number) → Destination (IP : port number)
```

The incoming packets belonging to a particular conversation will always have the same four values for these coordinates, and the replies going the other way will simply have the two IP numbers and two port numbers swapped in their source and destination fields.

To make this idea concrete, imagine you set up a DNS server (Chapter 4) on one of your machines with the IP address 192.168.1.9. To allow other computers to find the service, the server will ask the operating system for permission to receive packets arriving at the UDP port with the standard DNS port number: port 53. Assuming that a process is not already running that has claimed that port number, the DNS server will be granted that port.

Next, imagine that a client machine with the IP address 192.168.1.30 wants to issue a query to the server. It will craft a request in memory and then ask the operating system to send that block of data as a UDP packet. Since there will need to be some way to identify the client when the packet returns and since the client has not explicitly requested a port number, the operating system assigns it a random one—say, port 44137.

The packet will therefore wing its way toward port 53 with addresses that look like this:

```
Source (192.168.1.30:44137) → Destination (192.168.1.9:53)
```

Once it has formulated a response, the DNS server will ask the operating system to send a UDP packet in response that has these two addresses flipped around the other way so that the reply returns directly to the sender.

```
Source (192.168.1.9:53) → Destination (192.168.1.30:44137)
```

Thus, the UDP scheme is really quite simple; only an IP address and port are necessary to direct a packet to its destination.

But how can a client program learn the port number to which it should connect? There are three general approaches.

- *Convention*: The Internet Assigned Numbers Authority (IANA) has designated many port numbers as the official, well-known ports for specific services. That is why DNS was expected at UDP port 53 in the foregoing example.

- *Automatic configuration*: Often the IP addresses of critical services such as DNS are learned when a computer first connects to a network, using a protocol such as DHCP. By combining these IP addresses with well-known port numbers, programs can reach these essential services.

- *Manual configuration*: For all of the situations that are not covered by the previous two cases, manual intervention by an administrator or user will have to deliver an IP address or the corresponding hostname of a service. Manual configuration in this sense is happening, for example, every time you type a web server name into your web browser.

When making decisions about defining port numbers, such as 53 for DNS, IANA thinks of them as falling into three ranges—and this applies to both UDP and TCP port numbers.

- *Well-known ports* (0–1023) are for the most important and widely used services. On many Unix-like operating systems, normal user programs cannot listen on these ports. In the old days, this prevented troublesome undergraduates on multiuser university machines from running programs that masqueraded as important system services. Today the same caution applies when hosting companies hand out command-line Linux accounts.

- *Registered ports* (1024–49151) are not usually treated as special by operating systems—any user can write a program that grabs port 5432 and pretends to be a PostgreSQL database, for example—but they can be registered by IANA for specific services, and IANA recommends you avoid using them for anything but their assigned service.

- The remaining port numbers (49152–65535) are free for any use. They, as you will see, are the pool on which modern operating systems draw in order to generate arbitrary port numbers when a client does not care what port it is assigned for its outgoing connection.

When you craft programs that accept port numbers from user input such as the command line or configuration files, it is friendly to allow not just numeric port numbers but human-readable names for well-known ports. These names are standard, and they are available through the getservbyname() function inside Python's standard socket module. If you want to ask the port for the Domain Name Service, you can find out this way:

```
>>> import socket
>>> socket.getservbyname('domain')
53
```

As you will see in Chapter 4, port names can also be decoded by the more complicated getaddrinfo() function, which is also provided by the socket module.

The database of well-known service names and port numbers is usually kept in the file /etc/services on Linux and Mac OS X machines, which you can peruse at your leisure. The first few pages of the file, in particular, are littered with ancient protocols that still have reserved numbers despite not having had an actual packet addressed to them anywhere in the world for many years. An up-to-date (and typically much more extensive) copy is also maintained online by IANA at www.iana.org/assignments/port-numbers.

Sockets

Rather than trying to invent its own API for network programming, Python made an interesting decision. At bottom, Python's Standard Library simply provides an object-based interface to all of the normal, gritty, low-level operating system calls that are normally used to accomplish networking tasks on POSIX-compliant operating systems. The calls even have the same names as the underlying operations they wrap. Python's willingness to expose the traditional system calls that everyone already understood before it came on the scene is one of the reasons that Python came as such a breath of fresh air to those of us toiling in lower-level languages in the early 1990s. Finally, a higher-level language had arrived that let us make low-level operating system calls when we needed them, without insisting that we use an awkward, underpowered but ostensibly "prettier" language-specific API instead. It was much easier to remember a single set of calls that worked in both C and Python.

The underlying system calls for networking, on both Windows and POSIX systems (like Linux and Mac OS X), center around the idea of a communications endpoint called a *socket*. The operating system uses integers to identify sockets, but Python instead returns a more convenient socket.socket object to your Python code. It remembers the integer internally (you can call its fileno() method to peek at it) and uses it automatically every time you call one of its methods to request that a system call be run on the socket.

■ **Note**   On POSIX systems, the fileno() integer that identifies a socket is also a *file descriptor* drawn from the pool of integers representing open files. You might run across code that, assuming a POSIX environment, fetches this integer and then uses it to perform non-networking calls like os.read() and os.write() on the file descriptor to do filelike things with what is actually a network communications endpoint. However, because the code in this book is designed to work on Windows as well, you will perform only true socket operations on your sockets.

What do sockets look like in operation? Take a look at Listing 2-1, which shows a simple UDP server and client. You can see already that it makes only one Python Standard Library call, to the function socket.socket(), and that all of the other calls are to the methods of the socket object it returns.

Listing 2-1. UDP Server and Client on the Loopback Interface

```python
#!/usr/bin/env python3
# Foundations of Python Network Programming, Third Edition
# https://github.com/brandon-rhodes/fopnp/blob/m/py3/chapter02/udp_local.py
# UDP client and server on localhost

import argparse, socket
from datetime import datetime

MAX_BYTES = 65535

def server(port):
    sock = socket.socket(socket.AF_INET, socket.SOCK_DGRAM)
    sock.bind(('127.0.0.1', port))
    print('Listening at {}'.format(sock.getsockname()))
    while True:
        data, address = sock.recvfrom(MAX_BYTES)
        text = data.decode('ascii')
        print('The client at {} says {!r}'.format(address, text))
        text = 'Your data was {} bytes long'.format(len(data))
        data = text.encode('ascii')
        sock.sendto(data, address)

def client(port):
    sock = socket.socket(socket.AF_INET, socket.SOCK_DGRAM)
    text = 'The time is {}'.format(datetime.now())
    data = text.encode('ascii')
    sock.sendto(data, ('127.0.0.1', port))
    print('The OS assigned me the address {}'.format(sock.getsockname()))
    data, address = sock.recvfrom(MAX_BYTES)  # Danger!
    text = data.decode('ascii')
    print('The server {} replied {!r}'.format(address, text))
```

```
if __name__ == '__main__':
    choices = {'client': client, 'server': server}
    parser = argparse.ArgumentParser(description='Send and receive UDP locally')
    parser.add_argument('role', choices=choices, help='which role to play')
    parser.add_argument('-p', metavar='PORT', type=int, default=1060,
                        help='UDP port (default 1060)')
    args = parser.parse_args()
    function = choices[args.role]
    function(args.p)
```

You should be able to run this script right on your own computer, even if you are not currently in the range of a network, because both the server and the client use only the localhost IP address, which should be available whether you are connected to a real network or not. Try starting the server first.

```
$ python udp_local.py server
Listening at ('127.0.0.1', 1060)
```

After printing this line of output, the server waits for an incoming message.

In the source code, you can see that it took three steps for the server to get up and running.

It first created a plain socket with the socket() call. This new socket is not yet bound to an IP address or port number, is not yet connected to anything, and will raise an exception if you attempt to use it to communicate. However, the socket is, at least, marked as being of a particular type: its family is AF_INET, the Internet family of protocols, and it is of the SOCK_DGRAM datagram type, which means it will use UDP on an IP network. Note that the term *datagram* (and not *packet*) is the official term for an application-level block of transmitted data because the operating system networking stack does not guarantee that a single packet on the wire will actually represent a single datagram. (See the following section, where I do insist on a one-to-one correspondence between datagrams and packets so that you can measure the maximum transmission unit [MTU].)

Next, this simple server uses the bind() command to request a UDP network address, which you can see is a simple Python tuple combining a str IP address (a hostname, you will see later, is also acceptable) and an int UDP port number. This step could fail with an exception if another program is already using that UDP port and the server script cannot obtain it. Try running another copy of the server—you will see that it complains as follows:

```
$ python udp_local.py server
Traceback (most recent call last):
  ...
OSError: [Errno 98] Address already in use
```

Of course, there is a small chance that you received this exception the first time you ran the server because UDP port 1060 is already in use on your machine. It happens that I found myself in a bit of a bind when choosing the port number for this first example. It had to be above 1023, of course, or you could not have run the script without being a system administrator—and, while I do like my little example scripts, I really do not want to encourage anyone to run them as the system administrator! I could have let the operating system choose the port number (as I did for the client, as you will see in a moment), had the server print it out, and then made you type it into the client as one of its command-line arguments. However, then I would not have gotten to show you the syntax for asking for a particular port number yourself. Finally, I considered using a port from the high-numbered "ephemeral" range previously described, but those are precisely the ports that might randomly already be in use by some other application on your machine, such as your web browser or SSH client.

So, my only option seemed to be a port from the reserved-but-not-well-known range above 1023. I glanced over the list and made the gamble that you, gentle reader, are not running SAP BusinessObjects Polestar on the laptop or desktop or server where you are running my Python scripts. If you are, then try giving the server a -p option to select a different port number.

Note that the Python program can always use a socket's getsockname() method to retrieve a tuple that contains the current IP address and port to which the socket is bound.

Once the socket has been bound successfully, the server is ready to start receiving requests! It enters a loop and repeatedly runs recvfrom(), telling the routine that it will happily receive messages up to a maximum length of 65,535 bytes—a value that happens to be the greatest length that a UDP datagram can possibly have, so that you will always be shown the full content of each datagram. Until you send a message with a client, your recvfrom() call will wait forever.

Once a datagram arrives, recvfrom() will return the address of the client that has sent you a datagram as well as the datagram's contents as bytes. Using Python's ability to translate bytes directly to strings, you print the message to the console and then return a reply datagram to the client.

So, let's start up our client and examine the result. The client code is also shown in Listing 2-1.

(I hope, by the way, that it is not confusing that this example—like some of the others in the book—combines the server and client code into a single listing, selected by command-line arguments. I often prefer this style since it keeps server and client logic close to each other on the page, and it makes it easier to see which snippets of server code go with which snippets of client code.)

While the server is still running, open another command window on your system, and try running the client twice in a row like this:

```
$ python udp_local.py client
The OS assigned me the address ('0.0.0.0', 46056)
The server ('127.0.0.1', 1060) replied 'Your data was 46 bytes long'
$ python udp_local.py client
The OS assigned me the address ('0.0.0.0', 39288)
The server ('127.0.0.1', 1060) replied 'Your data was 46 bytes long'
```

Over in the server's command window, you should see it reporting each connection that it serves.

```
The client at ('127.0.0.1', 46056) says 'The time is 2014-06-05 10:34:53.448338'
The client at ('127.0.0.1', 39288) says 'The time is 2014-06-05 10:34:54.065836'
```

Although the client code is slightly simpler than that of the server—there are only three lines of networking code—it introduces two new concepts. The client call to sendto() provides both a message and a destination address. This simple call is all that is necessary to send a datagram winging its way toward the server! But, of course, you need an IP address and port number, on the client end, if you are going to be communicating. So, the operating system assigns one automatically, as you can see from the output of the call to getsockname(). As promised, the client port numbers are each from the IANA range for "ephemeral" port numbers. (At least they are here, on my laptop, under Linux; under a different operating system, you might get a different result.)

When you are done with the server, you can kill it by pressing Ctrl+C in the terminal where it is running.

Promiscuous Clients and Unwelcome Replies

The client program in Listing 2-1 is actually dangerous! If you review its source code, you will see that although recvfrom() returns the address of the incoming datagram, the code never checks the source address of the datagram it receives to verify that it is actually a reply from the server.

You can see this problem by delaying the server's reply and seeing whether someone else can send a response that this naïve client will trust. On a less capable operating system such as Windows, you will probably have to add a long time.sleep() call in between the server's receive and send to simulate a server that takes a long time to answer. On Mac OS X and Linux, however, you can much more simply suspend the server with Ctrl+Z once it has set up its socket to simulate a server that takes a long time to reply.

So, start up a fresh server but then suspend it using Ctrl+Z.

```
$ python udp_local.py server
Listening at ('127.0.0.1', 1060)
^Z
[1]  + 9370 suspended  python udp_local.py server
$
```

If you now run the client, it will send its datagram and then hang, waiting to receive a reply.

```
$ python udp_local.py client
The OS assigned me the address ('0.0.0.0', 39692)
```

Assume that you are now an attacker who wants to forge a response from the server by jumping in and sending your datagram before the server has a chance to send its own reply. Since the client has told the operating system that it is willing to receive any datagram whatsoever and is doing no sanity checks against the result, it should trust that your fake reply in fact originated at the server. You can send such a packet using a quick session at the Python prompt.

```
$ python3
Python 3.4.0 (default, Apr 11 2014, 13:05:18)
[GCC 4.8.2] on linux
Type "help", "copyright", "credits" or "license" for more information.
>>> import socket
>>> sock = socket.socket(socket.AF_INET, socket.SOCK_DGRAM)
>>> sock.sendto('FAKE'.encode('ascii'), ('127.0.0.1', 39692))
4
```

The client will immediately exit and happily interpret this third-party reply as being the response for which it was waiting.

```
The server ('127.0.0.1', 37821) replied 'FAKE'
```

You can kill the server now by typing fg to unfreeze it and let it keep running (it will now see the client packet that has been queued and waiting for it and will send its reply to the now-closed client socket). Press Ctrl+C as usual to kill it.

Note that the client is vulnerable to anyone who can address a UDP packet to it. This is not an instance where a man-in-the-middle attacker has control of the network and can forge packets from false addresses, a situation that can be protected against only by using encryption (see Chapter 6). Rather, an unprivileged sender operating completely within the rules and sending a packet with a legitimate return address nevertheless has its data accepted.

A listening network client that will accept or record every single packet that it sees, without regard for whether the packet is correctly addressed, is known technically as a *promiscuous* client. Sometimes we write these deliberately, as when we are doing network monitoring and want to see all of the packets arriving at an interface. In this case, however, promiscuity is a problem.

Only good, well-written encryption should really convince your code that it has talked to the right server. Short of that, there are two quick checks you can do. First, design or use protocols that include a unique identifier or request ID in the request that gets repeated in the reply. If the reply contains the ID you are looking for, then—so long as the range of IDs is large enough that someone could not simply be quickly flooding you with thousands or millions of packets containing every possible ID—someone who saw your request must at least have composed it. Second, either check the address of the reply packet against the address that you sent it to (remember that tuples in Python can simply be == compared) or use connect() to forbid other addresses from sending you packets. See the following sections "Connecting UDP Sockets" and "Request IDs" for more details.

Unreliability, Backoff, Blocking, and Timeouts

Because the client and server in the previous sections were both running on the same machine and talking through its loopback interface—which is not a physical network card that could experience a signaling glitch—there was no real way that packets could get lost, and so you did not actually see any of the inconvenience of UDP in Listing 2-1. How does code become more complicated when packets can really be lost?

Take a look at Listing 2-2. Instead of always answering client requests, this server randomly chooses to answer only half of the requests coming in from clients, which will let you see how to build reliability into your client code without waiting what might be hours for a real dropped packet to occur on your network!

Listing 2-2. UDP Server and Client on Different Machines

```python
#!/usr/bin/env python3
# Foundations of Python Network Programming, Third Edition
# https://github.com/brandon-rhodes/fopnp/blob/m/py3/chapter02/udp_remote.py
# UDP client and server for talking over the network

import argparse, random, socket, sys

MAX_BYTES = 65535

def server(interface, port):
    sock = socket.socket(socket.AF_INET, socket.SOCK_DGRAM)
    sock.bind((interface, port))
    print('Listening at', sock.getsockname())
    while True:
        data, address = sock.recvfrom(MAX_BYTES)
        if random.random() < 0.5:
            print('Pretending to drop packet from {}'.format(address))
            continue
        text = data.decode('ascii')
        print('The client at {} says {!r}'.format(address, text))
        message = 'Your data was {} bytes long'.format(len(data))
        sock.sendto(message.encode('ascii'), address)
```

```
def client(hostname, port):
    sock = socket.socket(socket.AF_INET, socket.SOCK_DGRAM)
    hostname = sys.argv[2]
    sock.connect((hostname, port))
    print('Client socket name is {}'.format(sock.getsockname()))

    delay = 0.1  # seconds
    text = 'This is another message'
    data = text.encode('ascii')
    while True:
        sock.send(data)
        print('Waiting up to {} seconds for a reply'.format(delay))
        sock.settimeout(delay)
        try:
            data = sock.recv(MAX_BYTES)
        except socket.timeout:
            delay *= 2  # wait even longer for the next request
            if delay > 2.0:
                raise RuntimeError('I think the server is down')
        else:
            break   # we are done, and can stop looping

    print('The server says {!r}'.format(data.decode('ascii')))

if __name__ == '__main__':
    choices = {'client': client, 'server': server}
    parser = argparse.ArgumentParser(description='Send and receive UDP,'
                                     ' pretending packets are often dropped')
    parser.add_argument('role', choices=choices, help='which role to take')
    parser.add_argument('host', help='interface the server listens at;'
                        'host the client sends to')
    parser.add_argument('-p', metavar='PORT', type=int, default=1060,
                        help='UDP port (default 1060)')
    args = parser.parse_args()
    function = choices[args.role]
    function(args.host, args.p)
```

While the server in the earlier example told the operating system that it wanted only packets, which arrived from other processes on the same machine through the private 127.0.0.1 interface, you can make this server more generous by specifying the server IP address as the empty string. This means "any local interface," which my Linux laptop means asking the operating system for the IP address 0.0.0.0.

```
$ python udp_remote.py server ""
Listening at ('0.0.0.0', 1060)
```

Each time a request is received, the server will use a random() flip of the coin to decide whether this request will be answered so that you do not have to keep running the client all day while waiting for a real dropped packet. Whichever decision it makes, it prints a message to the screen so that you can keep up with its activity.

How do we write a "real" UDP client, one that has to deal with the fact that packets might be lost?

First, UDP's unreliability means that the client has to perform its request inside a loop. It either has to be prepared to wait forever for a reply or else be somewhat arbitrary in deciding when it has waited "too long" for a reply and that it needs to send another one. This difficult choice is necessary because there is generally no way for the client to distinguish between these three quite different events:

- The reply is taking a long time to come back, but it will soon arrive.

- The reply will never arrive because it, or the request, was lost.

- The server is down, and it is not replying to anyone.

So, a UDP client has to choose a schedule on which it will send duplicate requests if it waits a reasonable period of time without getting a response. Of course, it might wind up wasting the server's time by doing this because the first reply might be about to arrive and the second copy of the request might cause the server to perform needless duplicate work. At some point, however, the client must decide to resend the request or it risks waiting forever.

Thus, rather than letting the operating system leave it forever paused in the recv() call, this client first does a settimeout() on the socket. This informs the system that the client is unwilling to stay stuck waiting inside a socket operation for more than delay seconds, and it wants the call interrupted with a socket.timeout exception once a call has waited for that long.

A call that waits for a network operation to complete is said to *block* the caller. The term *blocking* is used to describe a call like recv() that makes the client wait until new data arrives. When you get to Chapter 7 where server architecture is discussed, the distinction between blocking and nonblocking network calls will loom very large!

This particular client starts with a modest tenth-of-a-second wait. For my home network, where ping times are usually a few dozen milliseconds, this will rarely cause the client to send a duplicate request simply because the reply is delayed in getting back.

An important feature of this client program is what happens if the timeout is reached. It does *not* simply start sending out repeat requests over and over again at a fixed interval! Since the leading cause of packet loss is congestion—as anyone knows who has tried sending normal data upstream over a DSL modem at the same time that photographs or videos are uploading—the last thing you want to do is to respond to a possibly dropped packet by sending even more of them.

Therefore, this client uses a technique known as *exponential backoff*, where its attempts become less and less frequent. This serves the important purpose of surviving a few dropped requests or replies, while making it possible that a congested network will slowly recover as all of the active clients back off on their demands and gradually send fewer packets. Although there exist fancier algorithms for exponential backoff—for example, the Ethernet version of the algorithm adds some randomness so that two competing network cards are unlikely to back off on exactly the same schedule—the basic effect can be achieved quite simply by doubling the delay each time that a reply is not received.

Please note that if the requests are being made to a server that is, say, 200 milliseconds away, this naive algorithm will always send at least two copies of each request, every time, because it will never learn that requests to this server always take more than 0.1 seconds. If you are writing a UDP client that lives a long time, think about having it remember how long the last few requests have taken to complete so that it can delay its first retry until the server has had enough time to reply.

When you run the Listing 2-2 client,, give it the hostname of the other machine on which you are running the server script, as shown previously. Sometimes, this client will get lucky and get an immediate reply.

```
$ python udp_remote.py client guinness
Client socket name is ('127.0.0.1', 45420)
Waiting up to 0.1 seconds for a reply
The server says 'Your data was 23 bytes long'
```

However, often it will find that one or more of its requests never results in replies, and it will have to retry. If you watch its repeated attempts carefully, you can even see the exponential backoff happening in real time, as the print statements that echo to the screen come more and more slowly as the delay timer ramps up.

```
$ python udp_remote.py client guinness
Client socket name is ('127.0.0.1', 58414)
Waiting up to 0.1 seconds for a reply
Waiting up to 0.2 seconds for a reply
Waiting up to 0.4 seconds for a reply
Waiting up to 0.8 seconds for a reply
The server says 'Your data was 23 bytes long'
```

You can see in the terminal where you are running the server whether the requests are actually making it or whether, by any chance, you hit a real packet drop on your network. When I ran the foregoing test, I could look over at the server's console and see that all of the packets had actually made it.

```
Pretending to drop packet from ('192.168.5.10', 53322)
Pretending to drop packet from ('192.168.5.10', 53322)
Pretending to drop packet from ('192.168.5.10', 53322)
Pretending to drop packet from ('192.168.5.10', 53322)
The client at ('192.168.5.10', 53322) says, 'This is another message'
```

What if the server is down entirely? Unfortunately, UDP gives us no way to distinguish between a server that is down and a network that is simply in such poor condition that it is dropping all of our packets or their replies. Of course, I suppose we should not blame UDP for this problem. The world itself, after all, gives us no way to distinguish between something that we cannot detect and something that does not exist! So, the best that the client can do is to give up once it has made enough attempts. Kill the server process, and try running the client again.

```
$ python udp_remote.py client guinness
Client socket name is ('127.0.0.1', 58414)
Waiting up to 0.1 seconds for a reply
Waiting up to 0.2 seconds for a reply
Waiting up to 0.4 seconds for a reply
Waiting up to 0.8 seconds for a reply
Waiting up to 1.6 seconds for a reply
Traceback (most recent call last):
  ...
socket.timeout: timed out

The above exception was the direct cause of the following exception:

Traceback (most recent call last):
  ...
RuntimeError: I think the server is down
```

Of course, giving up makes sense only if your program is trying to perform some brief task and needs to produce output or return some kind of result to the user. If you are writing a daemon program that runs all day—like, say, a weather icon in the corner of the screen that displays the temperature and forecast fetched from a remote UDP service—then it is fine to have code that keeps retrying "forever." After all, a desktop or laptop machine might be off the network for long periods of time, and your code might have to wait patiently for hours or days until the forecast server can be contacted again.

If you are writing daemon code that retries all day, then do not adhere to a strict exponential backoff, or you will soon have ramped the delay up to a value of like two hours, and then you will probably miss the entire half-hour period during which the laptop owner sits down in a coffee shop and you could actually have gotten to the network. Instead, choose some maximum delay—like, say, five minutes—and once the exponential backoff has reached that period, keep it there so that you are always guaranteed to attempt an update once the user has been on the network for five minutes after a long time disconnected.

If your operating system lets your process be signaled for events like the network coming back up, then you will be able to do much better than to play with timers and guess about when the network might come back. But system-specific mechanisms like that are, sadly, beyond the scope of this book, so let's now return to UDP and a few more issues that it raises.

Connecting UDP Sockets

Listing 2-2, which you examined in the previous section, introduced another new concept that needs explanation. I have already discussed binding—both the explicit bind() call that a server uses to grab the address that it wants to use and the implicit binding that takes place when the client first tries to use a socket and is assigned a random ephemeral port number by the operating system.

But the remote UDP client in Listing 2-2 also uses a new call that I have not discussed before: the connect() socket operation. You can see easily enough what it does. Instead of having to use sendto() with an explicit address tuple every time you want to send something to the server, the connect() call lets the operating system know ahead of time the remote address to which you want to send packets so that you can simply supply data to the send() call and not have to repeat the server address again.

But connect() does something else important, which will not be obvious at all from reading Listing 2-2: it solves the problem of the client being promiscuous! If you perform the test that you performed in the "Promiscuity" section on this client, you will find that the Listing 2-2 client is not susceptible to receiving packets from other servers. This is because of the second, less-obvious effect of using connect() to configure a UDP socket's preferred destination: once you have run connect(), the operating system will discard any incoming packets to your port whose return address does not match the address to which you have connected.

There are, then, two ways to write UDP clients that are careful about the return addresses of the packets arriving back.

- You can use sendto() and direct each outgoing packet to a specific destination, then use recvfrom() to receive the replies and carefully check each return address against the list of servers to which you have made outstanding requests.

- You can instead connect() your socket right after creating it and communicate with send() and recv(). The operating system will filter out unwanted packets for you. This works only for speaking to one server at a time because running connect() again on the same socket does not add a second destination address. Instead, it wipes out the first address entirely so that no further replies from the earlier address will be delivered to your program.

After you have connected a UDP socket using connect(), you can use the socket's getpeername() method to remember the address to which you have connected it. Be careful about calling this on a socket that is not yet connected. Rather than returning 0.0.0.0 or some other wildcard response, the call will raise socket.error instead.

Two last points should be made about the connect() call.

First, doing a connect() on a UDP socket does *not* send *any* information across the network or do anything to warn the server that packets might be coming. It simply writes the address into the operating system's memory for use when you later call send() and recv().

Second, please remember that doing a connect()—or even filtering out unwanted packets yourself using the return address—is not a form of security! If there is someone on the network who is really malicious, it is usually easy enough for their computer to forge packets with the server's return address so that their faked replies will make it past your address filter just fine.

Sending packets with another computer's return address is called *spoofing*, and it is one of the first things that protocol designers have to think about when designing protocols that are supposed to be safe against interference. See Chapter 6 for more information about this.

Request IDs: A Good Idea

The messages sent in both Listings 2–1 and 2–2 were simple ASCII text. But if you ever design a scheme of your own for doing UDP requests and responses, you should strongly consider adding a sequence number to each request and making sure that the reply you accept uses the same number. On the server side, just copy the number from each request into the corresponding reply. This has at least two big advantages.

First, it protects you from being confused by duplicate answers to requests that were repeated several times by a client performing an exponential backoff loop.

You can see easily enough how duplication could happen. You send request A. You get bored waiting for an answer, so you repeat request A. Then you finally get an answer, reply A. You assume that the first copy got lost, so you continue merrily on your way.

However, what if both requests made it to the server and the replies have been just a bit slow in making it back? You received one of the two replies, but is the other about to arrive? If you now send request B to the server and start listening, you will almost immediately receive the duplicate reply A and perhaps think that it is the answer to the question you asked in request B, and you will become confused. You could, from then on, wind up completely out of step, interpreting each reply as corresponding to a different request than the one you think it does!

Request IDs protect you against that. If you gave every copy of request A the request ID #42496 and request B the ID #16916, then the program loop waiting for the answer to B can simply keep discarding replies whose IDs do not equal #16916 until it finally receives one that matches. This protects against duplicate replies, which arise not only in the case where you repeated the question, but also in the rare circumstance where a redundancy in the network fabric accidentally generates two copies of the packet somewhere between the server and the client.

The other purpose that request IDs can serve, as mentioned in the section "Promiscuity," is to provide a deterrent against spoofing, at least in the case where the attackers cannot see your packets. If they can, of course, then you are completely lost: they will see the IP, port number, and request ID of every single packet you send and can try sending fake replies—hoping that their answers arrive before those of the server, of course—to any request that they like! But in the case where the attackers cannot observe your traffic and have to shoot UDP packets at your server blindly, a good-sized request ID number can make it much less likely that your client will accept their answer.

You will note that the example request IDs that I used in the story I just told were neither sequential nor easy to guess. These features mean that an attacker will have no idea what is a likely sequence number. If you start with 0 or 1 and count upward from there, you make an attacker's job much easier. Instead, try using the random module to generate large integers. If your ID number is a random number between 0 and N, then an attacker's chance of hitting you with a valid packet—even assuming that the attacker knows the server's address and port—is at most 1/N and may be much less if he or she has to try wildly hitting all possible port numbers on your machine.

But, of course, none of this is real security—it just protects against naive spoofing attacks from people who cannot observe your network traffic. Real security protects you even if attackers can both observe your traffic and insert their own messages whenever they like. In Chapter 6, you will look at how real security works.

Binding to Interfaces

So far, you have seen two possibilities for the IP address used in the bind() call that the server makes. You can use '127.0.0.1' to indicate that you want packets from other programs running only on the same machine, or you can use an empty string ' ' as a wildcard to indicate that you are willing to receive packets arriving at the server via any of its network interfaces.

There is a third choice. You can provide the IP address of one of the machine's external IP interfaces, such as its Ethernet connection or wireless card, and the server will listen only for packets destined for those IPs. You might have noticed that Listing 2-2 actually allows you to provide a server string for the bind() call, which will now let you do a few experiments.

What if you bind solely to an external interface? Run the server like this, using whatever your operating system tells you is the external IP address of your system:

```
$ python udp_remote.py server 192.168.5.130
Listening at ('192.168.5.130', 1060)
```

Connecting to this IP address from another machine should still work just fine.

```
$ python udp_remote.py client guinness
Client socket name is ('192.168.5.10', 35084)
Waiting up to 0.1 seconds for a reply
The server says 'Your data was 23 bytes'
```

But if you try connecting to the service through the loopback interface by running the client script on the same machine, the packets will never be delivered.

```
$ python udp_remote.py client 127.0.0.1
Client socket name is ('127.0.0.1', 60251)
Waiting up to 0.1 seconds for a reply
Traceback (most recent call last):
  ...
socket.error: [Errno 111] Connection refused
```

Actually, on my operating system at least, the result is even better than the packets never being delivered. Because the operating system can see whether one of its own ports is opened without sending a packet across the network, it immediately replies that a connection to that port is impossible! But beware that this ability for UDP to return "Connection refused" is a superpower of the loopback that you will never see on the real network. There the packet must simply be sent with no indication of whether there is a destination port to receive it.

Try running the client again on the same machine, but this time use the external IP address of the box.

```
$ python udp_remote.py client 192.168.5.130
Client socket name is ('192.168.5.130', 34919)
Waiting up to 0.1 seconds for a reply
The server says 'Your data was 23 bytes'
```

Do you see what happened? Programs running locally are allowed to send requests that originate from any of the machine's IP addresses that they want—even if they are just using that IP address to talk back to another service on the same machine!

So, binding to an IP interface might limit which external hosts can talk to you. But it will certainly not limit conversations with other clients on the same machine, so long as they know the IP address to which they should connect.

What happens if you try to run two servers at the same time? Stop all of the scripts that are running and try running two servers on the same box. You will connect one to the loopback.

```
$ python udp_remote.py server 127.0.0.1
Listening at ('127.0.0.1', 1060)
```

Now that that address is occupied, you cannot run a second server at that address, because then the operating system would not know which process should get any given packet arriving at that address.

```
$ python udp_remote.py server 127.0.0.1
Traceback (most recent call last):
  ...
OSError: [Errno 98] Address already in use
```

But what might be more surprising is that you will not be able to run a server on the wildcard IP address either.

```
$ python udp_remote.py server
Traceback (most recent call last):
  ...
OSError: [Errno 98] Address already in use
```

This fails because the wildcard address includes 127.0.0.1, and therefore it conflicts with the address that the first server process has already grabbed. But what if instead of trying to run the second server against all IP interfaces, you just ran it against an external IP interface—one that the first copy of the server is not listening to? Let's try.

```
$ python udp_remote.py server 192.168.5.130
Listening at ('192.168.5.130', 1060)
```

It worked! There are now two servers running on this machine with the same UDP port number, one of which is bound to the inward-looking loopback interface and the other is looking outward for packets arriving on the network to which my wireless card has connected. If you happen to be on a box with several remote interfaces, you can start up even more servers, one on each remote interface.

Once you have these servers running, try to send them some packets with your UDP client. You will find that only one server receives each request, and in each case it will be the server that holds the particular IP address to which you have directed the UDP request packet.

The lesson of all of this is that an IP network stack never thinks of a UDP port as a lone entity that is either entirely available or else in use, at any given moment. Instead, it thinks in terms of UDP "socket names" that are always a pair linking an IP interface—even if it is the wildcard interface—with a UDP port number. It is these socket names that must not conflict among the listening servers at any given moment, rather than the bare UDP ports that are in use.

One last warning is in order. Since the foregoing discussion indicated that binding your server to the interface 127.0.0.1 protects you from possibly malicious packets generated on the external network, you might think that binding to one external interface will protect you from malicious packets generated by malcontents on other external networks. For example, on a large server with multiple network cards, you might be tempted to bind to a private subnet that faces your other servers and think therefore that you will avoid spoofed packets arriving at your Internet-facing public IP address.

Sadly, life is not so simple. It actually depends on your choice of operating system and how it is configured whether inbound packets addressed to one interface are allowed to arrive at another interface. It might be that your system will quite happily accept packets that claim to be from other servers on your network if they appear over your public Internet connection! Check with your operating system documentation, or your system administrator, to find out more about your particular case. Configuring and running a firewall on your box could also provide protection if your operating system does not.

UDP Fragmentation

I have been speaking so far in this chapter as though UDP lets you, as a user, send raw datagrams that are simply packaged up as IP packets with just a little bit of additional information—a port for both the sender and receiver. But you might already have become suspicious because the foregoing program listings have suggested that a UDP packet can be up to 64kB in size, whereas you probably already know that your Ethernet or wireless card can only handle packets of around 1,500 bytes instead.

The actual truth is that while UDP does send small datagrams as single IP packets, it has to split larger UDP datagrams into several small IP packets so that they can traverse the network (as was briefly discussed in Chapter 1). This means that large packets are more likely to be dropped, since if any one of their pieces fails to make its way to the destination, then the whole packet can never be reassembled and delivered to the listening operating system.

Except for the higher chance of failure, this process of fragmenting large UDP packets so that they will fit on the wire should be invisible to your application. There are three ways, however, in which it might be relevant.

- If you are thinking about efficiency, you might want to limit your protocol to small packets to make retransmission less likely and to limit how long it takes the remote IP stack to reassemble your UDP packet and give it to the waiting application.

- If the ICMP packets are wrongfully blocked by a firewall that would normally allow your host to autodetect the MTU between you and the remote host (a common situation in the late 1990s), then your larger UDP packets might disappear into oblivion without your ever knowing. The MTU is the "maximum transmission unit" or "largest packet size" that all of the network devices between two hosts will support.

If your protocol can make its own choices about how it splits up data between different datagrams and you want to be able to auto-adjust this size based on the actual MTU between two hosts, then some operating systems let you turn off fragmentation and receive an error if a UDP packet is too big. You could then be careful to fashion datagrams that fall under the minimum unit.

Linux is one operating system that supports this last option. Take a look at Listing 2-3, which sends a large datagram.

Listing 2-3. Sending a Large UDP Packet

```
#!/usr/bin/env python3
# Foundations of Python Network Programming, Third Edition
# https://github.com/brandon-rhodes/fopnp/blob/m/py3/chapter02/big_sender.py
# Send a big UDP datagram to learn the MTU of the network path.

import IN, argparse, socket
```

```
if not hasattr(IN, 'IP_MTU'):
    raise RuntimeError('cannot perform MTU discovery on this combination'
                       ' of operating system and Python distribution')

def send_big_datagram(host, port):
    sock = socket.socket(socket.AF_INET, socket.SOCK_DGRAM)
    sock.setsockopt(socket.IPPROTO_IP, IN.IP_MTU_DISCOVER, IN.IP_PMTUDISC_DO)
    sock.connect((host, port))
    try:
        sock.send(b'#' * 65000)
    except socket.error:
        print('Alas, the datagram did not make it')
        max_mtu = sock.getsockopt(socket.IPPROTO_IP, IN.IP_MTU)
        print('Actual MTU: {}'.format(max_mtu))
    else:
        print('The big datagram was sent!')

if __name__ == '__main__':
    parser = argparse.ArgumentParser(description='Send UDP packet to get MTU')
    parser.add_argument('host', help='the host to which to target the packet')
    parser.add_argument('-p', metavar='PORT', type=int, default=1060,
                        help='UDP port (default 1060)')
    args = parser.parse_args()
    send_big_datagram(args.host, args.p)
```

If I run this program against a server elsewhere on my home network, then I discover that my wireless network allows physical packets that are no bigger than the 1,500 bytes typically supported by Ethernet-style networks.

```
$ python big_sender.py guinness
Alas, the datagram did not make it
Actual MTU: 1500
```

It is slightly more surprising that the loopback interface on my laptop, which presumably could support packets as large as my RAM, also imposes an MTU.

```
$ python big_sender.py 127.0.0.1
Alas, the datagram did not make it
Actual MTU: 65535
```

But the ability to check the MTU is not available everywhere; check your operating system documentation for details.

Socket Options

The POSIX socket interface supports all sorts of socket options that control specific behaviors of network sockets. The IP_MTU_DISCOVER option that you saw in Listing 2-3 is just the tip of the iceberg. Options are accessed through the Python socket methods getsockopt() and setsockopt(), using the options that your operating system's documentation lists for these two system calls. On Linux, try viewing the manual pages *socket*(7), *udp*(7), and—when you progress to the next chapter—*tcp*(7).

When setting socket options, you first have to name the option group in which they live and then, as a subsequent argument, name the actual option you want to set. Consult your operating system manual for the names of these groups. Just like the Python calls `getattr()` and `setattr()`, the set call simply takes one more argument than does the get.

```
value = s.getsockopt(socket.SOL_SOCKET, socket.SO_BROADCAST)
s.setsockopt(socket.SOL_SOCKET, socket.SO_BROADCAST, value)
```

Many options are specific to particular operating systems, and they may be finicky about how their options are presented. Here are some of the more common options:

- SO_BROADCAST: This allows broadcast UDP packets to be sent and received, which I cover in the next section.

- SO_DONTROUTE: Only be willing to send packets that are addressed to hosts on subnets to which this computer is connected directly. My laptop, for example, at this moment would be willing to send packets to the networks 127.0.0.0/8 and 192.168.5.0/24 if this socket option were set, but it would not be willing to send them anywhere else because the packets would then have to be routed through a gateway.

- SO_TYPE: When passed to `getsockopt()`, this returns to you whether a socket is of type SOCK_DGRAM and can be used for UDP or whether it is of type SOCK_STREAM and instead supports the semantics of TCP (see Chapter 3).

The next chapter will introduce some further socket options that apply specifically to TCP sockets.

Broadcast

If UDP has a superpower, it is its ability to support broadcast. Instead of sending a datagram to some other specific host, you can address it to an entire subnet to which your machine is attached and have the physical network card broadcast the datagram so that all attached hosts see it without its having to be copied separately to each one of them.

It should be immediately mentioned that broadcast is considered passé these days because a more sophisticated technique called *multicast* has been developed that lets modern operating systems take better advantage of the intelligence built into many networks and network interface devices. Also, multicast can work with hosts that are not on the local subnet. But if you want an easy way to keep something such as gaming clients or automated scoreboards up-to-date on the local LAN and each client can survive the occasional dropped packet, then UDP broadcast is an easy choice.

Listing 2-4 shows an example of a server that can receive broadcast packets and a client that can send them. If you look closely, you will see that there is pretty much just one difference between this listing and the techniques used in previous listings. Before using this socket object, you call its `setsockopt()` method to turn on broadcast. Aside from that, both server and client use the socket quite normally.

Listing 2-4. UDP Broadcast

```
#!/usr/bin/env python3
# Foundations of Python Network Programming, Third Edition
# https://github.com/brandon-rhodes/fopnp/blob/m/py3/chapter02/udp_broadcast.py
# UDP client and server for broadcast messages on a local LAN

import argparse, socket

BUFSIZE = 65535
```

```python
def server(interface, port):
    sock = socket.socket(socket.AF_INET, socket.SOCK_DGRAM)
    sock.bind((interface, port))
    print('Listening for datagrams at {}'.format(sock.getsockname()))
    while True:
        data, address = sock.recvfrom(BUFSIZE)
        text = data.decode('ascii')
        print('The client at {} says: {!r}'.format(address, text))

def client(network, port):
    sock = socket.socket(socket.AF_INET, socket.SOCK_DGRAM)
    sock.setsockopt(socket.SOL_SOCKET, socket.SO_BROADCAST, 1)
    text = 'Broadcast datagram!'
    sock.sendto(text.encode('ascii'), (network, port))

if __name__ == '__main__':
    choices = {'client': client, 'server': server}
    parser = argparse.ArgumentParser(description='Send, receive UDP broadcast')
    parser.add_argument('role', choices=choices, help='which role to take')
    parser.add_argument('host', help='interface the server listens at;'
                        ' network the client sends to')
    parser.add_argument('-p', metavar='port', type=int, default=1060,
                        help='UDP port (default 1060)')
    args = parser.parse_args()
    function = choices[args.role]
    function(args.host, args.p)
```

When trying this server and client, the first thing you should notice is they behave exactly like a normal client and server if you simply use the client to send packets that are addressed to the IP address of a particular server. Turning on broadcast for a UDP socket does not disable or change its normal ability to send and receive specifically addressed packets.

The magic happens when you view the settings for your local network and use its IP "broadcast address" as the destination for the client. First bring up one or two servers on your network, using commands like the following:

```
$ python udp_broadcast.py server ""
Listening for broadcasts at ('0.0.0.0', 1060)
```

Then, while those servers are running, first use the client to send messages to each server. You will see that only one server gets each message.

```
$ python udp_broadcast.py client 192.168.5.10
```

But when you use the local network's broadcast address, suddenly you will see that all of the broadcast servers get the packet at the same time! (But no normal servers will see it—run a few copies of the normal udp_remote.py server while making broadcasts to be convinced.) On my local network at the moment, the ifconfig command tells me that the broadcast address is this:

```
$ python udp_broadcast.py client 192.168.5.255
```

And, sure enough, both servers immediately report that they see the message. In case your operating system makes it difficult to determine the broadcast address and you do not mind doing a broadcast out of every single network port of your host, Python lets you use the special hostname '<broadcast>' when sending with a UDP socket. Be careful to quote that name when passing it to your client, since the < and > characters are quite special to any normal POSIX shell.

```
$ python udp_broadcast.py client "<broadcast>"
```

If there were any platform-independent way to learn each connected subnet and its broadcast address, I would show you. Unfortunately, you will have to consult your own operating system documentation if you want to do anything more specific than use this special '<broadcast>' string.

When to Use UDP

You might think that UDP would be efficient for sending small messages. Actually, UDP is efficient only if your host sends only one message at a time and then waits for a response. If your application might send several messages in a burst, then using an intelligent message queue like ØMQ will actually be more efficient because it will set a short timer that lets it bundle several small messages together into a single transmission, probably on a TCP connection that does a much better job of splitting the payload into fragments than you would!

There are, however, a few good reasons to use UDP.

- Because you are implementing a protocol that already exists and it uses UDP.

- Because you are designing a time-critical media stream whose redundancy allows for occasional packet loss and you never want this second's data getting hung up waiting for old data from several seconds ago that has not yet been delivered (as happens with TCP).

- Because unreliable LAN subnet multicast is a great pattern for your application and UDP supports it perfectly.

Outside of these three situations, you should probably look at the latter chapters of this book for inspiration about how to construct the communication for your application. There is an old saying that by the time you have a UDP protocol kind of working for your application, you have probably just reinvented TCP—badly.

Summary

The User Datagram Protocol lets user-level programs send individual packets across an IP network. Typically, a client program sends a packet to a server, which then replies using the return address built into every UDP packet.

The POSIX network stack gives you access to UDP through the idea of a "socket," which is a communications endpoint that can sit at an IP address and UDP port number—these two things together are called the socket's *name* or *address*—and send and receive datagrams. Python offers these primitive network operations through the built-in socket module.

The server needs to bind() to an address and port before it can receive incoming packets. Client UDP programs can just start sending, and the operating system will choose a port number for them automatically.

Since UDP is built atop the actual behavior of network packets, it is unreliable. Packets can be dropped either because of a glitch on a network transmission medium or because a network segment becomes too busy. Clients have to compensate for this by being willing to retransmit a request until they receive a reply. To prevent making a busy network even worse, clients should use exponential backoff as they encounter repeated failure, and they should also make their initial wait time longer if they find that round-trips to the server are taking longer than they were initially willing to wait.

Request IDs are crucial to combat the problem of reply duplication, where a reply you thought was lost arrives later after all and could be mistaken for the reply to your current question. If randomly chosen, request IDs can also help protect against naive spoofing attacks.

When using sockets, it is important to distinguish the act of *binding*—by which you grab a particular UDP port for your own use—from the act that the client performs by *connecting*, which limits all replies received so that they can come only from the particular server to which you want to talk.

Among the socket options available for UDP sockets, the most powerful is broadcast, which lets you send packets to every host on your subnet without having to send to each host individually. This can help when programming local LAN games or other cooperative computation, and it is one of the few reasons that you would select UDP for new applications.

CHAPTER 3

TCP

The Transmission Control Protocol (officially TCP/IP but referred to as TCP throughout the rest of this book) is the workhorse of the Internet. First defined in 1974, it builds upon the packet transmission technology of the Internet Protocol (IP, described in Chapter 1) to let applications communicate using continuous streams of data. Unless a connection dies or freezes because of a network problem, TCP guarantees that the data stream will arrive intact, without any information lost, duplicated, or out of order.

Protocols that carry documents and files nearly always ride atop TCP. This includes the delivery of web pages to your browser, file transmission, and all of the major mechanisms for transmitting e-mail. TCP is also the foundation of choice for protocols that carry on long conversations between people or computers, such as SSH terminal sessions and many popular chat protocols.

When the Internet was younger, it was sometimes tempting to try to squeeze a little more performance out of a network by building an application atop UDP (see Chapter 2) and carefully choosing the size and timing of each individual datagram yourself. But modern TCP implementations tend to be sophisticated, having benefited from more than 30 years of improvement, innovation, and research. It is rare that anyone but an expert in protocol design can improve upon the performance of a modern TCP stack. These days, even performance-critical applications like message queues (Chapter 8) usually choose TCP as their medium.

How TCP Works

As you learned in Chapters 1 and 2, networks are fickle creatures. They sometimes drop the packets you try to transmit across them. They occasionally create extra copies of a packet. Plus, they often deliver packets out of order. With a bare datagram facility like UDP, your own application code has to worry about whether each datagram arrives and have a plan for recovering if it does not. But with TCP, the packets themselves are hidden beneath the protocol, and your application can simply stream data toward its destination, confident that lost information will be retransmitted until it finally arrives successfully.

The classic definition of TCP/IP is RFC 793 from 1981, though many subsequent RFCs have detailed extensions and improvements.

How does TCP provide a reliable connection? Here are its basic tenets:

- Every TCP packet is given a sequence number so that the system on the receiving end can put them back together in the right order and can also notice missing packets in the sequence and ask that they be retransmitted.

- Instead of using sequential integers (1, 2, 3...) to sequence packets, TCP uses a counter that counts the number of bytes transmitted. A 1,024-byte packet with a sequence number of 7,200, for example, would be followed by a packet with a sequence number of 8,224. This means that a busy network stack does not have to remember how it broke up a data stream into packets. If asked for a retransmission, it can break up the stream into new packets some other way (which might let it fit more data into a packet if more bytes are now waiting for transmission), and the receiver can still put the packets back together.

- The initial sequence number, in good TCP implementations, is chosen randomly so that villains cannot assume that every connection starts at byte zero. Predictable sequence numbers unfortunately make it easier to craft forged packets that might interrupt a conversation by looking like they are a legitimate part of its data.

- Rather than running very slowly in lock step by needing every packet to be acknowledged before it sends the next one, TCP sends whole bursts of packets at a time before expecting a response. The amount of data that a sender is willing to have on the wire at any given moment is called the size of the TCP *window*.

- The TCP implementation on the receiving end can regulate the window size of the transmitting end and thus slow or pause the connection. This is called *flow control.* This lets a receiver forbid the transmission of additional packets in cases where its input buffer is full, and it would have to discard more data anyway even if it were to arrive.

- Finally, if TCP believes that packets are being dropped, it assumes that the network is becoming congested and reduces how much data it sends every second. This can be something of a disaster on wireless networks and other media where packets are lost simply because of noise. It can also ruin connections that are running fine until a router reboots and the endpoints cannot talk for, say, 20 seconds. By the time the network comes back up, the two TCP peers will have decided that the network is extraordinarily overloaded with traffic, and upon reestablishing contact, they will at first refuse to send each other data at anything other than a trickle.

The design of TCP involves many other nuances and details beyond the behaviors just described, but ideally this description gives you a good feel for how it will work—even though, you will remember, all that your application will see is a stream of data, with the actual packets and sequence numbers cleverly hidden away by your operating system network stack.

When to Use TCP

If your network programs are at all like mine, then most of the network communications you perform from Python will use TCP. You might, in fact, spend an entire career without ever deliberately generating a UDP packet from your code. (Though, as you will see in Chapter 5, UDP is probably involved in the background every time your program needs to look up a DNS hostname.)

Although TCP has nearly become the universal default when two Internet programs need to communicate, I will cover a few instances in which its behavior is *not* optimal, in case an application you are writing ever falls into one of these categories.

First, TCP is unwieldy for protocols where clients want to send single, small requests to a server, and then they are done and will not talk to it further. It takes three packets for two hosts to set up a TCP connection—the famous sequence of SYN, SYN-ACK, and ACK.

- *SYN*: "I want to talk; here is the packet sequence number I will be starting with."

- *SYN-ACK*: "Okay, here is the initial sequence number I will be using in my direction."

- *ACK*: "Okay!"

Another three or four packets are necessary to shut the connection down when it is finished—either a quick FIN, FIN-ACK, and ACK, or else a slightly longer pair of separate FIN and ACK packets in each direction. Altogether, a minimum of six packets is necessary just to deliver a single request! Protocol designers quickly turn to UDP in such cases.

One question to ask, though, is whether a client might want to open a TCP connection and then use it over several minutes or hours to make many separate requests to the same server. Once the connection is going and the cost of the handshake had been paid, each actual request and response will require only a single packet in each direction, which will benefit from all of TCP's intelligence about retransmission, exponential backoff, and flow control.

Where UDP really shines, then, is where a long-term relationship will not exist between client and server, especially where there are so many clients that a typical TCP implementation would run out of memory if it had to keep up with a separate data stream for each active client.

The second situation where TCP is inappropriate is when an application can do something much smarter than simply retransmit data when a packet has been lost. Imagine an audio chat conversation, for example. If a second's worth of data is lost because of a dropped packet, then it will do little good simply to resend that same second of audio, over and over, until it finally arrives. Instead, the client should just fill that awkward second with whatever audio it can piece together from the packets that did arrive (a clever audio protocol will begin and end each packet with a bit of heavily compressed audio from the preceding and following moments of time to cover exactly this situation) and then keep going after the interruption as though it did not occur. This is impossible with TCP, which will keep stubbornly retransmitting the lost information even when it is far too old to be of any use. UDP datagrams are often the foundation of live-streaming multimedia over the Internet.

What TCP Sockets Mean

As was the case with UDP in Chapter 2, TCP uses port numbers to distinguish different applications running at the same IP address, and it follows exactly the same conventions regarding well-known and ephemeral port numbers. Reread the section "Port Numbers" in that chapter if you want to review the details.

As you saw in the previous chapter, it takes only a single socket to speak UDP: a server can open a UDP port and then receive datagrams from thousands of different clients. While it is certainly possible to connect() a datagram socket to a particular peer so that the socket will always send() to only that peer and recv()packets sent back from that peer, the idea of a connection is just a convenience. The effect of connect() is exactly the same as your application simply deciding, on its own, to send to only one address with sendto() calls and then ignore responses from any but that same address.

But with a stateful stream protocol like TCP, the connect() call becomes the opening step upon which all further network communication hinges. It is the moment when your operating system's network stack kicks off the handshake protocol described in the previous section that, if successful, will make both ends of the TCP stream ready for use.

This means that a TCP connect(), unlike the same call on a UDP socket, can fail. The remote host might not answer, or it might refuse the connection. Or more obscure protocol errors might occur, like the immediate receipt of a RST ("reset") packet. Because a stream connection involves setting up a persistent connection between two hosts, the other host needs to be listening and ready to accept your connection.

On the "server side"—which, by definition, is the conversation partner not doing the connect() call but receiving the SYN packet that the connect call initiates—an incoming connection generates an even more momentous event for a Python application: the creation of a new socket! This is because the standard POSIX interface to TCP actually involves two completely different kinds of sockets: "passive" listening sockets and active "connected" ones.

- The *passive socket* or *listening socket* maintains the "socket name"—the address and port number—at which the server is ready to receive connections. No data can ever be received or sent by this kind of socket. It does not represent any actual network conversation. Instead, it is how the server alerts the operating system to its willingness to receive incoming connections at a given TCP port number in the first place.

- An active, *connected socket* is bound to one particular remote conversation partner with a particular IP address and port number. It can be used only for talking back and forth with that one partner, and it can be read and written to without worrying about how the resulting data will be split up into packets. The stream looks so much like a pipe or file that, on Unix systems, a connected TCP socket can be passed to another program that expects to read from a normal file, and that program will never even know that it is talking over the network.

Note that while a passive socket is made unique by the interface address and port number at which it is listening—no one else is allowed to grab that same address and port—there can be many active sockets that all share the same local socket name. A busy web server to which a thousand clients have all made HTTP connections, for example, will have a thousand active sockets all bound to its public IP address at TCP port 80. What makes an active socket unique is, rather, the four-part coordinate, shown here:

```
(local_ip, local_port, remote_ip, remote_port)
```

It is this four-tuple by which the operating system names each active TCP connection, and incoming TCP packets are examined to see whether their source and destination address associate them with any of the currently active sockets on the system.

A Simple TCP Client and Server

Take a look at Listing 3-1. As I did in the previous chapter, I have here combined what could have been two separate programs into a single listing—both because they share a bit of common code and so that the client and server code can be read together more easily.

Listing 3-1. Simple TCP Server and Client

```python
#!/usr/bin/env python3
# Foundations of Python Network Programming, Third Edition
# https://github.com/brandon-rhodes/fopnp/blob/m/py3/chapter03/tcp_sixteen.py
# Simple TCP client and server that send and receive 16 octets

import argparse, socket

def recvall(sock, length):
    data = b''
    while len(data) < length:
        more = sock.recv(length - len(data))
        if not more:
            raise EOFError('was expecting %d bytes but only received'
                           ' %d bytes before the socket closed'
                           % (length, len(data)))
        data += more
    return data

def server(interface, port):
    sock = socket.socket(socket.AF_INET, socket.SOCK_STREAM)
    sock.setsockopt(socket.SOL_SOCKET, socket.SO_REUSEADDR, 1)
    sock.bind((interface, port))
    sock.listen(1)
    print('Listening at', sock.getsockname())
    while True:
        sc, sockname = sock.accept()
        print('We have accepted a connection from', sockname)
        print('  Socket name:', sc.getsockname())
        print('  Socket peer:', sc.getpeername())
        message = recvall(sc, 16)
        print('  Incoming sixteen-octet message:', repr(message))
        sc.sendall(b'Farewell, client')
        sc.close()
        print('  Reply sent, socket closed')
```

```
def client(host, port):
    sock = socket.socket(socket.AF_INET, socket.SOCK_STREAM)
    sock.connect((host, port))
    print('Client has been assigned socket name', sock.getsockname())
    sock.sendall(b'Hi there, server')
    reply = recvall(sock, 16)
    print('The server said', repr(reply))
    sock.close()

if __name__ == '__main__':
    choices = {'client': client, 'server': server}
    parser = argparse.ArgumentParser(description='Send and receive over TCP')
    parser.add_argument('role', choices=choices, help='which role to play')
    parser.add_argument('host', help='interface the server listens at;'
                        ' host the client sends to')
    parser.add_argument('-p', metavar='PORT', type=int, default=1060,
                        help='TCP port (default 1060)')
    args = parser.parse_args()
    function = choices[args.role]
    function(args.host, args.p)
```

In Chapter 2, I approached the subject of bind() quite carefully, since the address you provide as its argument makes an important choice: it determines whether remote hosts can try connecting to our server or whether your server is protected against outside connections and can be contacted only by other programs running on the same machine. Accordingly, Chapter 2 started with safe program listings that bound themselves only to the loopback interface and then progressed to more dangerous program listings that accepted connections from other hosts on the network.

But here I have combined both possibilities into a single listing. With the host argument that you provide from the command line, either you can make the safer choice of binding to 127.0.0.1 or you can choose to bind to one of your machine's external IP addresses instead—or you can supply a blank string to indicate that you will accept connections at any of your machine's IP addresses whatsoever. Again, review Chapter 2 if you want to remember all of the rules, which apply equally to TCP and UDP connections and sockets.

Your choice of port number also carries the same weight as it did when you chose port numbers for UDP in Chapter 2, and, again, the symmetry between TCP and UDP on the subject of port numbers is similar enough that you can simply apply the reasoning you used there to understand why the same choice has been used here in this chapter.

So, what are the differences between the earlier efforts with UDP and this new client and server that are instead built atop TCP?

The client actually looks much the same. It creates a socket, it runs connect() with the address of the server with which it wants to communicate, and then it is free to send and receive data. But beyond that, there are several differences.

First, the TCP connect() call—as I discussed a moment ago—is not the innocuous bit of local socket configuration that it is in the case of UDP, where it merely sets a default remote address to be used with any subsequent send() or recv() calls. Here, connect() is a real live network operation that kicks off the three-way handshake between the client and server machine so that they are ready to communicate. This means that connect() can fail, as you can verify quite easily by executing the client when the server is not running.

```
$ python tcp_deadlock.py client localhost
Sending 16 bytes of data, in chunks of 16 bytes
Traceback (most recent call last):
  ...
ConnectionRefusedError: [Errno 111] Connection refused
```

Second, you will see that this TCP client is in one way much simpler than the UDP client, because it does not need to make any provision for dropped packets. Because of the assurances that TCP provides, it can send() data without even stopping to check whether the remote end receives it and run recv() without having to consider the possibility of retransmitting its request. The client can rest assured that the network stack will perform any necessary retransmission to get its data through.

Third, there is a direction in which this program is actually more complicated than the equivalent UDP code—and this might surprise you because, with all of its guarantees, it sounds like TCP streams would be uniformly simpler for the programmer than UDP datagrams. But precisely because TCP considers your outgoing and incoming data to be, simply, streams with no beginning or end, it feels free to split them up into packets however it wants. And therefore send() and recv() mean something different than they meant before. In the case of UDP, they simply meant, "send this datagram" or "receive a datagram," and each datagram was atomic: it either arrived or not as a self-contained unit of data. An application will never see UDP datagrams that are only half-sent or half-received. Only fully intact datagrams are ever delivered to a UDP application.

But TCP might split its data stream into packets of several different sizes during transmission and then gradually reassemble them on the receiving end. Although this is vanishingly unlikely with the small 16-octet messages in Listing 3-1, your code still needs to be prepared for the possibility. What are the consequences of TCP streaming for both the send() and recv() calls?

Start by considering send(). When you perform a TCP send(), your operating system's networking stack will face one of three situations.

- The data can be immediately accepted by the local system's networking stack, either because the network card is immediately free to transmit or because the system has room to copy the data to a temporary outgoing buffer so that your program can continue running. In these cases, send() returns immediately, and it will return the length of your data string as its return value because the whole string is being transmitted.

- Another possibility is that the network card is busy and that the outgoing data buffer for this socket is full and the system cannot—or will not—allocate any more space. In this case, the default behavior of send() is simply to block, pausing your program until the data can be accepted for transmission.

- There is a final, intermediate possibility: that the outgoing buffers are *almost* full, but not quite, and so *part* of the data that you are trying to send can be immediately queued. But the rest of the block of data will have to wait. In this case, send() completes immediately and returns the number of bytes accepted from the beginning of your data string but leaves the rest of the data unprocessed.

Because of this last possibility, you cannot simply call send() on a stream socket without checking the return value. You have to put a send() call inside a loop that, in the case of a partial transmission, will keep trying to send the remaining data until the entire byte string has been sent. You will sometimes see this expressed in networking code using a loop like the following:

```
bytes_sent = 0
while bytes_sent < len(message):
    message_remaining = message[bytes_sent:]
    bytes_sent += s.send(message_remaining)
```

Fortunately, Python does not force you to do this dance yourself every time you have a block of data to send. As a special convenience, the Standard Library socket implementation provides a friendly sendall() method(), which Listing 3-1 uses instead. Not only is sendall() faster than doing it yourself, because it is implemented in C, but (for those readers who know what this means) it releases the Global Interpreter Lock during its loop so that other Python threads can run without contention until all of the data has been transmitted.

Unfortunately, no equivalent Standard Library wrapper is provided for the recv() call, even though it suffers from the same possibility of incomplete transmission. Internally, the operating system implementation of recv() uses logic very close to that used when sending.

- If no data is available, then recv() blocks, and your program pauses until data arrives.

- If plenty of data is available already in the incoming buffer, then you are given as many bytes as you gave recv() permission to deliver.

- If the buffer contains only *some* waiting data but not as much as you gave recv() permission to return, then you are immediately returned what does happen to be there even if it is not as much as you have requested.

That is why the recv() call has to be inside a loop. The operating system has no way of knowing that this simple client and server are using fixed-width 16-octet messages. Since it cannot guess when the incoming data might finally add up to what your program will consider a complete message, it gives you whatever data it can as soon as possible.

Why does the Python Standard Library include sendall() but no equivalent for the recv() method? It is probably because fixed-length messages are so uncommon these days. Most protocols have far more complicated rules about how part of an incoming stream is delimited than a simple decision that "the message is always 16 bytes long." In most real-world programs, the loop that runs recv() is more complicated than the one in Listing 3-1, because a program often has to read or process part of the message before it can guess how much more is coming. For example, an HTTP response consists of headers, a blank line, and then however many further bytes of data were specified in the Content-Length header. You do not know how many times to keep running recv() until you had at least received the headers and then parsed them to find out the content length, and this kind of detail is best left to your application instead of the Standard Library.

One Socket per Conversation

Turning to the server code in Listing 3-1, you see a very different pattern than you witnessed earlier, and the difference hinges on the very meaning of a TCP stream socket. Recall the our previous discussion that there are two different kinds of stream sockets: *listening* sockets, with which servers make a port available for incoming connections, and *connected* sockets, which represent a conversation that a server is having with a particular client.

In Listing 3-1, you can see how this distinction is carried through in actual server code. The link, which might strike you as odd at first, is that a listening socket actually returns a new, connected socket as the value that you get by calling accept()! Let's follow the steps in the program listing to see the order in which the socket operations occur.

First, the server runs bind() to claim a particular port. Note that this does not yet decide whether the program will be a client or server, that is, whether it will be actively making a connection or passively waiting to receive incoming connections. It simply claims a particular port, either on a particular interface or all interfaces, for the use of this program. Even clients can use this call if, for some reason, they want to reach out to a server from a particular port on their machine rather than simply using whatever ephemeral port number they would otherwise be assigned.

The real moment of decision comes with the next method call, when the server announces that it wants to use the socket to listen(). Running this on a TCP socket utterly transforms its character. After listen() has been called, the socket is irrevocably changed and can never, from this point on, be used to send or receive data. This particular socket object will now never be connected to any specific client. Instead, the socket can now be used only to receive incoming connections through its accept() method—a method that you have not seen yet in this book because its purpose is solely to support listening TCP sockets—and each of these calls waits for a new client to connect and then returns an entirely *new* socket that governs the new conversation that has just started with them.

As you can see from the code, getsockname() works fine against both listening and connected sockets, and in both cases, it lets you find out what local TCP port the socket is using. To learn the address of the client to which a connected socket is linked, you can run the getpeername() method at any time, or you can store the socket name that is returned as the second return value from accept(). When you run this server, you see that both values give you the same address.

```
$ python tcp_sixteen.py server ""
Listening at ('0.0.0.0', 1060)
Waiting to accept a new connection
We have accepted a connection from ('127.0.0.1', 57971)
  Socket name: ('127.0.0.1', 1060)
  Socket peer: ('127.0.0.1', 57971)
  Incoming sixteen-octet message: b'Hi there, server'
  Reply sent, socket closed
Waiting to accept a new connection
```

Having the client make one connection to the server, like this, produced the preceding output:

```
$ python3 tcp_sixteen.py client 127.0.0.1
Client has been assigned socket name ('127.0.0.1', 57971)
The server said b'Farewell, client'
```

You can see from the rest of the server code that once a connected socket has been returned by accept(), it works exactly like a client socket with no further asymmetries evident in their pattern of communication. The recv() call returns data as it becomes available, and sendall() is the best way to send a whole block of data when you want to make sure it all gets transmitted.

You will note that an integer argument was provided to listen() when it was called on the server socket. This number indicates how many waiting connections, which have not yet had sockets created for them by accept() calls, should be allowed to stack up before the operating system starts ignoring new connections and deferring any further three-way handshakes. I am using the very small value 1 here in the examples because I support only one example client connecting at a time, but I will consider larger values for this call when I talk about network server design in Chapter 7.

Once the client and server have said everything that they need to, they close() their end of the socket which tells the operating system to transmit any remaining data still left in their output buffer and then conclude the TCP session with the FIN-packet shutdown procedure mentioned previously.

Address Already in Use

There is one last detail in Listing 3-1 about which you may be curious. Why is the server careful to set the socket option SO_REUSEADDR before trying to bind to a port?

You can see the consequences of failing to set this option if you comment out that line and then try running the server. At first, you might think that it has no consequence. If all you are doing is stopping and starting the server, then you will see no effect at all (here I am starting the server and then terminating it with a simple Ctrl+C at the terminal's prompt):

```
$ python tcp_sixteen.py server ""
Listening at ('127.0.0.1', 1060)
Waiting to accept a new connection
^C
Traceback (most recent call last):
  ...
KeyboardInterrupt
$ python tcp_sixteen.py server ""
Listening at ('127.0.0.1', 1060)
Waiting to accept a new connection
```

But you will see a big difference if you bring up the server, run the client against it, and then try killing and rerunning the server. When the server starts back up, you will get an error:

```
$ python tcp_sixteen.py server
Traceback (most recent call last):
  ...
OSError: [Errno 98] Address already in use
```

How mysterious! Why would a bind() that can be repeated over and over again suddenly become impossible merely because a client has connected? If you keep trying to run the server without the SO_REUSEADDR option, you will find that the address does not become available again until several minutes after your last client connection.

The reason for this restriction is extreme caution on the part of your operating system's network stack. A server socket that is merely listening can immediately be shut down and forgotten. But a connected TCP socket, which is actually talking to a client, cannot immediately disappear even though both client and server may have closed their connection and sent FIN packets in each direction. Why? Because even after the network stack sends the last packet shutting the socket down, it has no way ever to be sure that it was received. If it happens to have been dropped by the network, then the remote end might at any moment wonder what is taking the last packet so long and retransmit its FIN packet in the hope of finally receiving an answer.

A reliable protocol like TCP obviously has to have some point like this where it stops talking; some final packet must, logically, be left hanging with no acknowledgment, or systems would have to commit to an endless exchange of "Okay, we both agree that we are all done, right?" messages until the machines were finally powered off. Yet even the final packet might get lost and need to be retransmitted a few times before the other end finally receives it. What is the solution?

The answer is that once a connected TCP connection is finally closed from the point of view of your application, the operating system's network stack actually keeps a record of it around for up to four minutes in a waiting state. The RFC names these states CLOSE-WAIT and TIME-WAIT. While the closed socket is still in either of these states, any final FIN packets can be properly replied to. If the TCP implementation were just to forget about the connection, then it could not reply to the FIN with a proper ACK.

So, a server that tries claiming a port on which a live connection was running within the last few minutes is, really, trying to claim a port that is in some sense still in use. That is why you are returned an error if you try a bind() to that address. By specifying the socket option SO_REUSEADDR, you are indicating that your application is okay about owning a port whose old connections might still be shutting down out on some client on the network. In practice, I always use SO_REUSEADDR when writing server code and have never had any problems.

Binding to Interfaces

As was explained in Chapter 2 when I discussed UDP, the IP address that you pair with a port number when you perform a bind() operation tells the operating system what are the network interfaces from which you are willing to receive connections. The example invocations of Listing 3-1 used the local IP address 127.0.0.1, which protects your code from connections originating on other machines.

You can verify this by running Listing 3-1 in server mode, as shown previously, and trying to connect with a client from another machine.

```
$ python tcp_sixteen.py client 192.168.5.130
Traceback (most recent call last):
  ...
ConnectionRefusedError: [Errno 111] Connection refused
```

You can see that the server, if you have it running, does not even react. The operating system does not even inform it that an incoming connection to its port was refused. (Note that if you have a firewall running on your machine, the client might just hang when it tries connecting, rather than getting a friendly "Connection refused" exception to tell it what is going on!)

But if you run the server with an empty string for the hostname, which tells the Python bind() routine that you are willing to accept connections through any of your machine's active network interfaces, then the client can connect successfully from another host (the empty string is supplied by giving the shell these two double quotes at the end of the command line).

```
$ python tcp_sixteen.py server ""
Listening at ('0.0.0.0', 1060)
Waiting to accept a new connection
We have accepted a connection from ('127.0.0.1', 60359)
  Socket name: ('127.0.0.1', 1060)
  Socket peer: ('127.0.0.1', 60359)
  Incoming sixteen-octet message: b'Hi there, server'
  Reply sent, socket closed
Waiting to accept a new connection
```

As noted before, my operating system uses the special IP address 0.0.0.0 to mean "accept connections on any interface," but this convention may be different on your operating system, and Python hides this difference by letting you use the empty string instead.

Deadlock

The term *deadlock* is used for all sorts of situations in computer science where two programs, sharing limited resources, can wind up waiting on each other forever because of poor planning. It turns out that it can happen fairly easily when using TCP.

I mentioned previously that typical TCP stacks use buffers—both so that they have somewhere to place incoming packet data until an application is ready to read it and so that they can collect outgoing data until the network hardware is ready to transmit an outgoing packet. These buffers are typically quite limited in size, and the system is not generally willing to let programs fill all of RAM with unsent network data. After all, if the remote end is not yet ready to process the data, it makes little sense to expend system resources generating more of it.

This limitation will generally not trouble you if you follow the client-server pattern shown in Listing 3-1, where each end always reads its partner's complete message before turning around and sending data in the other direction. But you can run into trouble quickly if you design a client and server that leave too much data waiting without having some arrangement for promptly reading it.

Take a look at Listing 3-2 for an example of a server and client that try to be a bit too clever without thinking through the consequences. Here the server author has done something that is actually quite intelligent. The server's job is to turn an arbitrary amount of text into uppercase. Recognizing that client requests can be arbitrarily large and that one could run out of memory trying to read an entire stream of input before trying to process it, the server reads and processes small blocks of 1,024 bytes of data at a time.

Listing 3-2. TCP Server and Client That Can Deadlock

```python
#!/usr/bin/env python3
# Foundations of Python Network Programming, Third Edition
# https://github.com/brandon-rhodes/fopnp/blob/m/py3/chapter03/tcp_deadlock.py
# TCP client and server that leave too much data waiting

import argparse, socket, sys

def server(host, port, bytecount):
    sock = socket.socket(socket.AF_INET, socket.SOCK_STREAM)
    sock.setsockopt(socket.SOL_SOCKET, socket.SO_REUSEADDR, 1)
    sock.bind((host, port))
    sock.listen(1)
    print('Listening at', sock.getsockname())
    while True:
        sc, sockname = sock.accept()
        print('Processing up to 1024 bytes at a time from', sockname)
        n = 0
        while True:
            data = sc.recv(1024)
            if not data:
                break
            output = data.decode('ascii').upper().encode('ascii')
            sc.sendall(output)  # send it back uppercase
            n += len(data)
            print('\r  %d bytes processed so far' % (n,), end=' ')
            sys.stdout.flush()
        print()
        sc.close()
        print('  Socket closed')

def client(host, port, bytecount):
    sock = socket.socket(socket.AF_INET, socket.SOCK_STREAM)
    bytecount = (bytecount + 15) // 16 * 16  # round up to a multiple of 16
    message = b'capitalize this!'  # 16-byte message to repeat over and over

    print('Sending', bytecount, 'bytes of data, in chunks of 16 bytes')
    sock.connect((host, port))
```

```
        sent = 0
        while sent < bytecount:
            sock.sendall(message)
            sent += len(message)
            print('\r  %d bytes sent' % (sent,), end=' ')
            sys.stdout.flush()

        print()
        sock.shutdown(socket.SHUT_WR)

        print('Receiving all the data the server sends back')

        received = 0
        while True:
            data = sock.recv(42)
            if not received:
                print('  The first data received says', repr(data))
            if not data:
                break
            received += len(data)
            print('\r  %d bytes received' % (received,), end=' ')

        print()
        sock.close()

if __name__ == '__main__':
    choices = {'client': client, 'server': server}
    parser = argparse.ArgumentParser(description='Get deadlocked over TCP')
    parser.add_argument('role', choices=choices, help='which role to play')
    parser.add_argument('host', help='interface the server listens at;'
                        ' host the client sends to')
    parser.add_argument('bytecount', type=int, nargs='?', default=16,
                        help='number of bytes for client to send (default 16)')
    parser.add_argument('-p', metavar='PORT', type=int, default=1060,
                        help='TCP port (default 1060)')
    args = parser.parse_args()
    function = choices[args.role]
    function(args.host, args.p, args.bytecount)
```

It can split the work up so easily—without needing to do framing or analysis—because it is merely trying to run the upper() string method on plain ASCII characters. This is an operation that can be performed separately on each block of input, without worrying about the blocks that came before or after. Things would not be this simple for the server if it were trying to run a more sophisticated string operation like title(), which would capitalize a letter in the middle of a word if the word happened to be split across a block boundary without being properly reassembled. For example, if a particular data stream got split into 16-byte blocks, then errors would creep in like this:

```
>>> message = 'the tragedy of macbeth'
>>> blocks = message[:16], message[16:]
>>> ''.join( b.upper() for b in blocks )    # works fine
'THE TRAGEDY OF MACBETH'
>>> ''.join( b.title() for b in blocks )    # whoops
'The Tragedy Of MAcbeth'
```

Processing text while splitting on fixed-length blocks would also not work for UTF-8 encoded Unicode data, since a multibyte character could get split across a boundary between two of the binary blocks. In such cases, the server would have to be more careful than in this example and carry some state between one block of data and the next.

In any case, handling input a block at a time like this is quite smart for the server, even if the 1,024-byte block size used here for illustration is actually a very small value for today's servers and networks. By handling the data in pieces and immediately sending out responses, the server limits the amount of data that it has to keep in memory at any one time. Servers designed like this could handle hundreds of clients at once, each sending streams totaling gigabytes, without taxing memory or other hardware resources.

And for small data streams, the client and server in Listing 3-2 seem to work fine. If you start the server and then run the client with a command-line argument specifying a modest number of bytes—say, asking it to send 32 bytes of data—then it will get its text back in all uppercase. For simplicity, it will round whatever value you supply up to a multiple of 16 bytes.

```
$ python tcp_deadlock.py client 127.0.0.1 32
Sending 32 bytes of data, in chunks of 16 bytes
  32 bytes sent
Receiving all the data the server sends back
  The first data received says b'CAPITALIZE THIS!CAPITALIZE THIS!'
  32 bytes received
```

The server will report that it indeed processed 32 bytes on behalf of its recent client. The server, by the way, needs to be running on the same machine, and this script uses the localhost IP address to make the example as simple as possible.

```
Processing up to 1024 bytes at a time from ('127.0.0.1', 60461)
  32 bytes processed so far
  Socket closed
```

So, this code appears to work well when tested with small amounts of data. In fact, it might also work for larger amounts. Try running the client with hundreds or thousands of bytes and see whether it continues to work.

This first example exchange of data, by the way, shows you the behavior of recv() that I have previously described. Even though the server asked for 1,024 bytes to be received, recv(1024) was quite happy to return only 16 bytes if that was the amount of data that became available and no further data had yet arrived from the client.

But this client and server can be pushed into dire territory. If you try a large enough value, then disaster strikes! Try using the client to send a large stream of data, say, one totaling a gigabyte.

```
$ python tcp_deadlock.py client 127.0.0.1 1073741824
```

You will see both the client and the server furiously updating their terminal windows as they breathlessly update you with the amount of data they have transmitted and received. The numbers will climb and climb until, quite suddenly, both connections freeze. Actually, if you watch carefully, you will see the server stop first, and then the client grinds to a halt soon afterward. The amount of data processed before they seize up varies on the Ubuntu laptop on which I am writing this chapter, but on the test run that I just completed here on my laptop, the Python script stopped with the server saying this:

```
$ python tcp_deadlock.py server ""
Listening at ('0.0.0.0', 1060)
Processing up to 1024 bytes at a time from ('127.0.0.1', 60482)
  4452624 bytes processed so far
```

And the client is frozen about 350,000 bytes farther ahead in writing its outgoing data stream.

```
$ python tcp_deadlock.py client "" 16000000
Sending 16000000 bytes of data, in chunks of 16 bytes
  8020912 bytes sent
```

Why have both client and server been brought to a halt?

The answer is that the server's output buffer and the client's input buffer have both finally filled, and TCP has used its window adjustment protocol to signal this fact and stop the socket from sending additional data that would have to be discarded and later resent.

Why has this resulted in deadlock? Consider what happens as each block of data travels. The client sends it with sendall(). Then the server accepts it with recv(), processes it, and transmits its capitalized version back out with another sendall() call. And then what? Well, nothing! The client is *never* running any recv() calls—not while it still has data to send—so more and more data backs up until the operating system buffers are not willing to accept any more.

During the run shown previous, about 4MB were buffered by the operating system in the client's incoming queue before the network stack decided that it was full. At that point, the server blocks in its sendall() call, and its process is paused by the operating system until the logjam clears and it can send more data. With the server no longer processing data or running any more recv() calls, it is now the client's turn to have data start backing up. The operating system seems to have placed a limit of around 3.5MB on the amount of data it is willing to queue up in that direction because the client got roughly that far into producing data before finally being brought to a halt as well.

On your own system, you will probably find that different limits are reached; the foregoing numbers are arbitrary and based on the mood of my laptop at the moment. They are not at all inherent in the way TCP works.

The point of this example is to teach you two things—besides, of course, showing that recv(1024) indeed returns fewer bytes than 1,024 if a smaller number are immediately available!

First, this example should make much more concrete the idea that there are buffers sitting inside the TCP stacks on each end of a network connection. These buffers can hold data temporarily so that packets do not have to be dropped and eventually resent if they arrive at a moment that their reader does not happen to be inside of a recv() call. But the buffers are not limitless. Eventually, a TCP routine trying to write data that is never being received or processed is going to find itself no longer able to write, until some of the data is finally read and the buffer starts to empty.

Second, this example makes clear the dangers involved in protocols that do not alternate lock step with the client requesting a limited amount of data and then waiting for the server to answer or acknowledge. If a protocol is not strict about making the server read a complete request until the client is done sending and then sending a complete response in the other direction, then a situation like the one created here can cause both of them to freeze without any recourse other than killing the program manually and then rewriting it to improve its design.

But how, then, are network clients and servers supposed to process large amounts of data without entering deadlock? There are, in fact, two possible answers. First, they can use socket options to turn off blocking so that calls like send() and recv() return immediately if they find that they cannot send any data yet. You will learn more about this option in Chapter 7, where you will look in earnest at the possible ways to architect network server programs.

Or the programs can use one of several techniques to process data from several inputs at a time, either by splitting into separate threads or processes (one tasked with sending data into a socket, perhaps, and another tasked with reading data back out) or by running operating system calls such as select() or poll() that let them wait on busy outgoing and incoming sockets at the same time and respond to whichever is ready. These are also explored in Chapter 7.

Finally, note carefully that the foregoing scenario cannot ever happen when you are using UDP. This is because UDP does not implement flow control. If more datagrams are arriving than can be processed, then UDP can simply discard some of them and leave it up to the application to discover that they went missing.

Closed Connections, Half-Open Connections

There are two more points that should be made, on a different subject, from the foregoing example.

First, Listing 3-2 shows you how a Python socket object behaves when an end-of-file is reached. Just as a Python file object returns an empty string upon a read() when there is no more data left, a socket simply returns an empty string when the socket is closed.

I never worried about this in Listing 3-1, because in that case I had imposed a strict enough structure on the protocol—exchanging a pair of messages of exactly 16 bytes—that I did not need to close the socket to signal when communication was done. The client and server could send a message while lazily leaving the socket open and close their sockets later without worrying that anyone was hanging waiting on them to close.

But in Listing 3-2, the client sends—and thus the server also processes and sends back—an arbitrary amount of data whose length is decided only by the number the user enters on the command line. And so you can see in the code, twice, the same pattern: a while loop that runs until it finally sees an empty string returned from recv(). Note that this normal Pythonic pattern will not work once you reach Chapter 7 and explore nonblocking sockets, where recv() might raise an exception simply because no data is available at the moment. In that case, other techniques are used to determine whether the socket has closed.

Second, you will see that the client makes a shutdown() call on the socket after it finishes sending its transmission. This solves an important problem. If the server is going to read forever until it sees end-of-file, then how will the client avoid having to do a full close() on the socket and thus forbid itself from running the many recv() calls that it still needs to make to receive the server's response? The solution is to "half-close" the socket—that is, to shut down communication permanently in one direction without destroying the socket itself. In this state, the server can no longer read any data, but it can still send any remaining reply back in the other direction, which will still be open.

The shutdown() call can be used to end either direction of communication in a two-way socket as shown in Listing 3-2. Its argument can be one of three symbols.

- SHUT_WR: This is the most common value used, since in most cases a program knows when its own output is done but not necessarily when its conversation partner will be finished. This value says that the caller will be writing no more data into the socket and that reads from its other end should respond that there is no more data and indicate end-of-file.

- SHUT_RD: This is used to turn off the incoming socket stream so that an end-of-file error is encountered if your peer tries to send any more data to you on the socket.

- SHUT_RDWR: This closes communication in both directions on the socket. It might not, at first, seem useful because you can also just perform a close() on the socket, and communication is similarly ended in both directions. The difference between closing a socket and shutting it down in both directions is a rather advanced one. If several programs on your operating system are allowed to share a single socket, then close() merely ends your process's relationship with the socket but keeps it open as long as another process is still using it. The shutdown() method, on the other hand, will always immediately disable the socket for everyone using it.

Since you are not allowed to create unidirectional sockets through a standard `socket()` call, many programmers who need to send information in only one direction over a socket will first create it and then—as soon as it is connected—immediately run `shutdown()` for the direction they do not need. This means that no operating system buffers will be needlessly filled if the peer with which they are communicating accidentally tries to send data in a direction that it should not.

Running `shutdown()` immediately on sockets that should really be unidirectional also provides a more obvious error message for a peer that does get confused and tries to send data. Otherwise, the unexpected data either will be simply ignored or might even fill a buffer and cause a deadlock because it will never be read.

Using TCP Streams Like Files

Since TCP supports streams of data, they might have already reminded you of normal files, which also support reading and writing sequential data as fundamental operations. Python does a good job of keeping these concepts separate. File objects can `read()` and `write()`, while sockets can only `send()` and `recv()`. And no kind of object can do both. (This is actually a substantially cleaner and more portable conceptual split than is achieved by the underlying POSIX interface, which lets a C programmer call `read()` and `write()` on a socket indiscriminately as though it were a normal file descriptor.)

But sometimes you will want to treat a socket like a normal Python file object—often because you want to pass it to code like that, like the many Python modules such as `pickle`, `json`, and `zlib`, can read and write data directly from a file. For this purpose, Python provides a `makefile()` method on every socket that returns a Python file object that is really calling `recv()` and `send()` behind the scenes.

```
>>> import socket
>>> sock = socket.socket(socket.AF_INET, socket.SOCK_STREAM)
>>> hasattr(sock, 'read')
False
>>> f = sock.makefile()
>>> hasattr(f, 'read')
True
```

Sockets on a Unix-derived system like Ubuntu and Mac OS X, like normal Python files, also have a `fileno()` method that lets you discover their file descriptor number in case you need to supply it to lower-level calls. You will find this helpful when you explore `select()` and `poll()` in Chapter 7.

Summary

The TCP-powered "stream" socket does whatever is necessary—including retransmitting lost packets, reordering the ones that arrive out of sequence, and splitting large data streams into optimally sized packets for your network—to support the transmission and reception of streams of data over the network between two sockets.

As with UDP, port numbers are used by TCP to distinguish the many stream endpoints that might exist on a single machine. A program that wants to accept incoming TCP connections needs to `bind()` to a port, run `listen()` on the socket, and then go into a loop that runs `accept()` over and over to receive a new socket for each incoming connection with which it can talk to each particular client that connects. Programs that want to connect to existing server ports need only create a socket and `connect()` to an address.

Servers will usually want to set the SO_REUSEADDR option on the sockets they `bind()`, lest old connections still closing down on the same port from the last time the server was run prevent the operating system from allowing the binding.

Data is actually sent and received with `send()` and `recv()`. Some protocols running on top of TCP will mark up their data so that clients and servers know automatically when a communication is complete. Other protocols will treat the TCP socket as a true stream and send and receive until end-of-file is reached. The `shutdown()` socket method can be used to produce end-of-file in one direction on a socket (all sockets are bidirectional by nature) while leaving the other direction open.

Deadlock can occur if two peers are written such that the socket fills with more and more data that never gets read. Eventually, one direction will no longer be able to `send()` and might hang forever waiting for the backlog to clear.

If you want to pass a socket to a Python routine that knows how to read to or write from a normal file object, the `makefile()` socket method will give you a Python object that calls `recv()` and `send()` behind the scenes when the caller needs to read and write.

CHAPTER 4

Socket Names and DNS

Having spent the previous two chapters learning the basics of UDP and TCP, the two major data transports available on IP networks, it is time for me to step back and talk about two larger issues that need to be tackled, regardless of which data transport you are using. In this chapter, I will discuss the topic of network addresses, and I will describe the distributed service that allows names to be resolved to raw IP addresses.

Hostnames and Sockets

We rarely type raw IP addresses into our browser or e-mail client. Instead, we type domain names. Some domain names identify entire organizations, like python.org and bbc.co.uk, while others name specific hosts or services, like www.google.com or asaph.rhodesmill.org. Some sites let you abbreviate a hostname by simply typing asaph, and they will automatically fill in the rest of the name for you by assuming you mean the asaph machine there at the same site. However, it is always correct, regardless of any local customization, to specify a *fully qualified domain name* that includes all of the pieces up to and including the top-level domain.

The idea of a *top-level domain (TLD)* used to be simple: it was either .com, .net, .org, .gov, .mil, or a two-letter internationally recognized country code like .uk. But today many other, more frivolous, top-level domains like .beer are being added, which will make it a bit more difficult to distinguish fully qualified from partially qualified domain names at a glance (unless you try to keep the whole list of top-level names memorized!).

Typically, each TLD has its own set of servers and is run by an organization that is in charge of granting ownership to domains beneath the TLD. When you sign up for a domain, they add an entry for it to their servers. Then, when a client running anywhere in the world wants to resolve a name that is within your domain, the top-level servers can refer the client to your own domain servers so that your organization can return the addresses it wants for the various hostnames you create. The collection of servers worldwide that answer name requests using this system of top-level names and referrals together provide the *Domain Name Service (DNS)*.

The previous two chapters have already introduced you to the fact that sockets cannot be named with a single primitive Python value like a number or string. Instead, both TCP and UDP use integer port numbers to share a single machine's IP address among the many different applications that might be running there, and so the address and port number have to be combined in order to produce a socket name, like this:

('18.9.22.69', 80)

While you might have been able to pick up some scattered facts about socket names from the previous few chapters—like the fact that the first item can be either a hostname or a dotted IP address—it is time to approach the whole subject in more depth.

You will recall that socket names are important at several points in the creation and use of sockets. For your reference, here are all of the major socket methods that demand of you some sort of socket name as an argument:

- `mysocket.accept()`: Each time this is called on a listening TCP stream socket that has incoming connections ready to hand off to the application, it returns a tuple whose second item is the remote address that has connected (the first item in the tuple is the new socket connected to that remote address).

- `mysocket.bind(address)`: This assigns the given local address to the socket so that outgoing packets have an address from which to originate and so that any incoming connections from other machines have a name to which they can connect.

- `mysocket.connect(address)`: This establishes that data sent through this socket will be directed to the given remote address. For UDP sockets, this simply sets the default address used if the caller uses `send()` rather than `sendto()` or `recv()` instead of `recvfrom()` but does not immediately perform any network communication. However, for TCP sockets, this actually negotiates a new stream with another machine using a three-way handshake and raises a Python exception if the negotiation fails.

- `mysocket.getpeername()`: This returns the remote address to which this socket is connected.

- `mysocket.getsockname()`: This returns the address of this socket's own local endpoint.

- `mysocket.recvfrom(...)`: For UDP sockets, this returns a tuple that pairs a string of returned data with the address from which it was received.

- `mysocket.sendto(data, address)`: An unconnected UDP port uses this method to fire off a data packet at a particular remote address.

There you have it! Those are the major socket operations that care about socket addresses, all in one place, so that you have some context for the remarks that follow. In general, any of the foregoing methods can receive or return any of the sorts of addresses that follow, meaning they will work regardless of whether you are using IPv4, IPv6, or even one of the less common address families that I will not be covering in this book.

Five Socket Coordinates

When studying the sample programs in Chapter 2 and Chapter 3, you paid particular attention to the hostnames and IP addresses that their sockets used. But these are only the last two coordinates of five major decisions that were made during the construction and deployment of each socket object. Recall that the steps go something like this:

```
import socket
s = socket.socket(socket.AF_INET, socket.SOCK_DGRAM)
s.bind(('localhost', 1060))
```

You can see that you specify four values here: two to configure the socket and two to address the `bind()` call. There is actually a fifth possible coordinate because `socket()` takes a third, optional argument, making five choices in all. I will discuss them each in turn, starting with the three possible parameters to `socket()`.

First, the *address family* makes the biggest decision: it names what kind of network you want to talk to out of the many kinds to which a particular machine might be connected.

In this book, I will always use the value `AF_INET` for the address family because I believe that writing about IP networking will best serve the vast majority of Python programmers while at the same time giving you skills that will work on Linux, Mac OS, or even Windows. Nevertheless, if you import the `socket` module, print out `dir(socket)`, and look for the symbols that start with `AF_` ("Address Family"), you will see other choices whose names you might recognize, like AppleTalk and Bluetooth. Especially popular on POSIX systems is the AF_UNIX address family, which offers connections very much like Internet sockets but that run directly between programs on the same machine by "connecting" to filenames instead of hostnames and port numbers.

Second, after the address family comes the *socket type*. It chooses the particular kind of communication technique that you want to use on the network you have chosen. You might guess that every single address family presents entirely different socket types that you would have to go and look up for each one. After all, what address family besides AF_INET is going to present socket types like UDP and TCP?

Happily, this suspicion is misplaced. Although UDP and TCP are indeed quite specific to the AF_INET protocol family, the socket interface designers decided to create more generic names for the broad idea of a packet-based socket. This goes by the name SOCK_DGRAM, and the broad idea of a reliable flow-controlled data stream, which, as you have seen, is known as a SOCK_STREAM. Because many address families support either one or both of these kinds of mechanisms, only these two symbols are necessary to cover many protocols under a variety of different address families.

The third field in the socket() call, the *protocol*, is rarely used because once you have specified the address family and socket type, you have usually narrowed down the possible protocols to only one major option. Thus, programmers usually leave this unspecified, or they provide the value 0 to force it to be chosen automatically. If you want a stream under IP, the system knows to choose TCP. If you want datagrams, then it selects UDP. That is why none of the socket() calls in this book has a third argument: it is almost never needed in practice. Look inside the socket module for names starting with IPPROTO for some examples of protocols defined for the AF_INET family. Listed there you will see the two this book actually addresses, under the names IPPROTO_TCP and IPPROTO_UDP.

Finally, the fourth and fifth values used to make a connection are the IP address and port number that were explained in detail in the previous two chapters.

We should immediately step back and note that it is only because of our specific choices for the first three coordinates that our socket names have had two components: hostname and port. If you instead had chosen AppleTalk or ATM or Bluetooth for your address family, then some other data structure might have been required instead of a tuple with a string and an integer inside. So, the whole set of coordinates, which I have talked about as five coordinates in this section, is really the three fixed coordinates needed to create the socket, followed by however many more coordinates your particular address family requires you to use in order to make a network connection.

IPv6

Now, having explained all of that, it turns out that this book actually does need to introduce one additional address family beyond the AF_INET used so far: the address family for IPv6, named AF_INET6, which is the way forward into a future where the world does *not* ultimately run out of IP addresses.

Once the old ARPANET really started taking off, its choice of 32-bit address names—which made so much sense back when computer memory was measured by the kilobyte—became a clear and worrying limitation. Only 4 billion possible addresses available provides less than one IP address for every person on the earth, and that means real trouble once everyone has both a computer and a smartphone!

Even though only a small percentage of the computers on the Internet today are actually using IPv6 to communicate with the global network through their Internet service providers (where "today" is June 2014), the steps necessary to make your Python programs compatible with IPv6 are simple enough so that you should go ahead and try writing code that prepares you for the future.

In Python, you can test directly for whether the underlying platform supports IPv6 by checking the has_ipv6 Boolean attribute inside the socket module.

```
>>> import socket
>>> socket.has_ipv6
True
```

Note that this does *not* tell you whether an actual IPv6 interface is up and configured and can currently be used to send packets anywhere! It is purely an assertion about whether IPv6 support has been compiled into the operating system, not about whether it is in use.

The differences that IPv6 will make for your Python code might sound quite daunting if listed one right after the other.

- Your sockets have to be created with the family AF_INET6 if you are called upon to operate on an IPv6 network.

- No longer do socket names consist of just two pieces—an address and a port number. Instead, they can also involve additional coordinates that provide "flow" information and a "scope" identifier.

- The pretty IPv4 octets like 18.9.22.69 that you might already be reading from configuration files or from your command-line arguments will now sometimes be replaced by IPv6 host addresses instead, and you might not even have good regular expressions for these just yet. They have lots of colons, they can involve hexadecimal numbers, and in general they look quite ugly.

The benefits of the IPv6 transition are not only that it will make an astronomically large number of addresses available but also that the protocol has more complete support for things such as link-level security than do most implementations of IPv4.

But the changes just listed can sound like a lot of trouble if you are in the habit of writing clunky, old-fashioned code that scans or assembles IP addresses and hostnames through regular expressions of your own devising. In other words, if you have been in the business of interpreting addresses yourself in any form, you probably imagine that the transition to IPv6 will make you write even more complicated code than previously. Fear not: my actual recommendation is that you get *out* of address interpretation and scanning altogether! The next section will show you how.

Modern Address Resolution

To make your code simple, powerful, and immune from the complexities of the transition from IPv4 to IPv6, you should turn your attention to one of the most powerful tools in the Python socket user's arsenal: getaddrinfo().

The getaddrinfo() function sits in the socket module along with most other operations that involve addresses. Unless you are doing something specialized, it is probably the only routine that you will ever need to use to transform the hostnames and port numbers that your users specify into addresses that can be used by socket methods.

Its approach is simple. Rather than making you attack the addressing problem piecemeal, which is necessary when using the older routines in the socket module, it lets you specify everything you know about the connection that you need to make in a single call. In response, it returns all of the coordinates that I discussed earlier, which are necessary for you to create and connect a socket to the named destination.

Its basic use is simple, and it goes like this (note that the pprint "pretty print" module has nothing to do with networking, but it will simply do a better job of displaying a list of tuples than the normal print function):

```
>>> from pprint import pprint
>>> infolist = socket.getaddrinfo('gatech.edu', 'www')
>>> pprint(infolist)
[(2, 1, 6, '', ('130.207.244.244', 80)),
 (2, 2, 17, '', ('130.207.244.244', 80))]
>>> info = infolist[0]
>>> info[0:3]
(2, 1, 6)
>>> s = socket.socket(*info[0:3])
>>> info[4]
('130.207.244.244', 80)
>>> s.connect(info[4])
```

The variable named info here contains everything you need to create a socket and use it to make a connection. It provides a family, a type, a protocol, a canonical name, and finally an address. What are the arguments provided to getaddrinfo()? I have asked about the possible methods for connecting to the HTTP service of the host gatech.edu, and the two-element list that has been returned tells you that there are two ways to do it: either by creating a SOCK_STREAM socket (socket type 1) that uses IPPROTO_TCP (protocol number 6) or by using a SOCK_DGRAM (socket type 2) socket with IPPROTO_UDP (which is the protocol represented by the integer 17).

And yes, the foregoing answer is indicative of the fact that HTTP officially supports both TCP and UDP, at least according to the official organization that doles out port numbers. When you call getaddrinfo() later from scripts, you will generally specify which kind of socket you want instead of leaving the answer to chance.

If you use getaddrinfo() in your code, then unlike the listings in Chapter 2 and Chapter 3, which used real symbols like AF_INET just to make it clearer how the low-level socket mechanisms were working, your production Python code will not reference any symbols at all from the socket module except for those that explain to getaddrinfo() which kind of address you want. Instead, you will use the first three items in the getaddrinfo() return value as the arguments to the socket() constructor and then use the fifth item as the address to any of the address-aware calls like connect() that were listed in the first section of this chapter.

As you can see from the previous code snippet, getaddrinfo() generally allows not only the hostname but also the port name to be a symbol like 'www' rather than an integer, eliminating the need for older Python code to make extra calls if the user wants to provide a symbolic port number like www or smtp instead of 80 or 25.

Before tackling all of the options that getaddrinfo() supports, it will be more useful to see how it is used to support three basic network operations. I will tackle them in the order that you might perform operations on a socket: binding, connecting, and then identifying a remote host who has sent you information.

Using getaddrinfo() to Bind Your Server to a Port

If you want an address to provide to bind(), either because you are creating a server socket or because for some reason you want your client to be connecting to someone else but from a predictable address, then you will call getaddrinfo() with None as the hostname but with the port number and socket type filled in. Note that here, as in the following getaddrinfo() calls, zeros serve as wildcards in fields that are supposed to contain numbers:

```
>>> from socket import getaddrinfo
>>> getaddrinfo(None, 'smtp', 0, socket.SOCK_STREAM, 0, socket.AI_PASSIVE)
[(2, 1, 6, '', ('0.0.0.0', 25)), (10, 1, 6, '', ('::', 25, 0, 0))]
>>> getaddrinfo(None, 53, 0, socket.SOCK_DGRAM, 0, socket.AI_PASSIVE)
[(2, 2, 17, '', ('0.0.0.0', 53)), (10, 2, 17, '', ('::', 53, 0, 0))]
```

Here I asked two different questions using a string port identifier for the first but a raw numeric port number for the second. First, I asked to which address I should bind() a socket if I want to serve SMTP traffic using TCP. Second, I asked about serving port 53 (DNS) traffic using UDP. The answers I got back are the appropriate wildcard addresses that will let you bind to every IPv4 and every IPv6 interface on the local machine with all of the right values for the socket family, socket type, and protocol in each case.

If you instead want to bind() to a particular IP address that you know is configured as a local address for the machine on which you are running, then omit the AI_PASSIVE flag and just specify the hostname. For example, here are two ways that you might try binding to localhost:

```
>>> getaddrinfo('127.0.0.1', 'smtp', 0, socket.SOCK_STREAM, 0)
[(2, 1, 6, '', ('127.0.0.1', 25))]
>>> getaddrinfo('localhost', 'smtp', 0, socket.SOCK_STREAM, 0)
[(10, 1, 6, '', ('::1', 25, 0, 0)), (2, 1, 6, '', ('127.0.0.1', 25))]
```

You can see that supplying the IPv4 address for the local host locks you down to receiving connections only over IPv4, while using the symbolic name `localhost` (at least on my Linux laptop with a well-configured /etc/hosts file) makes available both the IPv4 and IPv6 local names for the machine.

By the way, one question you might already be asking at this point is what on Earth are you supposed to do when you assert that you want to supply a basic service and getaddrinfo() goes and gives you several addresses to use—you certainly cannot create a single socket and bind() it to more than one address! In Chapter 7, I will tackle the techniques that you can use if you are writing server code and want to have several bound server sockets going at once.

Using getaddrinfo() to Connect to a Service

Except when you are binding to a local address to provide a service yourself, you will use getaddrinfo() to learn about connecting to other services. When looking up services, you can either use an empty string to indicate that you want to connect back to the local host using the loopback interface or provide a string giving an IPv4 address, IPv6 address, or a hostname to name your destination.

When you are preparing to connect() or sendto() a service, call getaddrinfo() with the AI_ADDRCONFIG flag, which filters out any addresses that are impossible for your computer to reach. For example, an organization might have both an IPv4 and an IPv6 range of IP addresses. If your particular host supports only IPv4, then you will want the results filtered to include only addresses in that family. To prepare for the situation in which the local machine has only an IPv6 network interface but the service to which you are connecting supports only IPv4, you will also want to specify AI_V4MAPPED to return the IPv4 addresses reencoded as IPv6 addresses that you can actually use.

Putting these pieces together, you will usually use getaddrinfo() this way before connecting:

```
>>> getaddrinfo('ftp.kernel.org', 'ftp', 0, socket.SOCK_STREAM, 0,
...             socket.AI_ADDRCONFIG | socket.AI_V4MAPPED)
[(2, 1, 6, '', ('204.152.191.37', 21)),
 (2, 1, 6, '', ('149.20.20.133', 21))]
```

In return, you have gotten exactly what you wanted: a list of every way to connect to a host named `ftp.kernel.org` through a TCP connection to its FTP port. Note that several IP addresses were returned because, to spread load, this service is located at several different addresses on the Internet. When several addresses come back like this, you should generally use the first address returned, and only if your connection attempt fails should you try the remaining ones. By honoring the order in which the administrators of the remote service want you to try contacting their servers, you will offer the workload that they intend.

Here is another query that asks how I can connect from my laptop to the HTTP interface of the IANA, who assigns port numbers in the first place:

```
>>> getaddrinfo('iana.org', 'www', 0, socket.SOCK_STREAM, 0,
...             socket.AI_ADDRCONFIG | socket.AI_V4MAPPED)
[(2, 1, 6, '', ('192.0.43.8', 80))]
```

The IANA web site is actually a good one for demonstrating the utility of the AI_ADDRCONFIG flag because, like any other good Internet standards organization, its web site already supports IPv6. It just so happens that my laptop can speak only IPv4 on the wireless network to which it is currently connected, so the foregoing call was careful to return only an IPv4 address. However, if you take away the carefully chosen flags in the sixth parameter, then you can peek at their IPv6 address that you cannot use.

```
>>> getaddrinfo('iana.org', 'www', 0, socket.SOCK_STREAM, 0)
[(2, 1, 6, '', ('192.0.43.8', 80)),
 (10, 1, 6, '', ('2001:500:88:200::8', 80, 0, 0))]
```

This can be useful if you are not going to try to use the addresses yourself but if you are providing some sort of directory information to other hosts or programs.

Asking getaddrinfo() for a Canonical Hostname

One last circumstance that you will commonly encounter is that you either are making a new connection or maybe have just accepted an incoming connection on one of your own server sockets and you want to know the hostname that belongs officially to the IP address at the other end of your socket.

Although this desire is understandable, please note that it comes with a grave danger: the fact that the owner of an IP address can, when your machine performs the reverse lookup, have their DNS server return *anything* they want as the canonical name! They can claim to be google.com or python.org or whomever they want. They are in complete control of the string of characters parroted back to you when you ask them what hostname belongs to one of their IP addresses.

Before trusting a canonical name lookup—also known as a *reverse* DNS lookup, because it maps an IP address to a hostname instead of the other way around—you will therefore probably want to look up the name that has been returned and see whether it really resolves to the original IP address. If not, then either the hostname is deliberately misleading or it was a well intentioned answer from a domain whose forward and reverse names and IP addresses have not been correctly configured so that they match.

Canonical name lookups are costly. They incur an extra round-trip through the worldwide DNS service and are therefore often skipped when doing logging. Services that stop to reverse-lookup every single IP address that makes a connection tend to be slow and lumbering, and a classic move by system administrators trying to make a system respond better is to log bare IP addresses. If one of them is causing a problem, you can always look it up by hand later when you see it in the log file.

But if you have a good use for the canonical name of a host and want to attempt the lookup, then simply run getaddrinfo() with the AI_CANONNAME flag turned on, and the fourth item of any of the tuples that it returns—an item that was the empty string in the foregoing examples—will contain the canonical name:

```
>>> getaddrinfo('iana.org', 'www', 0, socket.SOCK_STREAM, 0,
...             socket.AI_ADDRCONFIG | socket.AI_V4MAPPED | socket.AI_CANONNAME)
[(2, 1, 6, '43-8.any.icann.org', ('192.0.43.8', 80))]
```

You can also supply getaddrinfo() with the name of a socket that is already connected to a remote peer and get a canonical name in return.

```
>>> mysock = server_sock.accept()
>>> addr, port = mysock.getpeername()
>>> getaddrinfo(addr, port, mysock.family, mysock.type, mysock.proto,
...             socket.AI_CANONNAME)
[(2, 1, 6, 'rr.pmtpa.wikimedia.org', ('208.80.152.2', 80))]
```

Again, this will work only if the owner of the IP address happens to have a name defined for it. Many IP addresses on the Internet do not provide a useful reverse name, so you have no way of knowing what host has really contacted you unless you use encryption to verify the peer with which you are communicating.

Other getaddrinfo() Flags

The examples just given demonstrate the operation of three of the most important getaddrinfo() flags. The flags available vary somewhat by operating system, and you should always consult your own computer's documentation (not to mention its configuration) if you are confused about a value that it chooses to return. But there are several flags that tend to be cross-platform. Here are some of the more important ones:

- AI_ALL: I have already discussed that the AI_V4MAPPED option protects you from the situation where you are on a purely IPv6-connected host, but the host to which you want to connect advertises only IPv4 addresses. It resolves this problem by rewriting the IPv4 addresses to their IPv6 equivalent. However, if some IPv6 addresses do happen to be available, then they will be the only ones shown, and none of the IPv4 addresses will be included in the return value. This is fixed by this option: if you want to see all of the addresses from your IPv6-connected host, even though some perfectly good IPv6 addresses are available, then combine this AI_ALL flag with AI_V4MAPPED, and the list returned to you will have every address known for the target host.

- AI_NUMERICHOST: This turns off any attempt to interpret the hostname parameter—the first parameter to getaddrinfo()—as a textual hostname like cern.ch, and it tries only to interpret the hostname string as a literal IPv4 or IPv6 hostname like 74.207.234.78 or fe80::fcfd:4aff:fecf:ea4e. This is much faster, as the user or config file supplying the address cannot cause your program to make a DNS round-trip to look up the name (see the next section) and prevents possibly untrusted user input from forcing your system to issue a query to a name server under someone else's control.

- AI_NUMERICSERV: This turns off symbolic port names like 'www', and it insists that port numbers like 80 be used instead. You do not need to use this to protect your programs against slow DNS lookups because port number databases are typically stored locally on IP-capable machines instead of incurring a remote lookup. On POSIX systems, resolving a symbolic port name typically requires only a quick scan of the /etc/services file (but check your /etc/nsswitch.conf file's services option to be sure). However, if you know that your port string should always be an integer, then activating this flag can be a useful sanity check.

One final note about flags: you do not have to worry about the IDN-related flags that some operating systems offer, which tell getaddrinfo() to resolve those fancy new domain names that have Unicode characters in them. Instead, Python will detect whether a string requires special encoding and will set whatever options are necessary to get it converted for you:

```
>>> getaddrinfo('παράδειγμα.δοκιμή', 'www', 0, socket.SOCK_STREAM, 0,
...             socket.AI_ADDRCONFIG | socket.AI_V4MAPPED)
[(2, 1, 6, '', ('199.7.85.13', 80))]
```

If you are curious about how this works behind the scenes, read up on the relevant international standards starting with RFC 3492, and note that Python now includes an 'idna' codec that can translate to and from internationalized domain names.

```
>>> 'παράδειγμα.δοκιμή'.encode('idna')
b'xn--hxajbheg2az3al.xn--jxalpdlp'
```

It is this resulting plain-ASCII string that is actually sent to the domain name service when you enter the Greek sample domain name shown in the previous example. Again, Python will hide this complexity for you.

Primitive Name Service Routines

Before getaddrinfo() was all the rage, programmers doing socket-level programming got by with a simpler collection of name service routines supported by the operating system. They should be avoided today since most of them are hardwired to speak only IPv4.

You can find their documentation in the Standard Library page on the socket module. Here, I will show a few quick examples to illustrate each call. Two calls return the hostname of the current machine.

```
>>> socket.gethostname()
'asaph'
>>> socket.getfqdn()
'asaph.rhodesmill.org'
```

And two more let you convert between IPv4 hostnames and IP addresses.

```
>>> socket.gethostbyname('cern.ch')
'137.138.144.169'
>>> socket.gethostbyaddr('137.138.144.169')
('webr8.cern.ch', [], ['137.138.144.169'])
```

Finally, three routines let you look up protocol numbers and ports using symbolic names known to your operating system.

```
>>> socket.getprotobyname('UDP')
17
>>> socket.getservbyname('www')
80
>>> socket.getservbyport(80)
'www'
```

If you want to try learning the primary IP address for the machine on which your Python program is running, you can try passing its fully qualified hostname into a gethostbyname() call, like this:

```
>>> socket.gethostbyname(socket.getfqdn())
'74.207.234.78'
```

However, since either call could fail and return an address error (see the section on error handling in Chapter 5), your code should have a backup plan in case this pair of calls fails to return a useful IP address.

Using getsockaddr() in Your Own Code

To put everything together, I have assembled a quick example of how getaddrinfo() looks in actual code. Take a look at Listing 4-1.

Listing 4-1. Using getaddrinfo() to Create and Connect a Socket

```
#!/usr/bin/env python3
# Foundations of Python Network Programming, Third Edition
# https://github.com/brandon-rhodes/fopnp/blob/m/py3/chapter04/www_ping.py
# Find the WWW service of an arbitrary host using getaddrinfo().
```

```python
import argparse, socket, sys

def connect_to(hostname_or_ip):
    try:
        infolist = socket.getaddrinfo(
            hostname_or_ip, 'www', 0, socket.SOCK_STREAM, 0,
            socket.AI_ADDRCONFIG | socket.AI_V4MAPPED | socket.AI_CANONNAME,
            )
    except socket.gaierror as e:
        print('Name service failure:', e.args[1])
        sys.exit(1)

    info = infolist[0]  # per standard recommendation, try the first one
    socket_args = info[0:3]
    address = info[4]
    s = socket.socket(*socket_args)
    try:
        s.connect(address)
    except socket.error as e:
        print('Network failure:', e.args[1])
    else:
        print('Success: host', info[3], 'is listening on port 80')

if __name__ == '__main__':
    parser = argparse.ArgumentParser(description='Try connecting to port 80')
    parser.add_argument('hostname', help='hostname that you want to contact')
    connect_to(parser.parse_args().hostname)
```

This script performs a simple "Are you there?" test of whatever web server you name on the command line by attempting a quick connection to port 80 with a streaming socket. Using the script would look something like this:

```
$ python www_ping.py mit.edu
Success: host mit.edu is listening on port 80
$ python www_ping.py smtp.google.com
Network failure: Connection timed out
$ python www_ping.py no-such-host.com
Name service failure: Name or service not known
```

Note three things about this script:

- It is completely general, and it contains no mention either of IP as a protocol or of TCP as a transport. If the user happened to type a hostname that the system recognized as a host to which it was connected through AppleTalk (if you can imagine that sort of thing in this day and age), then getaddrinfo() would be free to return the AppleTalk socket family, type, and protocol, and that would be the kind of socket that you would wind up creating and connecting.

- getaddrinfo() failures cause a specific name service error, which Python calls a gaierror, rather than a plain socket error of the kind used for the normal network failure detected at the end of the script. You will learn more about error handling in Chapter 5.

- You have not given the socket() constructor a list of three separate items. Instead, the parameter list is introduced by an asterisk, which means that the three elements of the socket_args list are passed as three separate parameters to the constructor. This is the opposite of what you need to do with the actual address returned, which is instead passed as a single unit into all of the socket routines that need it.

The DNS Protocol

The *Domain Name System (DNS)* is the scheme by which millions of Internet hosts cooperate to answer the question of what hostnames resolve to which IP addresses. The DNS is behind the fact that you can type python.org into your web browser instead of always having to remember 82.94.164.162 for those of you on IPv4, or 2001:888:2000:d::a2 if you are already enjoying IPv6.

THE DNS PROTOCOL

Purpose: Resolve hostnames by returning IP addresses

Standard: RFC 1034 and RFC 1035 (from 1987)

Runs atop: UDP/IP and TCP/IP

Port number: 53

Libraries: Third-party, including dnspython3

The messages that computers send to perform this resolution traverse a hierarchy of servers. If your local computer and name server cannot resolve a hostname because it neither is local to your organization nor has it been seen recently enough to still be in the name server's cache, then the next step is to query one of the world's top-level name servers to find out which machines are responsible for the domain about which you need to inquire. Once the DNS server IP addresses have been returned, they in turn can be queried for the domain name itself.

Before examining the details, we should first step back for a moment and see how this operation is usually set in motion.

Consider the domain name www.python.org. If your web browser needs to know this address, then the browser runs a call like getaddrinfo() to ask the operating system to resolve that name. Your system itself will know either that it is running a name server of its own or that the network to which it is attached provides name service. Your machine typically configures name server information automatically through DHCP these days when it connects to the network—whether to a LAN in a corporate office or an educational institution, on a wireless network, or over a home cable or DSL connection. In other cases, the DNS server IP addresses will have been configured by hand when a system administrator set up your machine. Either way, the DNS servers must be specified by their raw IP addresses since you obviously cannot perform any DNS queries until you know some other way to reach the servers.

Sometimes people are unhappy with their ISP's DNS behavior or performance and they choose to configure a third-party DNS server of their own choosing, like the servers at 8.8.8.8 and 8.8.4.4 run by Google. In some rare cases, the local DNS domain name servers are known through some other set of names in use by the computer like the WINS Windows naming service. One way or another, however, a DNS server must be identified for name resolution to be possible.

Your computer knows some hostnames without even consulting the domain name service. Querying DNS for a hostname is not actually the first thing that an operating system usually does when you make a call like getaddrinfo(). In fact, because making a DNS query can be time-consuming, it is often the last choice! Depending on the hosts entry in your /etc/nsswitch.conf file if you are on a POSIX box, or else depending on your Windows Control Panel settings, there might be one or several other places that the operating system looks first before turning to DNS. On my Ubuntu laptop, for example, the /etc/hosts file is checked first on every single hostname lookup. Then a specialized protocol called multicast DNS is used, if possible. Only if that fails or is unavailable is full-blown DNS cranked up to answer the hostname query.

To continue our example, imagine that the name www.python.org is not defined locally on your machine and has not been queried recently enough to be in any local cache on the machine where you are running your web browser. In that case, the computer will look up the local DNS server and, typically, send it a single DNS request packet over UDP.

Now the question is in the hands of a real DNS server. For the rest of this discussion, I will call it "your DNS server," in the sense "the particular DNS server that is doing hostname lookups for you." Of course, the server itself probably belongs to someone else, like your employer or your ISP or Google, and is therefore not actually yours in the sense of your owning it.

The first act of your DNS server will be to check its own cache of recently queried domain names to see whether www.python.org has already been checked by some other machine served by the DNS server in the last few minutes or hours. If an entry is present and has not yet expired (and the owner of each domain name gets to choose its expiration timeout because some organizations like to change IP addresses quickly if they need to, while others are happy to have old IP addresses linger for hours or days in the world's DNS caches), then it can be returned immediately. But imagine that it is morning and you are the first person in your office or in the coffee shop to try talking to www.python.org today, so the DNS server has to go find the hostname from scratch.

Your DNS server will now begin a recursive process of asking about www.python.org at the top of the world's DNS server hierarchy, the "root-level" name servers that know all of the top-level domains (TLDs) like .com, .org, .net, and which know the groups of servers that are responsible for each. Name server software generally comes with the IP addresses of these top-level servers built in, so as to solve the bootstrapping problem of how you find any domain name servers before you are actually connected to the domain name system. With this first UDP round-trip, your DNS server will learn (if it did not know already from another recent query) which servers keep the full index of .org domain.

Now a second DNS request will be made, this time to one of the .org servers, asking who runs the python.org domain. You can find out what those top-level servers know about a domain by running the whois command-line program on a POSIX system or use one of the many "whois" web pages online if you do not have the command installed locally.

```
$ whois python.org
Domain Name:PYTHON.ORG
Created On:27-Mar-1995 05:00:00 UTC
Last Updated On:07-Sep-2006 20:50:54 UTC
Expiration Date:28-Mar-2016 05:00:00 UTC
...
Registrant Name:Python Software Foundation
...
Name Server:NS2.XS4ALL.NL
Name Server:NS.XS4ALL.NL
```

And that provides our answer! Wherever you are in the world, your DNS request for any hostname within python.org must be passed on to one of the two DNS servers named in that entry. Of course, when your DNS server makes this request to a top-level domain name server, it does not really get back only two names like those just given. Instead, it is also given their IP addresses so that it can contact them directly without incurring another expensive round of DNS lookups.

Your DNS server is now finished talking to both the root-level DNS server and the top-level .org DNS server, and it can communicate directly with NS2.XS4ALL.NL or NS.XS4ALL.NL to ask about the python.org domain. In fact, it will try one of them and then fall back to trying the other if the first one is unavailable. This increases the chances of you getting an answer, but, of course, a failure will increase the amount of time that you sit there staring at your web browser before the page can actually be displayed.

Depending on how python.org has its name servers configured, the DNS server might require just one more query to get its answer, or it might require several more queries if the organization is a large one with many departments and subdepartments that all run their own DNS servers to which requests need to be delegated. In this case, the www.python.org query can be answered directly by either of the two servers just named, and your DNS server can now return a UDP packet to your browser telling it which IP addresses belong to that hostname.

Note that this process required four separate network round-trips. Your machine made a request and got a response from your own DNS server, and in order to answer that request, your DNS server had to make a recursive query that consisted of three different round-trips to other servers. No wonder your browser sits there spinning when you enter a domain name for the first time.

Why Not to Use Raw DNS

The foregoing explanation of a typical DNS query has, I hope, made clear that your operating system is doing quite a lot for you when you need a hostname looked up. For this reason, I am going to recommend that unless you absolutely need to speak DNS for a very particular reason, you always rely on getaddrinfo() or some other system-supported mechanism for resolving hostnames. Consider these benefits of letting your operating system look up names for you:

- The DNS is often not the only way that a system gets name information. If your application runs off and tries to use DNS on its own as its first choice for resolving a domain name, then users will notice that some computer names that work everywhere else on your system—in their browser, in file share paths, and so forth—suddenly do not work when they use your application because you are not consulting mechanisms like WINS or /etc/hosts like the operating system itself does.

- The local machine probably has a cache of recently queried domain names that might already contain the host whose IP address you need. If you try speaking DNS yourself to answer your query, you will be duplicating work that has already been done.

- The system on which your Python script is running already knows about the local domain name servers, thanks either to manual configuration by your system administrator or to a network setup protocol like DHCP. To crank up DNS inside your Python program, you will have to learn how to query your particular operating system for this information—an operating-system-specific action that I will not be covering in this book.

- If you do not use the local DNS server, then you will not be able to benefit from its own cache that would prevent your application and other applications running on the same network from repeating requests about a hostname that is in frequent use at your location.

- From time to time, adjustments are made to the world DNS infrastructure, and operating system libraries and daemons are gradually updated to accommodate this. If your program makes raw DNS calls of its own, then you will have to follow these changes yourself and make sure your code stays up-to-date with the latest changes in TLD server IP addresses, conventions involving internationalization, and tweaks to the DNS protocol itself.

Finally, note that Python does not come with any DNS facilities built into the Standard Library. If you are going to talk DNS using Python, then you must choose and learn a third-party library for doing so.

Making a DNS Query from Python

There is, however, a solid and legitimate reason to make a DNS call from Python. It is because you are a mail server, or at the least a client trying to send mail directly to your recipients without needing to run a local mail relay, and you want to look up the MX records associated with a domain so that you can find the correct mail server for your friends at @example.com.

Thus, let's take a look at one of the third-party DNS libraries for Python as we bring this chapter to a close. The best one that currently seems to be available for Python 3 is dnspython3, which you can install using the standard Python packaging tool.

```
$ pip install dnspython3
```

The library uses its own tricks to find out what domain name servers your Windows or POSIX operating system is currently using, and then it asks those servers to go and do recursive queries on its behalf. Thus, there is not a single piece of code in this chapter that avoids needing a correctly configured host that an administrator or network configuration service has already configured with working name servers.

Listing 4-2 illustrates a simple and comprehensive lookup.

Listing 4-2. A Simple DNS Query Doing Its Own Recursion

```python
#!/usr/bin/env python3
# Foundations of Python Network Programming, Third Edition
# https://github.com/brandon-rhodes/fopnp/blob/m/py3/chapter04/dns_basic.py
# Basic DNS query

import argparse, dns.resolver

def lookup(name):
    for qtype in 'A', 'AAAA', 'CNAME', 'MX', 'NS':
        answer = dns.resolver.query(name, qtype, raise_on_no_answer=False)
        if answer.rrset is not None:
            print(answer.rrset)

if __name__ == '__main__':
    parser = argparse.ArgumentParser(description='Resolve a name using DNS')
    parser.add_argument('name', help='name that you want to look up in DNS')
    lookup(parser.parse_args().name)
```

You can see that only one type of DNS query can be attempted at a time, so this small script runs in a loop asking for different types of records pertaining to the single hostname that has been given as its command-line argument. Running this against python.org will immediately teach you several things about DNS.

```
$ python dns_basic.py python.org
python.org. 42945 IN A 140.211.10.69
python.org. 86140 IN MX 50 mail.python.org.
python.org. 86146 IN NS ns4.p11.dynect.net.
python.org. 86146 IN NS ns3.p11.dynect.net.
python.org. 86146 IN NS ns1.p11.dynect.net.
python.org. 86146 IN NS ns2.p11.dynect.net.
```

As you can see from the program, each "answer" in the reply that has been returned is represented by a sequence of objects. In order, the keys that get printed on each line are as follows:

- The name looked up.
- The time in seconds that you are allowed to cache the name before it expires.
- The "class" like IN, which indicates that you are being returned Internet address responses.

- The "type" of record. Some common ones are A for an IPv4 address, AAAA for an IPv6 address, NS for a record that lists a name server, and MX for a reply giving the mail server that should be used for a domain.

- Finally, the "data" provides the information you need to connect to or contact a service.

In the query just quoted, you learn three things about the python.org domain. First, the A record tells you that if you want to connect to an actual python.org machine—to make an HTTP connection, start an SSH session, or to do anything else because the user has supplied python.org as the machine to which he or she wants to connect—then you should direct your packets at IP address 140.211.10.69. Second, the NS records tell you that if you want to query the names of any hosts beneath python.org, then you should ask the name servers ns1.p11.dynect.net through ns4.p11.dynect.net (preferably in the order given, rather than in numeric order) to resolve those names for you. Finally, if you want to send e-mail to someone at the e-mail domain @python.org, then you will need to go look up the hostname mail.python.org.

A DNS query can also return a record type CNAME, which indicates that the hostname about which you have queried is actually just an alias for another hostname—that you then have to go and look up separately! Because it often requires two round-trips, this record type is unpopular these days, but you still might run across it.

Resolving Mail Domains

I mentioned previously that resolving an e-mail domain is a legitimate use of raw DNS in most Python programs. The rules for doing this resolution were specified most recently in RFC 5321. They are, briefly, that if MX records exist, then you *must* try to contact those SMTP servers and return an error to the user (or put the message on a retry queue) if none of them will accept the message. Attempt them in order from lowest- to highest-priority number, if their priorities are not equal. If no MX records exist but an A or AAAA record is provided for the domain, then you are allowed to try an SMTP connection to that address. If neither record exists but a CNAME is specified, then the domain name it provides should be searched for MX or A records using the same rules.

Listing 4-3 shows how you might implement this algorithm. By doing a series of DNS queries, it works its way through the possible destinations, printing its decisions as it goes. By adjusting a routine like this to return addresses rather than just printing them, you could power a Python mail dispatcher that needed to deliver e-mail to remote hosts.

Listing 4-3. Resolving an E-mail Domain Name

```
#!/usr/bin/env python3
# Foundations of Python Network Programming, Third Edition
# https://github.com/brandon-rhodes/fopnp/blob/m/py3/chapter04/dns_mx.py
# Looking up a mail domain - the part of an email address after the `@`

import argparse, dns.resolver

def resolve_hostname(hostname, indent=''):
    "Print an A or AAAA record for `hostname`; follow CNAMEs if necessary."
    indent = indent + '    '
    answer = dns.resolver.query(hostname, 'A')
    if answer.rrset is not None:
        for record in answer:
            print(indent, hostname, 'has A address', record.address)
        return
    answer = dns.resolver.query(hostname, 'AAAA')
```

```
    if answer.rrset is not None:
        for record in answer:
            print(indent, hostname, 'has AAAA address', record.address)
        return
    answer = dns.resolver.query(hostname, 'CNAME')
    if answer.rrset is not None:
        record = answer[0]
        cname = record.address
        print(indent, hostname, 'is a CNAME alias for', cname) #?
        resolve_hostname(cname, indent)
        return
    print(indent, 'ERROR: no A, AAAA, or CNAME records for', hostname)

def resolve_email_domain(domain):
    "For an email address `name@domain` find its mail server IP addresses."
    try:
        answer = dns.resolver.query(domain, 'MX', raise_on_no_answer=False)
    except dns.resolver.NXDOMAIN:
        print('Error: No such domain', domain)
        return
    if answer.rrset is not None:
        records = sorted(answer, key=lambda record: record.preference)
        for record in records:
            name = record.exchange.to_text(omit_final_dot=True)
            print('Priority', record.preference)
            resolve_hostname(name)
    else:
        print('This domain has no explicit MX records')
        print('Attempting to resolve it as an A, AAAA, or CNAME')
        resolve_hostname(domain)

if __name__ == '__main__':
    parser = argparse.ArgumentParser(description='Find mailserver IP address')
    parser.add_argument('domain', help='domain that you want to send mail to')
    resolve_email_domain(parser.parse_args().domain)
```

Of course, the implementation of resolve_hostname() shown here is rather fragile since it should really make a dynamic decision between A and AAAA records based on whether the current host is connected to an IPv4 or to an IPv6 network. In fact, it is likely that our friend getsockaddr() should really be deferred to here instead of trying to resolve the mail server hostname ourselves! But since Listing 4-3 is designed to show off how the DNS works, I thought I might as well follow through with the logic using pure DNS so that you could see how the queries are resolved.

Instead of printing the mail server addresses, a real mail server implementation would obviously attempt to deliver mail to them instead and stop once the first success was achieved. (If it kept going through the server list after the success, then several copies of the e-mail would be generated, one for each server to which it was delivered successfully.) Nonetheless, this simple script gives you a good idea of the process. You can see that python.org at the moment has but a single mail server IP address.

```
$ python dns_mx.py python.org
This domain has 1 MX records
Priority 50
    mail.python.org has A address 82.94.164.166
```

Whether that IP belongs to one machine or is shared by a cluster of hosts, is, of course, something that you cannot easily see from outside. Other organizations are more aggressive in giving incoming e-mails several places to land. The IANA currently has no fewer than six e-mail servers (or, at least it offers six IP addresses with which you can connect to, however many servers it in fact is running).

```
$ python dns_mx.py iana.org
This domain has 6 MX records
Priority 10
    pechora7.icann.org has A address 192.0.46.73
Priority 10
    pechora5.icann.org has A address 192.0.46.71
Priority 10
    pechora8.icann.org has A address 192.0.46.74
Priority 10
    pechora1.icann.org has A address 192.0.33.71
Priority 10
    pechora4.icann.org has A address 192.0.33.74
Priority 10
    pechora3.icann.org has A address 192.0.33.73
```

By trying this script against many different domains, you will be able to see how both big and small organizations arrange for incoming e-mails to be routed to IP addresses.

Summary

Python programs often have to turn hostnames into socket addresses to which they can actually make connections.

Most hostname lookup should occur through the getsockaddr() function in the socket module, since its intelligence is usually supplied by your operating system and it will know not only how to look up domain names using all of the mechanisms available to it but also what flavor of address (IPv4 or IPv6) the local IP stack is configured to support.

Traditional IPv4 addresses are still the most prevalent on the Internet, but IPv6 is becoming more and more common. By deferring all hostname and port name lookup to getsockaddr(), your Python program can treat addresses as opaque strings and not have to worry about parsing or interpreting them.

Behind most name resolution is the DNS, a worldwide-distributed database that forwards domain name queries directly to the servers of the organization that owns a domain. While not often used directly from Python, it can be helpful in determining where to direct e-mail based on the e-mail domain named after the @ sign in an e-mail address.

Now that you understand how to name the hosts to which you will then connect sockets, Chapter 5 will explore the different options for encoding and delimiting the data payloads that you then transmit.

CHAPTER 5

Network Data and Network Errors

The first four chapters of this book showed how hosts are named on an IP network and how to set up and tear down both TCP streams and UDP datagram connections between hosts. But how should you prepare data for transmission? How should it be encoded and formatted? And for what kinds of errors will Python programs need to be prepared?

These questions are relevant regardless of whether you are using streams or datagrams, and this chapter provides all of the basic answers to them.

Bytes and Strings

Computer memory chips and network cards both support the *byte* as their common currency. This tiny 8-bit package of information has become our global unit of information storage. There is a difference between memory chips and network cards, however. Python is able to completely conceal from you the choices that it makes about how to represent numbers, strings, lists, and dictionaries in memory as your program runs. Unless you use special debugging tools, you cannot even see the bytes with which these data structures are stored, only how they behave from the outside.

Network communication is different because the socket interface exposes bytes and makes them visible to both the programmer and the application. When doing network programming, you generally cannot avoid thinking about how data will be represented on the wire, which raises questions that a high-level language like Python otherwise lets you avoid.

So, now let's consider the properties of bytes.

- A *bit* is the smallest unit of information. It is a digit that can be either zero or one. In electronics, a bit is often implemented as a wire whose voltage is either hot or tied to ground.

- Eight bits together make a *byte*.

The bits need to be ordered so that you can tell which is which. When you write a binary number like 01100001, you order the digits in the same direction as you do when writing base-ten numbers, with the most significant bit first (just as in the decimal number 234, the 2 is the most significant and the 4 is the least significant, because the hundreds place makes a bigger difference to the number's magnitude than the tens or ones places).

One way to interpret a lone byte is as a number between 00000000 and 11111111. If you do the math, these are the values 0 and 255 in decimal.

You can also interpret the highest byte values in the 0 through 255 range as negative numbers since you can reach them by wrapping around backward from 0. A common choice is to interpret 10000000 through 11111111, which would normally be 128 through 255, as -128 through -1 instead, because then the most significant digit tells you whether the number is negative. (This is called *two's-complement arithmetic*.) Or you can interpret a byte using a variety of more complicated rules that will either assign some symbol or meaning to the byte through means of a table or build even larger numbers by putting the byte together with other bytes.

Network standards use the term *octet* for the 8-bit byte since in the old days a byte could have a variety of different lengths on different computers.

In Python, you will normally represent bytes in one of two ways: either as an integer whose value happens to be between 0 and 255 or as a length-1 byte string where the byte is the single value that it contains. You can type a byte-valued number using any of the typical bases supported in Python source code—binary, octal, decimal, and hexadecimal.

```
>>> 0b1100010
98
>>> 0b1100010 == 0o142 == 98 == 0x62
True
```

You can convert a list of such numbers to a byte string by passing them to the bytes() type inside a sequence, and you can convert back by attempting to iterate across the byte string.

```
>>> b = bytes([0, 1, 98, 99, 100])
>>> len(b)
5
>>> type(b)
<class 'bytes'>
>>> list(b)
[0, 1, 98, 99, 100]
```

What can be a bit confusing is that the repr() of a byte string object uses ASCII characters as a shorthand for the array elements whose byte values happen to correspond to printable character codes, and it uses the explicit hexadecimal format \xNN only for bytes that do not correspond to a printable ASCII character.

```
>>> b
b'\x00\x01bcd'
```

Do not be fooled, however: byte strings are in no way inherently ASCII in their semantics, and they are intended to represent mere sequences of 8-bit bytes.

Character Strings

If you really do want to transmit a string of symbols over a socket, you need an encoding that assigns each symbol to a valid byte value. The most popular such encoding is ASCII, which stands for American Standard Code for Information Interchange, and it defines character codes 0 through 127, which can fit into 7 bits. Therefore, when ASCII is stored in bytes, the most significant bit is always zero. Codes 0 through 31 represent control commands for an output display, not actual glyphs such as letters, numbers, and punctuation, so they cannot be displayed in a quick chart like the one that follows. The three subsequent 32-character tiers of ASCII characters that do represent glyphs are, as you can see, a first tier of punctuation and digits, then a tier that includes the uppercase letters, and finally a tier of the lowercase letters:

```
>>> for i in range(32, 128, 32):
...     print(' '.join(chr(j) for j in range(i, i+32)))
...
  ! " # $ % & ' ( ) * + , - . / 0 1 2 3 4 5 6 7 8 9 : ; < = > ?
@ A B C D E F G H I J K L M N O P Q R S T U V W X Y Z [ \ ] ^ _
` a b c d e f g h i j k l m n o p q r s t u v w x y z { | } ~
```

The character in the upper-left corner is the space, by the way, at character code 32. (The invisible character at the lower-right corner is, oddly enough, one last control character: Delete at position 127.) Note two clever tricks in this 1960 encoding. First, the digits are ordered so that you can compute any digit's mathematical value by subtracting the code for the digit zero. Plus, by flipping the 32's bit, you can switch between the uppercase and lowercase letters or can force letters to one case or the other by setting or clearing the 32's bit on a whole string of letters.

But Python 3 goes far beyond ASCII in the character codes its strings can include. Thanks to a more recent standard named Unicode, we now have character code assignments for numbers reaching beyond the 128 ASCII codes and up into the thousands and even millions. Python considers strings to be made of a sequence of Unicode characters and, as is usual for Python data structures, the actual representation of Python strings in RAM is carefully concealed from you while you are working with the language. But when dealing with data in files or on the network, you will have to think about external representation and about two terms that help you keep straight the meaning of your information versus how it is transmitted or stored:

> *Encoding* characters means turning a string of real Unicode characters into bytes that can be sent out into the real world outside your Python program.

> *Decoding* byte data means converting a byte string into real characters.

It might help you remember to which conversions these words refer if you think of the outside world as consisting of bytes that are stored in a secret code that has to be interpreted or cracked if your Python program is going to process them correctly. To move data outside your Python program, it must become code; to move back in, it must be decoded.

There are many possible encodings in use in the world today. They fall into two general categories.

The simplest encodings are *single-byte encodings* that can represent at most 256 separate characters but that guarantee every character fits into a single byte. These are easy to work with when writing network code. You know ahead of time that reading *n* bytes from a socket will generate *n* characters, for example, and you also know when a stream gets split into pieces that each byte is a stand-alone character that can safely be interpreted without knowing what byte will follow it. Also, you can seek immediately to character *n* in your input by looking at the *n*th byte.

Multibyte encodings are more complicated and lose each of these benefits. Some, like UTF-32, use a fixed number of bytes per character, which is wasteful when data consists mostly of ASCII characters but carries the benefit that each character is always the same length. Others, like UTF-8, vary how many bytes each character occupies and therefore require a great deal of caution; if the data stream is delivered in pieces, then there is no way ahead of time to know whether a character has been split across the boundary or not, and you cannot find character *n* without starting at the beginning and reading until you have read that many characters.

You can find a list of all the encodings that Python supports by looking up the Standard Library documentation for the codecs module.

Most of the single-byte encodings built in to Python are extensions of ASCII that use the remaining 128 values for region-specific letters or symbols:

```
>>> b'\x67\x68\x69\xe7\xe8\xe9'.decode('latin1')
'ghiçèé'
>>> b'\x67\x68\x69\xe7\xe8\xe9'.decode('latin2')
'ghiç
é'
>>> b'\x67\x68\x69\xe7\xe8\xe9'.decode('greek')
'ghiηθι'
>>> b'\x67\x68\x69\xe7\xe8\xe9'.decode('hebrew')
'ghiׇטׁ'
```

The same is true of the many Windows code pages that you will see listed in the Standard Library. A few single-byte encodings, however, share nothing in common with ASCII because they are based on alternative standards from the old days of big IBM mainframes.

```
>>> b'\x67\x68\x69\xe7\xe8\xe9'.decode('EBCDIC-CP-BE')
'ÅÇÑXYZ'
```

The multibyte encodings that you are most likely to encounter are the old UTF-16 scheme (which had a brief heyday back when Unicode was much smaller and could fit into 16 bits), the modern UTF-32 scheme, and the universally popular variable-width UTF-8 that looks like ASCII unless you start including characters with codes greater than 127. Here is what a Unicode string looks like using all three:

```
>>> len('Namárië!')
8
>>> 'Namárië!'.encode('UTF-16')
b'\xff\xfeN\x00a\x00m\x00\xe1\x00r\x00i\x00\xeb\x00!\x00'
>>> len(_)
18
>>> 'Namárië!'.encode('UTF-32')
b'\xff\xfe\x00\x00N\x00\x00\x00a\x00\x00\x00m\x00\x00\x00\xe1\x00\x00\x00r\x00\x00\x00i\x00\x00\x00\xeb\x00\x00\x00!\x00\x00\x00'
>>> len(_)
36
>>> 'Namárië!'.encode('UTF-8')
b'Nam\xc3\xa1ri\xc3\xab!'
>>> len(_)
10
```

If you peer hard into each encoding, you should be able to find the bare ASCII letters N, a, m, r, and i scattered among the byte values representing the non-ASCII characters.

Note that the multibyte encodings each include an extra character, bringing the UTF-16 encoding to a full $(8 \times 2) + 2$ bytes and UTF-32 to $(8 \times 4) + 4$ bytes. This special character \xfeff is the byte order marker (BOM) and can allow readers to autodetect whether the several bytes of each Unicode character are stored with the most significant or least significant byte first. (See the next section for more about byte order.)

There are two characteristic errors that you will encounter when working with encoded text: attempting to load from an encoded byte string that does not in fact follow the encoding rules that you are trying to interpret and attempting to encode characters that cannot actually be represented in the encoding you are requesting.

```
>>> b'\x80'.decode('ascii')
Traceback (most recent call last):
  ...
UnicodeDecodeError: 'ascii' codec can't decode byte 0x80 in position 0: ordinal not in range(128)
>>> 'ghiηθι'.encode('latin-1')
Traceback (most recent call last):
  ...
UnicodeEncodeError: 'latin-1' codec can't encode characters in position 3-5: ordinal not in range(256)
```

You will generally want to fix such errors either by determining that you are using the wrong encoding or by working out why your data is not conforming to the encoding that you expect of it. If neither fix works, however, and you find that your code must routinely survive mismatches between declared encodings and actual strings and data, then you will want to read the Standard Library documentation to learn about alternative approaches to errors rather than having to handle exceptions.

```
>>> b'ab\x80def'.decode('ascii', 'replace')
'ab�def'
>>> b'ab\x80def'.decode('ascii', 'ignore')
'abdef'
>>> 'ghiηθι'.encode('latin-1', 'replace')
b'ghi???'
>>> 'ghiηθι'.encode('latin-1', 'ignore')
b'ghi'
```

These are described in the Standard Library documentation for the codecs module, and you can find more examples in Doug Hellman's Python Module of the Week entry on codecs as well.

Note again that it is dangerous to decode a partially received message if you are using an encoding that encodes some characters using multiple bytes, since one of those characters might have been split between the part of the message that you have already received and the packets that have not yet arrived. See the "Framing and Quoting" section later in this chapter for some approaches to this issue.

Binary Numbers and Network Byte Order

If all you ever want to send across the network is text, then encoding and framing (which you will tackle in the next section) will be your only worries.

However, sometimes you might want to represent your data in a more compact format than text makes possible. Or you might be writing Python code to interface with a service that has already made the choice to use raw binary data. In either case, you will probably have to start worrying about a new issue: network byte order.

To understand the issue of byte order, consider the process of sending an integer over the network. To be specific, think about the integer 4253.

Of course, many protocols will simply transmit this integer as the string '4253'—that is, as four distinct characters. The four digits will require at least four bytes to transmit, at least in any of the usual text encodings. Using decimal digits will also involve some computational expense: since numbers are not stored inside computers in base 10, it will take repeated division—with inspection of the remainder—for the program transmitting the value to determine that this number is in fact made of 4 thousands, plus 2 hundreds, plus 5 tens, plus 3 left over. And when the four-digit string '4253' is received, repeated addition and multiplication by powers of ten will be necessary to put the text back together into a number.

Despite its verbosity, the technique of using plain text for numbers may actually be the most popular on the Internet today. Every time you fetch a web page, for example, the HTTP protocol expresses the Content-Length of the result using a string of decimal digits just like '4253'. Both the web server and the client do the decimal conversion without a second thought, despite a bit of expense. Much of the story of the past 20 years in networking, in fact, has been the replacement of dense binary formats with protocols that are simple, obvious, and human-readable—even if computationally expensive compared to their predecessors.

Of course, multiplication and division are also cheaper on modern processors than back when binary formats were more common—not only because processors have experienced a vast increase in speed but because their designers have become much more clever about implementing integer math so that the same operation requires far fewer cycles today than on the processors of, say, the early 1980s.

79

CHAPTER 5 ■ NETWORK DATA AND NETWORK ERRORS

In any case, the string '4253' is not how your computer represents this number as an integer variable in Python. Instead, it will store it as a binary number, using the bits of several successive bytes to represent the ones place, twos place, fours place, and so forth of a single large number. You can glimpse the way that the integer is stored by using the hex() built-in function at the Python prompt.

```
>>> hex(4253)
'0x109d'
```

Each hex digit corresponds to four bits, so each pair of hex digits represents a byte of data. Instead of being stored as four decimal digits (4, 4, 2, and 3), with the first 4 being the "most significant" digit (since tweaking its value would throw the number off by a thousand) and 3 being its least significant digit, the number is stored as a most significant byte 0x10 and a least significant byte 0x9d, adjacent to one another in memory.

But in which order should these two bytes appear? Here we reach a point of great difference among the architectures of different brands of computer processors. While they will all agree that the bytes in memory have an order and they will all store a string like Content-Length: 4253 in exactly that order starting with C and ending with 3, they do not share a single idea about the order in which the bytes of a binary number should be stored.

We describe the difference this way: some computers are "big-endian" (for example, older SPARC processors) and put the *most* significant byte first, just like we do when writing decimal digits; other computers (like the nearly ubiquitous x86 architecture) are "little-endian" and put the *least* significant byte first (where "first" means "at the byte with the lower memory address").

For an entertaining historical perspective on this issue, be sure to read Danny Cohen's paper IEN-137, "On Holy Wars and a Plea for Peace," which introduced the words *big-endian* and *little-endian* in a parody of Jonathan Swift: www.ietf.org/rfc/ien/ien137.txt.

Python makes it easy to see the difference between the two endians. Simply use the struct module, which provides a variety of operations for converting data to and from popular binary formats. Here is the number 4253 represented first in a little-endian format and then in a big-endian order:

```
>>> import struct
>>> struct.pack('<i', 4253)
b'\x9d\x10\x00\x00'
>>> struct.pack('>i', 4253)
b'\x00\x00\x10\x9d'
```

Here I used the struct formatting code 'i', which uses four bytes to store an integer, and this leaves the two upper bytes zero for a small number like 4253. You can think of the struct endianness codes '<' and '>' for these two orders as little arrows pointing toward the least significant end of a string of bytes, if that helps you to remember which one to use. See the struct module documentation in the Standard Library for the full array of data formats that it supports. It also supports an unpack() operation, which converts the binary data back to Python numbers.

```
>>> struct.unpack('>i', b'\x00\x00\x10\x9d')
(4253,)
```

If the big-endian format makes more sense to you intuitively, then you may be pleased to learn that it "won" the contest of which endianness would become the standard for network data. Therefore, the struct module provides another symbol, '!', which means the same thing as '>' in pack() and unpack() but says to other programmers (and, of course, to yourself as you read the code later), "I am packing this data so that I can send it over the network."

In summary, here is my advice for preparing binary data for transmission across a network socket:

- Use the struct module to produce binary data for transmission on the network and to unpack it upon arrival.

- Select network byte order with the '!' prefix if you control the data format.

- If someone else has designed the protocol and specified little-endian, then you will have to use '<' instead.

Always test struct to see how it lays out your data compared to the specification for the protocol you are speaking; note that 'x' characters in the packing format string can be used to insert padding bytes.

You might see older Python code use a cadre of awkwardly named functions from the socket module in order to turn integers into byte strings in network order. These functions have names like ntohl() and htons(), and they correspond to functions of the same name in the POSIX networking library, which also supplies calls such as socket() and bind(). I suggest you ignore these awkward functions and use the struct module instead; it is more flexible, it is more general, and it produces more readable code.

Framing and Quoting

If you are using UDP datagrams for communication, then the protocol itself will deliver your data in discrete and identifiable chunks. However, you will have to reorder and retransmit those chunks yourself if anything goes wrong on the network, as outlined in Chapter 2.

Nevertheless, if you have chosen the far more common option of using a TCP stream for communication, then you will face the issue of *framing*—of how to delimit your messages so that the receiver can tell where one message ends and the next one begins. Since the data you supply to sendall() might be broken up into several packets for actual transmission on the network, the program that receives your message might have to make several recv() calls before your whole message has been read—or it might not, if all the packets arrive by the time the operating system has the chance to schedule the process again!

The issue of framing asks the question: when is it safe for the receiver finally to stop calling recv() because an entire message or datum has arrived intact and complete, and it can now be interpreted or acted upon as a whole?

As you might imagine, there are several approaches.

First, there is a pattern that can be used by extremely simple network protocols that involve only the delivery of data—no response is expected, so there never has to come a time when the receiver decides "Enough!" and turns around to send a response. In this case, the sender can loop until all of the outgoing data has been passed to sendall() and then close() the socket. The receiver need only call recv() repeatedly until the call finally returns an empty string indicating that the sender has finally closed the socket. You can see this pattern in Listing 5-1.

Listing 5-1. Simply Send All Data and Then Close the Connection

```
#!/usr/bin/env python3
# Foundations of Python Network Programming, Third Edition
# https://github.com/brandon-rhodes/fopnp/blob/m/py3/chapter05/streamer.py
# Client that sends data then closes the socket, not expecting a reply.

import socket
from argparse import ArgumentParser

def server(address):
    sock = socket.socket(socket.AF_INET, socket.SOCK_STREAM)
    sock.setsockopt(socket.SOL_SOCKET, socket.SO_REUSEADDR, 1)
    sock.bind(address)
    sock.listen(1)
    print('Run this script in another window with "-c" to connect')
```

```
    print('Listening at', sock.getsockname())
    sc, sockname = sock.accept()
    print('Accepted connection from', sockname)
    sc.shutdown(socket.SHUT_WR)
    message = b''
    while True:
        more = sc.recv(8192)  # arbitrary value of 8k
        if not more: # socket has closed when recv() returns ''
            print('Received zero bytes - end of file')
            break
        print('Received {} bytes'.format(len(more)))
        message += more
    print('Message:\n')
    print(message.decode('ascii'))
    sc.close()
    sock.close()

def client(address):
    sock = socket.socket(socket.AF_INET, socket.SOCK_STREAM)
    sock.connect(address)
    sock.shutdown(socket.SHUT_RD)
    sock.sendall(b'Beautiful is better than ugly.\n')
    sock.sendall(b'Explicit is better than implicit.\n')
    sock.sendall(b'Simple is better than complex.\n')
    sock.close()

if __name__ == '__main__':
    parser = ArgumentParser(description='Transmit & receive a data stream')
    parser.add_argument('hostname', nargs='?', default='127.0.0.1',
                        help='IP address or hostname (default: %(default)s)')
    parser.add_argument('-c', action='store_true', help='run as the client')
    parser.add_argument('-p', type=int, metavar='port', default=1060,
                        help='TCP port number (default: %(default)s)')
    args = parser.parse_args()
    function = client if args.c else server
    function((args.hostname, args.p))
```

If you run this script as a server and then, at another command prompt, run the client version, you will see that all of the client's data makes it intact to the server, with the end-of-file event generated by the client closing the socket serving as the only framing that is necessary.

```
$ python streamer.py
Run this script in another window with "-c" to connect
Listening at ('127.0.0.1', 1060)
Accepted connection from ('127.0.0.1', 49057)
Received 96 bytes
Received zero bytes - end of file
Message:

Beautiful is better than ugly.
Explicit is better than implicit.
Simple is better than complex.
```

Note the nicety that since this socket is not intended to receive any data, the client and server both go ahead and shut down communication in the direction they do not plan on using. This prevents any accidental use of the socket in the other direction—use that could eventually queue up enough unread data to produce a deadlock, as you saw in Listing 3-2 in Chapter 3. It is really necessary only for either the client or the server to call shutdown() on the socket, but doing so from both directions provides both symmetry and redundancy.

A second pattern is a variant on the first: streaming in both directions. The socket is initially left open in both directions. First, data is streamed in one direction—exactly as shown in Listing 5-1—and then that one direction is shut down. Second, data is then streamed in the other direction, and the socket is finally closed. Again, Listing 3-2 from Chapter 3 illustrates an important warning: always finish the data transfer in one direction before turning around to stream data back in the other, or you could produce a client and server that are deadlocked.

A third pattern, which was also illustrated in Chapter 3, is to use fixed-length messages, as illustrated in Listing 3-1. You can use the Python sendall() method to transmit your byte string and then use a recv() loop of your own devising to make sure that you receive the whole message.

```python
def recvall(sock, length):
    data = ''
    while len(data) < length:
        more = sock.recv(length - len(data))
        if not more:
            raise EOFError('socket closed {} bytes into a {}-byte'
                           ' message'.format(len(data), length))
        data += more
    return data
```

Fixed-length messages are a bit rare since so little data these days seems to fit within static boundaries. However, when transmitting binary data in particular (think of a struct format that always produces data blocks of the same length, for example), you might find it to be a good fit for certain situations.

A fourth pattern is somehow to delimit your messages with special characters. The receiver would wait in a recv() loop like the one just shown but not exit the loop until the reply string it was accumulating finally contained the delimiter indicating the end-of-message. If the bytes or characters in the message are guaranteed to fall within some limited range, then the obvious choice is to end each message with a symbol chosen from outside that range. If you were sending ASCII strings, for example, you might choose the null character '\0' as the delimiter or a character entirely outside the range of ASCII like '\xff'.

If instead the message can include arbitrary data, then using a delimiter is a problem: what if the character you are trying to use as the delimiter turns up as part of the data? The answer, of course, is quoting—just like having to represent a single-quote character as \' in the middle of a Python string that is itself delimited by single-quote characters.

```python
'All\'s well that ends well.'
```

Nevertheless, I recommend using a delimiter scheme only where your message alphabet is constrained; it is usually too much trouble to implement correct quoting and unquoting if you have to handle arbitrary data. For one thing, your test for whether the delimiter has arrived now has to make sure that you are not confusing a quoted delimiter for a real one that actually ends the message. A second complexity is that you then have to make a pass over the message to remove the quote characters that were protecting literal occurrences of the delimiter. Finally, it means that message length cannot be measured until you have performed decoding; a message of length 400 could be 400 symbols long, or it could be 200 instances of the delimiter accompanied by the quoting character, or anything in between.

A fifth pattern is to prefix each message with its length. This is a popular choice for high-performance protocols since blocks of binary data can be sent verbatim without having to be analyzed, quoted, or interpolated. Of course, the length itself has to be framed using one of the techniques given previously—often the length is given as a simple fixed-width binary integer or else a variable-length decimal string followed by a textual delimiter. Either way, once the length has been read and decoded, the receiver can enter a loop and call recv() repeatedly until the whole message has arrived. The loop can look exactly like the one in Listing 3-1, but with a length variable in place of the number 16.

Finally, what if you want the simplicity and efficiency of this fifth pattern but you do not know ahead of time the length of each message—perhaps because the sender is reading data from a source whose length they cannot predict? In such cases, do you have to abandon elegance and slog through the data looking for delimiters?

Unknown lengths are no problem if you use the sixth, and final, pattern. Instead of sending just one, try sending several blocks of data that are each prefixed with their length. This means that as each chunk of new information becomes available to the sender, it can be labeled with its length and placed on the outgoing stream. When the end finally arrives, the sender can emit an agreed-upon signal—perhaps a length field giving the number zero—that tells the receiver that the series of blocks is complete.

A simple example of this idea is shown in Listing 5-2. Like the previous listing, this sends data in only one direction—from the client to the server—but the data structure is much more interesting than in the previous listing. Each message is prefixed with a 4-byte length contained in a struct. Since 'I' means a 32-bit unsigned integer, each frame can be up to 4GB in length. This sample code sends a series of three blocks to the server followed by a zero-length message, which is just a length field with zeros inside and then no message data after it, to signal that the series of blocks is over.

Listing 5-2. Framing Each Block of Data by Preceding It with Its Length

```
#!/usr/bin/env python3
# Foundations of Python Network Programming, Third Edition
# https://github.com/brandon-rhodes/fopnp/blob/m/py3/chapter05/blocks.py
# Sending data over a stream but delimited as length-prefixed blocks.

import socket, struct
from argparse import ArgumentParser

header_struct = struct.Struct('!I')  # messages up to 2**32 - 1 in length

def recvall(sock, length):
    blocks = []
    while length:
        block = sock.recv(length)
        if not block:
            raise EOFError('socket closed with %d bytes left'
                           ' in this block'.format(length))
        length -= len(block)
        blocks.append(block)
    return b''.join(blocks)

def get_block(sock):
    data = recvall(sock, header_struct.size)
    (block_length,) = header_struct.unpack(data)
    return recvall(sock, block_length)

def put_block(sock, message):
    block_length = len(message)
    sock.send(header_struct.pack(block_length))
    sock.send(message)

def server(address):
    sock = socket.socket(socket.AF_INET, socket.SOCK_STREAM)
    sock.setsockopt(socket.SOL_SOCKET, socket.SO_REUSEADDR, 1)
    sock.bind(address)
```

```
    sock.listen(1)
    print('Run this script in another window with "-c" to connect')
    print('Listening at', sock.getsockname())
    sc, sockname = sock.accept()
    print('Accepted connection from', sockname)
    sc.shutdown(socket.SHUT_WR)
    while True:
        block = get_block(sc)
        if not block:
            break
        print('Block says:', repr(block))
    sc.close()
    sock.close()

def client(address):
    sock = socket.socket(socket.AF_INET, socket.SOCK_STREAM)
    sock.connect(address)
    sock.shutdown(socket.SHUT_RD)
    put_block(sock, b'Beautiful is better than ugly.')
    put_block(sock, b'Explicit is better than implicit.')
    put_block(sock, b'Simple is better than complex.')
    put_block(sock, b'')
    sock.close()

if __name__ == '__main__':
    parser = ArgumentParser(description='Transmit & receive blocks over TCP')
    parser.add_argument('hostname', nargs='?', default='127.0.0.1',
                        help='IP address or hostname (default: %(default)s)')
    parser.add_argument('-c', action='store_true', help='run as the client')
    parser.add_argument('-p', type=int, metavar='port', default=1060,
                        help='TCP port number (default: %(default)s)')
    args = parser.parse_args()
    function = client if args.c else server
    function((args.hostname, args.p))
```

Note how careful you must be! Even though the 4-byte length field is such a tiny amount of data that you might not be able to imagine recv() not returning it all at once, the code is correct only if you carefully wrap recv() in a loop that (just in case) will keep demanding more data until all four bytes have arrived. This is the kind of caution that is necessary when writing network code.

Thus, you have at least six options for dividing up an unending stream of data into digestible chunks so that clients and servers know when a message is complete and can turn around and respond. Note that many modern protocols mix them together, and you are free to do the same thing.

A good example of a mashup between different framing techniques is the HTTP protocol, which you will learn more about later in this book. It uses a delimiter—the blank line '\r\n\r\n'—to signal when its headers are complete. Because the headers are text, line endings can safely be treated as special characters this way. However, since the actual payload can be pure binary data, such as an image or compressed file, a Content-Length measured in bytes is provided in the headers to determine how much more data to read off the socket past the end of the headers. Thus, HTTP mixes the fourth and fifth patterns you have seen here. In fact, it can also use the sixth option: if a server is streaming a response whose length it cannot predict, then HTTP can use a "chunked encoding," which sends a series of blocks that are each prefixed with their length. A zero-length field marks the end of the transmission, just as it does in Listing 5-2.

Pickles and Self-delimiting Formats

Note that some kinds of data you might send across the network already include some form of built-in delimiting. If you are transmitting such data, then you might not have to impose your own framing atop what the data is already doing.

Consider Python "pickles," for example, the native form of serialization that comes with the Standard Library. Using a quirky mix of text commands and data, a pickle stores the contents of a Python data structure so that you can reconstruct it later or on a different machine.

```
>>> import pickle
>>> pickle.dumps([5, 6, 7])
b'\x80\x03]q\x00(K\x05K\x06K\x07e.'
```

The interesting thing about this output data is the '.' character that you see at the end of the foregoing string. It is the format's way of marking the end of a pickle. Upon encountering it, the loader can stop and return the value without reading any further. Thus, you can take the foregoing pickle, stick some ugly data on the end, and see that loads() will completely ignore the extra data and give you the original list back.

```
>>> pickle.loads(b'\x80\x03]q\x00(K\x05K\x06K\x07e.blahblahblah')
[5, 6, 7]
```

Of course, using loads() this way is not useful for network data since it does not tell you how many bytes it processed in order to reload the pickle; you still do not know how much of the string is pickle data. But if you switch to reading from a file and use the pickle load() function, then the file pointer will remain right at the end of the pickle data, and you can start reading from there if you want to read what came after the pickle.

```
>>> from io import BytesIO
>>> f = BytesIO(b'\x80\x03]q\x00(K\x05K\x06K\x07e.blahblahblah')
>>> pickle.load(f)
[5, 6, 7]
>>> f.tell()
14
>>> f.read()
b'blahblahblah'
```

Alternately, you could create a protocol that just consisted of sending pickles back and forth between two Python programs. Note that you would not need the kind of loop that you put into the recvall() function in Listing 5-2 because the pickle library knows all about reading from files and how it might have to do repeated reads until an entire pickle has been read. Use the makefile() socket method (discussed in Chapter 3) if you want to wrap a socket in a Python file object for consumption by a routine like the pickle load() function.

Note that there are many subtleties involved in pickling large data structures, especially if they contain Python objects beyond simple built-in types such as integers, strings, lists, and dictionaries. See the pickle module documentation for more details.

XML and JSON

If your protocol needs to be usable from other programming languages or if you simply prefer universal standards instead of formats specific to Python, then the JSON and XML data formats are each a popular choice. Note that neither of these formats supports framing, so you will first have to figure out how to extract a complete string of text from over the network before you can then process it.

JSON is among the best choices available today for sending data between different computer languages. Since Python 2.6, it has been included in the Standard Library as a module named json. It offers a universal technique for serializing simple data structures.

```
>>> import json
>>> json.dumps([51, 'Namárië!'])
'[51, "Nam\\u00e1ri\\u00eb!"]'
>>> json.dumps([51, 'Namárië!'], ensure_ascii=False)
'[51, "Namárië!"]'
>>> json.loads('{"name": "Lancelot", "quest": "Grail"}')
{u'quest': u'Grail', u'name': u'Lancelot'}
```

Note from this example that JSON not only allows Unicode characters in its strings but can even include Unicode characters literally inline in its payload if you tell the Python json module that it need not restrict its output to ASCII characters. Also note that the JSON representation is defined as producing a string, which is why full strings and not simply Python byte objects are being used here as input and output from the json module. Per the JSON standard, you will want to encode its strings as UTF-8 for transmission on the wire.

The XML format is better for documents since its basic structure is to take strings and mark them up by wrapping them in angle-bracketed elements. In Chapter 10, you will take an extensive look at the various options available in Python for processing documents written in XML and related formats. For now, however, simply keep in mind that you do not have to limit your use of XML to when you are actually using the HTTP protocol. There might be a circumstance when you need markup in text and you find XML useful in conjunction with some other protocol.

Among the many other formats that developers might want to consider are binary formats like Thrift and Google Protocol Buffers, which are a bit different from the formats just defined because both the client and the server need to have a code definition available to them of what each message will contain. However, these systems contain provisions for different protocol versions so that new servers can be brought into production still talking to other machines with an older protocol version until they can all be updated to the new one. They are efficient, and they pass binary data with no problem.

Compression

Since the time necessary to transmit data over the network is often more significant than the time your CPU spends preparing the data for transmission, it is often worthwhile to compress data before sending it. The popular HTTP protocol, as you will see in Chapter 9, lets a client and server figure out whether they can both support compression.

An interesting fact about the GNU zlib facility, which is available through the Python Standard Library and is one of the most ubiquitous forms of compression on the Internet today, is that it is self-framing. If you start feeding it a compressed stream of data, then it can tell you when the compressed data has ended and give you access to the uncompressed payload that might follow.

Most protocols choose to do their own framing and then, if desired, pass the resulting block to zlib for decompression. However, you could conceivably promise yourself that you will always tack a bit of uncompressed data onto the end of each zlib compressed string (here, I will use a single b'.' byte) and watch for your compression object to split out that "extra data" as the signal that you are done.

Consider this combination of two compressed data streams:

```
>>> import zlib
>>> data = zlib.compress(b'Python') + b'.' + zlib.compress(b'zlib') + b'.'
>>> data
b'x\x9c\x0b\xa8,\xc9\xc8\xcf\x03\x00\x08\x97\x02\x83.x\x9c\xab\xca\xc9L\x02\x00\x04d\x01\xb2.'
>>> len(data)
28
```

Note that most compression schemes, when given tiny payloads, tend to make them longer instead of shorter because the overhead of the compression format overwhelms any tiny bit of compressibility in the payload.

Imagine that these 28 bytes arrive at their destination in 8-byte packets. After processing the first packet, you will find the decompression object's unused_data slot still empty, telling you that there is still more data coming.

```
>>> d = zlib.decompressobj()
>>> d.decompress(data[0:8]), d.unused_data
(b'Pytho', b'')
```

So, you would want to recv() on the socket again. The second block of eight characters, when fed to the decompress object, will both finish out the compressed data for which you were waiting and return a nonempty unused_data value that shows you that you finally received the b'.' byte:

```
>>> d.decompress(data[8:16]), d.unused_data
('n', '.x')
```

The character following the period must be the first byte of whatever payload is coming after this first bit of compressed data. Since here you are expecting further compressed data, you will feed the 'x' to a fresh decompress object to which you can then feed the final 8-byte "packets" you are simulating:

```
>>> d = zlib.decompressobj()
>>> d.decompress(b'x'), d.unused_data
(b'', b'')
>>> d.decompress(data[16:24]), d.unused_data
(b'zlib', b'')
>>> d.decompress(data[24:]), d.unused_data
(b'', b'.')
```

At this point, unused_data is again nonempty to show you that you have read past the end of this second bout of compressed data and can examine its content knowing that it has arrived complete and intact.

Again, most protocol designers make compression optional and simply do their own framing. Nonetheless, if you know ahead of time that you will always want to use zlib, then a convention like this will let you take advantage of the stream termination built into zlib and autodetect the end of each compressed stream.

Network Exceptions

The example scripts in this book are generally designed to catch only those exceptions that are integral to the feature being demonstrated. Thus, when I illustrated socket timeouts in Listing 2-2, I was careful to catch the exception socket.timeout since that is how timeouts are signaled. However, I ignored all of the other exceptions that will occur if the hostname provided on the command line is invalid, a remote IP is used with bind(), the port used with bind() is already busy, or the peer cannot be contacted or stops responding.

What errors can result from working with sockets? Though the number of errors that can take place while using a network connection is quite large—involving every possible misstep that can occur at every stage of the complex TCP/IP protocol—the number of actual exceptions with which socket operations can hit your programs is fortunately quite few. The exceptions that are specific to socket operations are as follows:

> OSError: This is the workhorse of the socket module, and it will be raised for nearly every failure that can happen at any stage in network transmission. This can occur during nearly any socket call, even when you least expect it. When a previous send(), for example, has elicited a reset (RST) packet from the remote host, you will actually see the error raised by whatever socket operation you next attempt on that socket.

socket.gaierror: This exception is raised when getaddrinfo() cannot find a name or service about which you ask, which is the reason for the letters *g*, *a*, and *i* in its name. It can be raised not only when you make an explicit call to getaddrinfo() but also if you supply a hostname instead of an IP address to a call like bind() or connect() and the hostname lookup fails. If you catch this exception, you can look inside of the exception object for the error number and message.

```
>>> import socket
>>> s = socket.socket(socket.AF_INET, socket.SOCK_STREAM)
>>> try:
...     s.connect(('nonexistent.hostname.foo.bar', 80))
... except socket.gaierror as e:
...     raise
...
Traceback (most recent call last):
  ...
socket.gaierror: [Errno -2] Name or service not known
>>> e.errno
-2
>>> e.strerror
'Name or service not known'
```

socket.timeout: This exception is raised only if you, or a library that you are using, decides to set a timeout on a socket rather than be willing to wait forever for a send() or recv() to complete. It indicates that the timeout indeed expired before the operation could complete normally.

You will see that the Standard Library documentation for the socket module also describes an herror exception. Fortunately, it can occur only if you use certain old-fashioned address lookup calls instead of following the practices outlined in Chapter 4.

A big question when using higher-level socket-based protocols from Python is whether they allow raw socket errors to hit your own code or whether they catch them and turn them into their own kind of error. Examples of both approaches exist within the Python Standard Library itself! For example, httplib considers itself low level enough that it can let you see the raw socket error that results from connecting to an unknown hostname.

```
>>> import http.client
>>> h = http.client.HTTPConnection('nonexistent.hostname.foo.bar')
>>> h.request('GET', '/')
Traceback (most recent call last):
  ...
socket.gaierror: [Errno -2] Name or service not known
```

But urllib2, probably because it wants to preserve the semantics of being a clean and neutral system for resolving URLs to documents, hides this same error and raises URLError instead.

```
>>> import urllib.request
>>> urllib.request.urlopen('http://nonexistent.hostname.foo.bar/')
Traceback (most recent call last):
  ...
socket.gaierror: [Errno -2] Name or service not known
```

During handling of the above exception, another exception occurred:

Traceback (most recent call last):
  ...
urllib.error.URLError: <urlopen error [Errno -2] Name or service not known>

So, depending on the protocol implementation you are using, you might have to deal only with exceptions specific to that protocol, or you might have to deal with both protocol-specific exceptions and with raw socket errors. Consult the documentation carefully if you are in doubt about the approach taken by a particular library. For the major packages that I cover in subsequent chapters of this book, I have tried to provide insets that list the possible exceptions to which each library can subject your code.

Of course, you can always fire up the library in question, provide it with a nonexistent hostname, or even run it when disconnected from the network and see what kind of exception comes out.

When writing a network program, how should you handle all of the errors that can occur? Of course, this question is not really specific to networking. All sorts of Python programs have to handle exceptions, and the techniques that I discuss briefly in this chapter are applicable to many other kinds of programs. Your approach will differ whether you are packaging up exceptions for processing by other programmers who call your API or whether you are intercepting exceptions to report them appropriately to an end user.

Raising More Specific Exceptions

There are two approaches to delivering exceptions to the users of an API that you are writing. Of course, in many cases you will be the only customer of a module or routine you are writing. However, it is still worthwhile to think of your future self as a customer who will have forgotten nearly everything about this module and will very much appreciate simplicity and clarity in its approach toward exceptions.

One option is not to handle network exceptions at all. They will then be visible for processing by the caller, who can catch or report them as they choose. This approach is a good match for networking routines that are fairly low level, where the caller can vividly picture why you are setting up a socket and why its setup or use might have run into an error. Only if the mapping between API callables and low-level networking actions is clear will the developer writing the calling code expect a network error.

The other approach is wrapping the network errors in an exception of your own. This can be much easier on authors who know little about how you implement your routines because their code can now catch exceptions specific to the operations your code performs without having to know the details of how you use sockets. Custom exceptions also give you the opportunity to craft error messages that describe exactly what your library was trying to accomplish when it ran afoul of the network.

If, for example, you write a little mycopy() method that copies a file from one remote machine to another, a socket.error will not help the caller know whether the error was with the connection to the source or the destination machine or whether it was some other problem altogether. In this case, it could be much better to define your own exceptions—perhaps SourceError and DestinationError—which have a tight semantic relationship to your API. You can always include the original socket error through raise...from exception chaining, in case some users of your API will want to investigate further.

```
class DestinationError(Exception):
    def __str__(self):
        return '%s: %s' % (self.args[0], self.__cause__.strerror)

# ...

try:
    host = sock.connect(address)
except socket.error as e:
    raise DestinationError('Error connecting to destination') from e
```

This code assumes, of course, that `DestinationError` will only ever be wrapping `OSError` descendants like `socket.error`. Otherwise, the `__str__()` method would have to be more complicated to handle the case where the cause exception holds its textual information in an attribute other than `strerror`. But this at least illustrates the pattern. The caller who catches a `DestinationError` can then examine its `__cause__` to learn about the network error behind the semantically richer exception they have actually caught.

Catching and Reporting Network Exceptions

There are two basic approaches to catching exceptions: granular exception handlers and blanket exception handlers.

The granular approach to exceptions is to wrap a `try...except` clause around every single network call that you ever make and print out a pithy error message in its place. While suitable for short programs, this can become repetitive in long programs without necessarily providing much more information for the user. When you wrap the hundredth network operation in your program with yet another `try...except` and specific error message, ask yourself whether you are really providing more information.

The other approach is using blanket exception handlers. This involves stepping back from your code and identifying big regions that do specific things, like these:

- "This whole routine is about connecting to the license server."

- "All of the socket operations in this function are fetching a response from the database."

- "This last part is all cleanup and shutdown code."

Then the outer parts of your program—the ones that collect input, command-line arguments, and configuration settings and then set big operations in motion—can wrap those big operations with handlers like the following:

```
import sys

...

try:
    deliver_updated_keyfiles(...)
except (socket.error, socket.gaierror) as e:
    print('cannot deliver remote keyfiles: {}'.format(e), file=sys.stderr)
    exit(1)
```

Better yet, have your code raise an error of your own devising that indicates an error that specifically needs to halt the program and print error output for the user.

```
except:
    FatalError('cannot send replies: {}'.format(e))
```

Then, at the very top level of your program, catch all the `FatalError` exceptions that you throw and print the error messages out there. That way, when the day comes that you want to add a command-line option that sends fatal errors to the system error logs instead of to the screen, you have to adjust only one piece of code instead of a dozen!

There is one final reason that might dictate where you add an exception handler to your network program: you might want intelligently to retry an operation that failed. In long-running programs, this is common. Imagine a utility that periodically sent out e-mails with its status. If it suddenly cannot send them successfully, then it probably does not want to shut down for what might be just a transient error. Instead, the e-mail thread might log the error, wait several minutes, and try again.

In such cases, you will add exception handlers around specific sequences of network operations that you want to treat as having succeeded or failed as a single combined operation. "If anything goes wrong in here, then I will just give up, wait ten minutes, and then start the attempt to send that e-mail all over again." Here the structure and logic of the network operations that you are performing—and not user or programmer convenience—will guide where you deploy `try...except` clauses.

Summary

For machine information to be placed on the network, it has to be transformed so that regardless of whatever private and idiosyncratic storage mechanism is used inside your machine, the data is presented using a public and reproducible representation that can be read on other systems, by other programs, and perhaps even by other programming languages.

For text, the big question will be choosing an encoding so that the symbols you want to transmit can be changed into bytes, since 8-bit octets are the common currency of an IP network. Binary data will require your attention to make sure that bytes are ordered in such a way that is compatible between different machines; the Python `struct` module will help you with this. Finally, data structures and documents are sometimes best sent using something like JSON or XML, which provides a common way to share structured data between machines.

When using TCP/IP streams, a big question you will face is about framing: how, in the long stream of data, will you tell where a particular message starts and ends? There are many possible techniques for accomplishing this, all of which must be handled with care since `recv()` might return only part of an incoming transmission with each call. Special delimiter characters or patterns, fixed-length messages, and chunked-encoding schemes are all possible ways to festoon blocks of data so that they can be distinguished.

Not only will Python pickles transform data structures into strings that you can send across the network, but also the `pickle` module will know where an incoming pickle ends. This lets you use pickles not only to encode data but also to frame the individual messages on a stream. The `zlib` compression module, which is often used with HTTP, also can tell when a compressed segment comes to an end and thus can provide you with inexpensive framing.

Sockets can raise several kinds of exceptions, as can network protocols that your code uses. The choice of when to use `try...except` clauses will depend on your audience—are you writing a library for other developers or a tool for end users? It will also depend on semantics: you can wrap a whole section of your program in a `try...except` if all of that code is doing one big thing from the point of view of the caller or end user.

Finally, you will want to wrap operations separately with a `try...except` that can be automatically retried in case the error is transient and the call might be able to succeed later.

CHAPTER 6

TLS/SSL

Originally known as the Secure Sockets Layer (SSL) when first released by Netscape in 1995, Transport Layer Security (TLS) became an Internet standard in 1999 and may be the most widely deployed form of encryption used on the Internet today. As you will learn in this chapter, it is used with many basic protocols on the modern Internet to verify server identity and to protect data in transit.

The correct use and deployment of TLS is a moving target. Each year, new attacks are suggested against its encryption algorithms, and new ciphers and techniques are pioneered as a result. TLS 1.2 is the most current version as of this third edition of *Foundations of Python Network Programming*, but further versions will doubtlessly be issued in the years to come. I will try to keep the example scripts stored online in the book's source code repository updated as the state of the art advances Thus, be sure that you go to the URL at the top of each script shown in this chapter and cut and paste from the version of the code that you find there in version control.

This chapter will begin by clarifying what TLS accomplishes and outlining the techniques that it uses to do so. Then you will look at Python examples, both simple and complex, to learn how TLS can be activated and configured on a TCP socket. Finally, you will see how TLS is integrated into the real-world protocols that you will learn about in the rest of the book.

What TLS Fails to Protect

The data passing over a well-configured TLS socket should, as you will see later in this chapter, appear as gibberish to anyone watching. Furthermore, unless mathematics has failed the designers of TLS, it will be gibberish that is fairly impressively impenetrable even to a computer—and even to a government agency with a large budget. It should prevent any eavesdroppers of, say, an HTTPS connection from learning the URL that you request, the content that comes back, or any identifying information such as a password or cookie that might pass in either direction across the socket. (See Chapter 9 for more information about HTTP features such as passwords and cookies.)

Nonetheless, you should immediately step back and remember how much about a connection, besides its data, is *not* made secret by TLS and will still be observable by any third party.

- The addresses of both your machine and the remote host are visible, as plain bytes, in every single packet's IP header.

- The port number of your client and of the server also appears in every TCP header.

- The DNS request that your client made to learn the server's IP address in the first place probably passed across the network in the clear.

An observer can watch the size of the chunks of data that pass in each direction across the TLS-encrypted socket. Even though TLS will try to hide the exact number of bytes, it will still be possible to see in roughly what sized chunks data passes, as well as the overall pattern of requests and responses.

I'll illustrate the previous weaknesses with an example. Imagine that you use a secure HTTPS client (such as your favorite web browser) to fetch https://pypi.python.org/pypi/skyfield/ over a coffee shop's wireless network.

What would an observer know—where an "observer" could be anyone else connected to the coffee shop's wireless network or who has control of one of the routers between it and the rest of the Internet? The observer will first see your machine make a DNS query for `pypi.python.org`, and unless there are many other web sites hosted at the IP address that comes back, they will guess that your subsequent conversations with that IP address at port 443 are for the purpose of viewing `https://pypi.python.org` web pages. They will know the difference between your HTTP requests and the server's responses because HTTP is a lock-step protocol where each request gets written out in its entirety before a response is then written back. Furthermore, they will know roughly the size of each returned document, as well as the order in which they were fetched.

Think of what the observer could learn! Different pages at `https://pypi.python.org` will have different sizes, which the observer could catalog by scanning the site with a web scraper (see Chapter 11). Different genres of pages will involve different constellations of images and other resources that are referenced in the HTML and need to be downloaded on first viewing or if they have expired from your browser's cache. While the outside observer might not know exactly the searches that you enter and the packages that you eventually visit or download, they will often be able to make a good guess based on the rough sizes of the files that they see you fetch.

The big question about how to keep your browsing habits secret, or to conceal any other personal data that travels across the public Internet, is far beyond the scope of this book and will involve research into mechanisms such as online anonymity networks (Tor has been in the news lately, for example) and anonymous remailers. Even when such mechanisms are employed, your machine is still likely to send and receive blocks of data whose size might be used to guess what you are doing. A powerful enough adversary might even note that your pattern of requests corresponds with payloads exiting the anonymous network elsewhere to reach a particular destination.

The rest of this chapter will focus instead on the narrower question of what TLS *can* achieve and how your Python code can effectively use it.

What Could Possibly Go Wrong?

To tour the essential features of TLS, you will consider the series of challenges that the protocol itself faces when establishing a connection and learn how each hurdle is faced and overcome.

Let's presume you want to open a TCP conversation with a particular hostname and port number somewhere on the Internet and that you have reluctantly accepted that your DNS lookup of the hostname will be public knowledge, as will the port number to which you are connecting (which will reveal the protocol you are speaking, unless you are connecting to a service whose owner has bound it to a nonstandard or misleading port number). You would go ahead and make a standard TCP connection to the IP address and port. If the protocol you are speaking requires an introduction between turning on encryption, those first few bytes would pass in the clear for everyone to see. (Protocols vary in this detail—HTTPS does not send anything before turning on encryption, but SMTP exchanges several lines of text. You will learn the behavior of several major protocols later in this chapter.)

Once you have the socket up and running and have exchanged whatever pleasantries your protocol dictates to prepare the way for encryption, it is time for TLS to take over and begin to build strong guarantees about both to whom you are talking and how you and the *peer* (the other party) to whom you are speaking will protect data from prying eyes.

The first demand of your TLS client will be that the remote server provide a binary document called a *certificate*, which includes what cryptologists call a *public key*—an integer that can be used to encrypt data, such that only the possessor of the corresponding *private key* integer can decrypt the information and understand it. If the remote server is correctly configured and has never been compromised, then it will both possess a copy of the private key and be the only server on the Internet (with the possible exception of the other machines in its cluster) that holds such a copy. How can your TLS implementation verify that the remote server actually holds the private key? Simple! Your TLS library sends some information across the wire that has been encrypted using the public key, and it demands that the remote server provide a checksum demonstrating that the data was decrypted successfully with the secret key.

Your TLS stack must also turn its attention to the question of whether the remote certificate has been forged. After all, anyone with access to the `openssl` command-line tool (or any of a number of other tools) can create a certificate whose common name is `cn=www.google.com` or `cn=pypi.python.org` or anything else. Why would you trust such a claim? The solution is for your TLS session to keep a list of *certificate authorities (CAs)* that it trusts to verify Internet host identities. By default, your operating system TLS library or that of your web browser uses a standard worldwide CA list of a few hundred certificates that represent organizations in the business of performing trusted site verification. However, you can always provide a CA list of your own if you are not satisfied with the defaults or if you want to use a private CA that your organization has generated for signing your own private host certificates for free. This is a popular option when no outside clients are going to connect and you need to support connections only between your own services.

The mathematical mark that a CA makes upon a certificate to demonstrate its approval is called a *signature*. Your TLS library will verify the certificate's signature against the public key of the corresponding CA certificate before accepting that the certificate is valid.

Once TLS has verified that the body of the certificate was indeed submitted to and signed by the trusted third party, it will examine the data fields of the certificate itself. Two kinds of fields will be of special interest. First, certificates include a `notBefore` date and a `notAfter` date to bracket the time period in which they are valid so that the certificates belonging to stolen private keys do not last forever. Your TLS stack will check these using your system clock, which means that a bad or misconfigured clock can actually break your ability to communicate over TLS! Second, the certificate's common name should match the hostname to which you are trying to connect—after all, if you want to connect to `https://pypi.python.org`, you are hardly going to be reassured if the site responds with a certificate for a completely different hostname!

A single certificate can actually be shared among many hostnames. Modern certificates can supplement the single-value common name in their `subject` field with additional names stored in their `subjectAltName` field. Also, any of those names can include wildcards like `*.python.org` that match multiple hostnames instead of just one hostname each. Modern TLS algorithms will perform such matching for you automatically, and the Python `ssl` module has its own ability to do so as well.

Finally, the TLS agents on the client and server negotiate a shared secret key and cipher with which to encrypt the actual data that passes over the connection. This is one final point at which TLS can fail because correctly configured software will reject either a cipher or key length that it believes to be inadequate. In fact, this can happen at two levels: TLS can fail either because the version of the TLS protocol that the other end wants to speak is too hopelessly out-of-date and insecure or because the particular ciphers that the other end supports are not considered strong enough to trust.

Once the cipher is agreed upon and both peers have generated the keys, both for encrypting data and also for signing each block of data, control is handed back to the application at each end. Each chunk of data they transmit is encrypted with the encryption key, and then the resulting block is signed with the signing key to prove to the other end that it was really generated by the other peer and not someone who has jumped on to the network to attempt a *man-in-the-middle* attack. Data can flow in both directions without any restriction, just as on a normal TCP socket, until TLS shuts down and the socket either is closed or returns to plain-text mode.

In the sections that follow, you will learn how to control Python's `ssl` library because it makes every one of the major decisions outlined earlier. Please consult official references for further information, as well as resources such as Bruce Schneier's books, the Google Online Security blog, and blogs like Adam Langley's. I myself found Hynek Schlawack's "The Sorry State Of SSL" talk at PyCon 2014 helpful, which you can watch online. If even more recent talks on TLS have been featured at conferences by the time you read this book, they might be a good source of up-to-date information on the dynamic practice of cryptography.

Generating Certificates

The Python Standard Library does not concern itself with private key generation or with certificate signing. If you need to perform these steps, you will have to use other tools instead. One of the most widespread is the `openssl` command-line tool. If you want to see several examples of how it is invoked, see the Makefile in the `playground/certs` directory of this book's source code repository.

```
https://github.com/brandon-rhodes/fopnp/tree/m/playground/certs
```

The certs directory also contains several certificates used in the network playground itself (see Chapter 1), several of which you will use at the command line in this chapter's examples. The ca.crt certificate, which is a small self-contained certificate authority that you will tell Python to trust when using the other certificates with TLS, has signed all of the other certificates.

In brief, certificate creation generally begins with two pieces of information—one human-generated and the other machine-generated. These are, respectively, a textual description of the entity described by the certificate and a private key that has been carefully produced using sources of true randomness provided by the operating system. I usually save the handwritten identity description to a version-controlled file for later reference; however, some administrators simply type the fields into openssl when prompted for them. As one example, Listing 6-1 shows the www.cnf file used to generate the certificate for the network playground's www.example.com web server.

Listing 6-1. Configuration for an X.509 Certificate for Use by the OpenSSL Command Line

```
[ req ]
prompt = no
distinguished_name = req_distinguished_name

[ req_distinguished_name ]
countryName            = us
stateOrProvinceName    = New York
localityName           = New York
O.organizationName     = Example from Apress Media LLC
organizationalUnitName = Foundations of Python Network Programming 3rd Ed
commonName             = www.example.com
emailAddress           = root@example.com

[ ssl_client ]
basicConstraints = CA:FALSE
nsCertType = client
keyUsage = digitalSignature, keyEncipherment
extendedKeyUsage = clientAuth
```

Remember that the commonName and any subjectAltName entries (not present in this example) are the crucial fields that TLS will compare to the hostname to determine whether it is talking to the correct host.

Experts have several opinions today regarding the proper length and type for a private key backing up a certificate, with some administrators opting for RSA and others preferring Diffie-Hellman. Without entering that debate, here is a sample command line for creating an RSA key at what is currently considered a quite respectable key length:

```
$ openssl genrsa -out www.key 4096
Generating RSA private key, 4096 bit long modulus
.............................................................
............++
............++
e is 65537 (0x10001)
```

With these two pieces in place, the administrator is ready to create a certificate-signing request (CSR) for submission to a certificate authority—whether the administrator's own or one belonging to a third party.

```
$ openssl req -new -key www.key -config www.cnf -out www.csr
```

Consult the Makefile if you want to see the steps by which a private CA is created by the `openssl` tool and how it signs a CSR to produce a `www.crt` file corresponding to the request generated earlier. When dealing instead with a public certificate authority, you might receive your `www.crt` in an e-mail (before you panic, remember that the certificate is *supposed* to be public!) or perhaps download the signed certificate from your account on the authority's web site when it is ready. In any case, the final step to making your certificate easy to use with Python is to combine the certificate and secret key into a single file for convenience. If the files are in the standard PEM format produced by the previous commands, then combining them is as simple as running the Unix "concatenate" command.

```
$ cat www.crt www.key > www.pem
```

The resulting file should contain a textual summary of the certificate contents, then certificate itself, and finally the private key. Be careful with this file! If either `www.key` or this PEM file `www.pem` containing the private key were leaked or became available to a third party, then that third party would be able to impersonate your service for all of the months or years until the key expires. The three sections of the file should look something like Listing 6-2. (Note the ellipses—we are abbreviating the file, which would actually take two or three book pages!)

Listing 6-2. A Certificate and Private Key Bundled into a Single PEM File

```
Certificate:
    Data:
        Version: 1 (0x0)
        Serial Number: 3 (0x3)
    Signature Algorithm: sha1WithRSAEncryption
        Issuer: C=us, ST=New York, L=New York, O=Example CA from Apress Media LLC,
                OU=Foundations of Python Network Programming 3rd Ed,
                CN=ca/emailAddress=ca@example.com
        Validity
            Not Before: Mar  8 16:58:12 2014 GMT
            Not After : Feb 12 16:58:12 2114 GMT
        Subject: C=us, ST=New York, O=Example from Apress Media LLC,
                OU=Foundations of Python Network Programming 3rd Ed,
                CN=www.example.com/emailAddress=root@example.com
...
-----BEGIN CERTIFICATE-----
MIIE+zCCA2MCAQMwDQYJKoZIhvcNAQEFBQAwgcUxCzAJBgNVBAYTAnVzMREwDwYD
VQQIEwhOZXcgWW9yazERMA8GA1UEBxMITmV3IFlvcmsxKTAnBgNVBAoTIEV4YW1w
I7Ahb1Dobi7EoK9tXFMrXutOTQkoFe ... pT7/ivFnx+ZaxEOmcR8qyzyQqWTDQ
SBH14aSHQPSodSHC1AAAfB3B+CHII1TkAXUudh67swE2qvR/mFbFtHwuSVEbSHZ+
2ukF5Z8mSgkNlr6QnikCDIYbBWDOSiTzmX/zPorqlw==
-----END CERTIFICATE-----
-----BEGIN RSA PRIVATE KEY-----
MIIG5QIBAAKCAYEA3rM3H+kGaWhbbfqyKzoePLIiYBOLw3W+wuKigsU1qDPFJBKk
JF4UqCo6OfZuJLpAHAIPwb/OihA2hXK8/I9Rd75t3leiYER6Oefg9TRGuxloDOom
8ZFW8k3p4RA7uDBMjHF3tZqIGpHpY6 ... f8QJ7ZsdXLRsVmHM+95T1Sy6QgmW2
WorzOPhhWVzGT7MgSduYOc8efArdZC5aVo24Gvd3i+di2pRQaOg9rSL7VJrm4BdB
NmdPSZN/rGhvwbWbPVQ5ofhFOMod1qgAp626ladmlublPtFt9sRJESU=
-----END RSA PRIVATE KEY-----
```

There exist more complicated arrangements than a CA that directly signs certificates for server use. For example, some organizations want their servers to use only short-lived certificates that last a few days or weeks before expiring. This minimizes the damage if a server is compromised and its private key is stolen. Instead of having to contact (and pay) the CA organization every few days for a replacement, such an organization can have the CA sign a longer-lived *intermediate* certificate whose private key the organization holds as a close secret and uses to sign the user-visible certificates that actually get put on servers. The resulting *certificate chain* or *chain of trust* combines the flexibility of having your own CA (because you can sign new certificates whenever you please) with the benefit of a recognized public CA (because you do not have to install a custom CA certificate in every browser or client that wants to talk to you). As long as your TLS-powered server provides clients with both its own particular server certificate as well as with the intermediate certificate making the cryptographic link back to the CA certificate that the client knows to trust, client software should have no problem validating their identity.

Consult books or documentation about certificate signing if you find yourself tasked with establishing the cryptographic identity of your organization and its services.

Offloading TLS

Before showing you how to use TLS from Python—especially if you are about to write a server—I should note that many experts would ask why you want to perform encryption directly inside your Python application in the first place. After all, many tools already exist that have carefully implemented TLS and can take charge of answering client connections on your behalf and forwarding the unencrypted data to your application if you run it on another port.

A separate daemon or service that provides TLS termination for your Python application might be easier to upgrade and tweak than the combination of your own server code, Python, and the underlying OpenSSL library. In addition, a third-party tool will often expose TLS features that the Python `ssl` module, even under Python 3.4, does not yet allow you to customize. For example, the vanilla `ssl` module currently seems to make it impossible to use ECDSA elliptic curve signatures or to fine-tuning session renegotiation. Session renegotiation is a particularly important topic. It can significantly reduce the CPU cost of offering TLS, but if configured poorly, it can compromise your ability to promise Perfect Forward Security (see the "Hand-Picked Ciphers and Perfect Forward Security" section). The old 2013 blog post at `https://www.imperialviolet.org/2013/06/27/botchingpfs.html`, "How to botch TLS forward secrecy," is still one of the best introductions to the topic.

Front-end HTTPS servers are a good example of third-party daemons that provide TLS termination. It is particularly easy for a third-party tool to wrap HTTP because the HTTPS standard specifies that the client and server should go ahead and negotiate encryption first before any protocol-specific messages pass over the channel. Whether you deploy Apache, nginx, or some other reverse proxy in front of your Python web service as an extra level of defense or instead subscribe to a content delivery network like Fastly that tunnels requests through to your own servers, you will find that TLS can disappear from your Python code and into the surrounding infrastructure.

But even a raw socket protocol of your own, for which no third-party tools are available, could accept third-party TLS protection if you set up a simple daemon such as `stunnel` to run on your public TCP port and forward the connections to your service privately.

If you do choose the course of offloading TLS to another tool, then you can probably just skim the rest of this chapter (to get familiar with the knobs for which you will be looking) before getting started on the tool's documentation. It will be that tool, and not Python itself, which will load your certificate and private key, and it will need to be properly configured to provide the level of protection against weak ciphers that you require. The only question to ask is how your front end of choice will tell your Python service the remote IP address and (if you are using client certificates) the identity of each client that has connected. For HTTP connections, information about the client can be added to the request as additional headers. For more primitive tools like stunnel or haproxy that might not actually be speaking HTTP, extra information like the client IP address will have to be prepended as extra bytes in front of the incoming data stream. Either way, the tool itself will be providing the TLS superpowers that the rest of this chapter will illustrate using pure Python sockets instead.

Python 3.4 Default Contexts

Several open source implementations of TLS are available. The Python Standard Library opts to wrap the most popular, the OpenSSL library, which despite several recent security incidents still seems to be considered the best option for most systems and languages. Some Python distributions come with their own OpenSSL, while others simply wrap the version of OpenSSL that happens to come bundled with your operating system. The Standard Library module has the old and nostalgic name `ssl`. Although you will focus your attention on `ssl` in this book, be aware that other cryptography projects are underway in the Python community, including a `pyOpenSSL` project that reveals much more of the underlying library's API.

Through its introduction of the `ssl.create_default_context()` function, Python 3.4 makes it dramatically easier for Python applications to use TLS safely than did earlier versions of Python. It is an excellent example of the kind of "opinionated API" that most users need. We should thank Christian Heimes for adding the idea of a default context to the Standard Library, as well as Donald Stufft for pushing to give it strong and useful opinions. The other mechanisms that the `ssl` module offers for setting up TLS connections are forced to stick with older and less secure defaults because they had already made the promise not to break backward compatibility when new versions of Python come out. But `create_default_context()` is quite willing to raise an exception the next time you upgrade Python if the TLS cipher or key length that you have been using is now believed to be insecure.

By abandoning the promise that you can upgrade Python without changing your application's behavior, `create_default_context()` can carefully choose the ciphers it will support, which lets you off the hook—you will not have to become a TLS expert and read security blogs if you simply rely on its advice and then keep Python updated on your machine. Do retest your applications after each upgrade to make sure that they can still connect to their TLS peers. If an application fails, then investigate whether the peer at the other end of the problematic connection can also be upgraded to support more modern ciphers or mechanisms.

How is a default context created and used? Listing 6-3 shows how both a simple client and server can safely secure a TCP socket using TLS.

Listing 6-3. Securing a Socket with TLS for Both Client and Server in Python 3.4 or Newer

```
#!/usr/bin/env python3
# Foundations of Python Network Programming, Third Edition
# https://github.com/brandon-rhodes/fopnp/blob/m/py3/chapter06/safe_tls.py
# Simple TLS client and server using safe configuration defaults

import argparse, socket, ssl

def client(host, port, cafile=None):
    purpose = ssl.Purpose.SERVER_AUTH
    context = ssl.create_default_context(purpose, cafile=cafile)

    raw_sock = socket.socket(socket.AF_INET, socket.SOCK_STREAM)
    raw_sock.connect((host, port))
    print('Connected to host {!r} and port {}'.format(host, port))
    ssl_sock = context.wrap_socket(raw_sock, server_hostname=host)
```

```
    while True:
        data = ssl_sock.recv(1024)
        if not data:
            break
        print(repr(data))

def server(host, port, certfile, cafile=None):
    purpose = ssl.Purpose.CLIENT_AUTH
    context = ssl.create_default_context(purpose, cafile=cafile)
    context.load_cert_chain(certfile)

    listener = socket.socket(socket.AF_INET, socket.SOCK_STREAM)
    listener.setsockopt(socket.SOL_SOCKET, socket.SO_REUSEADDR, 1)
    listener.bind((host, port))
    listener.listen(1)
    print('Listening at interface {!r} and port {}'.format(host, port))
    raw_sock, address = listener.accept()
    print('Connection from host {!r} and port {}'.format(*address))
    ssl_sock = context.wrap_socket(raw_sock, server_side=True)

    ssl_sock.sendall('Simple is better than complex.'.encode('ascii'))
    ssl_sock.close()

if __name__ == '__main__':
    parser = argparse.ArgumentParser(description='Safe TLS client and server')
    parser.add_argument('host', help='hostname or IP address')
    parser.add_argument('port', type=int, help='TCP port number')
    parser.add_argument('-a', metavar='cafile', default=None,
                        help='authority: path to CA certificate PEM file')
    parser.add_argument('-s', metavar='certfile', default=None,
                        help='run as server: path to server PEM file')
    args = parser.parse_args()
    if args.s:
        server(args.host, args.port, args.s, args.a)
    else:
        client(args.host, args.port, args.a)
```

You can see in the listing that securing a socket requires only three steps. First, create a TLS *context* object that knows all of your preferences regarding certificate validation and choice of cipher. Second, use the context's wrap_ socket() method to let the OpenSSL library take control of your TCP connection, exchange the necessary greetings with the other end, and set up an encrypted channel. Finally, perform all further communication with the ssl_sock that has been returned to you so that the TLS layer always has the chance to encrypt your data before it actually hits the wire. This wrapper, you will note, offers all of the same methods as a normal socket, such as send() and recv() and close() that you learned about from your experience with normal TCP sockets in Chapter 3.

The choice of whether you are creating a context for a client trying to verify the server to which it connects (Purpose.SERVER_AUTH) or of a server needing to accept client connections (Purpose.CLIENT_AUTH) affects several settings in the new context that is returned. The theory behind having two different sets of settings is the guess, on the part of the Standard Library authors, that you want TLS clients to be a bit forgiving about older ciphers because they will sometimes find themselves connecting to servers that are outside of your control and might be a bit out-of-date. But surely, they think, you will want your *own* servers to insist on modern and secure ciphers! While the settings chosen by `create_default_context()` will change with each new version of Python, here are some of the choices that it makes under Python 3.4 to provide you with an illustration:

- Both your client and server will be willing to negotiate the TLS version that is spoken, thanks to the fact that `create_default_context()` sets the protocol to `PROTOCOL_SSLv23` when creating your new `SSLContext` object.

- Both your client and server will refuse to speak the old protocols SSLv2 and SSLv3 because of known weaknesses in each of them. Instead, they will insist that the peer to which they are speaking use a dialect at least as recent as TLSv1. (The most common client that this choice excludes is Internet Explorer 6 running on Windows XP—a combination so old that it is no longer even officially supported by Microsoft).

- TLS compression is turned off because of attacks that it makes possible.

- Here is the first difference between the client and server settings. Since most TLS conversations on the Internet involve a client without its own signed certificate (such as a typical web browser) talking to a server that *does* possess a valid and signed certificate (such as PyPI or Google or GitHub or your bank), Python tells the server not to even attempt peer certificate validation (the context's `verify_mode` is set to `ssl.CERT_NONE`), but it insists that a client always validate the remote certificate and fail with an exception if it cannot (`ssl.CERT_REQUIRED`).

- The other client-server difference is their choice of ciphers. The client settings support a larger list of possible ciphers, even down to the old RC4 stream cipher. The server settings are much stricter and strongly prefer modern ciphers that provide Perfect Forward Security (PFS) so that a compromised server key—whether captured by criminals or released by court order—cannot lead to old conversations being divulged.

It was easy to compile the previous list: I simply opened `ssl.py` in the Standard Library and read the source code of `create_default_context()` to learn the choices it makes. You can do so yourself, especially as new Python versions come out and the previous list begins to grow out-of-date. The `ssl.py` source code even includes the raw list of ciphers for both client and server operations, currently named `_DEFAULT_CIPHERS` and `_RESTRICTED_SERVER_CIPHERS`, if you are curious enough to want to review them. You can consult recent OpenSSL documentation to learn about what the options in each string mean.

The `cafile` option provided when building the context in Listing 6-3 determines which certificate authorities your script will be willing to trust when verifying a remote certificate. If its value is None, which is the default if you choose not to specify the cafile keyword, then `create_default_context()` will automatically call the `load_default_certs()` method of your new context before returning it. This attempts to load all of the default CA certificates that browsers on your operating system would trust when connecting to a remote site, and it should be sufficient to validate public web sites and other services that have bought a certificate from a well-known public certificate authority. If instead `cafile` is a string specifying a filename, then no certificates are loaded from the operating system, and only CA certificates provided in that file will be trusted to validate the remote end of your TLS connection. (Note that you can make both kinds of certificates available if you create the context with `cafile` set to None and then call `load_verify_locations()` to install any further certificates.)

Finally, there are two crucial options that are provided to `wrap_socket()` in Listing 6-3—one for the server and the other for the client. The server is given the option `server_side=True` simply because one of the two ends has to assume the responsibilities of the server or the negotiation will fail with an error. The client call needs something more specific: the name of the host to which you think you have connected with `connect()` so that it can be checked against the subject fields of the certificate being proffered by the server. This extremely important check is performed automatically, as long as you always provide the `server_hostname` keyword to `wrap_socket()`, as shown in the listing.

To keep the code simple, neither the client nor the server in Listing 6-3 runs inside a loop. Instead, they each make a single attempt at conversation. A simple localhost certificate and a CA that has signed it are available in the chapter06 directory where the listing is located online; if you would like to use them to test the scripts, they can be downloaded by visiting the following URLs and clicking the Raw button:

```
https://github.com/brandon-rhodes/fopnp/blob/m/py3/chapter06/ca.crt
https://github.com/brandon-rhodes/fopnp/blob/m/py3/chapter06/localhost.pem
```

If you have checked out the entire source code repository for the book's scripts, then you can skip downloading them separately and just cd into the chapter06 directory where you will find the scripts and certificates already sitting next to each other. Either way, Listing 6-3 can then be run successfully as long as the localhost alias is working correctly on your system as a synonym for the 127.0.0.1 IP address. Start by running the server with -s and the path to your server PEM file in one terminal window.

```
$ /usr/bin/python3.4 safe_tls.py -s localhost.pem '' 1060
```

Remember from Chapter 2 and Chapter 3 that the empty hostname '' tells Python that you want your server to listen on all available interfaces. Now open another terminal window and, first, run the client with your normal system list of CA certificates that is used when your browser is operating on the public Internet.

```
$ /usr/bin/python3.4 safe_tls.py localhost 1060
Connected to host 'localhost' and port 1060
Traceback (most recent call last):
  ...
ssl.SSLError: [SSL: CERTIFICATE_VERIFY_FAILED] certificate verify failed (_ssl.c:598)
```

Because no public authority has signed the certificate inside of localhost.pem, your client is refusing to trust the server. You will also see that the server has died, with a message indicating that the client started a connection attempt but then abandoned it. Next, restart the server and then rerun the client with the -a option, which tells it to trust any certificate that the ca.crt has signed.

```
$ /usr/bin/python3.4 safe_tls.py -a ca.crt localhost 1060
Connected to host 'localhost' and port 1060
b'Simple is better than complex.'
```

This time, you can see that the conversation has been a complete success, with a simple message having been delivered from server to client. If you turn on a packet sniffer like tcpdump, you will find it impossible to decipher the plain text of the message from the packet contents you capture. On my system, I can monitor the conversation by running the following command as root (check your operating system documentation for how you might perform packet capture on your own machine with tcpdump or WireShark or some other tool):

```
# tcpdump -n port 1060 -i lo -X
```

The first few packets will include a bit of legible information: the certificate and public key, which can be safely sent in the clear since it is, after all, a *public* key. My packet dump shows me fragments of legible public keys as the packets pass by.

```
0x00e0:   5504 0a13 2045 7861 6d70 6c65 2043 4120   U....Example.CA.
0x00f0:   6672 6f6d 2041 7072 6573 7320 4d65 6469   from.Apress.Medi
0x0100:   6120 4c4c 4331 3930 3706 0355 040b 1330   a.LLC1907..U...O
0x0110:   466f 756e 6461 7469 6f6e 7320 6f66 2050   Foundations.of.P
0x0120:   7974 686f 6e20 4e65 7477 6f72 6b20 5072   ython.Network.Pr
0x0130:   6f67 7261 6d6d 696e 6720 3372 6420 4564   ogramming.3rd.Ed
```

But once the encrypted cipher is put into use, it is no longer possible (assuming no bugs or weakness in the encryption) for a third party to examine. Here is the packet that just carried the bytes 'Simple is better than complex' from the server to the client on my machine:

```
16:49:26.545897 IP 127.0.0.1.1060 > 127.0.0.1.40220:
  Flags [P.], seq 2082:2141, ack 426, win 350, options
  [nop,nop,TS val 51288448 ecr 51285953], length 59
        0x0000:   4500 006f 645f 4000 4006 d827 7f00 0001   E..od_@.@..'....
        0x0010:   7f00 0001 0424 9d1c dbbf f412 f4d0 24a3   .....$........$.
        0x0020:   8018 015e fe63 0000 0101 080a 030e 9980   ...^.c..........
        0x0030:   030e 8fc1 1703 0300 367f 9b5d e6c3 dfbd   ........6..]....
        0x0040:   8f21 d83f 8b61 569f 78a0 2ac3 090b bc9f   .!.?.aV.x.*.....
        0x0050:   101d 2cb1 1c07 ee08 f784 f277 b11e 9214   ..,........w....
        0x0060:   ce02 8e2b 1c0b b630 9c2d f323 3674 f5     ...+...0.-.#6t.
```

Note again what I warned about earlier in this chapter: the server and client IP addresses and port numbers pass completely in the clear. Only the data payload itself has been protected from any outside observer.

Variations on Socket Wrapping

All the scripts in this chapter present simple and universal steps to achieving TLS with the ssl module: creating a configured SSLContext object that describes your security requirements, making the connection from client to server yourself using a plain socket, and then calling the context's wrap_socket() method to perform the actual TLS negotiation. The reason that my examples always use this pattern is because it is robust, efficient, and the most flexible approach to using the module's API. It is the pattern that you can always use with success in a Python application, and by always using it, you will craft clients and servers that are easy to read because their approach is consistent and their code is easy to compare to the examples here and to each other.

However, the Standard Library ssl module provides a few variant shortcuts that you might see used in other code, which I should therefore mention. Let me describe each of them along with their shortcomings.

The first alternative you will run into is the invocation of the module-level function ssl.wrap_socket() without creating a context first. You will see this especially often in older code since it was actually the only way to create a TLS connection before context objects were added in Python 3.2! It has at least four shortcomings.

- It is less efficient because, underneath the hood, it creates a new context object full of settings every single time it is called. By instead building and configuring your own context, you can reuse it over and over again and incur the expense of creating it only once.

- It fails to provide the flexibility of a real context—even though it offers nine (!) different optional keyword arguments in a desperate attempt to provide enough knobs and buttons—it still manages to omit things such as letting you specify the ciphers that you are willing to use.

- It is woefully permissive with respect to the weak ciphers that it will allow because of the promise of backward compatibility with versions of Python that are now a decade old.

- And, finally, it fails to provide actual security because it performs no hostname checking! Unless you remember to follow up after a "successful" connection by running match_hostname(), you will not even know whether the certificate that your peer has offered is even for the same hostname to which you think you are connected.

For all of these reasons, you should avoid ssl.wrap_socket() and be prepared to migrate away from it in any old code that you might be maintaining. Instead, use practices like those shown in Listing 6-3.

The other major shortcut you will see is wrapping a socket before it is connected, by wrapping either a client socket before it runs connect() or a server socket before it runs accept(). In both cases, the wrapped socket cannot really negotiate TLS immediately, but it will wait until the socket is connected to perform TLS negotiation. Obviously, this will work only for protocols such as HTTPS that do their TLS activation as the first step after connecting. A protocol like SMTP that needs to start the conversation with some cleartext cannot use this approach, so a keyword option do_handshake_on_connect is available when wrapping, which you can set to False if you want to wait until later to trigger TLS negotiation with the socket's do_handshake() method.

It is true that prewrapping a socket does not by itself reduce your security, but I recommend against it for these three reasons involving code readability:

- First, it puts the wrapping call somewhere else in your code than where the actual TLS negotiation takes place, which can hide from someone reading your eventual connect() or accept() call that the TLS protocol is even involved.

- Related to the previous problem is the fact that connect() and accept() will now be able to fail not only with their usual socket or DNS exceptions but also with TLS errors if the negotiation goes poorly. Any try...except clause wrapping those calls will now have to worry about two entirely separate classes of error because two quite different operations will be hidden under the covers of a single method call.

- Finally, you will find that you now possess an SSLSocket object that might not, in fact, be doing any encryption. Only once a connection is made or when an explicit do_handshake() is called (if you turned autonegotiation off) will the so-called SSLSocket be providing any actual encryption! In contrast, the pattern offered in the program listings in this book transitions to an SSLSocket only at the moment that encryption actually becomes active, making a far cleaner semantic link between the class of your current socket object and the state of the underlying connection.

The only case in which I have seen prewrapping put to interesting use is when trying to use an old, naïve library that only supports cleartext communication. By providing a prewrapped socket and leaving the do_handshake_on_connect keyword argument set to its default value of True, you can provide TLS protection to the protocol without its even knowing. However, this is a special case and is better handled (if possible) by making the underlying library TLS-aware and able to accept a TLS context as an argument.

Hand-Picked Ciphers and Perfect Forward Security

If you are picky about data security, then you might find yourself wanting to specify exactly the ciphers that OpenSSL can use instead of relying on the defaults provided by the create_default_context() function.

As the field of encryption continues to advance, there will doubtless be concerns, vulnerabilities, and countermeasures of which we do not yet dream. But one important concern as this book is going to press is the question of Perfect Forward Security (PFS), that is, the question of whether someone who in the future acquires (or cracks) an old private key of yours will then be able to read old TLS conversations that they captured and kept archived for future decryption. The most popular ciphers today are those that protect against this possibility by using an *ephemeral* (temporary) key to perform the encryption of each new socket. The desire to guarantee PFS is one of the most popular reasons for wanting to hand-specify the properties of your context object.

Note that although the `ssl` module's default contexts do not *require* a PFS-capable cipher, you will probably get one anyway if both your client and server are running against recent-enough versions of OpenSSL. For example, if I start up the `safe_tls.py` script given in Listing 6-3 in its server mode and connect to it with the `test_tls.py` script you will meet in Listing 6-4, then (given my particular laptop, operating system, and OpenSSL version) I can see that the Python scripts have given priority to the PFS-capable *elliptic curve Diffie–Hellman exchange* (ECDHE) cipher without my even my asking.

```
$ python3.4 test_tls.py -a ca.crt localhost 1060
...
Cipher chosen for this connection... ECDHE-RSA-AES256-GCM-SHA384
Cipher defined in TLS version....... TLSv1/SSLv3
Cipher key has this many bits....... 256
Compression algorithm in use........ none
```

Thus, Python will often make good choices without your having to be specific. Nonetheless, if you want a guarantee that a particular protocol version or algorithm is put into use, simply lock down the context to your specific choices. As this book is going to press, for example, a good server configuration (for a server that will not be expecting clients to offer TLS certificates and thus can choose CERT_NONE as its verification mode) is as follows:

```
context = ssl.SSLContext(ssl.PROTOCOL_TLSv1_2)
context.verify_mode = ssl.CERT_NONE
context.options |= ssl.OP_CIPHER_SERVER_PREFERENCE  # choose *our* favorite cipher
context.options |= ssl.OP_NO_COMPRESSION            # avoid CRIME exploit
context.options |= ssl.OP_SINGLE_DH_USE             # for PFS
context.options |= ssl.OP_SINGLE_ECDH_USE           # for PFS
context.set_ciphers('ECDH+AES128 ')                 # choose over AES256, says Schneier
```

You can substitute these lines of code into a program like Listing 6-3 whenever a server socket is being created. Here the exact TLS version and cipher have been locked down to only a few explicit options. Any client trying to connect that cannot support these choices will fail instead of establishing the connection successfully. If you add the previous code to Listing 6-3 in place of the default context, then a client attempting a connection with an even slightly older version of TLS (like 1.1) or a slightly weaker cipher (like 3DES) will be rejected.

```
$ python3.4 test_tls.py -p TLSv1_1 -a ca.crt localhost 1060
Address we want to talk to.......... ('localhost', 1060)
Traceback (most recent call last):
  ...
ssl.SSLError: [SSL: TLSV1_ALERT_PROTOCOL_VERSION] tlsv1 alert protocol version (_ssl.c:598)

$ python3.4 test_tls.py -C 'ECDH+3DES' -a ca.crt localhost 1060
Address we want to talk to.......... ('localhost', 1060)
Traceback (most recent call last):
  ...
ssl.SSLError: [SSL: SSLV3_ALERT_HANDSHAKE_FAILURE] sslv3 alert handshake failure (_ssl.c:598)
```

The server in each of these cases will also raise a Python exception diagnosing the failure from its own point of view. And thus the resulting connection, if it succeeds, is guaranteed to be using the latest and most capable version of TLS (1.2) with one of the best ciphers available to protect your data.

The problem with switching from the `ssl` module's default contexts to hand-picked settings like this is that you not only have to do the research to determine your needs and choose a TLS version and cipher when you first write an application, but you—or your successor who maintains the software in the future—must continue to stay up-to-date in case your choices are later discovered to be vulnerable to a new exploit. TLS version 1.2 combined with elliptic curve Diffie–Hellman looks great, at least as this book goes to press. However, someday the choice will probably look dated or even quaint. Or look positively insecure. Will you be in a position to learn this quickly and get the manual selections in your software projects updated to better ones?

Unless `create_default_context()` someday gains an option that lets you insist on Perfect Forward Security, you will find yourself stuck between these two options. Either you will have to trust the default context and accept that some clients (or servers) with which you communicate might not receive PFS protection or you will have to lock down the choice of cipher and then stay abreast of news from the cryptography community.

Note that PFS is only as "perfect" as your mechanism for regularly discarding the session state or session ticket key that the server maintains. In the simplest case, simply restarting your server process every evening should make sure that new keys are generated, but do further research if you have a whole fleet of servers to deploy and want them to be able to support a pool of TLS clients efficiently, which take advantage of session restart. (However, this case—wanting a whole cluster whose session-restart keys are coordinated without compromising PFS—is one of those where it might begin to make more sense to look at tools beyond Python to perform your TLS termination!)

One last consideration is that locking down the choice of cipher is far easier if you are the one writing, or at least configuring, both the client and the server, as might be the case if you are setting up encrypted communications within your own machine room or between your own servers. When other pieces of software, administered by other parties, come into play, a less flexible cipher set might make it harder for others to interoperate with your services, especially if their tools use other implementations of TLS. If you do lock things down to only a few options, try to document these clearly and prominently for the people who write and configure the clients so that they can diagnose why older clients might have problems connecting.

Protocol Support for TLS

Most of the widely used Internet protocols have by now added TLS support. When using these protocols from either a Python Standard Library module or a third-party library, the important feature to search for is how you can configure the TLS cipher and options to prevent peers from connecting with weak protocol versions, weak ciphers, or options such as compression that weaken the protocol. This configuration might take the form of library-specific API calls or might simply allow you to pass an `SSLContext` object with your configuration choices.

Here are the TLS-aware protocols that come with the Python Standard Library:

- `http.client`: When you build an `HTTPSConnection` object (see Chapter 9), you can use the constructor's `context` keyword to pass in an `SSLContext` with your own settings. Unfortunately, neither `urllib.request` nor the third-party Requests library documented in Chapter 9 currently accept an `SSLContext` argument as part of their APIs.

- `smtplib`: When you build an `SMTP_SSL` object (see Chapter 13), you can use the constructor's `context` keyword to pass in an `SSLContext` with your own settings. If instead you create a plain `SMTP` object and only later call its `starttls()` method, then you provide the `context` parameter to that method call.

- `poplib`: When you build a `POP3_SSL` object (see Chapter 14), you can use the constructor's `context` keyword to pass in an `SSLContext` with your own settings. If instead you create a plain `POP3` object and only later call its `stls()` method, then you would provide the `context` parameter to that method call.

- `imaplib`: When you build an `IMAP4_SSL` object (see Chapter 15), you can use the constructor's `ssl_context` keyword to pass in an `SSLContext` with your own settings. If instead you create a plain `IMAP4` object and only later call its `starttls()` method, then you would provide the `ssl_context` parameter to that method call.

- ftplib: When you build an FTP_TLS object (see Chapter 17), you can use the constructor's context keyword to pass in an SSLContext with your own settings. Note that the first line or two of the FTP conversation will always pass in the clear (such as the "220" welcome message that often includes the server hostname) before you have the chance to turn on encryption. An FTP_TLS object will automatically turn on encryption before the login() method sends a username and password. If you are not logging in to the remote server but want encryption turned on anyway, you will have to call the auth() method manually as the first action you take after connecting.

- nntplib: Although the NNTP network news (Usenet) protocol is not covered in this book, I should note that it too can be secured. If you build an NNTP_SSL, you can use the constructor's ssl_context keyword to pass in an SSLContext with your own settings. If instead you create a plain NNTP object and only later call its starttls() method, then you would provide the context parameter to that method call.

Note that the common theme running across nearly all of these protocols is that an older plain-text protocol can be extended with TLS in one of two different ways. One way is for a new command to be added to the protocol that allows an upgrade to TLS in mid-conversation, after an old-fashioned plain-text connection is made using the protocol's traditional port number. The other approach is for the Internet standard to allocate a second well-defined TCP port number specifically for the TLS-protected version of the protocol, in which case TLS negotiation can happen immediately upon connecting without having to ask. Most of the previously mentioned protocols support both options, but HTTP opted for only the second because the protocol is stateless by design.

If you are connecting to a server configured by another team or organization that supports the TLS version of one of the previous protocols, then you may simply have to test (in the absence of any documentation that they might offer) to determine whether they opened the protocol's new TLS port or simply support TLS upgrades atop the old plain-text protocol.

If instead of relying on the Standard Library for your network communication you are using a third-party package that you learned about either from this book or elsewhere, you will want to consult its documentation for how to provide your own SSLContext. If no mechanism is provided—and, as I type this, even popular third-party libraries are typically not yet offering this ability for users of Python 3.4 and newer—then you will have to experiment with whatever knobs and settings the package does provide and test the result (perhaps using Listing 6-4, introduced in the next section) to see whether the third-party library guarantees a strong enough protocol and cipher for the privacy required by your data.

Learning Details

To help you learn more about the TLS protocol version and cipher choices that your clients and servers can make, Listing 6-4 offers a Python 3.4 script that makes an encrypted connection and then reports on its features. To do this, it uses several recent features of the Standard Library ssl module's SSLSocket object that now allow Python scripts to introspect the state of their OpenSSL-powered connections to see how they are configured.

The methods that it uses to perform its reporting are as follows:

- getpeercert(): A long-standing feature of SSLSocket that is available in several previous Python versions, this method returns a Python dictionary of fields picked out of the X.509 certificate of the peer to which the TLS session is connected. But recent Python versions have been expanding the range of certificate features that are exposed.

- cipher(): Returns the name of the cipher that OpenSSL and the peer's TLS implementation finally agreed upon and that is currently in use over the connection.

- compression(): Returns the name of the compression algorithm in use or else the Python singleton None.

To make its reporting as complete as possible, the script in Listing 6-4 also attempts a bit of magic using ctypes in a desperate attempt to learn the TLS protocol in use (which will ideally be a native feature of the ssl module by the time Python 3.5 is released). By pulling these pieces together, Listing 6-4 lets you connect to a client or server that you have constructed and learn what ciphers and protocols it will or will not negotiate.

Listing 6-4. Connect to Any TLS Endpoint and Report the Cipher Negotiated

```python
#!/usr/bin/env python3
# Foundations of Python Network Programming, Third Edition
# https://github.com/brandon-rhodes/fopnp/blob/m/py3/chapter06/test_tls.py
# Attempt a TLS connection and, if successful, report its properties

import argparse, socket, ssl, sys, textwrap
import ctypes
from pprint import pprint

def open_tls(context, address, server=False):
    raw_sock = socket.socket(socket.AF_INET, socket.SOCK_STREAM)
    if server:
        raw_sock.setsockopt(socket.SOL_SOCKET, socket.SO_REUSEADDR, 1)
        raw_sock.bind(address)
        raw_sock.listen(1)
        say('Interface where we are listening', address)
        raw_client_sock, address = raw_sock.accept()
        say('Client has connected from address', address)
        return context.wrap_socket(raw_client_sock, server_side=True)
    else:
        say('Address we want to talk to', address)
        raw_sock.connect(address)
        return context.wrap_socket(raw_sock)

def describe(ssl_sock, hostname, server=False, debug=False):
    cert = ssl_sock.getpeercert()
    if cert is None:
        say('Peer certificate', 'none')
    else:
        say('Peer certificate', 'provided')
        subject = cert.get('subject', [])
        names = [name for names in subject for (key, name) in names
                 if key == 'commonName']
        if 'subjectAltName' in cert:
            names.extend(name for (key, name) in cert['subjectAltName']
                         if key == 'DNS')

        say('Name(s) on peer certificate', *names or ['none'])
        if (not server) and names:
            try:
                ssl.match_hostname(cert, hostname)
            except ssl.CertificateError as e:
                message = str(e)
            else:
                message = 'Yes'
            say('Whether name(s) match the hostname', message)
```

```
        for category, count in sorted(context.cert_store_stats().items()):
            say('Certificates loaded of type {}'.format(category), count)

    try:
        protocol_version = SSL_get_version(ssl_sock)
    except Exception:
        if debug:
            raise
    else:
        say('Protocol version negotiated', protocol_version)

    cipher, version, bits = ssl_sock.cipher()
    compression = ssl_sock.compression()

    say('Cipher chosen for this connection', cipher)
    say('Cipher defined in TLS version', version)
    say('Cipher key has this many bits', bits)
    say('Compression algorithm in use', compression or 'none')

    return cert

class PySSLSocket(ctypes.Structure):
    """The first few fields of a PySSLSocket (see Python's Modules/_ssl.c)."""

    _fields_ = [('ob_refcnt', ctypes.c_ulong), ('ob_type', ctypes.c_void_p),
                ('Socket', ctypes.c_void_p), ('ssl', ctypes.c_void_p)]

def SSL_get_version(ssl_sock):
    """Reach behind the scenes for a socket's TLS protocol version."""

    lib = ctypes.CDLL(ssl._ssl.__file__)
    lib.SSL_get_version.restype = ctypes.c_char_p
    address = id(ssl_sock._sslobj)
    struct = ctypes.cast(address, ctypes.POINTER(PySSLSocket)).contents
    version_bytestring = lib.SSL_get_version(struct.ssl)
    return version_bytestring.decode('ascii')

def lookup(prefix, name):
    if not name.startswith(prefix):
        name = prefix + name
    try:
        return getattr(ssl, name)
    except AttributeError:
        matching_names = (s for s in dir(ssl) if s.startswith(prefix))
        message = 'Error: {!r} is not one of the available names:\n {}'.format(
            name, ' '.join(sorted(matching_names)))
        print(fill(message), file=sys.stderr)
        sys.exit(2)

def say(title, *words):
    print(fill(title.ljust(36, '.') + ' ' + ' '.join(str(w) for w in words)))

def fill(text):
    return textwrap.fill(text, subsequent_indent='    ',
                         break_long_words=False, break_on_hyphens=False)
```

```
if __name__ == '__main__':
    parser = argparse.ArgumentParser(description='Protect a socket with TLS')
    parser.add_argument('host', help='hostname or IP address')
    parser.add_argument('port', type=int, help='TCP port number')
    parser.add_argument('-a', metavar='cafile', default=None,
                        help='authority: path to CA certificate PEM file')
    parser.add_argument('-c', metavar='certfile', default=None,
                        help='path to PEM file with client certificate')
    parser.add_argument('-C', metavar='ciphers', default='ALL',
                        help='list of ciphers, formatted per OpenSSL')
    parser.add_argument('-p', metavar='PROTOCOL', default='SSLv23',
                        help='protocol version (default: "SSLv23")')
    parser.add_argument('-s', metavar='certfile', default=None,
                        help='run as server: path to certificate PEM file')
    parser.add_argument('-d', action='store_true', default=False,
                        help='debug mode: do not hide "ctypes" exceptions')
    parser.add_argument('-v', action='store_true', default=False,
                        help='verbose: print out remote certificate')
    args = parser.parse_args()

    address = (args.host, args.port)
    protocol = lookup('PROTOCOL_', args.p)

    context = ssl.SSLContext(protocol)
    context.set_ciphers(args.C)
    context.check_hostname = False
    if (args.s is not None) and (args.c is not None):
        parser.error('you cannot specify both -c and -s')
    elif args.s is not None:
        context.verify_mode = ssl.CERT_OPTIONAL
        purpose = ssl.Purpose.CLIENT_AUTH
        context.load_cert_chain(args.s)
    else:
        context.verify_mode = ssl.CERT_REQUIRED
        purpose = ssl.Purpose.SERVER_AUTH
        if args.c is not None:
            context.load_cert_chain(args.c)
    if args.a is None:
        context.load_default_certs(purpose)
    else:
        context.load_verify_locations(args.a)

    print()
    ssl_sock = open_tls(context, address, args.s)
    cert = describe(ssl_sock, args.host, args.s, args.d)
    print()
    if args.v:
        pprint(cert)
```

You can most easily learn the command-line options supported by this tool by running it with the standard –h help option. It tries to expose all of the major features of an SSLContext through its command-line options so that you can experiment with them and learn how they affect negotiation. For example, you can investigate how the default settings of a server that uses Python 3.4's create_default_context() are stricter than the settings of a client that uses it. In one terminal window, start up the script from Listing 6-3 as a server. I will again presume that you have available the certificate files ca.crt and localhost.pem from the chapter06 directory of the book's source code repository.

```
$ /usr/bin/python3.4 safe_tls.py -s localhost.pem '' 1060
```

This server is happy to accept connections using recent protocol versions and ciphers; in fact, it will negotiate a strong configuration with Perfect Forward Security enabled if it has the opportunity. Simply taking Python's defaults, watch what happens if you connect using Listing 6-4, shown here:

```
$ /usr/bin/python3.4 test_tls.py -a ca.crt localhost 1060

Address we want to talk to.......... ('localhost', 1060)
Peer certificate.................... provided
Name(s) on peer certificate......... localhost
Whether name(s) match the hostname.. Yes
Certificates loaded of type crl..... 0
Certificates loaded of type x509.... 1
Certificates loaded of type x509_ca. 0
Protocol version negotiated......... TLSv1.2
Cipher chosen for this connection... ECDHE-RSA-AES128-GCM-SHA256
Cipher defined in TLS version....... TLSv1/SSLv3
Cipher key has this many bits....... 128
Compression algorithm in use........ none
```

The combination ECDHE-RSA-AES128-GCM-SHA256 is one of the best that OpenSSL currently offers! But the safe_tls.py server will refuse to talk to a client that supports only Windows XP levels of encryption. Start the safe_tls.py server up again for another run, and this time connect with the following options:

```
$ /usr/bin/python3.4 test_tls.py -p SSLv3 -a ca.crt localhost 1060

Address we want to talk to.......... ('localhost', 1060)
Traceback (most recent call last):
  ...
ssl.SSLError: [SSL: SSLV3_ALERT_HANDSHAKE_FAILURE] sslv3 alert handshake failure (_ssl.c:598)
```

The old SSLv3 protocol is flatly refused by the careful server settings that Python has provided. Old end-of-lifetime ciphers like RC4 will also result in failure, even if used in combination with modern protocols.

```
$ /usr/bin/python3.4 test_tls.py -C 'RC4' -a ca.crt localhost 1060

Address we want to talk to.......... ('localhost', 1060)
Traceback (most recent call last):
  ...
ssl.SSLError: [SSL: SSLV3_ALERT_HANDSHAKE_FAILURE] sslv3 alert handshake failure (_ssl.c:598)
```

But the behavior of the "safe" script changes considerably if you place it in the role of a client because of the theory, discussed earlier, that it is really the server that is responsible for deciding how secure the connection should be, while client authors generally just want things to work if they can possibly do so without completely exposing the data. Remember that the safe server, when tested earlier, would refuse to speak RC4. Watch what happens when you instead try the tls_safe.py *client* with RC4. First, close any server that you already have running and run the test script as the server, setting the cipher with -C.

```
$ /usr/bin/python3.4 test_tls.py -C 'RC4' -s localhost.pem '' 1060

Interface where we are listening.... ('', 1060)
```

Then go to another terminal window and try connecting with the safe_tls.py script that uses Python 3.4's default context.

```
$ /usr/bin/python3.4 safe_tls.py -a ca.crt localhost 1060
```

Even using the safe default context, the connection happens successfully! Over in the server window, you will see that RC4 was indeed chosen as the streaming cipher. However, by providing the –C option with different strings, you can confirm that RC4 is as low as the safe script is willing to stoop. Ciphers or algorithms like MD5 will be rejected outright as not even reasonable for a client that is trying to ensure maximum compatibility with any server with which the user might want to communicate.

Consult the ssl module documentation and then the official OpenSSL documentation to learn more about crafting a custom choice of protocol and cipher. A helpful tool as you experiment is the native OpenSSL command line, if your system includes it, which can print out all of the ciphers that match a particular cipher string—the same string that you might provide to Listing 6-3 with its –C option or specify with the set_cipher() method in your own code. Plus, the command line will let you test how various cipher rules change their effect through time as cryptography continues to advance and OpenSSL on your system is upgraded. At the moment, to show one example of its use, here are the ciphers that match the ECDH+AES128 cipher string when it is used here on the Ubuntu laptop on which I am typing this:

```
$ openssl ciphers -v 'ECDH+AES128'
ECDHE-RSA-AES128-GCM-SHA256 TLSv1.2 Kx=ECDH     Au=RSA  Enc=AESGCM(128) Mac=AEAD
ECDHE-ECDSA-AES128-GCM-SHA256 TLSv1.2 Kx=ECDH    Au=ECDSA Enc=AESGCM(128) Mac=AEAD
ECDHE-RSA-AES128-SHA256 TLSv1.2 Kx=ECDH     Au=RSA  Enc=AES(128)  Mac=SHA256
ECDHE-ECDSA-AES128-SHA256 TLSv1.2 Kx=ECDH     Au=ECDSA Enc=AES(128)  Mac=SHA256
ECDHE-RSA-AES128-SHA    SSLv3 Kx=ECDH     Au=RSA  Enc=AES(128)  Mac=SHA1
ECDHE-ECDSA-AES128-SHA  SSLv3 Kx=ECDH     Au=ECDSA Enc=AES(128)  Mac=SHA1
AECDH-AES128-SHA        SSLv3 Kx=ECDH     Au=None Enc=AES(128)  Mac=SHA1
ECDH-RSA-AES128-GCM-SHA256 TLSv1.2 Kx=ECDH/RSA Au=ECDH Enc=AESGCM(128) Mac=AEAD
ECDH-ECDSA-AES128-GCM-SHA256 TLSv1.2 Kx=ECDH/ECDSA Au=ECDH Enc=AESGCM(128) Mac=AEAD
ECDH-RSA-AES128-SHA256  TLSv1.2 Kx=ECDH/RSA Au=ECDH Enc=AES(128)  Mac=SHA256
ECDH-ECDSA-AES128-SHA256 TLSv1.2 Kx=ECDH/ECDSA Au=ECDH Enc=AES(128)  Mac=SHA256
ECDH-RSA-AES128-SHA     SSLv3 Kx=ECDH/RSA Au=ECDH Enc=AES(128)  Mac=SHA1
ECDH-ECDSA-AES128-SHA   SSLv3 Kx=ECDH/ECDSA Au=ECDH Enc=AES(128)  Mac=SHA1
```

The OpenSSL library will consider any of these combinations to be fair game under the setting `set_cipher('ECDH+AES128')`. Again, my recommendation is to use the default context if at all possible and otherwise to test the specific client and server that you expect to use, trying to choose one or two strong ciphers that they both support. But if you wind up doing more experimenting and debugging than that, then I hope Listing 6-4 will be a useful tool as you experiment and narrow down OpenSSL's behavior. Be sure to download a fresh version of Listing 6-4 from the URL in the comment at its top when you have the chance because the version in the book will grow out-of-date; I will work to keep the one online updated with recent developments both in cryptography and in the Python `ssl` API.

Summary

This chapter addresses a topic on which few people are truly expert: the use of cryptography to protect data as it is in flight across a TCP socket and, specifically, the use of the TLS protocol (once named SSL) from Python.

In a typical TLS exchange, the client demands a certificate from the server—a digital document that asserts an identity. An authority that both the client and the server trust should sign it, and it must include a public key of which the server then needs to prove it actually possesses a copy. The client should verify that the identity stated in the certificate matches the hostname to which it thinks it has connected. Finally, the client and server negotiate settings such as the cipher, compression, and keys, which are then used to protect the data passing in both directions over the socket.

Many administrators do not even attempt to support TLS in their applications. Instead, they hide the applications behind industrial-strength front ends such as Apache, nginx, or HAProxy that can perform TLS on their behalf. Services that have content delivery networks in front of them must also offload TLS responsibility instead of embedding it in their own application.

Though a web search will suggest third-party libraries that can perform TLS in Python, the language's built-in abilities come from its OpenSSL-powered `ssl` module in the Standard Library. Assuming that `ssl` is available and working properly on your operating system and version of Python, basic encrypted channels can be set up, needing only a server certificate to operate.

Python applications written for Python 3.4 and newer (I strongly recommend using at least version 3.4, if your application is going to do its own TLS) will generally follow the pattern of creating a "context" object, opening a connection, and then calling the context's `wrap_socket()` method to turn the connection over to the control of the TLS protocol. Although the `ssl` module does provide one or two shortcut functions that you will see used in older code, the context-connect-wrap pattern is the most universal and flexible.

Many Python clients and servers can simply accept the settings provided by the default "context" object returned by `ssl.create_default_context()` that tries to make servers slightly strict in the settings that they will accept but make clients a little more lenient so that they can successfully connect to servers with only old versions of TLS available. Other Python applications will want to instantiate `SSLContext` themselves so as to tailor the protocol and cipher to their specific requirements. In any case, either the test script shown in this chapter or another TLS tool can be used to explore the behaviors that result from the settings.

The Standard Library supports a number of protocols that can be optionally secured with TLS, most of which are explored in later chapters of this book. They all support an `SSLContext` object if you can provide one. Third-party libraries, at the moment, provide poor support for contexts, since Python 3.4 has only recently been released and since most Python programmers are still using Python 2 in any case. Ideally, both situations will improve over the years.

Once you have implemented TLS in your application, it is always worthwhile to test it using tools that will attempt various kinds of connections with varying sets of parameters. Both third-party tools and web sites are available outside of Python for testing both TLS clients and servers, and the tool shown in Listing 6-4 can be used with Python 3.4 right on your own machine if you want to throw different settings at OpenSSL to see how it negotiates and behaves.

CHAPTER 7

■ ■ ■

Server Architecture

There are two challenges facing the author of a network service. The first is the core challenge of writing code that will correctly respond to incoming requests and craft the appropriate responses. The second is the task of installing this network code inside a Windows service or Unix daemon that starts automatically when the system boots, logs its activity to a persistent store, raises an alert if it cannot connect to its database or back-end data store, and either protects itself completely against all possible failure modes or can be quickly restarted should it fail.

This book focuses on the first of these two challenges. Not only is the second challenge, that of keeping a process up and running on your operating system of choice, a topic to which an entire book could be dedicated, but it is one that would take this book far afield from its central topic of network programming. This chapter, therefore, will spend only one section introducing the topic of deployment before moving on to its real topic of how network servers can be crafted as pieces of software.

Our treatment of network servers will then fall naturally into three topics. I will first cover a simple single-threaded server, similar to the UDP servers (covered in Chapter 2) and TCP servers (covered in Chapter 3), and focus on its limitations: it can serve only one client at a time, making any other clients wait, and even when talking to that client, it will probably keep the system CPU almost entirely idle. Once you understand this challenge, you will proceed to study the two competing solutions: either duplicating the single-threaded server in multiple threads or processes or taking the duty of multiplexing away from the operating system and doing it in your own code by using asynchronous network operations.

While studying threaded versus asynchronous network code, you will first implement each pattern from the ground up, and then you will look at frameworks that implement each pattern on your behalf. All of the frameworks that I illustrate will be from the Python Standard Library, but the text will also point out major third-party competitors to the Standard Library where they exist.

Most of the scripts in this chapter can also run under Python 2, but the most advanced framework introduced—the new `asyncio` module—is specific to Python 3, and it is a big advance in standardization that can be enjoyed only by programmers ready to make the upgrade.

A Few Words About Deployment

You will deploy a network service either to a single machine or to several machines. Clients can use a service that lives on a single machine by simply connecting to its IP address. A service running on several machines requires a more complicated approach. You could give each client the address or hostname of a single instance of the service, for example the instance that is running in the same machine room as a particular client, but you will gain no redundancy. If that instance of the service goes down, then the clients that were hardwired to its hostname or IP address will fail to connect.

A more robust approach is to have your DNS server return every IP address at which the service lives when its name is accessed and write clients that fall back to the second or third IP address that they are given if the first one fails. The approach that scales best in the industry today is to place your services behind a *load balancer* to which clients connect directly and that then forwards each incoming connection to an actual server sitting behind it. If a server fails, then the load balancer simply stops forwarding requests there until it comes back up, which can make server failures nearly invisible to a large client base. The biggest Internet services combine these approaches: a load balancer and server farm in each machine room with a public DNS name that returns the IP addresses for the load balancer whose machine room appears to be closest to you geographically.

However simple or grandiose your service architecture, you will need some way of running your Python server code on a physical or virtual machine, a process called *deployment*. There are two schools of thought regarding deployment. The old-fashioned technique is to suit up every single server program you write with all of the features of a service: double-forking to become a Unix daemon (or registering itself as a Windows service), arranging for system-level logging, supporting a configuration file, and offering a mechanism by which it can be started up, shut down, and restarted. You can do this either by using a third-party library that has solved these problems already or by doing it all over again in your own code.

A competing approach has been popularized by manifestos like *The Twelve-Factor App*. They advocate a minimalist approach in which each service is written as a normal program that runs in the foreground and makes no effort to become a daemon. Such a program takes any configuration options that it needs from its environment (the sys.environ dictionary in Python) instead of expecting a system-wide configuration file. It connects to any back-end services that the environment names. And it prints its logging messages directly to the screen—even through as naïve a mechanism as Python's own print() function. Network requests are accepted by opening and listening at whatever port the environment configuration dictates.

A service written in this minimalist style is easy for developers to run right at a shell prompt for testing. Yet it can then be made into a daemon or system service or deployed to a web-scale server farm by simply surrounding the application with the right scaffolding. The scaffolding could, for example, pull the environment variable settings from a central configuration service, connect the application's standard output and standard error to a remote logging server, and restart the service if it either fails or seems to freeze up. Because the program itself does not know this and is simply printing to standard output as usual, the programmer has the confidence that the service code is running in production exactly as it runs when under development.

There are now large platform-as-a-service providers that will host such applications for you, spinning up dozens or even hundreds of copies of your application behind a single public-facing domain name and TCP load balancer and then aggregating all of the resulting logs for analysis. Some providers allow you to submit Python application code directly. Others prefer that you bundle up your code, a Python interpreter, and any dependencies you need inside a container ("Docker" containers in particular are becoming a popular mechanism) that can be tested on your own laptop and then deployed, assuring you that your Python code will run in production from an image that is byte-for-byte identical to the one you use in testing. Either way, you are absolved from writing a service that spawns multiple processes itself; all redundancy/duplication of your service is handled by the platform.

More modest efforts at getting programmers out of the business of having to write stand-alone services have long existed in the Python community. The popular supervisord tool is an excellent example. It can run one or more copies of your program, divert your standard output and error to log files, restart a process if it fails, and even send alerts if a service begins failing too frequently.

If, despite all of these temptations, you do decide to write a process that knows how to turn itself into a daemon, you should find good patterns for doing so available in the Python community. A good starting point is PEP 3143 (available at http://python.org) whose section "Other daemon implementations" is a well-curated list of resources on the steps required. The supervisord source code might also be of interest, along with the documentation for Python's Standard Library module logging.

Whether you have a stand-alone Python process or a platform-powered web-scale service, the question of how you can most efficiently use an operating system network stack plus an operating system process to serve network requests is the same. It is to this problem that you will turn your attention for the rest of the chapter, with the goal of keeping the system as busy as possible so that clients wait as little as possible before having their network requests answered.

A Simple Protocol

To keep your attention on the various options presented by server design, the examples in this chapter feature a minimalist TCP protocol where the client asks one of three plain-text ASCII questions and then waits for the server to complete its answer. As in HTTP, the client may ask as many questions as it wants while the socket remains open and then close the connection without any warning when it has no more questions. The end of each question is delimited with the ASCII question mark character.

Beautiful is better than?

The answer is then sent back delimited by a period.

Ugly.

Each of the three question-and-answer pairs is based on one of the aphorisms of the Zen of Python, a poem about the inner consistent design of the Python language. Run Python and type `import this` any time that you need inspiration and want to reread the poem.

To build a client and several servers around this protocol, a number of routines are defined in Listing 7-1, which you will note has no command-line interface of its own. The module exists solely to be imported as a support module by the subsequent listings so that they can reuse its patterns without having to repeat them.

Listing 7-1. Data and Routines to Support the Toy Zen-of-Python Protocol

```python
#!/usr/bin/env python3
# Foundations of Python Network Programming, Third Edition
# https://github.com/brandon-rhodes/fopnp/blob/m/py3/chapter07/zen_utils.py
# Constants and routines for supporting a certain network conversation.

import argparse, socket, time

aphorisms = {b'Beautiful is better than?': b'Ugly.',
             b'Explicit is better than?': b'Implicit.',
             b'Simple is better than?': b'Complex.'}

def get_answer(aphorism):
    """Return the string response to a particular Zen-of-Python aphorism."""
    time.sleep(0.0)  # increase to simulate an expensive operation
    return aphorisms.get(aphorism, b'Error: unknown aphorism.')

def parse_command_line(description):
    """Parse command line and return a socket address."""
    parser = argparse.ArgumentParser(description=description)
    parser.add_argument('host', help='IP or hostname')
    parser.add_argument('-p', metavar='port', type=int, default=1060,
                        help='TCP port (default 1060)')
    args = parser.parse_args()
    address = (args.host, args.p)
    return address
```

```python
def create_srv_socket(address):
    """Build and return a listening server socket."""
    listener = socket.socket(socket.AF_INET, socket.SOCK_STREAM)
    listener.setsockopt(socket.SOL_SOCKET, socket.SO_REUSEADDR, 1)
    listener.bind(address)
    listener.listen(64)
    print('Listening at {}'.format(address))
    return listener

def accept_connections_forever(listener):
    """Forever answer incoming connections on a listening socket."""
    while True:
        sock, address = listener.accept()
        print('Accepted connection from {}'.format(address))
        handle_conversation(sock, address)

def handle_conversation(sock, address):
    """Converse with a client over `sock` until they are done talking."""
    try:
        while True:
            handle_request(sock)
    except EOFError:
        print('Client socket to {} has closed'.format(address))
    except Exception as e:
        print('Client {} error: {}'.format(address, e))
    finally:
        sock.close()

def handle_request(sock):
    """Receive a single client request on `sock` and send the answer."""
    aphorism = recv_until(sock, b'?')
    answer = get_answer(aphorism)
    sock.sendall(answer)

def recv_until(sock, suffix):
    """Receive bytes over socket `sock` until we receive the `suffix`."""
    message = sock.recv(4096)
    if not message:
        raise EOFError('socket closed')
    while not message.endswith(suffix):
        data = sock.recv(4096)
        if not data:
            raise IOError('received {!r} then socket closed'.format(message))
        message += data
    return message
```

The three questions that a client can expect a server to understand are listed as keys in the aphorisms dictionary, and their answers are stored as the values. The get_answer() function is a quick shorthand for doing a safe lookup into this dictionary for an answer, with a short error message returned if the aphorism is not recognized. Note that the client requests always end with a question mark and that answers—even the fallback error message—always end with a period. These two pieces of punctuation provide the tiny protocol with its framing.

The next two functions provide some common startup code that will be shared among the servers. The parse_command_line() function provides a common scheme for reading command-line arguments, while create_srv_socket() can build the listening TCP socket that a server needs in order to receive incoming connections.

But it is in the final four routines that the listing begins to demonstrate the central patterns of a server process. The cascade of four functions simply repeats gestures which you have already learned about in Chapter 3, which was about creating a TCP server for a listening socket, and in Chapter 5, which was about framing data and handling errors.

- accept_connections_forever() is a simple listen() loop that announces each connecting client with print() before handing its socket over to the next function for action.

- handle_conversation() is an error-catching routine to wrap an unlimited number of request-response cycles in a way that is designed to make it impossible for any problems with the client socket to crash the program. The exception EOFError is caught in its own specific except clause because it is how the innermost data-reception loop will signal that a client has finished making requests and has finally hung up—which, in this particular protocol (as in HTTP), is normal and not a truly an exceptional event. But all other exceptions are treated as errors and are reported with print() after being caught. (Recall that all normal Python errors inherit from Exception and will therefore be intercepted by this except clause!) The finally clause makes sure that the client socket is always closed, regardless of the code path by which this function exits. Running close() like this is always safe because already-closed file and socket objects in Python allow close() to be called again for good measure as many times as a program wants.

- handle_request() performs a single back-and-forth with the client, reading its question and then replying with an answer. Note the careful use of send_all() because the send() call by itself cannot guarantee the delivery of an entire payload.

- recv_until() performs the framing, using the practice outlined in Chapter 5. Repeated calls are made to the socket's recv() until the accumulated byte string finally qualifies as a complete question.

These routines are the tool chest from which you will build several servers.

To exercise the various servers in this chapter, you need a client program. One is provided in Listing 7-2 as a simple command-line tool.

Listing 7-2. Client Program for Example Zen-of-Python Protocol

```
#!/usr/bin/env python3
# Foundations of Python Network Programming, Third Edition
# https://github.com/brandon-rhodes/fopnp/blob/m/py3/chapter07/client.py
# Simple Zen-of-Python client that asks three questions then disconnects.

import argparse, random, socket, zen_utils

def client(address, cause_error=False):
    sock = socket.socket(socket.AF_INET, socket.SOCK_STREAM)
    sock.connect(address)
    aphorisms = list(zen_utils.aphorisms)
    if cause_error:
        sock.sendall(aphorisms[0][:-1])
        return
```

```
    for aphorism in random.sample(aphorisms, 3):
        sock.sendall(aphorism)
        print(aphorism, zen_utils.recv_until(sock, b'.'))
    sock.close()

if __name__ == '__main__':
    parser = argparse.ArgumentParser(description='Example client')
    parser.add_argument('host', help='IP or hostname')
    parser.add_argument('-e', action='store_true', help='cause an error')
    parser.add_argument('-p', metavar='port', type=int, default=1060,
                        help='TCP port (default 1060)')
    args = parser.parse_args()
    address = (args.host, args.p)
    client(address, args.e)
```

In the normal case, where cause_error is False, this client creates a TCP socket and transmits three aphorisms, waiting after each one for the server to reply with an answer. But in case you want to see what any of the servers in this chapter do in the case of an error, the -e option to this client will make it send an incomplete question and then hang up abruptly on the server. Otherwise, you should see three questions with their answers if a server is up and running correctly.

```
$ python client.py 127.0.0.1
b'Beautiful is better than?' b'Ugly.'
b'Simple is better than?' b'Complex.'
b'Explicit is better than?' b'Implicit.'
```

As with many other examples in this book, this client and the servers in this chapter use port 1060 but accept a -p option that can specify an alternative if that port is not available on your system.

A Single-Threaded Server

The rich set of utilities provided in the zen_utils module of Listing 7-1 reduces the task of writing a simple single-threaded server—the simplest possible design, which you saw already in Chapter 3—to only the three-line function of Listing 7-3.

Listing 7-3. The Simplest Possible Server Is Single-Threaded

```
#!/usr/bin/env python3
# Foundations of Python Network Programming, Third Edition
# https://github.com/brandon-rhodes/fopnp/blob/m/py3/chapter07/srv_single.py
# Single-threaded server that serves one client at a time; others must wait.

import zen_utils

if __name__ == '__main__':
    address = zen_utils.parse_command_line('simple single-threaded server')
    listener = zen_utils.create_srv_socket(address)
    zen_utils.accept_connections_forever(listener)
```

As usual with the server programs you wrote in Chapter 2 and Chapter 3, this server demands a single command-line argument: the interface on which the server should listen for incoming connections. To protect the server from other people on your LAN or network, specify the standard local host IP address.

```
$ python srv_single.py 127.0.0.1
Listening at ('127.0.0.1', 1060)
```

Or be more daring and offer the service on all your machine's interfaces by specifying the empty string, which Python interprets as meaning every interface on the current machine.

```
$ python srv_single.py ''
Listening at ('', 1060)
```

Either way, the server prints a line to announce that it opened its server port successfully and then waits for incoming connections. The server also supports an -h help option and a -p option to choose a port other than 1060, if you want to play with those. Once it is up and running, try executing the client script documented in the previous section to see the server operate. As your clients connect and disconnect, you will see the server reporting client activity in the terminal window where it is running.

```
Accepted connection from ('127.0.0.1', 40765)
Client socket to ('127.0.0.1', 1060) has closed
Accepted connection from ('127.0.0.1', 40768)
Client socket to ('127.0.0.1', 1060) has closed
```

If your network service has only a single client making a single connection at a time, then this design is all you need. As soon as the previous connection closes, this server is ready for the next. For as long as a connection exists, either this server sits blocked in a recv() call, waiting for the operating system to wake it back up when more data arrives, or it is putting together an answer as quickly as it can and transmitting it without further delay. The only circumstance in which send() or sendall() can block is when the client is not ready to receive data yet, in which case the data will be sent—and the server unblocked to return to its recv()—as soon as the client is ready. In all situations, therefore, responses are provided to the client as quickly as they can be computed and received.

The weakness of this single-threaded design is apparent the moment that a second client tries to connect while the server is still in conversation with the first. If the integer argument to listen() was greater than zero, then the operating system will at least be willing to acknowledge the second incoming client with a three-way TCP handshake to set up a connection, which saves a bit of time when the server is finally ready to talk. But that connection will then sit in the operating system's listen queue until the server's conversation with the first client is complete. Only once the first client conversation is complete and the server code has looped back to its next call to accept() will the second client's connection be available to the server and its first request over that socket be able to be answered.

Performing a denial-of-service attack against this single-threaded server is trivial: connect and never close the connection. The server will remain permanently blocked in recv() waiting for your data. If the server author gets clever and tries setting a timeout with sock.settimeout() to avoid waiting forever, then adjust your denial-of-service tool so that it sends a request often enough that the timeout is never reached. No other clients will ever be able to use the server.

Finally, the single-threaded design makes poor use of the server CPU and system resources because it cannot take other actions while waiting for the client to send the next request. You can time how long each line of the single-threaded server takes by running it under the control of the trace module from the Standard Library. To limit the output to only the server code itself, tell the tracer to ignore Standard Library modules (on my system, Python 3.4 is installed beneath the /usr directory).

```
$ python3.4 -m trace -tg --ignore-dir=/usr srv_single.py ''
```

Each line of output gives the moment, counted in seconds from when the server is launched, at which a line of Python code starts executing. You will see that most lines start executing as soon as the previous line is finished, falling either in the same hundredth of a second or in the next hundredth. But every time the server needs to wait on the client, execution stops and has to wait. Here is a sample run:

```
3.02 zen_utils.py(40):        print('Accepted connection...'...)
3.02 zen_utils.py(41):        handle_conversation(sock, address)
⋮
3.02 zen_utils.py(57):    aphorism = recv_until(sock, b'?')
3.03 zen_utils.py(63):    message = sock.recv(4096)
3.03 zen_utils.py(64):    if not message:
3.03 zen_utils.py(66):    while not message.endswith(suffix):
⋮
3.03 zen_utils.py(57):    aphorism = recv_until(sock, b'?')
3.03 zen_utils.py(63):    message = sock.recv(4096)
3.08 zen_utils.py(64):    if not message:
3.08 zen_utils.py(66):    while not message.endswith(suffix):
⋮
3.08 zen_utils.py(57):    aphorism = recv_until(sock, b'?')
3.08 zen_utils.py(63):    message = sock.recv(4096)
3.12 zen_utils.py(64):    if not message:
3.12 zen_utils.py(66):    while not message.endswith(suffix):
⋮
3.12 zen_utils.py(57):    aphorism = recv_until(sock, b'?')
3.12 zen_utils.py(63):    message = sock.recv(4096)
3.16 zen_utils.py(64):    if not message:
3.16 zen_utils.py(65):        raise EOFError('socket closed')
⋮
3.16 zen_utils.py(48):    except EOFError:
3.16 zen_utils.py(49):        print('Client socket...has closed'...)
3.16 zen_utils.py(53):        sock.close()
3.16 zen_utils.py(39):    sock, address = listener.accept()
```

This is an entire conversation—three requests and responses—with the client.py program. During a total of 0.14 seconds of processing time between the first and last lines of this trace, it has to wait on the client three different times for a total of around 0.05 + 0.04 + 0.04 = 0.13 seconds spent idle! This means that the CPU is only about 0.01 / 0.14 = 7 percent occupied during this exchange. This is, of course, only a rough number. The fact that we are running under trace slows the server down and increases its CPU usage, and the resolution of these numbers is approximate in the first place. But it is a result you will find confirmed if you use more sophisticated tools. Single-threaded servers, unless they are doing a large amount of in-CPU work during each request, are measurably poor at using the server machine to its full potential. The CPU is sitting idle while other clients are waiting in line to be served.

There are two interesting technical details worth commenting on. One is the fact that the first recv() returns immediately—it is only the second and third recv() calls that show a delay before returning data, as does the final recv() before learning that the socket has been closed. This is because the operating system's network stacks are cleverly going ahead and including the text of the first request in the same three-way handshake that sets up the TCP connection. Thus, by the time the connection officially exists and accept() can return, there is already data waiting that can be returned immediately from recv()!

The other detail is that send() causes no delay. This is because its semantics on a POSIX system are that it returns as soon as the outgoing data has been enrolled in the operating system network stack's outgoing buffers. There is never a guarantee that the system has really sent any data just because send() has returned! Only by turning around and listening for more client data can the program force the operating system to block its progress and wait to see the result of sending.

Let's get back to the topic at hand. How can these limitations of a single-threaded server be overcome? The rest of this chapter explores two competing techniques for preventing a single client from monopolizing a server. Both techniques allow the server to talk to several clients at once. First, I will cover the use of threads (processes work too), giving the operating system the job of switching the server's attention between different clients. Then I will turn to asynchronous server design, where I show how to handle the switches of attention yourself to converse with several clients at once in a single thread of control.

Threaded and Multiprocess Servers

If you want your server to converse with several clients simultaneously, a popular solution is to leverage your operating system's built-in support for allowing several threads of control to proceed independently through the same section of code, either by creating threads that share the same memory footprint or by creating processes that run independently of one another.

The advantage of this approach is its simplicity: take the same code that runs your single-threaded server and launch several copies of it.

Its disadvantage is that the number of clients to which you can talk is limited by how your operating system concurrency mechanisms scale. Even an idle or slow client will occupy the attention of an entire thread or process, which even if blocked in recv() will both occupy system RAM and a slot in the process table. Operating systems rarely scale well to thousands or more threads running simultaneously, and the context switches required as the system's attention turns from one client to the next will begin to bog down your service as it becomes busy.

You might expect that a multithreaded or multiprocess server would need to be composed of a master thread of control that runs a tight accept() loop that then hands off the new client sockets to some sort of waiting queue of workers. Happily, the operating system makes things much easier on you: it is perfectly permissible for every thread to have a copy of the listening server socket and to run its own accept() statement. The operating system will hand each new client connection to whichever thread is waiting for its accept() to complete, or else keep the connection queued if all the threads are currently busy until one of them is ready. Listing 7-4 shows an example.

Listing 7-4. Multithreaded Server

```
#!/usr/bin/env python3
# Foundations of Python Network Programming, Third Edition
# https://github.com/brandon-rhodes/fopnp/blob/m/py3/chapter07/srv_threaded.py
# Using multiple threads to serve several clients in parallel.

import zen_utils
from threading import Thread
```

```
def start_threads(listener, workers=4):
    t = (listener,)
    for i in range(workers):
        Thread(target=zen_utils.accept_connections_forever, args=t).start()

if __name__ == '__main__':
    address = zen_utils.parse_command_line('multi-threaded server')
    listener = zen_utils.create_srv_socket(address)
    start_threads(listener)
```

Note that this is only one possible design for a multithreaded program: the main thread starts *n* server threads and then exits, confident that those *n* threads will run forever and thus keep the process alive. Other options are possible. The main thread could stay alive, for example, and become a server thread itself. Or it could act as a monitor, checking periodically to make sure that the *n* server threads are still up and restarting replacement threads if any of them die. A switch from threading.Thread to multiprocessing.Process would give each thread of control its own separate memory image and file descriptor space, increasing expense from an operating system point of view but better isolating the threads and making it much more difficult for them to crash a main monitor thread.

However, all of these patterns, which you can learn about in the documentation to the threading and multiprocessing modules as well as in books and guides to Python concurrency, share the same essential feature: dedicating a somewhat expensive operating system–visible thread of control to every connected client, whether or not that client is busy making requests at the moment. But since your server code can remain unchanged while being put under the control of several threads (assuming that each thread establishes its own database connection and open files so that no resource coordination is needed between threads), it is simple enough to try the multithreaded approach on your server's workload. If it proves capable of being able to handle your request load, then its simplicity makes it an especially attractive technique for in-house services not touched by the public, where an adversary cannot simply open idle connections until you have exhausted your pool of threads or processes.

The Legacy SocketServer Framework

The pattern established in the previous section of using operating system–visible threads of control for handling multiple client conversations at the same time is popular enough that there is a framework implementing the pattern built into the Python Standard Library. While by now it is showing its age, with a 1990s design fraught with object orientation and multiple inherited mix-ins, it is worth a quick example both to show how the multithreaded pattern can be generalized and to make you familiar with the module, in case you ever need to maintain old code that uses it.

The socketserver module (known as SocketServer in the days of Python 2) breaks out the *server* pattern, which knows how to open a listening socket and accept new client connections, from the *handler* pattern, which knows how to converse over an open socket. These two patterns are combined by instantiating a server object that is given a handler class as one of its arguments, as you can see in Listing 7-5.

Listing 7-5. Threaded Server Built Atop the Standard Library Server Pattern

```
#!/usr/bin/env python3
# Foundations of Python Network Programming, Third Edition
# https://github.com/brandon-rhodes/fopnp/blob/m/py3/chapter07/srv_legacy1.py
# Uses the legacy "socketserver" Standard Library module to write a server.

from socketserver import BaseRequestHandler, TCPServer, ThreadingMixIn
import zen_utils
```

```
class ZenHandler(BaseRequestHandler):
    def handle(self):
        zen_utils.handle_conversation(self.request, self.client_address)

class ZenServer(ThreadingMixIn, TCPServer):
    allow_reuse_address = 1
    # address_family = socket.AF_INET6  # uncomment if you need IPv6

if __name__ == '__main__':
    address = zen_utils.parse_command_line('legacy "SocketServer" server')
    server = ZenServer(address, ZenHandler)
    server.serve_forever()
```

By substituting ForkingMixIn for ThreadingMixIn, the programmer can instead have fully isolated processes serve incoming clients instead of threads.

The vast weakness of this approach should be apparent by comparing it with the earlier Listing 7-4, which started a fixed number of threads that could be chosen by a server administrator based on how many threads of control a given server and operating system can easily manage without a significant degradation in performance. Listing 7-5, by contrast, lets the pool of connecting clients determine how many threads are started—with no limit on how many threads ultimately wind up running on the server! This makes it easy for an attacker to bring the server to its knees. This Standard Library module, therefore, cannot be recommended for production and customer-facing services.

Async Servers

How can you keep the CPU busy during the delay between sending an answer to a client and then receiving its next request without incurring the expense of an operating system–visible thread of control per client? The answer is that you can write your server using an *asynchronous* pattern, where instead of blocking and waiting for data to arrive or depart from one particular client, the code instead is willing to hear from a whole list of waiting client sockets and respond whenever one of those clients is ready for more interaction.

This pattern is made possible by two features of modern operating system network stacks. The first is that they offer a system call that lets a process block waiting on a whole list of client sockets, instead of on only a single client socket, which allows a single thread to serve hundreds or thousands of client sockets at a time. The second feature is that a socket can be configured as nonblocking, where it promises to never, ever make the calling thread block in a send() or recv() call but will always return from the send() or recv() system call immediately whether or not further progress can be made in the conversation. If progress is delayed, then it is up to the caller to try again later when the client looks ready for further interaction.

The name *asynchronous* means that the client code never stops to wait for a particular client and that the thread of control running the code is not *synchronized*, or made to wait in lockstep, with the conversation of any one particular client. Instead, it switches freely among all connected clients to do the work of serving.

There are several calls by which operating systems support asynchronous mode. The oldest is the POSIX call select(), but it suffers from several inefficiencies that have inspired modern replacements like poll() on Linux and epoll() on BSD. The book *UNIX Network Programming* by W. Richard Stevens (Prentice Hall, 2003) is the standard reference on the subject. Here I will focus on poll() and skip the others because the intention of this chapter is not really that you implement your own asynchronous control loop. Instead, you are taking a poll()-powered loop merely as an example so that you understand what happens under the hood of a full asynchronous framework, which is how you will really want to implement asynchrony in your programs. Several frameworks are illustrated in the following sections.

Listing 7-6 shows the complete internals of a raw asynchronous server for your simple Zen protocol.

Listing 7-6. A Raw Asynchronous Event Loop

```python
#!/usr/bin/env python3
# Foundations of Python Network Programming, Third Edition
# https://github.com/brandon-rhodes/fopnp/blob/m/py3/chapter07/srv_async.py
# Asynchronous I/O driven directly by the poll() system call.

import select, zen_utils

def all_events_forever(poll_object):
    while True:
        for fd, event in poll_object.poll():
            yield fd, event

def serve(listener):
    sockets = {listener.fileno(): listener}
    addresses = {}
    bytes_received = {}
    bytes_to_send = {}

    poll_object = select.poll()
    poll_object.register(listener, select.POLLIN)

    for fd, event in all_events_forever(poll_object):
        sock = sockets[fd]

        # Socket closed: remove it from our data structures.

        if event & (select.POLLHUP | select.POLLERR | select.POLLNVAL):
            address = addresses.pop(sock)
            rb = bytes_received.pop(sock, b'')
            sb = bytes_to_send.pop(sock, b'')
            if rb:
                print('Client {} sent {} but then closed'.format(address, rb))
            elif sb:
                print('Client {} closed before we sent {}'.format(address, sb))
            else:
                print('Client {} closed socket normally'.format(address))
            poll_object.unregister(fd)
            del sockets[fd]

        # New socket: add it to our data structures.

        elif sock is listener:
            sock, address = sock.accept()
            print('Accepted connection from {}'.format(address))
            sock.setblocking(False) # force socket.timeout if we blunder
            sockets[sock.fileno()] = sock
            addresses[sock] = address
            poll_object.register(sock, select.POLLIN)
```

```
        # Incoming data: keep receiving until we see the suffix.

        elif event & select.POLLIN:
            more_data = sock.recv(4096)
            if not more_data:  # end-of-file
                sock.close()  # next poll() will POLLNVAL, and thus clean up
                continue
            data = bytes_received.pop(sock, b'') + more_data
            if data.endswith(b'?'):
                bytes_to_send[sock] = zen_utils.get_answer(data)
                poll_object.modify(sock, select.POLLOUT)
            else:
                bytes_received[sock] = data

        # Socket ready to send: keep sending until all bytes are delivered.

        elif event & select.POLLOUT:
            data = bytes_to_send.pop(sock)
            n = sock.send(data)
            if n < len(data):
                bytes_to_send[sock] = data[n:]
            else:
                poll_object.modify(sock, select.POLLIN)

if __name__ == '__main__':
    address = zen_utils.parse_command_line('low-level async server')
    listener = zen_utils.create_srv_socket(address)
    serve(listener)
```

The essence of this event loop is that it takes charge of maintaining the state of each client conversation in its own data structures instead of relying on the operating system to switch contexts when activity turns from one client to another. The server is actually two loops deep: a while loop to call poll() over and over and then an inner loop to process each event that poll() returns since it can return many events per call. You hide these two levels of iteration inside a generator to prevent the main server loop from being buried needlessly two levels of indentation deep.

A dictionary of sockets is maintained so that when poll() tells you that file descriptor n is ready for more activity, you can find the corresponding Python socket. You also remember the addresses of your sockets so that you can print diagnostic messages with the correct remote address, even after the socket has closed and the operating system will no longer remind you of the endpoint to which it was connected.

But the real core of the asynchronous server are its buffers: the bytes_received dictionary where you stuff incoming data while waiting for a request to complete and the bytes_to_send dictionary where outgoing bytes wait until the operating system can schedule them for transmission. Together with the event for which you tell poll() you are waiting on each socket, these data structures form a complete state machine for handling a client conversation one tiny step at a time.

1. A client ready to connect manifests itself first as activity on the listening server socket, which you leave permanently in the POLLIN ("poll input") state. You respond to such activity by running accept(), squirreling away the socket and its address in your dictionaries and telling the poll object you are ready to receive data from the new client socket.

2. When the client socket itself is then presented to you with a `POLLIN` event, you `recv()` up to 4KB of data. If the request is not yet framed with a concluding question mark, then you save the data to the `bytes_received` dictionary and continue back to the top of the loop to `poll()` further. Otherwise, you have a complete question, and you can act on the client's request by looking up the corresponding reply and putting it in your `bytes_to_send` dictionary. This involves a crucial pivot: switching the socket from `POLLIN` mode, where you want to know when more data arrives, to `POLLOUT` mode, where you want to be notified as soon as the outgoing buffers are free because you are now using the socket to send instead of receive.

3. The `poll()` call now notifies you immediately with `POLLOUT` whenever the outgoing buffers on the client socket can accept at least one byte, and you respond by attempting a `send()` of everything you have left to transmit and by keeping only the bytes that `send()` could not squeeze into the outgoing buffers.

4. Finally, a `POLLOUT` arrives whose `send()` lets you complete the transmission of all remaining outward-bound data. At this point, a request-response cycle is complete, and you pivot the socket back into `POLLIN` mode for another request.

5. When a client socket finally gives you an error or closing status, you dispose of it and any outgoing or incoming buffers. Of all the simultaneous conversations you may be having, that one, at least, is now complete.

The key to the asynchronous approach is that this single thread of control can handle hundreds, or eventually thousands, of client conversations. As each client socket becomes ready for its next event, the code steps forward into that socket's next operation, receives or sends what data it can, and then immediately returns to `poll()` to watch for more activity. Without requiring a single operating system context switch (aside from the privilege-mode escalations and de-escalations involved in entering the operating system itself for the `poll()`, `recv()`, `send()`, and `close()` system calls), this single thread of control can handle a large number of clients by keeping all client-conversation states in one set of dictionaries, indexed by client socket. Essentially, you substitute the key lookup supported by Python dictionaries for the full-fledged operating system context-switch that a multithreaded or multiprocess server would require to switch its attention from one client to another.

Technically, the previous code can run correctly even without setting every new client socket to nonblocking mode with `sock.setblocking(False)`. Why? Because Listing 7-6 never calls `recv()` unless there is waiting data, and `recv()` never blocks if at least one byte of input is ready; and it never calls `send()` unless data can be transmitted, and `send()` never blocks if at least one byte can be written to the operating system's outgoing network buffers. But the `setblocking()` call is prudent anyway in case you make an error. In its absence, a misplaced call to `send()` or `recv()` would block and make you unresponsive to all but the one client on which you were blocked. With the `setblocking()` call in place, a mix-up on your part will raise `socket.timeout` and alert you to the fact that you have somehow managed to make a call that cannot be immediately acted upon by the operating system.

If you unleash several clients against this server, you will see that its single thread juggles all of the simultaneous conversations with great aplomb. But you had to dive into quite a few operating system internals with Listing 7-6. What if you want to focus on your client code and let someone else worry about the details of `select()`, `poll()`, or `epoll()`?

Callback-Style asyncio

Python 3.4 introduced the new `asyncio` framework to the Standard Library, designed in part by Python inventor Guido van Rossum. It provides a standard interface for event loops based on `select()`, `epoll()`, and similar mechanisms in an attempt to unify a field that had become fragmented in the era of Python 2.

After considering Listing 7-6 and noticing how little of its code is specific to the sample question-and-answer protocol that you are studying in this chapter, you can probably already imagine the responsibilities that such a framework undertakes. It maintains a central select-style loop. It keeps a table of sockets on which I/O activity is expected, and it adds or removes them from the attention of the select loop as necessary. It cleans up and abandons the sockets once they closed. Finally, when actual data has arrived, it defers to user code to determine the correct response.

The asyncio framework supports two programming styles. One, which reminds programmers of the old Twisted framework under Python 2, lets the user keep up with each open client connection by means of an object instance. In this design pattern, the steps that Listing 7-6 took to advance a client conversation become method calls on the object instance. You can see the familiar steps of reading in a question and reeling off a response in Listing 7-7, written in a way that plugs directly into the asyncio framework.

Listing 7-7. An asyncio Server in the Callback Style

```python
#!/usr/bin/env python3
# Foundations of Python Network Programming, Third Edition
# https://github.com/brandon-rhodes/fopnp/blob/m/py3/chapter07/srv_asyncio1.py
# Asynchronous I/O inside "asyncio" callback methods.

import asyncio, zen_utils

class ZenServer(asyncio.Protocol):

    def connection_made(self, transport):
        self.transport = transport
        self.address = transport.get_extra_info('peername')
        self.data = b''
        print('Accepted connection from {}'.format(self.address))

    def data_received(self, data):
        self.data += data
        if self.data.endswith(b'?'):
            answer = zen_utils.get_answer(self.data)
            self.transport.write(answer)
            self.data = b''

    def connection_lost(self, exc):
        if exc:
            print('Client {} error: {}'.format(self.address, exc))
        elif self.data:
            print('Client {} sent {} but then closed'
                    .format(self.address, self.data))
        else:
            print('Client {} closed socket'.format(self.address))

if __name__ == '__main__':
    address = zen_utils.parse_command_line('asyncio server using callbacks')
    loop = asyncio.get_event_loop()
    coro = loop.create_server(ZenServer, *address)
    server = loop.run_until_complete(coro)
    print('Listening at {}'.format(address))
    try:
        loop.run_forever()
    finally:
        server.close()
        loop.close()
```

You can see that the actual socket object is carefully protected from the protocol code in Listing 7-7. You ask the framework, not the socket, for the remote address. Data is delivered via a method call that shows you only the string that has arrived. The answer you want transmitted is handed off to the framework with its transport.write() method call, leaving your code out of the loop—quite literally—about when, exactly, that data will be handed off to the operating system for transmission back to the client. The framework assures you that it will happen as soon as possible, so long as it does not block progress on other client connections that need attention.

Asynchronous workers usually become more complicated than this. A common example is when responses to the client cannot be composed trivially, as they can here, but involve reading from files on the file system or consultation with back-end services such as databases. In that case, your client code will have to face in two different directions: it will defer to the framework both when sending and receiving data to the client, and when sending and receiving data from the filesystem or database. In such cases, your callback methods might themselves build futures objects that provide yet further callbacks, to be invoked when the database or filesystem I/O has finally completed. See the official asyncio documentation for details.

Coroutine-Style asyncio

The other means of constructing protocol code for the asyncio framework is to construct a *coroutine*, which is a function that pauses when it wants to perform I/O—returning control to its caller—instead of blocking in an I/O routine itself. The canonical form in which the Python language supports coroutines is through *generators*: functions that have one or more yield statements inside of them and that therefore reel off a sequence of items instead of terminating with a single return value when called.

If you have written generic generators before, whose yield statements simply offer up items for consumption, then you will be a bit surprised at how asyncio-targeted generators look. They take advantage of the extended yield syntax developed in PEP 380. The extended syntax not only allows a running generator to reel off all the items yielded by another generator with the yield from statement but allows yield to return a value to the inside of the coroutine, and even to raise an exception if the consumer demands it. This allows a pattern in which the coroutine does a result = yield of an object describing some operation that it would like performed—maybe a read on another socket or access to the filesystem—and either receive back the result of the successful operation in result or experience, right there in the coroutine, an exception indicating that the operation failed.

Listing 7-8 illustrates the protocol implemented as a coroutine.

Listing 7-8. An asyncio Server in the Coroutine Style

```
#!/usr/bin/env python3
# Foundations of Python Network Programming, Third Edition
# https://github.com/brandon-rhodes/fopnp/blob/m/py3/chapter07/srv_asyncio2.py
# Asynchronous I/O inside an "asyncio" coroutine.

import asyncio, zen_utils

@asyncio.coroutine
def handle_conversation(reader, writer):
    address = writer.get_extra_info('peername')
    print('Accepted connection from {}'.format(address))
    while True:
        data = b''
        while not data.endswith(b'?'):
            more_data = yield from reader.read(4096)
```

```
        if not more_data:
            if data:
                print('Client {} sent {!r} but then closed'
                        .format(address, data))
            else:
                print('Client {} closed socket normally'.format(address))
            return
        data += more_data
    answer = zen_utils.get_answer(data)
    writer.write(answer)

if __name__ == '__main__':
    address = zen_utils.parse_command_line('asyncio server using coroutine')
    loop = asyncio.get_event_loop()
    coro = asyncio.start_server(handle_conversation, *address)
    server = loop.run_until_complete(coro)
    print('Listening at {}'.format(address))
    try:
        loop.run_forever()
    finally:
        server.close()
        loop.close()
```

Comparing this listing with the earlier efforts at servers, you will recognize all of the code. The while loop calling recv() repeatedly is the old framing maneuver, followed by a write of the reply to the waiting client, all wrapped up in a while loop that is happy to keep responding to as many requests as the client would like to make. But there is a crucial difference that prevents you from simply reusing the earlier implementations of this same logic. Here it takes the form of a generator that does a yield from everywhere that the earlier code simply performed a blocking operation and waited for the operating system to respond. It is this difference that lets this generator plug into the asyncio subsystem without blocking it and preventing more than one worker from making progress at a time.

PEP 380 recommends this approach for coroutines because it makes it easy to see where your generator might get paused. It could stop running for an indefinite period of time every time it does a yield. Some programmers dislike festooning their code with explicit yield statements, and in Python 2 there are frameworks like gevent and eventlet that take normal networking code with normal blocking I/O calls and specially intercept those calls to perform what is really asynchronous I/O under the hood. These frameworks have not, as of this writing, been ported to Python 3, and if ported, they will still face competition from the fact that asyncio is now built into the Standard Library. If they ever arrive, then programmers will have to choose between the verbose but explicit approach of an asyncio coroutine where you can see a "yield" everywhere a pause might take place and the implicit but more compact code possible when calls like recv() return control to the asynchronous I/O loop while looking like innocent method calls in the code itself.

The Legacy Module asyncore

In case you run across any services written against the asyncore Standard Library module, Listing 7-9 uses it to implement the sample protocol.

Listing 7-9. Using the Old asyncore Framework

```python
#!/usr/bin/env python3
# Foundations of Python Network Programming, Third Edition
#   https://github.com/brandon-rhodes/fopnp/blob/m/py3/chapter07/srv_legacy2.py
# Uses the legacy "asyncore" Standard Library module to write a server.

import asyncore, asynchat, zen_utils

class ZenRequestHandler(asynchat.async_chat):

    def __init__(self, sock):
        asynchat.async_chat.__init__(self, sock)
        self.set_terminator(b'?')
        self.data = b''

    def collect_incoming_data(self, more_data):
        self.data += more_data

    def found_terminator(self):
        answer = zen_utils.get_answer(self.data + b'?')
        self.push(answer)
        self.initiate_send()
        self.data = b''

class ZenServer(asyncore.dispatcher):

    def handle_accept(self):
        sock, address = self.accept()
        ZenRequestHandler(sock)

if __name__ == '__main__':
    address = zen_utils.parse_command_line('legacy "asyncore" server')
    listener = zen_utils.create_srv_socket(address)
    server = ZenServer(listener)
    server.accepting = True  # we already called listen()
    asyncore.loop()
```

This listing will raise red flags if you are an experienced Python programmer. The ZenServer object is never handed to the asyncore.loop() method or explicitly registered in any way, yet the control loop seems magically to know that the service is available! Clearly this module is trafficking in module-level globals or some other nefariousness to build links between the main control loop, the server object, and the request handlers that it creates but is doing so in a way you cannot quite see.

However, you can see that many of the same steps are accomplished under the hood, which asyncio had put out in the open. New client connections each result in the creation of a new instance of ZenRequestHandler in whose instance variables you can store any kind of state necessary to keep up with how the client conversation is going. Furthermore, as is normal with these asynchronous frameworks that you have been examining, there is an asymmetry between receiving and sending. Receiving data involves returning and handing control back to the framework and then getting called back for each block of new bytes that arrives as input. But sending data is a fire-and-forget operation—you hand the whole outgoing payload to the framework and can return control, confident that the framework will make as many send() calls as necessary to get the data transmitted.

One last time, you see that asynchronous frameworks, unless they do invisible magic like gevent or eventlet (which are currently Python 2 only), force you to write your server code using different idioms than you use in a simple server like the one shown in Listing 7-3. While multithreading and multiprocessing simply ran your single-threaded code without modification, an asynchronous approach forces you to break up your code into little pieces that can each run without ever blocking. A callback style forces each unblockable code snippet to live inside a method; a coroutine style has you wedge each basic unblockable operation in between yield or yield from statements.

The Best of Both Worlds

These asynchronous servers can switch nimbly between one client's traffic and another's by simply glancing from one protocol object to another (or, in the case of the more primitive Listing 7-6, between one dictionary entry and another). This can serve clients with far less expense than when the operating system needs to be involved in the context switches.

But an asynchronous server has a hard limit. Precisely because it does all of its work within a single operating system thread, it hits a wall and can process no further client work once it has maxed out the CPU that it is running at 100 percent utilization. It is a pattern, at least in its pristine form, which is always confined to a single processor regardless of how many cores your server features.

Fortunately, a solution is ready at hand. When you need high performance, write your service using an asynchronous callback object or coroutine and launch it under an asynchronous framework. Then step back and configure your server operating system to start as many of these event loop processes as you have CPU cores! (Consult with your server administrator about one detail: should you leave one or two cores free for the operating system instead of occupying them all?) You will now have the best of both worlds. On a given CPU, the asynchronous framework can blaze away, swapping between active client sockets as often as its heart desires without incurring a single context switch into another process. But the operating system can distribute new incoming connections among all of the active server processes, ideally balancing the load adequately across the entire server.

As discussed in the section "A Few Words About Deployment," you will probably want to corral these processes inside a daemon that can monitor their health and restart them, or notify staff, if they fail. Any of the mechanisms discussed there should work just fine for an asynchronous service, from supervisord all the way up to full platform-as-a-service containerization.

Running Under inetd

I should not close this chapter without mentioning the venerable inetd daemon, available for nearly all BSD and Linux distributions. Invented in the early days of the Internet, it solves the problem of needing to start *n* different daemons when the system boots if you want to offer *n* different network services on a given server machine. In its /etc/inetd.conf file, you simply list every port that you want listening on the machine.

The inetd daemon does a bind() and listen() on every one of them, but it kicks off a server process only if a client actually connects. This pattern makes it easy to support low-port-number services that run under a normal user account, since inetd itself is the process that is opening the low-numbered port. For a TCP service like the one in this chapter (see your inetd(8) documentation for the more complicated case of a UDP datagram service), the inetd daemon can either launch one process per client connection or expect your server to stay up and continue listening for new connections once it has accepted the first one.

Creating one process per connection is more expensive and presents the server with a higher load, but it is also simpler. Single-shot services are designated by the string nowait in the fourth field of a service's inetd.conf entry.

```
1060 stream tcp nowait brandon /usr/bin/python3 /usr/bin/python3 in_zen1.py
```

Such a service will start up and find that its standard input, output, and error are already connected to the client socket. The service needs to converse only with that one client and then exit. Listing 7-10 gives an example, which can be used in conjunction with the inetd.conf line just given.

Listing 7-10. Answer a Single Client, Whose Socket Is the stdin/stdout/stderr

```
#!/usr/bin/env python3
# Foundations of Python Network Programming, Third Edition
# https://github.com/brandon-rhodes/fopnp/blob/m/py3/chapter07/in_zen1.py
# Single-shot server for the use of inetd(8).

import socket, sys, zen_utils

if __name__ == '__main__':
    sock = socket.fromfd(0, socket.AF_INET, socket.SOCK_STREAM)
    sys.stdin = open('/dev/null', 'r')
    sys.stdout = sys.stderr = open('log.txt', 'a', buffering=1)
    address = sock.getpeername()
    print('Accepted connection from {}'.format(address))
    zen_utils.handle_conversation(sock, address)
```

This script is careful to replace the Python standard input, output, and error objects with more appropriate open files because you rarely want raw tracebacks and status messages—that either Python or one of its libraries might direct toward standard out or especially standard error—interrupting your conversation with the client. Note that this maneuver fixes only I/O attempted from within Python itself because it touches the file objects only inside of sys but not the real file descriptors. If your server calls any low-level C libraries that do their own standard I/O, then you will want to close the underlying file descriptors 0, 1, and 2 as well. However, in that case, you are beginning to undertake the kind of sandboxing that is really better accomplished through supervisord, a daemonization module, or platform-style containerization as described in the previous "A Few Words About Deployment" section.

You can test Listing 7-10 at your normal user command line, so long as the port you have chosen is not a low-numbered one, by running inetd -d inet.conf against a tiny configuration file that contains the line given earlier and then connecting to the port as usual with client.py.

The other pattern is to specify the string wait in the fourth field of your inetd.conf entry, which means that your script will be given the listener socket itself. This gives your script the task of calling accept() for the client that is currently waiting. The advantage of this is that your server can then choose to stay alive and keep running accept() to receive further client connections without inetd having to be involved. This can be more efficient than starting a whole new process for every single incoming connection. If clients stop connecting for a while, your server can feel free to exit() to reduce the server machine's memory footprint until a client needs the service again; inetd will detect that your service has exited and take over the job of listening again.

Listing 7-11 is designed to be used in wait mode. It is capable of accepting new connections forever, but it can also time out and exit—absolving the server of the need to keep it in memory any longer—if several seconds go by without any new client connections.

Listing 7-11. Answer One or More Client Connections, but Eventually Get Bored and Time Out

```
#!/usr/bin/env python3
# Foundations of Python Network Programming, Third Edition
# https://github.com/brandon-rhodes/fopnp/blob/m/py3/chapter07/in_zen2.py
# Multi-shot server for the use of inetd(8).

import socket, sys, zen_utils

if __name__ == '__main__':
    listener = socket.fromfd(0, socket.AF_INET, socket.SOCK_STREAM)
    sys.stdin = open('/dev/null', 'r')
    sys.stdout = sys.stderr = open('log.txt', 'a', buffering=1)
```

```
listener.settimeout(8.0)
try:
    zen_utils.accept_connections_forever(listener)
except socket.timeout:
    print('Waited 8 seconds with no further connections; shutting down')
```

Of course, this server is of the same primitive single-threaded design with which I started this chapter. In production, you are likely to want a more robust design, and you can use any of the approaches discussed in this chapter. The only requirement is that they be able to take an already-listening socket and run `accept()` on it over and over again, forever. This is simple if you are happy for your server process, once launched by `inetd`, never to exit. It can get a bit more complicated (and beyond the scope of this book) if you want the server to be able to time out and shut down after a period of inactivity since it can be tricky for a group of threads or processes to confirm that none of them are currently talking to a client and that none of them have received a client connection recently enough to warrant keeping the server alive.

There is also a simple access control mechanism based on IP address and hostname that is built into some versions of `inetd`. The mechanism is the descendent of an old program named `tcpd` that once worked in conjunction with `inetd` before being rolled into the same process. Its `/etc/hosts.allow` and `/etc/hosts.deny` files can, depending on their rules, prevent some (or all!) IP addresses from connecting to one of your services. Be sure to read your system documentation and review how your system administrator has configured these files if you are debugging a problem where clients cannot reach one of your `inetd`-powered services!

Summary

The example network servers of Chapter 2 and Chapter 3 were capable of interacting with only one client at a time, while all others had to wait until the previous client socket had closed. There are two techniques for expanding beyond this roadblock.

From a programming perspective, the simplest is multithreading (or multiprocessing) where the server code can usually remain unchanged, and the operating system is tasked with the job of switching invisibly between workers so that waiting clients get responses quickly while idle clients consume no server CPU. This technique not only allows several client conversations to make progress simultaneously but also makes better use of a server CPU that might otherwise sit idle most of the time waiting for more work from one client.

The more complicated but powerful approach is to embrace an asynchronous programming style that lets a single thread of control switch its attention between as many clients as it wants, by giving the operating system the full list of sockets with which it is currently having conversations. The complication is that this requires the logic of reading a client request and building a response to be split into small, nonblocking pieces of code that can hand control back to the asynchronous framework when it is time to wait on the client again. While an asynchronous server can be written manually using a mechanism like `select()` or `poll()`, most programmers will want to rely on a framework, like the `asyncio` framework built into the Standard Library in Python 3.4 and newer.

Arranging for a service you have written to get installed on a server and to start running when the system boots is called *deployment*, and it can be automated using many modern mechanisms, either by using tools like `supervisord` or by handing control to a platform-as-a-service container. The simplest possible deployment for a baseline Linux server may be the old `inetd` daemon, which provides a bare-bones way to make sure your service is launched the moment that a client first needs it.

You will see the topic of servers again in this book. After Chapter 8 tackles a number of basic network-based services upon which modern Python programmers rely, Chapter 9 through Chapter 11 will look at the design of the HTTP protocol and the Python tools for acting as both a client and a server, where you will see the designs presented by this chapter available all over again in the choice between a forking web server such as Gunicorn and an asynchronous framework like Tornado.

CHAPTER 8

Caches and Message Queues

This chapter, though brief, might be one of the most important in this book. It surveys two technologies—caches and messages queues—that have become fundamental building blocks for services under heavy load. The book reaches a turning point here. The previous chapters have explored the sockets API and how Python can use primitive IP network operations to build communication channels. All of the subsequent chapters, as you will see if you peek ahead, are about particular protocols built atop sockets—how to fetch documents from the World Wide Web, send e-mail, and submit commands to remote servers.

What sets apart the two tools that you will be looking at in this chapter? They share several characteristics.

- Each of these technologies is popular because it is a powerful tool. The point of using Memcached, or a message queue, is that it is a well-written service that will solve a particular problem for you, not because it implements an interesting protocol that lets you interoperate with any other tools.

- The problems solved by these tools tend to be internal to an organization. You often cannot tell from the outside which caches, queues, and load distribution tools are being used to power a particular web site or network service.

- While protocols such as HTTP and SMTP were built with specific payloads in mind—hypertext documents and e-mail messages, respectively—caches and message queues tend to be completely agnostic about the data they carry for you.

This chapter is not intended to be a manual for any of these technologies. Ample documentation for each of the libraries mentioned exists online, and for the more popular ones, you can even find entire books that have been written about them. Instead, this chapter's purpose is to introduce you to the problem that each tool solves, explain how to use the service to address that issue, and give a few hints about using the tool from Python.

After all, the greatest challenge that a programmer often faces—aside from the basic, lifelong process of learning to program itself—is to recognize common problems for which quick prebuilt solutions exist. Programmers have an unfortunate habit of laboriously reinventing the wheel. Think of this chapter as offering you two finished wheels in the hope that you can avoid building them yourself.

Using Memcached

Memcached is the "memory cache daemon." It combines the free, idle RAM on the servers on which it is installed into a single, large least-recently used (LRU) cache. Its impact on many large Internet services has been, by all accounts, revolutionary. After glancing at how to use it from Python, I will discuss its implementation, which will teach you about an important modern network concept called *sharding*.

The actual procedure for using Memcached is designed to be simple.

- You run a Memcached daemon on every server with some spare memory.

- You make a list of the IP address and port numbers of your new Memcached daemons and distribute this list to all of the clients that will be using the cache.

- Your client programs now have access to an organization-wide, blazingly fast key-value cache that acts something like a big Python dictionary that all of your servers can share. The cache operates on an LRU basis, dropping old items that have not been accessed for a while so that it has room to both accept new entries and keep records that are being frequently accessed.

Enough Python clients are currently listed for Memcached that I had better just send you to the page that lists them, rather than try to review them here: http://code.google.com/p/memcached/wiki/Clients.

The client listed first is written in pure Python, and thus it will not need to compile against any libraries. It should install quite cleanly into a virtual environment (see Chapter 1), thanks to being available on the Python Package Index. The version for Python 3 can be installed with a single command.

```
$ pip install python3-memcached
```

The API for this package is straightforward. Though you might have expected an interface that more strongly resembles a Python dictionary with native methods like __getitem__(), the author of this API chose instead to use the same method names as are used in other languages supported by Memcached. This was a good decision since it makes it easier to translate Memcached examples into Python. A simple interaction at the Python prompt, if you have Memcached installed and running on your machine at its default port of 11211, might run as follows:

```
>>> import memcache
>>> mc = memcache.Client(['127.0.0.1:11211'])
>>> mc.set('user:19', 'Simple is better than complex.')
True
>>> mc.get('user:19')
'Simple is better than complex.'
```

You can see that the interface here is very much like that of a Python dictionary. When you submit a string as a value like this, the string gets written directly to Memcached as UTF-8 and is then decoded again when you fetch it later. Any other kind of Python object besides a simple string will trigger the memcache module to auto-pickle the value for you (see Chapter 5) and store the binary pickle in Memcached. Keep this difference in mind in case you ever write a Python application that is sharing a Memcached cache with clients written in other languages. Only the values you save as strings will be decipherable to clients written in other languages.

Always keep in mind that data stored in Memcached can be thrown away at the server's discretion. The cache is designed to speed up operations by remembering results that are expensive to recompute. It is not designed to store data that you cannot reconstruct from other sources of information! If the previous commands were run against a busy enough Memcached and if enough time elapsed between the set() and the get() operation, then the get() could easily find that the string had expired from the cache and was no longer present.

Listing 8-1 shows the basic pattern by which Memcached is used from Python. Before embarking on an (artificially) expensive integer-squaring operation, this code checks Memcached to see whether the answer is already stored in the cache. If so, then the answer can be returned immediately without needing to be recomputed. If not, then it is computed and stored in the cache before being returned.

Listing 8-1. Using Memcached to Accelerate an Expensive Operation

```python
#!/usr/bin/env python3
# Foundations of Python Network Programming, Third Edition
# https://github.com/brandon-rhodes/fopnp/blob/m/py3/chapter08/squares.py
# Using memcached to cache expensive results.

import memcache, random, time, timeit

def compute_square(mc, n):
    value = mc.get('sq:%d' % n)
    if value is None:
        time.sleep(0.001)  # pretend that computing a square is expensive
        value = n * n
        mc.set('sq:%d' % n, value)
    return value

def main():
    mc = memcache.Client(['127.0.0.1:11211'])

    def make_request():
        compute_square(mc, random.randint(0, 5000))

    print('Ten successive runs:')
    for i in range(1, 11):
        print(' %.2fs' % timeit.timeit(make_request, number=2000), end='')
    print()

if __name__ == '__main__':
    main()
```

Again, the Memcached daemon needs to be running on your machine at port 11211 for this example to succeed. For the first few hundred requests, of course, the program will run at its usual speed; every time it asks the square of a particular integer for the first time, it will find it missing from the RAM cache and have to compute it instead. However, as the program runs and begins to encounter the same integers over and over again, it will start speeding up as it finds squares that are still present in the cache from the last time it saw a particular integer.

After a few thousand requests drawn from the domain of 5,000 possible input integers, the program should show a substantial speedup. On my machine, the tenth batch of 2,000 squares runs more than six times faster than the initial batch.

```
$ python squares.py
Ten successive runs:
 2.87s 2.04s 1.50s 1.18s 0.95s 0.73s 0.64s 0.56s 0.48s 0.45s
```

This pattern is generally characteristic of caching. The runtime gradually improves as the cache begins to learn enough keys and values, and then the rate of improvement levels off as Memcached fills and as the percent coverage of the input domain reaches its maximum.

In a real application, what kind of data might you want to write to the cache?

Many programmers simply cache the lowest level of expensive call, such as queries to a database, reads from the filesystem, or queries to an external service. At this level, it is often easy to understand which items can be cached for how long without making information too out-of-date. And if a database row changes, then perhaps the cache can even be preemptively cleared of stale items related to the changed value. But sometimes there can be great value in caching intermediate results at higher levels of the application such as data structures, snippets of HTML, or even entire web pages. That way, a cache hit prevents not only a database access but also the cost of turning the result into a data structure and then into rendered HTML.

There are many good introductions and in-depth guides that are linked to from the Memcached site, as well as a surprisingly extensive FAQ; it's as though the Memcached developers have discovered that catechism is the best way to teach people about their service. I will just make some general points here.

First, keys have to be unique, and consequently developers tend to use prefixes and encodings to keep distinct the various classes of objects they are storing. You often see things like `user:19`, `mypage:/node/14`, or even the entire text of a SQL query used as a key. Keys can be only 250 characters long, but by using a strong hash function, you can get away with lookups that support longer strings. The values stored in Memcached, by the way, can be longer than keys but are limited to 1MB in length.

Second, you must always remember that Memcached is a cache. It is ephemeral, it uses RAM for storage, and if restarted, it remembers nothing that you have ever stored! Your application should always be able to recover and rebuild all of its data if the cache should disappear.

Third, make sure that your cache does not return data that is too old to be accurately presented to your users. "Too old" depends entirely upon your problem domain. A bank balance probably needs to be absolutely up-to-date, while "today's top headline" can probably be a few minutes old on a news site's front page.

There are three approaches to solving the problem of stale data and making sure that it gets cleaned up and is not returned forever far past its useful shelf life.

- Memcached will let you set an expiration date and time on each item that you place in the cache, and it will take care of dropping these items silently when the time comes.

- You can reach in and actively invalidate particular cache entries the moment that they become invalid—if you have a way to map from the identity of a piece of information to all of the keys in the cache that could possibly have included it.

- You can rewrite and replace entries that are invalid instead of simply removing them, which works well for entries that might be hit dozens of times per second. Instead of all of those clients finding the missing entry and all trying to recompute it simultaneously, they find the rewritten entry there instead. For the same reason, prepopulating the cache when an application first comes up can be a crucial survival skill for large sites.

As you might guess, decorators are a popular way to add caching in Python since they wrap function calls without changing their names or signatures. If you look at the Python Package Index, you will find several decorator cache libraries that can take advantage of Memcached.

Hashing and Sharding

The design of Memcached illustrates an important principle that is used in several other kinds of databases and that you might want to employ in architectures of your own. When faced with several Memcached instances in a list, a Memcached client will *shard* the database by hashing each key's string value and letting the hash determine which server in the Memcached cluster is used to store that particular key.

To understand why this is effective, consider a particular key-value pair—such as the key `sq:42` and the value 1764 that might be stored by Listing 8-1. To make the best use of the RAM it has available, the Memcached cluster wants to store this key and value exactly once. But to make the service fast, it wants to avoid duplication without requiring any coordination between the different servers or communication between all of the clients.

This means that all of the clients, without any other information to go on than (a) the key and (b) the list of Memcached servers with which they are configured, need some scheme for working out where that piece of information belongs. If they fail to make the same decision, then not only might the key and value be copied to several servers and reduce the overall memory available but also a client's attempt to remove an invalid entry could leave other invalid copies elsewhere.

The solution is that the clients all implement a single, stable algorithm that can turn a key into an integer n that selects one of the servers from their list. They do this by using a "hash" algorithm, which mixes the bits of a string when forming a number so that any pattern in the string is, ideally, obliterated.

To see why patterns in key values must be obliterated, consider Listing 8-2. It loads a dictionary of English words (you might have to download a dictionary of your own or adjust the path to make the script run on your own machine) and explores how those words would be distributed across four servers if they were used as keys. The first algorithm tries to divide the alphabet into four roughly equal sections and distributes the keys using their first letter; the other two algorithms use hash functions.

Listing 8-2. Two Schemes for Assigning Data to Servers: Patterns in the Data and Bits from a Hash

```python
#!/usr/bin/env python3
# Foundations of Python Network Programming, Third Edition
# https://github.com/brandon-rhodes/fopnp/blob/m/py3/chapter08/hashing.py
# Hashes are a great way to divide work.

import hashlib

def alpha_shard(word):
    """Do a poor job of assigning data to servers by using first letters."""
    if word[0] < 'g':           # abcdef
        return 'server0'
    elif word[0] < 'n':         # ghijklm
        return 'server1'
    elif word[0] < 't':         # nopqrs
        return 'server2'
    else:                       # tuvwxyz
        return 'server3'

def hash_shard(word):
    """Assign data to servers using Python's built-in hash() function."""
    return 'server%d' % (hash(word) % 4)

def md5_shard(word):
    """Assign data to servers using a public hash algorithm."""
    data = word.encode('utf-8')
    return 'server%d' % (hashlib.md5(data).digest()[-1] % 4)

if __name__ == '__main__':
    words = open('/usr/share/dict/words').read().split()
    for function in alpha_shard, hash_shard, md5_shard:
        d = {'server0': 0, 'server1': 0, 'server2': 0, 'server3': 0}
        for word in words:
            d[function(word.lower())] += 1
        print(function.__name__[:-6])
        for key, value in sorted(d.items()):
            print('   {} {} {:.2}'.format(key, value, value / len(words)))
        print()
```

The hash() function is Python's own built-in hash routine, which is designed to be blazingly fast because it is used internally to implement Python dictionary lookup. The MD5 algorithm is much more sophisticated because it was actually designed as a cryptographic hash. Although it is now considered too weak for security use, using it to distribute load across servers is fine (though slower than Python's built-in hash).

The results show quite plainly the danger of trying to distribute load using any method that could directly expose the patterns in your data.

```
$ python hashing.py
alpha
    server0 35285 0.36
    server1 22674 0.23
    server2 29097 0.29
    server3 12115 0.12

hash
    server0 24768 0.25
    server1 25004 0.25
    server2 24713 0.25
    server3 24686 0.25

md5
    server0 24777 0.25
    server1 24820 0.25
    server2 24717 0.25
    server3 24857 0.25
```

You can see that distributing load by first letters, where each of the four bins has a roughly equal number of letters assigned to it, results in server 0 getting more than three times the load of server 3, even though it was assigned only six letters instead of seven letters! The hash routines, however, both performed like champions. Despite all of the strong patterns that characterize not only the first letters but also the entire structure and endings of English words, the hash functions scattered the words evenly across these four fictional servers.

Though many data sets are not as skewed as the letter distributions of English words, sharded databases like Memcached always have to contend with the appearance of patterns in their input data.

Listing 8-1, for example, was not unusual in its use of keys that always began with a common prefix and that were followed by characters from a restricted alphabet: the decimal digits. These kinds of obvious patterns are why sharding should always be performed through a hash function.

Of course, this is an implementation detail that you can often ignore when you use a database system like Memcached whose client libraries support sharding internally. But if you ever need to design a service of your own that automatically assigns work or data to nodes in a cluster in a way that needs to be reproducible between several clients of the same data store, then you will find the same technique useful in your own code.

Message Queues

Message queue protocols let you send reliable chunks of data that the protocols call *messages* instead of *datagrams* since, as you saw in Chapter 2, the idea of a datagram is specific to unreliable services where data can be lost, duplicated, or reordered by the underlying network. Typically, a message queue promises to transmit messages reliably and to deliver them atomically: a message either arrives whole and intact, or it does not arrive at all. Framing is performed by the message queue protocol itself. Your clients using the message queue never have to loop and keep calling something like recv() until a whole message has arrived.

The other innovation message queues offer is that instead of supporting only the point-to-point connections that are possible with an IP transport like TCP, you can set up all kinds of topologies between messaging clients. There are many possible uses to which message queues are put.

- When you sign up for an account at a new web site using your email address, the site typically responds immediately with a page saying "Thank you, please watch your inbox for a confirmation e-mail," without making you wait the several minutes that it might take the site to reach your e-mail service provider to deliver it. The site typically accomplishes this by putting your e-mail address into a message queue from which back-end servers can retrieve the address when they are ready to attempt a new outgoing SMTP connection (Chapter 13). If a delivery attempt experiences a temporary failure, then your e-mail address can simply be placed back on the queue with a longer timeout for a re-try attempt later.

- Message queues can be used as the basis for a custom *remote procedure call (RPC)* (see Chapter 18) service, a pattern in which busy front-end servers can offload difficult work by placing requests on a message queue that might have dozens or hundreds of back-end servers listening to it and then waiting for a response.

- High-volume event data that needs to be aggregated or centrally stored and analyzed is often streamed as tiny efficient messages over a message queue. On some sites, this entirely replaces both on-machine logging to local hard drives and older log transmission mechanisms such as syslog.

The hallmark of a message queue application design is this ability to mix and match entire populations of clients and servers, or publisher and subscriber processes, by having them all attach to the same messaging fabric.

The use of message queues can produce a bit of a revolution in how you write programs. Typical monolithic applications are composed of layer upon layer of APIs through which a single thread of control might pass from reading HTTP data from a socket to authenticating and interpreting the request to calling an API to perform bespoke image processing and finally to writing the result to disk. Every API used by that single thread of control has to be present on a single machine, loaded into a single instance of the Python runtime. But once message queues are part of your toolkit, you start to ask why something as intensive, specialized, and web-agnostic as image processing should be sharing the CPU and disk drive with your front-end HTTP service. Instead of building services from large machines with dozens of heterogeneous libraries installed, you start pivoting toward single-purpose machines grouped into clusters that provide a single service. Your operations folks can easily start taking down, upgrading, and reattaching the image processing servers, say, without needing even to touch the load-balanced pool of HTTP services that sit out in front of your message queue, so long as operations understands the messaging topology and the protocol for detaching a server such that no messages are lost.

Each brand of message queue typically supports several topologies.

- A *pipeline* topology is the pattern that perhaps best resembles the picture you have in your head when you think of a queue: a producer creates messages and submits them to the queue from which the messages can then be received by a consumer. For example, the front-end web machines of a photo-sharing web site might accept image uploads from end users and enroll the incoming files on an internal queue. A machine room full of thumbnail generators could then read from the queue, with each agent receiving one message at a time containing the image for which it should generate several thumbnails. The queue might get long during the day when the site is busy and then grow short or empty again during periods of relatively low use, but either way the front-end web servers are freed to return a response quickly to the waiting customer, telling the customer that their upload is successful and that their image will soon appear in their photo stream.

- A *publisher-subscriber* or *fanout* topology looks like a pipeline but with a key difference. While the pipeline makes sure that every queued message is delivered to exactly one consumer—since, after all, it would be wasteful for two thumbnail servers to be assigned the same photograph—subscribers typically want to receive all of the messages that are being queued the publishers. Alternatively, subscribers can specify a filter that narrows their interest to messages with a particular format. This kind of queue can be used to power external services that need to push events to the outside world. It can also form a fabric that a machine room full of servers can use to advertise which systems are up, which are going down for maintenance, and which can even publish the addresses of other message queues as they are created and destroyed.

- Finally, the *request-reply* pattern is the most complex because messages have to make a round-trip. Both of the previous patterns placed very little responsibility on the producer of a message: the producer connects to the queue and transmits its message, and it is done. But a message queue client that makes a request has to stay connected and wait for the reply to be delivered to it. The queue, to support this, has to feature some sort of addressing scheme by which replies can be directed to the correct client, perhaps out of thousands of connected clients, which is still sitting and waiting for it. But for all of its underlying complexity, this is probably the most powerful pattern of all. It allows the load of dozens or hundreds of clients to be spread equally across large numbers of servers without any effort beyond setting up the message queue. Since a good message queue will allow servers to attach and detach without losing messages, this topology also allows servers to be brought down for maintenance in a way that is invisible to the population of client machines.

Request-reply queues are a great way to connect lightweight workers that can run together by the hundreds on a particular machine—say like the threads of a web server front end—to database clients or file servers that sometimes need to be called in to do heavier work on the front end's behalf. The request-reply pattern is a natural fit for RPC mechanisms, with an added benefit not usually offered by simpler RPC systems; that is, many consumers or producers can all be attached to the same queue in a fan-in or fan-out work pattern, without either group of clients knowing the difference.

Using Message Queues from Python

The most popular message queues are implemented as stand-alone servers. All of the various tasks out of which you choose to build your application—producers, consumers, filters, and RPC services—can then attach to the message queue and not have to learn each other's addresses or even identity. The AMQP protocol is one of the most widely implemented language-agnostic message queue protocols, and it is supported by open source servers that you can install such as RabbitMQ, the Apache Qpid server, and a number of other projects.

Many programmers never learn a messaging protocol themselves. Instead, they lean on third-party libraries that package up the benefits of a message queue for easy consumption through an API. Many Python programmers who use the Django web framework, for example, use the popular Celery distributed task queue instead of learning AMQP themselves. A library can also offer protocol independence by supporting other back-end services. In Celery's case, you can use the simple Redis key-value store as your "message queue" instead of a dedicate messaging appliance.

However, for the purposes of this book, an example that does not require the installation of a full-fledged separate message queue server is more convenient, so I will cover ØMQ, the *Zero Message Queue,* which was created by the same company as AMQP but moves the messaging intelligence from a centralized broker into every one of your message client programs. Embedding the ØMQ library in each of your programs, in other words, lets your code spontaneously build a messaging fabric without the need for a centralized broker. This involves several differences in approach from an architecture based on a central broker that can provide reliability, redundancy, retransmission, and persistence to disk. A good summary of the advantages and disadvantages is provided at the ØMQ web site: `www.zeromq.org/docs:welcome-from-amqp`.

To keep the example in this section self-contained, Listing 8-3 tackles a simple problem that does not really need a message queue: computing the value of π by using a simple, if inefficient, Monte Carlo method. The messaging topology, which is the important thing, is shown in Figure 8-1. A bitsource routine produces strings of length $2n$ consisting of ones and zeros. I will use the odd bits as an n-digit integer x coordinate and the even bits as an n-digit integer y coordinate. Does this coordinate lie inside or outside the quarter-circle centered on the origin whose radius is the maximum value that either of these integers could take?

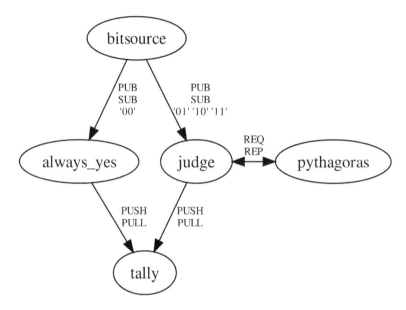

Figure 8-1. *The topology of the simple Monte Carlo estimate of* π

Using a publish-subscribe topology, you build an audience of two listeners for these binary strings. The always_yes listener will receive only digit strings starting with 00 and can therefore always push the answer Y because, if your two coordinates both start with the digit zero, then the point must lie in the lower-left quadrant of the field and therefore fall safely inside the circle. The other three possible patterns for the first two bits, however, must be processed by the judge routine that does the real test. It must ask pythagoras to compute the sum-of-the-squares of the two integer coordinates to determine whether the point that they name falls inside or outside the circle and push T or F to its outgoing queue accordingly.

The tally routine at the bottom of the topology receives either the T or F produced for every generated random bit pattern, and by comparing the number of T answers to the total number of T and F answers together, it can estimate the value of π. Do a web search for *monte carlo estimate of pi* if you are curious about the math.

Listing 8-3 implements this five-worker topology, which it lets run for 30 seconds before letting the program exit. It requires ØMQ, which you can most easily make available to Python by creating a virtual environment and then typing the following:

```
$ pip install pyzmq
```

This package might already be installed if you are using an operating system that has packaged Python for you or a stand-alone Python installation like Anaconda. In either case, Listing 8-3 will be able to run out of the box without an import error.

Listing 8-3. A ØMQ Messaging Fabric Linking Five Different Workers

```python
#!/usr/bin/env python3
# Foundations of Python Network Programming, Third Edition
# https://github.com/brandon-rhodes/fopnp/blob/m/py3/chapter08/queuecrazy.py
# Small application that uses several different message queues

import random, threading, time, zmq
B = 32  # number of bits of precision in each random integer

def ones_and_zeros(digits):
    """Express `n` in at least `d` binary digits, with no special prefix."""
    return bin(random.getrandbits(digits)).lstrip('0b').zfill(digits)

def bitsource(zcontext, url):
    """Produce random points in the unit square."""
    zsock = zcontext.socket(zmq.PUB)
    zsock.bind(url)
    while True:
        zsock.send_string(ones_and_zeros(B * 2))
        time.sleep(0.01)

def always_yes(zcontext, in_url, out_url):
    """Coordinates in the lower-left quadrant are inside the unit circle."""
    isock = zcontext.socket(zmq.SUB)
    isock.connect(in_url)
    isock.setsockopt(zmq.SUBSCRIBE, b'00')
    osock = zcontext.socket(zmq.PUSH)
    osock.connect(out_url)
    while True:
        isock.recv_string()
        osock.send_string('Y')

def judge(zcontext, in_url, pythagoras_url, out_url):
    """Determine whether each input coordinate is inside the unit circle."""
    isock = zcontext.socket(zmq.SUB)
    isock.connect(in_url)
    for prefix in b'01', b'10', b'11':
        isock.setsockopt(zmq.SUBSCRIBE, prefix)
    psock = zcontext.socket(zmq.REQ)
    psock.connect(pythagoras_url)
    osock = zcontext.socket(zmq.PUSH)
    osock.connect(out_url)
    unit = 2 ** (B * 2)
    while True:
        bits = isock.recv_string()
        n, m = int(bits[::2], 2), int(bits[1::2], 2)
        psock.send_json((n, m))
        sumsquares = psock.recv_json()
        osock.send_string('Y' if sumsquares < unit else 'N')
```

```python
def pythagoras(zcontext, url):
    """Return the sum-of-squares of number sequences."""
    zsock = zcontext.socket(zmq.REP)
    zsock.bind(url)
    while True:
        numbers = zsock.recv_json()
        zsock.send_json(sum(n * n for n in numbers))

def tally(zcontext, url):
    """Tally how many points fall within the unit circle, and print pi."""
    zsock = zcontext.socket(zmq.PULL)
    zsock.bind(url)
    p = q = 0
    while True:
        decision = zsock.recv_string()
        q += 1
        if decision == 'Y':
            p += 4
        print(decision, p / q)

def start_thread(function, *args):
    thread = threading.Thread(target=function, args=args)
    thread.daemon = True  # so you can easily Ctrl-C the whole program
    thread.start()

def main(zcontext):
    pubsub = 'tcp://127.0.0.1:6700'
    reqrep = 'tcp://127.0.0.1:6701'
    pushpull = 'tcp://127.0.0.1:6702'
    start_thread(bitsource, zcontext, pubsub)
    start_thread(always_yes, zcontext, pubsub, pushpull)
    start_thread(judge, zcontext, pubsub, reqrep, pushpull)
    start_thread(pythagoras, zcontext, reqrep)
    start_thread(tally, zcontext, pushpull)
    time.sleep(30)

if __name__ == '__main__':
    main(zmq.Context())
```

Every one of these threads is careful to create its own socket or sockets for communication since it is not safe for two threads to try to share a single messaging socket. But the threads do share a single *context* object, which assures they all exist within what you might call a shared arena of URLs, messages, and queues. You will typically want to create only a single ØMQ context per process.

Even though these sockets are offering methods with names similar to familiar socket operations such as recv() and send(), keep in mind that they have different semantics. Messages are kept in order and are never duplicated, but they are cleanly delimited as separate messages instead of being lost in a continuous stream.

This example is obviously contrived so that, within a few lines of code, you have an excuse to use most of the major messaging patterns offered by a typical queue. The connections that always_yes and the judge make to the bitsource form a publish-subscribe system, where every connected client receives its own copy of every message sent by the publisher (minus, in this case, any messages that wind up being filtered out). Each filter applied to a ØMQ socket adds, not subtracts, to the total number of messages received by opting in to every message whose first few digits match the filter string. Your pair of subscribers, then, are guaranteed to receive every bit string produced by the `bitsource` since among their four filters is every possible combination of two leading binary digits.

The relationship between `judge` and `pythagoras` is a classic RPC request-and-reply where the client holding the `REQ` socket must speak first in order to assign its message to one of the waiting agents that are attached to its socket. (In this case, of course, only one agent is attached.) The messaging fabric automatically adds a return address to the request behind the scenes. Once the agent is done with its work and replies, the return address can be used to transmit the reply over the `REP` socket so that it will arrive at the correct client, even if dozens or hundreds are currently attached.

Finally, the `tally` worker illustrates the way that a push-pull arrangement guarantees that each item pushed will be received by one, and only one, of the agents connected to the socket; if you were to start up several `tally` workers, then each new datum from upstream would arrive at only one of them, and they would each converge separately on π.

Note that, unlike in all of the other socket programming featured in in this book, this listing does not have to be at all careful about whether `bind()` or `connect()` occurs first! This is a feature of ØMQ, which uses timeouts and polling to keep retrying a failed `connect()` behind the scenes in case the endpoint described by the URL comes up later. This makes it robust against agents that come and go while an application is running.

The resulting system of workers, when run, is able to compute π to about three digits on my laptop by the time the program exits.

```
$ python queuepi.py
...
Y 3.1406089633937735
```

This modest example may make ØMQ programming look overly simple. In real life, you will typically want more sophisticated patterns than the ones provided here in order to assure the delivery of messages, persist them in case they cannot yet be processed, and do flow control to make sure that a slow agent will not be overwhelmed by the number of messages that eventually wind up queued and waiting for it. See the official documentation for extended discussions of how to implement these patterns for a production service. In the end, many programmers find that a full-fledged message broker like RabbitMQ, Qpid, or Redis behind Celery gives them the assurances that they want with the least work and potential for mistakes.

Summary

Serving thousands or millions of customers has become a routine assignment for application developers in the modern world. Several key technologies have emerged to help them meet this scale, and they can easily be accessed from Python.

One popular service is Memcached, which combines the free RAM across all of the servers on which it is installed into a single large LRU cache. As long as you have some procedure for invalidating or replacing entries that become out of date—or are dealing with data that can be expired on a fixed, predictable schedule—Memcached can remove a massive amount of load from your database or other back-end storage. It can be inserted at several different points in your processing. Instead of saving the result of an expensive database query, for example, it might be even better simply to cache the web widget that ultimately gets rendered.

Message queues are another general mechanism that provide a point of coordination and integration for different parts of your application, which may require different hardware, load balancing techniques, platforms, or even programming languages. They can take responsibility for distributing messages among many waiting consumers or servers in a way that is not possible with the single point-to-point links offered by normal TCP sockets, and they can also use a database or other persistent storage to assure that messages are not lost if the server goes down. Message queues also offer resilience and flexibility, since, if some part of your system temporarily becomes a bottleneck, the message queue can then absorb the shock by allowing many messages to queue up for that service. By hiding the population of servers or processes that serve a particular kind of request, the message queue pattern also makes it easy to disconnect, upgrade, reboot, and reconnect servers without the rest of your infrastructure noticing.

Many programmers use message queues behind a friendlier API, such as the Celery project, which is popular in the Django community. It can also use Redis as a back end. While not covered in this chapter, Redis deserves your attention. It is like Memcached in maintaining keys and values, it is like a database in that it can persist them to storage, and it is like a message queue in that a FIFO is one of the possible values that it can support.

If any of these patterns sound like they address a problem you have, then search the Python Package Index for good leads on Python libraries that might implement them. The state of the art in the Python community with respect to these general tools and techniques will continue to develop while this book is in print, and it can be explored through blogs, tweets, and especially Stack Overflow since there is a strong culture there of keeping answers up-to-date as solutions age and new ones emerge.

Having examined these simple and specific technologies built atop IP/TCP, you will turn your attention over the next three chapters to the protocol that has become so dominant that many people speak as though it is synonymous with the Internet itself: the HTTP protocol that implements the World Wide Web.

CHAPTER 9

■ ■ ■

HTTP Clients

This is the first of three chapters about HTTP. In this chapter, you will learn how to use the protocol from the point of view of a client program that wants to fetch and cache documents and perhaps submit queries or data to the server as well. In the process, you will learn the rules of how the protocol operates. Chapter 10 will then look at the design and deployment of HTTP servers. Both chapters will consider the protocol in its most pristine conceptual form, that is, simply as a mechanism for fetching or posting documents.

While HTTP can deliver many kinds of document—images, PDFs, music, and video—Chapter 11 examines the particular class of document that has made HTTP and the Internet world famous: the World Wide Web of hypertext documents, which are interlinked thanks to the invention of the URL, also described in Chapter 11. There you will learn about the programming patterns enabled by template libraries, forms, and Ajax, as well as about web frameworks that try to bring all of these patterns together into an easy-to-program form.

HTTP version 1.1, the most common version in use today, is defined in RFCs 7230-7235, to which you should refer in any cases where the text of these chapters seems ambiguous or leaves you wanting to know more. For a more technical introduction to the theory behind the protocol's design, you can consult Chapter 5 of Roy Thomas Fielding's famous PhD dissertation "Architectural Styles and the Design of Network-based Software Architectures."

For now your journey begins here, where you will learn to query a server and to get documents in response.

Python Client Libraries

The HTTP protocol and the massive data resources that it makes available are a perennially popular topic for Python programmers, and this has been reflected through the years in a long parade of third-party clients purporting to do a better job than the urllib built into the Standard Library.

Today, however, a single third-party solution stands alone, not only having thoroughly swept the field of contenders but also having replaced urllib as the go-to tool of the Python programmer who wants to speak HTTP. That library is Requests, written by Kenneth Reitz and backed by the connection pooling logic of urllib3, which is maintained by Andrey Petrov.

As you learn about HTTP in this chapter, you will return to both urllib and Requests to see what they do well, and what they do poorly, when faced with each HTTP feature. Their basic interfaces are quite similar—they provide a callable that opens an HTTP connection, makes a request, and waits for the response headers before returning a response object that presents them to the programmer. The response body is left queued on the incoming socket and read only when the programmer asks.

In most of the examples in this chapter, I will be testing the two HTTP client libraries against a small test web site named http://httpbin.org, which was designed by Kenneth Reitz and which you can run locally by installing it with pip and then running it inside a WSGI container (see Chapter 10) like Gunicorn. To run it on localhost port 8000

so that you can try the examples in this chapter on your own machine without needing to hit the public version of
httpbin.org, simply type the following:

```
$ pip install gunicorn httpbin requests
$ gunicorn httpbin:app
```

You should then be able to fetch one of its pages with both urllib and Requests to see how their interfaces, at first
glance, are similar.

```
>>> import requests
>>> r = requests.get('http://localhost:8000/headers')
>>> print(r.text)
{
  "headers": {
    "Accept": "*/*",
    "Accept-Encoding": "gzip, deflate",
    "Host": "localhost:8000",
    "User-Agent": "python-requests/2.3.0 CPython/3.4.1 Linux/3.13.0-34-generic"
  }
}
>>> from urllib.request import urlopen
>>> import urllib.error
>>> r = urlopen('http://localhost:8000/headers')
>>> print(r.read().decode('ascii'))
{
  "headers": {
    "Accept-Encoding": "identity",
    "Connection": "close",
    "Host": "localhost:8000",
    "User-Agent": "Python-urllib/3.4"
  }
}
```

Two differences are already visible, and they are a good foreshadowing of what is to come in this chapter. Requests
has declared up front that it supports gzip- and deflate-compressed HTTP responses, while urllib knows nothing about
them. Furthermore, while Requests has been able to determine the correct decoding to turn this HTTP response from
raw bytes into text, the urllib library has simply returned bytes and made you perform the decoding yourself.

There have been other attempts at powerful Python HTTP clients, many of them focused on trying to be more
browser-like. These wanted to go beyond the HTTP protocol described in this chapter and launch into concepts that
you will learn about in Chapter 11, bringing together the structure of HTML, the semantics of its forms, and the rules
of what a browser is supposed to do when you have completed a form and click Submit. The library mechanize, for
example, enjoyed a period of popularity.

In the end, however, web sites are often too sophisticated to interact with anything less than a full browser, as
forms are often valid today only because of annotations or adjustments made by JavaScript. Many modern forms do
not even have a real Submit button but activate a script to do their work. Technologies for controlling browsers have
proved more useful than mechanize, and I cover some of them in Chapter 11.

The goal of this chapter is for you to understand HTTP, to see how many of its features are accessible through
Requests and urllib, and to help you understand the boundaries in which you will operate if instead you use the urllib
package built in to the Standard Library. If you do ever find yourself in a situation where you cannot install third-party

libraries but need to perform advanced HTTP operations, then you will want to consult not only the urllib library's own documentation but also two other resources: its Python Module of the Week entry and the chapter on HTTP in the online *Dive Into Python* book.

```
http://pymotw.com/2/urllib2/index.html#module-urllib2
http://www.diveintopython.net/http_web_services/index.html
```

These resources were both written in the days of Python 2 and therefore call the library urllib2 instead of urllib.request, but you should find that they still work as a basic guide to urllib's awkward and outdated object-oriented design.

Ports, Encryption, and Framing

Port 80 is the standard port for plain-text HTTP conversations. Port 443 is the standard port for clients that want first to negotiate an encrypted TLS conversation (see Chapter 6) and then begin speaking HTTP only once the encryption has been established—a variant of the protocol that is named Hypertext Transfer Protocol Secure (HTTPS). Inside the encrypted channel, HTTP is spoken exactly as it would be normally over an unencrypted socket.

As you will learn in Chapter 11, the choice between HTTP and HTTPS and between the standard or a nonstandard port is generally expressed, from the point of view of the user, in the URLs that they construct or are given.

Remember that the purpose of TLS is not only to protect traffic from eavesdropping but also to verify the identity of the server to which the client is connecting (moreover, if a client certificate is presented, to allow the server to verify the client identity in return). Never use an HTTPS client that does not perform a check of whether the certificate presented by the server matches the hostname to which the client is attempting to connect. All of the clients covered in this chapter do perform such a check.

In HTTP, it is the client that speaks first, transmitting a *request* that names a document. Once the entire request is on the wire, the client then waits until it has received a complete *response* from the server that either indicates an error condition or provides information about the document that the client has requested. The client, at least in the HTTP/1.1 version of the protocol that is popular today, is not permitted to begin transmitting a second request over the same socket until the response is finished.

There is an important symmetry built into HTTP: the request and response use the same rules to establish formatting and framing. Here is an example request and response to which you can refer as you read the description of the protocol that follows:

```
GET /ip HTTP/1.1
User-Agent: curl/7.35.0
Host: localhost:8000
Accept: */*

HTTP/1.1 200 OK
Server: gunicorn/19.1.1
Date: Sat, 20 Sep 2014 00:18:00 GMT
Connection: close
Content-Type: application/json
Content-Length: 27
Access-Control-Allow-Origin: *
Access-Control-Allow-Credentials: true

{
  "origin": "127.0.0.1"
}
```

The request is the block of text that begins with GET. The response begins with the version HTTP/1.1, and it continues through the blank line below the headers to include the three lines of JSON text. Both the request and the response are called an HTTP *message* in the standard, and each message is composed of three parts.

- A first line that names a method and document in the request and names a return code and description in the response. The line ends with a carriage return and linefeed (CR-LF, ASCII codes 13 and 10).

- Zero or more headers that consist of a name, a colon, and a value. Header names are case-insensitive, so they can be capitalized however a client or server desires. Each header ends with a CR-LF. A blank line then terminates the entire list of headers—the four bytes CR-LF-CR-LF that form a pair of end-of-line sequences with nothing in between them. This blank line is mandatory whether any headers appear above it or not.

- An optional body that immediately follows the blank line that end the headers. There are several options for framing the entity, as you will learn shortly.

The first line and the headers are each framed by their terminal CR-LF sequences, and the whole assembly is framed as a unit by the blank line at the end, so the end can be discovered by a server or client by calling recv() until the four-character sequence CR-LF-CR-LF appears. No prior warning is provided about how long the line and headers might be, so many servers set commonsense maximums on their length to avoid running out of RAM when a troublemaker connects and sends infinite-length headers.

There are three different options for framing a body, if one has been attached to the message.

The most common framing is the presence of a Content-Length header, whose value should be a decimal integer giving the length of the body in bytes. This is simple enough to implement. The client can simply loop on a repeated recv() call until the accumulated bytes finally equal the stated length. But declaring a Content-Length is sometimes not feasible when data is being generated dynamically, and its length cannot be known until the process is complete.

A more complicated scheme is activated if the headers specify a Transfer-Encoding of "chunked." Instead of the body having its length specified up front, it is delivered in a series of smaller pieces that are each separately prefixed by their length. Each chunk consists of at least a hexadecimal (in contrast to the Content-Length header, which is decimal!) length field, the two characters CR-LF, a block of data of exactly the stated length, and again the two characters CR-LF. The chunks end with a final chunk that declares that it has zero length—minimally, the digit zero, a CR-LF, and then another CR-LF.

After the chunk length but before the CR-LF, the sender can insert a semicolon and then specify an "extension" option that applies to that chunk. At the end, after the last chunk has given its length of zero and its CR-LF, the sender can append a few last HTTP headers. You can refer to RFC 7230 for these details if you are implementing HTTP yourself.

The other alternative to Content-Length is quite abrupt: the server can specify "Connection: close," send as much or as little body as it wants, and then close the TCP socket. This introduces the danger that the client cannot tell whether the socket closed because the entire body was successfully delivered or whether the socket closed prematurely because of a server or network error, and it also makes the protocol less efficient by forcing the client to re-connect for every single request.

(The standard says that the "Connection: close" trick cannot be attempted by the client because then it could not receive the server's response. Had they not heard of the idea of a unidirectional shutdown() on the socket, allowing the client to end its direction while still being able to read data back from the server?).

Methods

The first word of an HTTP request specifies the action that the client is requesting of the server. There are two common methods, GET and POST, and a number of less common methods defined for servers that want to present a full document API to other computer programs that may be accessing them (typically, JavaScript that they themselves have delivered to a browser).

The two basic methods, GET and POST, provide the basic "read" and "write" operations of HTTP.

GET is the method performed when you type an HTTP URL into your web browser: it asks for the document named by the request path to be transmitted as the server's response. It cannot include a body. The standard insists that servers cannot, under any circumstances, let clients modify data with this method. Any parameters attached to the path (see Chapter 11 to learn about URLs) can only modify the document that is being returned, as in `?q=python` or `?results=10`, not ask that changes take place on the server. The restriction that GET cannot modify data lets a client safely re-attempt a GET if a first attempt is interrupted, allows GET responses to be cached (you learn about caching later in this chapter), and makes it safe for web scraping programs (see Chapter 11) to visit as many URLs as they want without fearing that they are creating or deleting content on the sites they are traversing.

POST is used when the client wants to submit new data to the server. Traditional web forms, if they do not simply copy your form fields into the URL, usually use POST to deliver your request. Programmer-oriented APIs also use POST for submitting new documents, comments, and database rows. Because running the same POST twice might perform an action on the server twice, like giving a merchant a second $100 payment, the results of a POST neither can be cached to satisfy future repeats of the POST nor can a POST be retried automatically if the response does not arrive.

The remaining HTTP methods can be categorized as being basically like GET or basically like POST.

The methods like GET are OPTIONS and HEAD. The *OPTIONS* method asks what header values will work with a particular path, and the *HEAD* method asks the server to go through the process of getting ready to transmit the resource but then to stop and transmit only the headers instead. This lets a client check on things such as Content-Type without incurring the cost of downloading the body.

The operations like POST are PUT and DELETE, in that they are expected to perform what might be irreversible changes to the content stored by the server. As you would expect from their names, *PUT* is intended to deliver a new document that will henceforth live at the path that the request specifies, and *DELETE* asks the server to destroy the path and any content associated with it. Interestingly, these two methods—while requesting "writes" of the server content—are safe in a way that POST is not: they are *idempotent* and can be retried as many times as the client wants because the effect of running either of them once ought to be the same as the effect of running them many times.

Finally, the standard specifies both a debugging method TRACE and a method CONNECT for switching protocols to something besides HTTP (which, as you will see in Chapter 11, is used to turn on WebSockets). They are, however, rarely used, and in neither case have they anything to do with the delivery of documents that is the core duty of HTTP, which you are learning about in this chapter. Refer to the standard for more information about them.

Note that one quirk of the Standard Library's `urlopen()` is that it chooses its HTTP verb invisibly: POST if the caller specifies a data parameter, or GET otherwise. This is an unfortunate choice because the correct use of HTTP verbs is crucial to safe client and server design. The Requests choice of `get()` and `post()` is much better for these essentially different methods.

Paths and Hosts

The first versions of HTTP allowed the request to consist solely of a verb and path.

```
GET /html/rfc7230
```

This worked well in the early era when every server hosted exactly one web site, but it broke down as soon as administrators wanted to be able to deploy large HTTP servers that could serve dozens or hundreds of sites. Given only a path, how could the server guess which hostname the user had typed in the URL—especially for a path like / that typically exists on every web site?

The solution was to make at least one header, the Host header, mandatory. Modern versions of the protocol also include the protocol version in a minimally correct request, which would read as follows:

```
GET /html/rfc7230 HTTP/1.1
Host: tools.ietf.org
```

Many HTTP servers will signal a client error unless the client supplies at least a Host header revealing which hostname was used in the URL. The result, in its absence, is often 400 Bad Request. See the following section for more about error codes and their meanings.

Status Codes

The response line starts with the protocol version instead of ending with it like the request line, and then it supplies a standard status code before concluding with an informal textual description of the status for presentation to the user or entry in a log file. When everything has gone perfectly, the status code is 200, in which case the response line often reads as follows:

```
HTTP/1.1 200 OK
```

Because the text following the code is merely informal, a server could replace OK with Okay or Yippee or It Worked or even with text that had been internationalized for the country in which the server was operating.

The standard—in particular, RFC 7231—specifies more than two dozen return codes for situations both general and specific. You may consult the standard if you need to learn the complete list. In general, the 200s indicate success, the 300s redirection, the 400s that the client request is unintelligible or illegal, and the 500s that something unexpected has gone wrong that is entirely the server's fault.

There are only a few that will concern you in this chapter.

- *200 OK*: The request was successful. If a POST, it had its intended effect.

- *301 Moved Permanently*: The path, while valid, is not the canonical one for the resource in question (though it might have been at some point in the past), and the client should instead request the URL specified in the Location header of the response. All future requests can skip this old URL and go straight to the new one, if the client wants to cache it.

- *303 See Other*: The client can learn the result of this particular, unique request by doing a GET against the URL specified in the Location header of the response. However, any future attempts to access this resource will need to return to this location. As you will see in Chapter 11, this status is crucial to the design of web sites—any form submitted successfully with POST should return 303 so that the actual page the client sees is fetched with a safe, idempotent GET operation instead.

- *304 Not Modified*: The document body does not need to be included in the response because the request headers make it clear that the client already has an up-to-date version of the document in its cache (see the "Caching and Validation" section).

- *307 Temporary Redirect*: Whatever request the client has made, whether GET or POST, should be attempted again against the different URL specified in the Location header of the response. But any future attempts to access this resource will need to return to this location. Among other things, this allows forms to be delivered to an alternative address in case a server is down or unavailable.

- *400 Bad Request*: The request does not appear to be valid HTTP.

- *403 Forbidden*: No password or cookie (for both, see later in this chapter) or other identifying data is present in the request that proves to the server that the client has permission to access it.

- *404 Not Found*: The path does not name an existing resource. This is probably the most famous exception code because users never see the 200 code displayed on their screen; they see a document instead.

- *405 Method Not Allowed*: The server recognizes the method and path, but this particular method does not make sense when run against this particular path.

- *500 Server Error*: Another familiar status. The server wants to fulfill the request but cannot at the moment because of some internal error.

- *501 Not Implemented*: The server does not recognize your HTTP verb.

- *502 Bad Gateway*: The server is a gateway or proxy (see Chapter 10), but it cannot contact the server behind it that is supposed to provide the response for this path.

While responses with 3*xx* status codes are not expected to carry a body, both 4*xx* and 5*xx* responses usually do so—generally offering some kind of human-readable description of the error. The less informative examples are typically unmodified error pages for the language or framework in which the web server has been written. Server authors have often handcrafted more informative pages to help users or developers know how to recover from the error.

As you are learning a particular Python HTTP client, there are two important questions to ask regarding status codes.

The first question is whether a library automatically follows redirects. If not, you have to detect 3*xx* status codes yourself and follow their Location header. While the low-level httplib module built into the Standard Library would make you follow redirects yourself, the urllib module will follow them for you in conformance with the standard. The Requests library does the same, and it additionally presents you with a history attribute that lists the whole series of redirects that brought you to the final location.

```
>>> r = urlopen('http://httpbin.org/status/301')
>>> r.status, r.url
(200, 'http://httpbin.org/get')
>>> r = requests.get('http://httpbin.org/status/301')
>>> (r.status, r.url)
(200, 'http://httpbin.org/get')
>>> r.history
[<Response [301]>, <Response [302]>]
```

The Requests library additionally lets you turn redirection off, if you prefer, with a simple keyword argument—a maneuver that is possible but much more difficult if attempted with urllib.

```
>>> r = requests.get('http://httpbin.org/status/301',
...                   allow_redirects=False)
>>> r.raise_for_status()
>>> (r.status_code, r.url, r.headers['Location'])
(301, 'http://localhost:8000/status/301', '/redirect/1')
```

It will reduce load on the servers that you query if your Python program takes the time to detect 301 errors and attempt to avoid those URLs in the future. If your program maintains a persistent state, then it might be able to cache 301 errors to avoid revisiting those paths, or directly rewrite the URL wherever you have it stored. If a user requested the URL interactively, then you might print a helpful message informing them of the new location of the page.

Two of the most common redirections involve whether the prefix www belongs at the front of the hostname you use to contact a server.

```
>>> r = requests.get('http://google.com/')
>>> r.url
'http://www.google.com/'
>>> r = requests.get('http://www.twitter.com/')
>>> r.url
'https://twitter.com/'
```

Here, two popular sites have taken opposite stances on whether the www prefix should be part of their official hostname. However, in both cases they are willing to use a redirect to enforce their preference and also to prevent the chaos of their site appearing to live at two different URLs. Unless your application is careful to learn these redirections and avoid repeating them, you will wind up doing two HTTP requests instead of one for every resource you fetch if your URLs are built from the wrong hostname.

The other question to investigate regarding your HTTP client is how it chooses to alert you if an attempt to fetch a URL fails with a 4*xx* or 5*xx* status code. For all such codes, the Standard Library urlopen() raises an exception, making it impossible for your code to accidentally process an error page returned from the server as though it were normal data.

```
>>> urlopen('http://localhost:8000/status/500')
Traceback (most recent call last):
...
urllib.error.HTTPError: HTTP Error 500: INTERNAL SERVER ERROR
```

How can you ever examine the details of the response if urlopen() interrupts you with an exception? The answer is by examining the exception object, which performs double duty by being both an exception and also a response object with headers and a body.

```
>>> try:
...     urlopen('http://localhost:8000/status/500')
... except urllib.error.HTTPError as e:
...     print(e.status, repr(e.headers['Content-Type']))
500 'text/html; charset=utf-8'
```

The situation presented by the Requests library is more surprising—even error status codes result in a response object being returned, without comment, to the caller. It is the responsibility of the caller either to test the status code of the response or to volunteer to call its raise_for_status() method that will trigger an exception on 4*xx* or 5*xx* status code.

```
>>> r = requests.get('http://localhost:8000/status/500')
>>> r.status_code
500
>>> r.raise_for_status()
Traceback (most recent call last):
...
requests.exceptions.HTTPError: 500 Server Error: INTERNAL SERVER ERROR
```

If you are worried about having to remember to perform a status check every time you call requests.get, then you might consider writing a wrapper function of your own that performs the check automatically.

Caching and Validation

HTTP includes several well-designed mechanisms for letting clients avoid the repeated GET of resources of which they are making frequent use, but they operate only if the server chooses to add headers to the resource allowing them. It is important for server authors to think through caching and allow it whenever possible since it reduces both network traffic and server load while also letting client applications run faster.

RFCs 7231 and 7232 describe all of these mechanisms in exhaustive detail. This section attempts only to provide a basic introduction.

The most important question that a service architect can ask when they want to add headers to turn on caching is whether two requests should really return the same document merely because their paths are identical. Is there anything else about a pair of requests that might result in their needing to return two different resources? If so, then a service needs to include a Vary header in every response listing the other headers on which document content depends. Common choices are `Host`, `Accept-Encoding`, and especially `Cookie` if the designer is returning different documents to different users.

Once the Vary header is set correctly, there are various levels of caching that can be activated.

Resources can be forbidden from being stored in a client cache at all, which forbids the client from making any kind of automatic copy of the response on nonvolatile storage. The intention is to leave the user in control of whether they select "save" to archive a copy of the resource to disk.

```
HTTP/1.1 200 OK
Cache-control: no-store
...
```

If the server opts instead to allow caching, then it will usually want to protect against the possibility that the client might keep presenting the cached copy of the resource every time the user asks for it until it has become quite out-of-date. The one case in which the server need not worry about whether a resource gets cached forever is when it is careful to use a given path only for a single permanent version of a document or image. If a version number or hash at the end of the URL is incremented or changed every time the designers come out with a new version of the corporate logo, for example, then any given version of the logo can be delivered with permission to store it forever.

There are two ways that the server can prevent the client copy of the resource from being used forever. First, it can specify an expiration date and time after which the resource cannot be reused without a request back to the server.

```
HTTP/1.1 200 OK
Expires: Thu, 01 Dec 1994 16:00:00 GMT
...
```

But the use of a date and time introduces the danger that an incorrectly set client clock will result in the cached copy of the resource being used for far too long. A much better method is the modern mechanism of specifying the number of seconds that the resource can be cached once it has been received, which will work as long as the client clock is not simply stalled.

```
HTTP/1.1 200 OK
Cache-control: max-age=3600
...
```

The two headers shown here grant the client the unilateral ability, for a limited period of time, to keep using an old copy of a resource without any consultation with the server.

But what if a server wants to retain a veto over whether a cached resource is used or a new version is fetched? In that case, it will have to require the client to use an HTTP request to check back every time it wants to use the resource. This will be more expensive than letting the client use the cached copy silently and without a network operation, but it can still save time because the server will have to send a new copy of the resource if the only old copy possessed by the client indeed proves to be out-of-date.

There are two mechanisms by which a server can make the client check back about every use of a resource but let the client reuse its cached copy of the resource if possible. These are called *conditional* requests in the standard because they will result in the transmission of a body only if the tests reveal the client cache to be out-of-date.

The first mechanism requires the server to know when resources were last modified. This can be easy to determine if the resources are backed by, say, a file on the file system, but it can be difficult or impossible to determine if the resources are pulled from a database table that does not feature an audit log or a date of last modification. If the information is available, the server can include it in every response.

```
HTTP/1.1 200 OK
Last-Modified: Tue, 15 Nov 1994 12:45:26 GMT
...
```

A client that wants to reuse a cached copy of the resource can also cache this date and then repeat it back to the server the next time it needs to use the resource. If the server sees that the resource has not been modified since the client last received it, then the server can opt out of transmitting a body by instead simply transmitting headers and the special status code 304.

```
GET / HTTP/1.1
If-Modified-Since: Tue, 15 Nov 1994 12:45:26 GMT
...

HTTP/1.1 304 Not Modified
...
```

The second mechanism deals with resource identity instead of modify time. The server in this case needs some way to create a unique tag for every version of a resource that is guaranteed to change to a new unique value every time the resource changes—checksums or database UUIDs are possible sources of such information. The server, whenever it builds a reply, will need to deliver the tag in an ETag header.

```
HTTP/1.1 200 OK
ETag: "d41d8cd98f00b204e9800998ecf8427e"
...
```

The client that has cached and possesses this version of the resource can, when it wants to reuse the copy again to satisfy a user action, make a request for the resource to the server and include the cached tag in case it still names the current version of the resource.

```
GET / HTTP/1.1
If-None-Match: "d41d8cd98f00b204e9800998ecf8427e"
...

HTTP/1.1 304 Not Modified
...
```

The quotation marks used in ETag and If-None-Match reflect the fact that the scheme can actually do more powerful comparisons than simply to compare the two strings for equality. Consult RFC 7232 Section 3.2 if you want the details.

Note again that both If-Modified-Since and If-None-Match save bandwidth only by preventing the resource from being transmitted again and thus also the time spent in transmission. They still incur at least a round-trip to the server and back before the client can proceed to use the resource.

Caching is powerful and crucial to the performance of the modern Web. However, neither of the client libraries for Python that you are looking at will perform caching by default. Both urllib and Requests believe that their job is to perform a real live network HTTP request when the time comes that you need one—not to manage a cache that might exempt you from needing to talk over the network in the first place. You will have to seek out third-party libraries if you want a wrapper that when pointed at some form of local persistent storage that you can provide, uses Expires and Cache-control headers, modify dates, and ETags to try to minimize the latency and network traffic that your client incurs.

Caching is also important to think about if you are configuring or running a proxy, a topic that I will discuss in Chapter 10.

Content Encoding

It is crucial to understand the difference between an HTTP transfer encoding and content encoding.

A *transfer encoding* is simply a scheme for turning a resource into an HTTP response body. By definition, the choice of transfer encoding makes no difference in the end. As an example, the client ought to find that same document or image has been delivered whether the response was framed with either a Content-Length or a chunked encoding. The resource should look the same whether the bytes were sent raw or compressed to make transmission faster. A transfer encoding is simply a wrapper used for data delivery, not a change in the underlying data itself.

Though modern web browsers support several transfer encodings, the most popular with programmers is probably gzip. A client able to accept this transfer encoding must declare so in an Accept-Encoding header and be prepared to examine the Transfer-Encoding header of the response to determine whether the server took it up on its offer.

```
GET / HTTP/1.1
Accept-Encoding: gzip
...

HTTP/1.1 200 OK
Content-Length: 3913
Transfer-Encoding: gzip
...
```

The urllib library has no support for this mechanism, and so it requires your own code to produce and detect these headers and then to uncompress the response body yourself if you want to take advantage of compressed transfer encodings.

The Requests library automatically declares an Accept-Encoding of `gzip,deflate`, and it uncompresses the body automatically if the server responds with an appropriate Transfer-Encoding. This makes compression both automatic when servers support it and invisible to the user of Requests.

Content Negotiation

Content type and *content encoding*, in contrast to transfer encoding, are entirely visible to the end user or client program that is performing an HTTP request. They determine both what file format will be selected to represent a given resource and—if the format is text—what encoding will be used to turn text code points into bytes.

These headers allow an old browser that cannot display new-fangled PNG images to indicate that it prefers GIF and JPG instead, and they allow resources to be delivered in a language that the user has indicated to their web browser that they prefer. Here is a sample of what such headers might look like when generated by a modern web browser:

```
GET / HTTP/1.1
Accept: text/html;q=0.9,text/plain,image/jpg,*/*;q=0.8
Accept-Charset: unicode-1-1;q=0.8
Accept-Language: en-US,en;q=0.8,ru;q=0.6
User-Agent: Mozilla/5.0 (X11; Linux i686) AppleWebKit/537.36 (KHTML)
...
```

The types and languages listed first have the strongest preference value of 1.0, while the ones that are listed later in the header are often demoted to q=0.9 or q=0.8 to make sure the server knows that they are not preferred over the best choices.

Many simple HTTP services and sites ignore these headers entirely and instead fall back to using a separate URL for each version of a resource they possess. A site's front page, for example, might exist in the two versions /en/index.html and /fr/index.html if the site supports both English and French. The same corporate logo might be located at both of the paths /logo.png and /logo.gif, and the user might be offered both for download when browsing the corporation's press kit. The documentation for a RESTful web service (see Chapter 10) will often specify that different URL query parameters, like ?f=json and ?f=xml, be used to select the representation that is returned.

But that is not how HTTP was designed to work.

The intention of HTTP was that a resource should have one path at which it lives, regardless of how many different machine formats—or human languages—might be used to render it, and that the server use those content negotiation headers to select that resource.

Why is content negotiation often ignored?

First, the use of content negotiation can leave the user with little control over their user experience. Imagine again a site that offers its pages in both English and French. If it displays a language based on the Accept-Language header and the user wants to see the other language, the server has no control over the situation—it would have to suggest to the user that they bring up the control panel for their web browser and change their default language. What if the user cannot find that setting? What if they are browsing from a public terminal and do not have permission to set preferences in the first place?

Instead of turning control of language selection over to a browser that might not be well written, coherent, or easily configurable, many sites simply build several redundant sets of paths, one for each human language that they want to support. They might, when the user first arrives, examine the Accept-Language header in order to autodirect the browser to the language most likely to be appropriate. But they want the user to be able to browse back in the other direction if the selection was inappropriate.

Second, content negotiation is often ignored (or sits alongside a URL-based mechanism for forcing the return of the correct version of the content) because HTTP client APIs (whether the API is used by JavaScript in a browser or the API is offered by other languages in their own runtimes) often make it difficult to control the Accepts headers. The pleasant thing about placing control elements into the path inside the URL is that anyone using even the most primitive tool for fetching a URL will be able to twiddle the knob by adjusting the URL.

Finally, content negotiation means that HTTP servers have to generate or select content by making choices among several axes. You might assume that server logic can always access the Accepts headers, which, alas, is not always the case. Programming on the server side is often easier if content negotiation is left off the table.

But for sophisticated services that want to support it, content negotiation can help prune the possible space of URLs while still offering a mechanism by which an intelligent HTTP client can get content that has been rendered with its data formatting or human reader's needs in mind. If you plan on using it, consult RFC 7231 for the details of the various Accept headers' syntax.

One final annoyance is the User-Agent string.

The User-Agent was not supposed to be part of content negotiation at all, but to serve only as an emergency stop-gap for working around the limitations of particular browsers. It was, in other words, a mechanism for targeting carefully designed fixes at specific clients while letting any other clients through to the page without any problem.

But the developers of applications backed by customer call centers quickly discovered that they could make compatibility problems impossible and reduce the number of support calls up front by forbidding any browser except, say, a single version of Internet Explorer from accessing their site. The arms race that ensued between clients and browsers resulted in the very long User-Agent strings you have today, as recounted somewhat fancifully at http://webaim.org/blog/user-agent-string-history/.

Both of the client libraries you are exploring, urllib and Requests, allow you to put any Accept headers into your request that you please. They also both support patterns for creating a client that will use your favorite headers automatically. Requests builds this feature right into its idea of a Session.

```
>>> s = requests.Session()
>>> s.headers.update({'Accept-Language': 'en-US,en;q=0.8'})
```

All subsequent calls to methods like `s.get()` will use this default value for the header unless they override it with a different value.

The urllib library offers its own patterns for setting up default handlers that can inject default headers, but, as they are labyrinthine and, alas, object-oriented, I refer you to the documentation.

Content Type

Once a server has inspected the various Accepts headers from the client and decided which representation of a resource to deliver, it sets the Content-Type header of the outgoing response accordingly.

Content types are selected from among the various MIME types that were already established for multimedia that is transmitted as part of e-mail messages (see Chapter 12). The types `text/plain` and `text/html` are both common along with image formats such as `image/gif`, `image/jpg`, and `image/png`. Documents can be delivered as types including `application/pdf`. A plain sequence of bytes for which the server can guarantee no more specific interpretation is given the content type of `application/octet-stream`.

There is one complication of which you should be aware when dealing with a Content-Type header delivered over HTTP. If the major type (the word to the left of the slash) is `text`, then the server has a number of options about how those text characters can be encoded for transmission to the client. It states its choice by appending to the Content-Type header, a semicolon, and a declaration of the character encoding used to turn the text into bytes.

```
Content-Type: text/html; charset=utf-8
```

This means you cannot simply compare the Content-Type header to a list of MIME types without first checking for the semicolon character and splitting it into two pieces. Most libraries will give you no help here. Whether you use urllib or whether you use Requests, you will have to be responsible for splitting on the semicolon if you write code that needs to inspect the content type (although Requests will at least use, if not tell you about, the content type's charset setting if you ask its `Response` object for its already-decoded `text` attribute).

The only library that you will examine in this book that allows the content type and character set to be manipulated separately by default is Ian Bicking's WebOb library (Chapter 10), whose `Response` objects offer separate attributes called `content_type` and `charset` that get put together with a semicolon in the Content-Type header per the standard.

HTTP Authentication

Just as the word *authentic* denotes something that is genuine, real, actual, or true, *authentication* describes any procedures for determining whether a request really comes from someone authorized to make it. Just as your telephone conversation with a bank or airline will be prefixed with questions about your address and personal identity in order to establish that it is really the account holder calling, so too an HTTP request often needs to carry built-in proof as to the identity of the machine or person making it.

The error code 401 Not Authorized is used by servers that want to signal formally, through the protocol itself, either that they cannot authenticate your identity or that the identity is fine but is not one authorized to view this particular resource.

Many real-world HTTP servers never actually deign to return a 401 because they are designed purely for human users. On these servers, an attempt to fetch a resource without the proper identification is likely to return a 303 See Other to their login page. This is helpful for a human but far less so for your Python program, which will have to learn distinguish between a 303 See Other that truly indicates a failure to authenticate from an innocent redirection that is really just trying to take you to the resource.

Because every HTTP request is stand-alone and independent of all other requests, even those that come right before and after it on the same socket, any authenticating information much be carried separately in every single request. This independence is what makes it safe for proxy servers and load balancers to distribute HTTP requests, even requests that arrive over the same socket, among as many servers as they want.

You can read RFC 7235 to learn about the most recent HTTP authentication mechanisms. The initial steps in the early days were not encouraging.

The first mechanism, Basic Authentication (or "Basic Auth"), involved the server including a string called a *realm* in its 401 Not Authorized headers. The realm string allows a single server to protect different parts of its document tree with different passwords because the browser can keep up with which user password goes with which realm. The client then repeats its request with an Authorization header giving the username and password (base-64 encoded, as though that helps), and it is ideally given a 200 reply.

```
GET / HTTP/1.1
...

HTTP/1.1 401 Unauthorized
WWW-Authenticate: Basic realm="engineering team"
...

GET / HTTP/1.1
Authorization: Basic YnJhbmRvbjphdGlnZG5nbmF0d3dhA==
...

HTTP/1.1 200 OK
...
```

Passing the username and password in the clear sounds unconscionable today, but in that earlier and more innocent era, there were as yet no wireless networks, and switching equipment tended to be solid-state instead of running software that could be compromised. As protocol designers began to contemplate the dangers, an updated "Digest access authentication" scheme was created where the server issues a challenge and the client replies with an MD5 hash of the challenge-plus-password instead. But the result is still something of a disaster. Even with Digest authentication in use, your username is still visible in the clear. All form data submitted and all resources returned from the web site are visible in the clear. An ambitious enough attacker can then launch a man-in-the-middle attack so that, thinking they are the server, you sign a challenge that they have just themselves received from the server and which they can turn around and use to impersonate you.

Web sites needed real security if banks wanted to show you your balance and if Amazon wanted you to type in your credit card information. Thus, SSL was invented to create HTTPS, and it was followed by the various versions of TLS that you enjoy today, as detailed in Chapter 6.

The addition of TLS meant, in principle, that there was no longer anything wrong with Basic Auth. Many simple HTTPS-protected APIs and web applications use it today. While urllib supports it only if you build a series of objects to install in your URL opener (see the documentation for details), Requests supports Basic Auth with a single keyword parameter.

```
>>> r = requests.get('http://example.com/api/',
...                  auth=('brandon', 'atigdngnatwwal'))
```

You can also prepare a Requests Session for authentication to avoid having to repeat it yourself with every get() or post().

```
>>> s = requests.Session()
>>> s.auth = 'brandon', 'atigdngnatwwal'
>>> s.get('http://httpbin.org/basic-auth/brandon/atigdngnatwwal')
<Response [200]>
```

Note that this mechanism, as implemented by Requests or other modern libraries, is not the full-fledged protocol! The username and password specified previously have not been tied to any specific realm. There is no 401 response involved that could even provide a realm because the username and password are being supplied unilaterally with the request without checking first whether the server even wants them. The auth keyword argument, or the equivalent Session setting, is merely a way to set the Authorization header without having to do any base-64 encoding yourself.

Modern developers prefer this simplicity to the full realm-based protocol. Typically, their only goal is for GET or POST requests to a programmer-targeted API to be authenticated independently with the identity of the user or application making the request. A unilateral Authorization header is perfect for this. It also has another advantage: time and bandwidth is not wasted getting an initial 401 when the client already has good reason to believe that the password will be required.

If you wind up talking to a true legacy system that needs you to use different passwords for different realms on the same server, then Requests gives you no help. It will be up to you to use the right password with the right URLs. This is a rare area in which urllib is capable of doing the right thing and Requests is not! But I have never heard a single complaint about this shortcoming in Requests, which is an indication of how rare true Basic Auth negotiation has become.

Cookies

HTTP-mediated authentication is rare today. It was, in the end, a losing proposition for HTTP resources that were designed to be visited by people using a web browser.

What was the problem with HTTP authentication and users? Web site designers typically want to perform their own authentication in their own way. They want a custom and friendly login page that follows their own user interaction guidelines. The sad little pop-up window that web browsers offer when challenged for in-protocol HTTP authentication are intrusive. They are not terribly informative, even at the best of times. They take the user completely out of the experience of a site. Also, any failure to type in the right username and password can result in the pop-up appearing over and over again, without the user knowing what is going wrong or how they can correct it.

And so cookies were invented.

A *cookie*, from the point of view of the client, is an opaque key-value pair. It can be delivered in any successful response that the client receives from the server.

```
GET /login HTTP/1.1
...

HTTP/1.1 200 OK
Set-Cookie: session-id=d41d8cd98f00b204e9800998ecf8427e; Path=/
...
```

When making all further requests to that particular server, the client includes that name and value in a Cookie header.

```
GET /login HTTP/1.1
Cookie: session-id=d41d8cd98f00b204e9800998ecf8427e
...
```

This made site-generated login pages possible. When a login form is submitted with invalid credentials, the server can present it again with as many helpful hints or support links as it pleases, all styled exactly like the rest of the site. Once the form is submitted correctly, it can grant the client a cookie that is specially crafted to convince the site of the user's identity during all subsequent requests.

More subtly, a login page that is not a true web form but that uses Ajax to stay on the same page (see Chapter 11) can still enjoy the benefit of cookies if the API lives at the same hostname. When the API call to do the login confirms the username and password and returns 200 OK along with a Cookie header, it is empowering all subsequent requests to the same site—not just API calls but requests for pages, images, and data—to supply the cookie and be recognized as coming from an authenticated user.

Note that cookies should be designed to be opaque. They should be either random UUID strings that lead the server to a database record giving the real username or encrypted strings that the server alone can decrypt to learn user identity. If they were user-parsable—if, for example, a cookie had the value THIS-USER-IS-brandon—then a clever user could edit the cookie to produce a forged value and submit it with their next request to impersonate some other user whose username they knew or were able to guess.

Real-world Set-Cookie headers can be much more complicated than the example given, as described at length in RFC 6265. I should mention the secure attribute. It instructs the HTTP client not to present the cookie when making unencrypted requests to the site. Without this attribute, a cookie could be exposed, allowing anyone else sharing the coffee-shop wi-fi with a user to learn the cookie's value and use it to impersonate the user. Some web sites give you a cookie simply for visiting. This lets them track your visit as you move around the site. The history collected can already be used to target ads as you browse and then can be copied into your permanent account history if you later log in with a username.

Many user-directed HTTP services will not operate without cookies keeping track of your identity and proving that you have authenticated. Tracking cookies with urllib requires object orientation; please read its documentation. Tracking cookies in Requests happens automatically if you create, and consistently use, a Session object.

Connections, Keep-Alive, and httplib

The three-way handshake that starts a TCP connection (see Chapter 3) can be avoided if a connection is already open, which even in the early days provided the impetus for HTTP to allow connections to stay open as a browser downloaded an HTTP resource, then its JavaScript, and then its CSS and images. With the emergence of TLS (see Chapter 6) as a best practice for all HTTP connections, the cost of setting up a new connection is even greater, increasing the benefit of connection reuse.

Protocol version HTTP/1.1 has made it the default for an HTTP connection to stay open after a request. Either the client or the server can specify Connection: close if they plan on hanging up once a request is completed, but otherwise a single TCP connection can be used repeatedly to pull as many resources from the server as the client wants. Web browsers often create four or more simultaneous TCP connections per site so that a page and all of its support files and images can be downloaded in parallel to try to get them in front of the user as quickly as possible.

Section 6 of RFC 7230 should be consulted to learn the complete connection control scheme, if you are an implementer who is interested in the details.

It is unfortunate that the urllib module makes no provision for connection reuse. Making two requests on the same socket is possible through the Standard Library only by using the lower-level httplib module.

```
>>> import http.client
>>> h = http.client.HTTPConnection('localhost:8000')
>>> h.request('GET', '/ip')
>>> r = h.getresponse()
>>> r.status
200
>>> h.request('GET', '/user-agent')
>>> r = h.getresponse()
>>> r.status
200
```

Note that an `HTTPConnection` object that gets hung up on will not return an error, but it will silently create a new TCP connection to replace the old one when you ask it to perform another request. The `HTTPSConnection` class offers a TLS-protected version of the same object.

The Requests library `Session` object, by contrast, is backed by a third-party package named urllib3 that will maintain a connection pool of open connections to HTTP servers with which you have recently communicated so that it can attempt to reuse them automatically when you ask it for another resource from the same site.

Summary

The HTTP protocol is used to fetch resources based on their hostname and path. The urllib client in the Standard Library will work in simple cases, but it is underpowered and lacks the features of Requests, an Internet sensation of a Python library that is the go-to tool of programmers wanting to fetch information from the Web.

HTTP runs in the clear on port 80, under the protection of TLS on port 443, and it uses the same basic layout on the wire for the client request and the server response: a line of information followed by name-value headers, finally followed by a blank line, and then, optionally, a body that can be encoded and delimited in several different ways. The client always speaks first, sending a request, and then it waits until the server has completed a response.

The most common HTTP methods are GET, for fetching a resource, and POST, for sending updated information to a server. Several other methods exist, but they each tend to be either something like GET or something like POST. The server returns a status code with each response indicating whether the request has simply succeeded or simply failed or whether the client needs to be redirected to go load another resource in order to finish.

There are several concentric layers of design built into HTTP. Caching headers might allow a resource to be cached and reused repeatedly on a client without being fetched again, or the headers might let the server skip redelivering a resource that has not changed. Both optimizations can be crucial to the performance of busy sites.

Content negotiation holds the promise of tailoring data formats and human languages to the exact preferences of the client and the human using it, but it runs into problems in practice that makes it less than universally employed. Built-in HTTP authentication was a poor design for interactive use, having been replaced with custom login pages and cookies, but Basic Auth is sometimes still used to authenticate requests to TLS-secured APIs.

HTTP/1.1 connections can survive and be reused by default, and the Requests library is careful to do so whenever possible.

In the next chapter, you will take all that you have learned here, and reversing the perspective, you will look at the task of programming from the point of view of writing a server.

## CHAPTER 10

HTTP Servers

How can a Python program run as a server responding to HTTP requests? In Chapter 7, you learned several basic socket and concurrency patterns for writing a TCP-based network server. With HTTP, it is unlikely that you will ever need to write anything that low-level because the protocol's popularity has resulted in off-the-shelf solutions for all of the major server patterns that you might need.

While this chapter will focus on third-party tools, the Standard Library does have an HTTP server implementation built in. It can even be invoked from the command line.

```
$ python3 -m http.server
Serving HTTP on 0.0.0.0 port 8000 ...
```

This server follows the old conventions established in the 1990s for serving up files from the filesystem. The path in the HTTP request is translated into a path to search in the local filesystem. The server is designed to serve files only at or beneath its current working directory. Files are served normally. When a directory is named, the server returns either the content of its index.html file if one exists or a dynamically generated listing of the files inside.

Having a small web server available wherever Python is installed has gotten me out of more than one awkward fix over the years when I have needed to transfer files between machines and none of the more specific file transfer protocols have been available. But what are the steps to take if you need something more—if you need to put your own software in charge of responding to HTTP requests?

This book tackles this question in two separate chapters. This chapter will look at server architecture and deployment, answering the questions that need solutions whether your code returns documents or a programmer-facing API. Chapter 11 will then describe the World Wide Web, and it will examine tools specific to returning HTML pages and interacting with a user's browser.

WSGI

In the earliest days of HTTP programming, many Python services were written as simple CGI scripts that were invoked once per incoming request. The server carved the HTTP request into pieces and made them available to the CGI script in its environment variables. Python programmers could either inspect these directly and print an HTTP response to standard output or get help from the cgi module in the Standard Library.

Launching a new process for every incoming HTTP request imposed a significant limitation on server performance, so language runtimes began implementing HTTP servers of their own. Python gained its http.server Standard Library module, which invites programmers to implement their services by adding do_GET() and do_POST() methods to their own subclass of BaseHTTPRequestHandler.

Other programmers wanted to serve dynamic pages from a web server that could also serve static content, such as images and stylesheets. So, mod_python was written: an Apache module that allowed properly registered Python functions to provide custom Apache handlers that could provide authentication, logging, and content. The API was unique to Apache. Handlers written in Python received a special Apache request object as their argument and could call special functions in the apache module to interact with the web server. Applications that used mod_python bore little resemblance to those written against either CGI or http.server.

This situation meant that each HTTP application written in Python tended to be anchored to one particular mechanism for interfacing with the web server. A service written for CGI would need, at the very least, a partial rewrite to work with http.server, and both would need modification before they could run under Apache. This made Python web services difficult to migrate to new platforms.

The community responded with PEP 333, the Web Server Gateway Interface (WSGI).

As David Wheeler famously said, "All problems in computer science can be solved by another level of indirection," and the WSGI standard created the extra level of indirection that was necessary for a Python HTTP service to interoperate with any web server. It specified a calling convention that, if implemented for all major web servers, would allow both low-level services and full web frameworks to be plugged into any web server that they wanted to use. The effort to implement WSGI everywhere succeeded quickly, and it is now the standard way for Python to speak HTTP.

The standard defines a WSGI application as a callable that takes two arguments. An example is shown in Listing 10-1, where the callable is a simple Python function. (Other possibilities would be a Python class, which is another kind of callable, or even class instance with a __call__() method.) The first parameter, environ, receives a dictionary that provides an extended version of the old familiar CGI set of environment variables. The second parameter is itself a callable, conventionally named start_response(), with which the WSGI app should declare its response headers. After it has been called, the app either can begin yielding byte strings (if it is itself a generator) or can return an iterable that yields byte strings when iterated across (returning a simple Python list is sufficient, for example).

Listing 10-1. A Simple HTTP Service Written as a WSGI Client

```
#!/usr/bin/env python3
# Foundations of Python Network Programming, Third Edition
# https://github.com/brandon-rhodes/fopnp/blob/m/py3/chapter10/wsgi_env.py
# A simple HTTP service built directly against the low-level WSGI spec.

from pprint import pformat
from wsgiref.simple_server import make_server

def app(environ, start_response):
    headers = {'Content-Type': 'text/plain; charset=utf-8'}
    start_response('200 OK', list(headers.items()))
    yield 'Here is the WSGI environment:\r\n\r\n'.encode('utf-8')
    yield pformat(environ).encode('utf-8')

if __name__ == '__main__':
    httpd = make_server('', 8000, app)
    host, port = httpd.socket.getsockname()
    print('Serving on', host, 'port', port)
    httpd.serve_forever()
```

Listing 10-1 might make WSGI appear simple, but that is only because the listing is choosing to behave in a simple manner and not make full use of the specification. The level of complexity is greater when implementing the server side of the specification because in that case the code must be prepared for applications that take full advantage of the many caveats and edge cases described in the standard. You can read PEP 3333, the modern Python 3 version of WSGI, if you want an idea of what is involved.

After the debut of WSGI, the idea of WSGI middleware enjoyed a heyday—the idea that Python HTTP services might in the future be designed from a series of concentric WSGI wrappers. One wrapper might provide authentication. Another might catch exceptions and log them before returning a 500 Internal Server Error page. Yet another might reverse-proxy legacy URLs to an old CMS still running in an organization and use Diazo (a project that survives to this day) to re-theme it to match the organization's more modern pages.

Although there are still developers who write and use WSGI middleware, most Python programmers today use WSGI only for the pluggability that it offers between an application or framework and the web server that listens for incoming HTTP requests.

Asynchronous Server-Frameworks

There is one application pattern, however, that has not been touched by the WSGI revolution, and that is asynchronous servers, which support coroutines or green threads.

The design of the WSGI callable targets a traditional multithreaded or multiprocess server, and so the callable is expected to block during any I/O that it needs to perform. WSGI offers no mechanism by which the callable could hand control back to the main server thread so that other callables can take turns making progress. (See the discussion of asynchrony in Chapter 7 to review how an asynchronous service splits its logic into small, nonblocking snippets of code.)

Each asynchronous server framework has therefore had to offer its own conventions for writing a web service. While these patterns vary in both brevity and convenience, they usually take responsibility for parsing the incoming HTTP requests, and they sometimes offer conveniences for doing URL dispatch and committing database connections automatically (see Chapter 11).

That is why the title of this section includes "Server-Frameworks." Projects exploring async in Python must both produce an HTTP web server atop their particular engine and then invent a calling convention whereby the request information that they have parsed can be handed off to your own code. Unlike in the WSGI ecosystem, you cannot pick an async HTTP server and web framework separately. Both are likely to come in the same package.

The Twisted server, which supports many different protocol handlers, has offered its own conventions for writing a web service for more than a decade. More recently, Facebook developed and open sourced its Tornado engine that, rather than support many protocols, focuses specifically on performance with HTTP alone. It supports a different set of callback conventions than does Twisted. And the Eventlet project, whose green threads are implicitly asynchronous instead of explicitly handing control back during each I/O operation, lets you write callables that look like normal WSGI but that will silently yield control when they attempt blocking operations.

Looking toward the future, the inventor of Python—Guido van Rossum—has championed the new `asyncio` engine in Python 3.4 (see Chapter 7) as providing a uniform interface by which different event-loop implementations can plug into different asynchronous protocol frameworks. While this might help unite the variegated world of low-level event loops, it does not appear that it will have any immediate effect on authors wanting to write asynchronous HTTP services because it does not specify an API that specifically speaks the language of HTTP requests and responses.

The limitation to keep in mind, if you are planning on writing an HTTP service using a specific async engine like `asyncio` or Tornado or Twisted, is that you choose both your HTTP server and the framework that will help you parse requests and compose responses. You will not be able to mix and match servers and frameworks.

Forward and Reverse Proxies

An HTTP proxy—whether forward or reverse—is an HTTP server that receives incoming requests and, at least for some paths, turns around and becomes a client making an outgoing HTTP request to a server behind it, finally passing that server's response back to the original client. Read RFC 7230 Section 2.3 for an introduction to proxies and how the design of HTTP anticipates their needs: `https://tools.ietf.org/html/rfc7230#section-2.3`.

Early descriptions of the Web seem to have imagined that *forward proxies* would be the most common proxying pattern. An employer, for example, might provide an HTTP proxy that their employees' web browsers request instead of speaking to remote servers directly. A hundred employee web browsers asking for the Google logo first thing in the morning might result in the proxy making but a single request to Google for the logo, which could then be cached and used to satisfy all of the subsequent employee requests. If Google was generous enough with its Expires and Cache-Control headers, then the employer would incur less bandwidth, and the employees would experience a faster Web.

But with the emergence of TLS as a universal best practice to protect user privacy and credentials, forward proxies become impossible. A proxy cannot inspect or cache a request that it cannot read.

Reverse proxies, on the other hand, are now ubiquitous among large HTTP services. A *reverse proxy* is operated as part of a web service itself and is invisible to HTTP clients. When clients think they are connecting to python.org, they are in fact speaking with a reverse proxy. The proxy can serve many resources, both static and dynamic, directly out of its cache if the core python.org servers were careful to include Expires or Cache-Control headers. A reverse proxy can often bear most of the load of running a service because HTTP requests need to be forwarded to the core servers only if a resource is either uncacheable or has expired from the proxy's cache.

A reverse proxy must necessarily perform TLS termination, and it must be the service that holds a certificate and private key for the service it proxies. Unless a proxy can examine each incoming HTTP request, it cannot perform either caching or forwarding.

If you adopt the use of a reverse proxy, either in the form of a front-end web server like Apache or nginx or with a dedicated daemon like Varnish, then caching-related headers such as Expires and Cache-Control become even more important than normal. Instead of being relevant only to the end user's browser, they become crucial signals between tiers of your own service architecture.

Reverse proxies can even help with data that you might think should not be cached, like a headline page or event log that needs up-to-the-second accuracy, as long as you can tolerate the results being at least a few seconds old. After all, it often takes clients a good fraction of a second to retrieve a resource anyway. Could it really hurt if the resource is one extra second old? Imagine putting a one-second maximum age in the Cache-Control header of a critical feed or event log that receives, say, a hundred requests per second. Your reverse proxy will go into action and, potentially, reduce your server load by a hundred-fold: it will only need to fetch the resource once at the beginning of every second, and then it can reuse that cached result for all of the other clients that ask.

If you will be designing and deploying a large HTTP service behind a proxy, you will want to consult RFC 7234 and its extended discussion of the design of HTTP caching and its intended benefits. You will find options and settings that are specifically targeted at intermediary caches such as Varnish rather than at the end user's HTTP client, like proxy-revalidate and s-maxage, which you should have in your toolbox as you approach a service design.

■ **Warning**   The content of a page often depends on not just its path and method but also on things such as the Host header, the identity of the user making the request, and perhaps the headers describing what content types their client can support. Review carefully the Vary header description in RFC 7231 section 7.1.4, as well as the description of the Vary header in Chapter 9. The value Vary: Cookie is, for reasons that will become clear, often necessary to ensure correct behavior.

Four Architectures

While architects seem capable of producing an unlimited number of complicated schemes for assembling an HTTP service from smaller parts, there are four primary designs that have become established as habits in the Python community (see Figure 10-1). What are your options for putting an HTTP service online if you have written Python code to produce the dynamic content and have chosen an API or framework that can speak WSGI?

- Run a server that is itself written in Python and that can call your WSGI endpoint directly from its own code. The Green Unicorn ("gunicorn") server is the most popular at the moment, but other production-ready, pure-Python servers are available. The old battle-tested CherryPy server, for example, is still used in projects today, and Flup still attracts users. (It is best to avoid prototype servers such as wsgiref, unless your service will be under light load and internal to an organization.) If you use an async server engine, then both the server and the framework will necessarily live in the same process.

- Run Apache with mod_wsgi configured to run your Python code inside of a separate WSGIDaemonProcess, producing a hybrid approach: two different languages are at work but within a single server. Static resources can be served directly from Apache's C-language engine, while dynamic paths are submitted to mod_wsgi so that it can call the Python interpreter to run your application code. (This option is not available for async web frameworks because WSGI provides no mechanism by which an application could yield control temporarily and then finish its work later.)

- Run a Python HTTP server like Gunicorn (or whatever server is dictated by your choice of async framework) behind a web server that can serve static files directly but also act a reverse proxy for the dynamic resources that you have written in Python. Both Apache and nginx are popular front-end servers for this task. They can also load-balance requests between several back-end servers if your Python application outgrows a single box.

- Run a Python HTTP server behind Apache or nginx that itself sits behind a pure reverse proxy like Varnish, creating a third tier that faces the real world. These reverse proxies can be geographically distributed so that cached resources are served from locations close to client machines instead of all from the same continent. *Content delivery networks* such as Fastly operate by deploying armies of Varnish servers to machine rooms on each continent and then using them to offer you a turnkey service that both terminates your externally facing TLS certificates and forwards requests to your central servers.

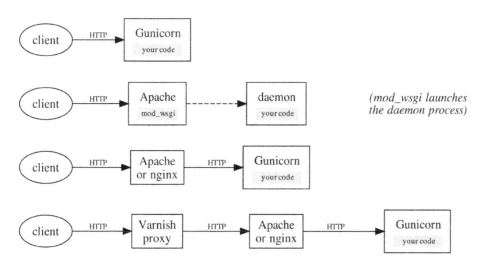

Figure 10-1. *Four common techniques for deploying Python code stand-alone or behind reverse HTTP proxies*

The choice between these four architectures has historically been driven by three features of the C Python runtime: the interpreter is large, it is slow, and its Global Interpret Lock prevents more than one thread at a time from executing Python bytecode.

The limitations of the interpreter lock encouraged the use of separate Python processes instead of multiple Python threads sharing the same process. But the size of the interpreter pushed back in the other direction: only a certain number of Python instances will easily fit into RAM, limiting the number of processes.

Running Python Under Apache

You can best appreciate the problems described earlier if you imagine an early Python-powered web site operating under Apache with the old mod_python. Most requests to a typical web site (see Chapter 11) are for static resources: for every request that asks Python to generate a page dynamically, there might be a dozen requests for the accompanying CSS, JavaScript, and images. Yet mod_python burdened every Apache worker with its own copy of the Python interpreter runtime, most of which sat idle. Only one out of every dozen workers might be running Python at a given moment while the rest spooled out files using Apache's core C code.

This impasse is broken if Python interpreters live in separate processes from the web server workers that shovel static content from disk out onto waiting sockets. This spawned two competing approaches.

The first way to avoid burdening each Apache thread with a Python interpreter is to use the modern mod_wsgi module with its "daemon process" feature activated. In this mode, Apache workers—whether threads or processes—are spared the expense of loading or executing Python, incurring only the cost of dynamically linking to mod_wsgi itself. Instead, mod_wsgi creates and manages a separate pool of Python worker processes to which it can forward requests and where the WSGI application will actually be invoked. Dozens of tiny Apache workers can be busily chattering out static files for each big Python interpreter that sits slowly building a dynamic page.

The Rise of Pure-Python HTTP Servers

However, once you have resigned yourself to the fact that Python will not live within the main server process itself but that HTTP requests will have to be serialized and forwarded from an Apache process and into a Python process, why not simply use HTTP? Why not configure Apache to reverse-proxy each dynamic request to Gunicorn, with your service running inside?

True, you will now have to start and manage two different daemons—Apache and Gunicorn—where before you only had to start Apache and let mod_wsgi take care of spawning your Python interpreters. But in return you gain a great deal of flexibility. To begin with, there is no longer any reason that Apache and Gunicorn need to live on the same box; you can run Apache on a server optimized for a huge number of simultaneous connections and sprawling filesystem access and run Gunicorn on a separate server optimized for a dynamic language runtime making back-end requests to a database.

Once Apache has been reduced from your application container to a mere static file server with reverse-proxy capabilities, you have the option of replacing it. After all, nginx can also serve files while reverse-proxying other paths just as well, as can many other modern web servers.

The mod_wsgi option, in the end, works out to a limited and proprietary version of real reverse proxying: you are speaking its own internal protocol between processes that have to live on the same machine, when you could be speaking real HTTP and have the option of running Python either on the same machine or on a different one as your needs evolve.

The Benefits of Reverse Proxies

What about HTTP applications that serve only dynamic content, generated by Python code, and involve no static resources? Apache or nginx might seem to have little work to do in such cases, and you might be tempted to ignore them and expose Gunicorn or another pure Python web server directly to the world.

In such cases, do consider the safety that a reverse proxy provides. To bring your web service to a halt, all someone needs to do is to connect to your n-worker service with n sockets, offer a few initial desultory bytes of request data, and then freeze. All of your workers will now be occupied waiting for a complete request that may never arrive. With Apache or nginx in front of your service, by contrast, requests that take a long time to arrive—whether through malice or because some of your clients run on mobile devices or are otherwise suffering low bandwidth—are slowly collected by the buffers of the reverse proxy, which will typically not forward the request along to you until it has been received in its entirety.

Of course, a proxy that collects full requests before forwarding them is no proof against a real denial-of-service attack—nothing, alas, is—but it does prevent your dynamic language runtime from stalling when data from a client is not yet forthcoming. It also insulates Python from many other kinds of pathological input, from megabyte-long header names to entirely malformed requests, because Apache or nginx will reject these outright with 4*xx* errors without your back-end application code even suspecting.

I currently gravitate toward three sweet spots on the spectrum of architectures in the previous list.

My default is Gunicorn behind nginx or, if a system administrator prefers, Apache.

If I am running a service that is really a pure API and does not involve any static components, then I will sometimes attempt to run Gunicorn by itself or perhaps directly behind Varnish if I want even my dynamic resources to benefit from its first-class caching logic.

It is only when architecting large web services that I go full-bore with three tiers: my Python running in Gunicorn, behind nginx or Apache, behind either a local or geographically distributed Varnish cluster.

Many other configurations are, of course, possible, and I hope that the previous discussion included enough caveats and trade-offs that you will be able to choose intelligently when the question comes up in your own projects and organizations.

One important question that looms on the horizon is the emergence of Python runtimes like PyPy that can run at machine speed. Once Python code can run as fast as Apache, why not have Python serve both static and dynamic content? It will be interesting to see whether servers powered by fast Python runtimes create any competition for old and reliable solutions like Apache and nginx. What incentives can Python servers offer for migration when the industry favorites are so well documented, understood, and beloved by system administrators?

There are, of course, variations possible on any of the previous patterns. Gunicorn can run directly behind Varnish, for example, if no static files need to be served or if you are happy to have Python pull them off of the disk itself. Another option is to use nginx or Apache with their reverse-caching options turned on so that they provide basic Varnish-like caching without the need for a third tier. Some sites experiment with alternative protocols for the conversation between the front-end server and Python, like those supported by the Flup and uwsgi projects. The four patterns featured in this section are merely among the most common. There are many other possible designs, most of which are in use somewhere today.

Platforms as a Service

Many of the topics raised in the previous section—load balancing, multiple tiers of proxy server, and application deployment—begin to veer in the direction of system administration and operations planning. Issues such as the selection of a front-end load balancer or the choices involved in making an HTTP service physically and geographically redundant are not unique to Python. If covered in this chapter, they would take you far afield from the subject of Python network programming.

As you make Python part of your strategy for providing a network service, I encourage you also to read about automated deployment, continuous integration, and high-performance scaling to learn about technologies that might be applicable to your own service and organization. There is not enough space to cover them here.

But one topic does bear mentioning: the emergence of platform-as-a-service (PaaS) providers and the question of how to package your applications for deployment on such services.

With PaaS, much of the tedium of establishing and running an HTTP service is automated away—or, at least, devolves upon your PaaS provider rather than upon yourself. You are exempted from having to rent servers, providing them with storage and IP addresses, configuring root access with which to administer and reboot them, installing the correct version of Python, and copying your application to every single server along with the system scripts necessary to start your service up automatically after a reboot or power failure.

Instead, these burdens are assumed by the PaaS provider that might install or rent thousands of machines, hundreds of database servers, and many dozens of load balancers in order to serve its customer base. Having automated all of these steps, all that the provider needs is a configuration file from you. The provider then can add your domain name to its DNS, point it at one of its load balancers, install the correct version of Python and all of your Python dependencies inside an operating system image, and have your application up and running. The process can make it easy to push new source code to them and easy to roll back if the new version of your application seems to generate errors when faced with real users. You get away without having to create a single /etc/init.d file or reboot a single machine.

Heroku is a current favorite in the PaaS space and provides first-class support for Python applications as part of their ecosystem. Heroku and its rivals are especially valuable for small organizations that lack the expertise or the time in-house to set up and administer tools such as load balancers.

The emerging Docker ecosystem is a potential rival to Heroku because it lets you create and run Heroku-style containers right on your own Linux machine, making it much easier to test and debug them than when every line of configuration that you want to tweak involves a long and slow push and rebuild on Heroku.

If you have only a vague familiarity with PaaS, you might expect such a service to take your WSGI-ready Python application and get it running for you without any additional effort.

It turns out that this is not the case. Under Heroku or inside a Docker instance, you will still have the responsibility of choosing a web server.

The reason for this is that while PaaS providers provide load balancing, containerization, version-controlled configuration, container image caching, and database administration, they still expect your application to provide the gold standard in HTTP interoperability: an open port to which the PaaS load balancer can connect and make HTTP requests. And to turn your WSGI application or framework into a listening network port, you are obviously going to need a server.

Some developers, satisfied that the PaaS service is going to be doing load balancing for them, select a simple single-threaded server and put the PaaS service in charge of spinning up as many instances of their application as they need.

But many developers instead opt for Gunicorn or one of its competitors so that each of their containers can have several workers running at once. This makes a single container able to accept several requests in case the round-robin logic of the PaaS load balancer makes it back to the same container before its first request is finished—which is a particular problem if some of the resources offered by your service might take several seconds to render and cause subsequent requests to be queued up until the first is complete.

Note that most PaaS providers do not make any provision for serving static content, unless you serve it from Python or else add Apache or nginx to your container. While you could design your URL space so that static resources come from an entirely different hostname than do dynamic pages and host those static resources elsewhere, many architects prefer to be able to mix static and dynamic resources in a single namespace.

GET and POST Patterns and the Question of REST

Dr. Roy Fielding, one of the principle authors of the current HTTP standards, wrote his Ph.D. dissertation on its design. He coined the term Representational State Transfer (REST) to name the architecture that emerges when all of the features of a hypertext system like HTTP are operating at full tilt. His dissertation is online if you want to consult it. Chapter 5 is where he builds up the concept of REST from a series of simpler concepts.

www.ics.uci.edu/~fielding/pubs/dissertation/rest_arch_style.htm

Dr. Fielding is specific that "REST is defined by four interface constraints," which he briefly enumerates at the end of section 5.1.5 of the dissertation.

- Identification of resources

- Manipulation of resources through representations

- Self-descriptive messages

- Hypermedia as the engine of application state

Many service designers, wanting their designs to run with the grain of HTTP's design instead of against it, have aspired to the creation of services that can properly earn the accolade "RESTful." Dr. Fielding is at pains to object that most of them do not. Where do they go wrong?

The first constraint, "identification of resources," rules out nearly all traditional forms of RPC. Neither JSON-RPC nor XML-RPC (see Chapter 18) exposes resource identities at the level of the HTTP protocol itself. Imagine a client that wants to fetch a blog post, update its title, and then fetch the post again to see the difference. If these steps were implemented as RPC method calls, the methods and paths visible to HTTP would be as follows:

```
POST /rpc-endpoint/ → 200 OK
POST /rpc-endpoint/ → 200 OK
POST /rpc-endpoint/ → 200 OK
```

Presumably somewhere inside the body of each POST, each of these requests names something like "post 1022" as the specific resource that the client wanted to fetch or edit. But RPC makes this opaque to the HTTP protocol. An interface aspiring to REST would instead use the resource path to specify which post was being manipulated, perhaps by naming it /post/1022/.

The second constraint, "Manipulation of resources through representations," prohibits the designer from specifying an ad-hoc mechanism, specific to their service, by which the title must be updated. That, after all, would require client authors to wade through service-specific documentation every time they wanted to learn how to perform an update. In REST, there is no need to learn a specific trick to changing a post's title because the representation of a post—whether it uses HTML, JSON, XML, or some other format—is the only form in which either reads or writes can be expressed. To update a blog post title, a client simply fetches the current representation, changes the title, and submits the new representation back to the service.

```
GET /post/1022/ → 200 OK
PUT /post/1022/ → 200 OK
GET /post/1022/ → 200 OK
```

The idea that fetching or updating a dozen resources must require a dozen round-trips to the service is a sore point for many designers and a strong temptation to make pragmatic exceptions to the architecture. But the advantages of REST, when followed, are symmetry between the operations of reading and writing a resource and the exposure of meaningful semantics in the HTTP protocol. The protocol can now see which requests are reads and which are writes, and if GET responses include the right headers, then caching and conditional requests become possible even when programs are speaking with each other without a browser involved.

Explicit caching headers bring us to the third constraint, "self-descriptive messages," because such headers make messages self-documenting. The programmer writing a client does not need to consult API documentation to learn, for example, that /post/1022/ is in JSON format or to learn that it can be cached only if conditional requests are used to assure that the cached copy is up-to-date, while a search like /post/?q=news can be served directly from cache for up to 60 seconds after retrieval. This knowledge is instead declared afresh in the headers of every HTTP response that is transmitted.

If the first three constraints of REST are achieved, then a service becomes radically transparent to the HTTP protocol and thus to the full slate of proxies, caches, and clients, which are written to take advantage of its semantics. Furthermore, they can do so whether the service is designed for human consumption, delivering HTML pages bristling with forms and JavaScript (see Chapter 11), or is designed for machine consumption with succinct URLs leading to JSON or XML representations.

But the last constraint is achieved far less often.

"Hypermedia as the engine of application state" has become contentious enough to need an acronym! While not being singled out for special attention in Dr. Fielding's thesis, it has since been abbreviated to "HATEOAS" in the subsequent literature and debates. He drew attention to the constraint with a blog post "REST APIs must be hypertext-driven" that complained about the announcement of a so-called REST API that, in fact, failed this final constraint.

```
http://roy.gbiv.com/untangled/2008/rest-apis-must-be-hypertext-driven
```

There he unpacks the HATEOAS constraint into no less than six separate bullet points, of which the last is perhaps the most sweeping. It begins, "A REST API should be entered with no prior knowledge beyond the initial URI (bookmark) and set of standardized media types that are appropriate for the intended audience."

This would disqualify almost all familiar HTTP-driven APIs. Whether purveyed by Google or GitHub, their documentation nearly always seems to start a discussion of each resource type with, "Each post lives at a URL like /post/1022/ that names the post's unique ID." With this maneuver, an API has departed from complete RESTfulness and has entered a murky realm where special rules embedded in documentation, and not hypertext links, are leading the client to the correct resource.

A fully RESTful API, by contrast, would have a single entry point. The media returned would include, perhaps, a series of forms, one of which could be used to submit a blog post ID to learn its URL. The service itself, then, and not human-readable documentation, would dynamically link the idea of "the post with ID 1022" with a particular path.

This encompassing concept of hypertext is, for Dr. Fielding, a crucial constraint for services aiming for decades of use, which will be capable of supporting many generations of HTTP clients and, later, data archaeology when the original users of an old service are all long gone. But because most of the benefits of HTTP—statelessness, redundancy, and cache acceleration—can be gained through the first three elements alone, it appears that few services have yet risen to the challenge of full REST compliance.

WSGI Without a Framework

Chapter 7 exhibited several patterns for writing a network service, any of which can be used to answer HTTP requests. But there is rarely any need to write your own low-level socket code to speak the protocol. Many of the protocol details can be delegated to your web server and, if you opt to use one, to your web framework. What is the difference between the two?

The web *server* is the code that will hold a listening socket, run accept() to receive new connections, and parse each incoming HTTP request. Without even needing to invoke your code, a server will handle cases like a client that connects but never finishes its request and a client whose request cannot be parsed as HTTP. Some servers will also time out and close a client socket that goes idle and rejects requests whose path or headers are unreasonably long. Only well-formed, complete requests are passed to your framework or code by invoking the WSGI callable that you have registered with the server. The server will typically, on its own authority, go ahead and produce HTTP response codes (see Chapter 9) like these:

- 400 Bad Request: If the incoming HTTP request is unintelligible or exceeds a size limit you have specified

- 500 Server Error: If your WSGI callable raises an exception instead of running successfully to completion

There are two ways to build the WSGI callable that your web server will invoke for HTTP requests that arrive and are parsed successfully. You can build the callable yourself, or you can write code that plugs into a web framework that provides its own WSGI callable. What is the difference?

The essential task of a web framework is to assume responsibility for *dispatch*. Each HTTP request names a coordinate in the space of possible methods, hostnames, and paths. You are probably running your service at only one or a couple of hostnames, not all possible hostnames. You might be prepared to process GET or POST, but a request can name whatever method it wants—even an invented one. There may be many paths for which you can produce useful responses but probably many more for which you cannot. The framework will let you declare which paths and methods you do support, so the framework can shoulder the burden of replying automatically for those that do not with status codes like these:

- 404 Not Found

- 405 Method Not Allowed

- 501 Not Implemented

Chapter 11 explores how both traditional and asynchronous frameworks assume responsibility for dispatch, and it surveys the other major features that they offer programmers. But what might your code look like without them? What if your own code interfaces directly with WSGI and takes charge of performing dispatch?

There are two ways of constructing such an application: either by reading the WSGI specification and learning to read its environment dictionary yourself or by using a wrapper like those provided by the competing WebOb and Werkzeug toolkits available from the Python Package Index. Listing 10-2 demonstrates the verbose coding style necessary with working in the raw WSGI environment.

Listing 10-2. Raw WSGI Callable for Returning the Current Time

```
#!/usr/bin/env python3
# Foundations of Python Network Programming, Third Edition
# https://github.com/brandon-rhodes/fopnp/blob/m/py3/chapter10/timeapp_raw.py
# A simple HTTP service built directly against the low-level WSGI spec.

import time

def app(environ, start_response):
    host = environ.get('HTTP_HOST', '127.0.0.1')
    path = environ.get('PATH_INFO', '/')
    if ':' in host:
        host, port = host.split(':', 1)
    if '?' in path:
        path, query = path.split('?', 1)
    headers = [('Content-Type', 'text/plain; charset=utf-8')]
    if environ['REQUEST_METHOD'] != 'GET':
        start_response('501 Not Implemented', headers)
        yield b'501 Not Implemented'
    elif host != '127.0.0.1' or path != '/':
        start_response('404 Not Found', headers)
        yield b'404 Not Found'
    else:
        start_response('200 OK', headers)
        yield time.ctime().encode('ascii')
```

In the absence of a framework, your code must do all of the negative work of determining which hostnames, paths, and methods do *not* match the services you intend to provide. To offer a GET of the path / at the hostname 127.0.0.1, you have to return an error for every deviation from that combination of request parameters that you are able to detect. Of course, for a tiny service like this, it might seem silly not to simply accept any hostname. But we are pretending that we might grow into a big service that offers different content at dozens of different hostnames, and so we are being careful to pay attention to them.

Note that you are responsible for breaking apart the hostname and port in case the client provides a Host header like 127.0.0.1:8000. Further, you have to split the path on the character ? in case the URL has a query string like /?name=value dangling off of the end. (The listing assumes that, per common practice, you want to ignore extraneous query strings instead of returning 404 Not Found.)

The next two listings demonstrate how these raw WSGI patterns can be made easier through third-party libraries, which can be installed with the standard "pip" installation tool (see Chapter 1).

```
$ pip install WebOb

$ pip install Werkzeug
```

The WebOb "Web Object" library, , initially written by Ian Bicking, is a lightweight object interface that wraps a standard WSGI dictionary to provide more convenient access to its information. Listing 10-3 shows how it eliminates several common patterns from the previous example.

Listing 10-3. WSGI Callable Written with WebOb for Returning the Current Time

```python
#!/usr/bin/env python3
# Foundations of Python Network Programming, Third Edition
# https://github.com/brandon-rhodes/fopnp/blob/m/py3/chapter10/timeapp_webob.py
# A WSGI callable built using webob.

import time, webob

def app(environ, start_response):
    request = webob.Request(environ)
    if environ['REQUEST_METHOD'] != 'GET':
        response = webob.Response('501 Not Implemented', status=501)
    elif request.domain != '127.0.0.1' or request.path != '/':
        response = webob.Response('404 Not Found', status=404)
    else:
        response = webob.Response(time.ctime())
    return response(environ, start_response)
```

WebOb already implements the two common patterns of wanting to examine the hostname from the Host header separately from any optional port number that might be attached and of looking at the path without its trailing query string. It also provides a Response object that knows all about content types and encodings—it defaults to plain text—so that you need only to provide a string for the response body, and WebOb will take care of everything else.

■ **Note** WebOb has a feature that makes it stand almost alone among the many Python HTTP response object implementations. The WebOb Response class lets you treat the two pieces of a Content-Type header like text/plain; charset=utf-8 as two separate values, which it exposes as the separate attributes content_type and charset.

Less popular than WebOb for pure WSGI coding but also supported by a loyal fan base is Armin Ronacher's Werkzeug library that is also the foundation of his Flask framework (discussed in Chapter 11). Its request and response objects are immutable, instead of allowing the underlying WSGI environment to be changed. Listing 10-4 shows how its conveniences differ in this case from those of WebOb.

Listing 10-4. WSGI Callable Written with Werkzeug for Returning the Current Time

```python
#!/usr/bin/env python3
# Foundations of Python Network Programming, Third Edition
# https://github.com/brandon-rhodes/fopnp/blob/m/py3/chapter10/timeapp_werkz.py
# A WSGI callable built using Werkzeug.

import time
from werkzeug.wrappers import Request, Response

@Request.application
def app(request):
    host = request.host
    if ':' in host:
        host, port = host.split(':', 1)
    if request.method != 'GET':
        return Response('501 Not Implemented', status=501)
    elif host != '127.0.0.1' or request.path != '/':
        return Response('404 Not Found', status=404)
    else:
        return Response(time.ctime())
```

Werkzeug has not even made you remember the correct signature for a WSGI callable, instead giving you a decorator that switches your function to a far simpler calling convention. You receive a Werkzeug Request object automatically as your only argument and are given the privilege of simply returning a Response object—the library will handle everything else for you.

The only slight regression from the code written with WebOb is that you have to split hostnames like 127.0.0.1:8000 in two yourself instead of having a convenience method split them out for you. Nevertheless, with this small difference, the two libraries are doing equivalent work to let you speak about HTTP requests and responses at a higher level than that exposed by the WSGI convention.

Usually, it will not be worth your time as a developer to operate at this low level instead of using a web framework. But writing in raw WSGI does come in handy when you want to perform some transform on incoming HTTP requests before handing them off to your web framework for processing. A straight WSGI application can also be appropriate if you are writing a custom reverse proxy, or another pure HTTP service, in the Python language.

Raw WSGI callables can be thought to have the same place in Python programming that forward proxies and reverse proxies have in the HTTP ecosystem at large. They are better for low-level tasks such as filtering, normalizing, and dispatching requests than they are for doing the positive work of providing resources at specific hostnames and paths that you want to provide as an HTTP service. For details on how a WSGI callable can modify a request before handing it off to a further callable, either read the specification or consult the patterns given in either the WebOb or Werkzeug documentation for writing middleware.

Summary

Python has an `http.server` module built in that, when launched from the command line, serves up files from beneath its current working directory. While convenient in emergencies or when examining a web site stored directly on disk, the module is rarely used any more for creating new HTTP services.

Normal, synchronous HTTP in Python is usually mediated by the WSGI standard. Servers parse the incoming request to produce a dictionary full of information, and applications examine the dictionary before returning HTTP headers and an optional response body. This lets you use any web server you want with any standard Python web framework.

Asynchronous web servers are an exception to the WSGI ecosystem. Because WSGI callables are not full coroutines, every async HTTP server has to adopt its own convention for how you write a service in its custom framework. The server and framework come as a bundle in this case, often without any possibility of wider interoperability.

Four architectures are popular for serving HTTP from Python. A stand-alone server can be run using Gunicorn or other pure-Python server implementations such as CherryPy. Other architects opt to run their Python under the control of Apache through `mod_wsgi`. However, now that the concept of a reverse proxy is a go-to pattern for web services of all kinds, many architects find it simpler to put Gunicorn or another pure-Python server directly behind nginx or Apache as a separate HTTP service to which they can forward requests for paths whose resources are generated dynamically.

Any of these patterns can then have Varnish or another reverse proxy put in front of them to provide a caching layer. The cache instances can be local to the same machine room (or even the same machine), but they will often be geographically distributed to put them closer to particular populations of HTTP clients.

Installing your service on a PaaS provider will often provide caching, reverse-proxying, and load balancing as part of the service. All that your application will be responsible for is answering HTTP requests, often using a simple container like Gunicorn.

A popular question that is asked of services is whether they are RESTful: whether they feature the properties that standards author Dr. Roy Fielding describes as having been intended by the design of HTTP. While many services today have pivoted away from opaque choices of method and path, which hid what the service was doing, few have adopted Fielding's full vision for powering semantics with hypertext instead of with programmer-directed documentation.

Small services, especially those that filter or transform an HTTP request, can be written as a WSGI callable. Either of two competing solutions, WebOb or Werkzeug, can reduce the raw WSGI environment to an easier-to-consume `Request` object, and they can also help you build your answer through their `Response` classes.

In the next chapter, you will go beyond both generic HTTP services and low-level WSGI programming by learning about the World Wide Web—the vast collection of interlinked documents that have made the Internet world famous. You will learn how to fetch and process hypertext documents and to implement web sites yourself using popular web frameworks.

CHAPTER 11

∎ ▨ ▨

The World Wide Web

Chapters 9 and 10 explained the Hypertext Transfer Protocol (HTTP) as a general mechanism by which clients can request documents and to which servers can respond by providing them.

Something, however, went unexplained. Why does the name of the protocol start with the word *hypertext*?

The answer is that HTTP was not designed simply as a new way to transfer files. It is not simply a fancy caching replacement for older file transfer protocols such as FTP (see Chapter 17). While it is certainly capable of delivering stand-alone documents such as books, images, and video, the purpose of HTTP is a much more ambitious one: to allow servers all over the world to publish documents that, through mutual cross-references, become a single interlinked fabric of information.

HTTP was built to deliver the World Wide Web.

Hypermedia and URLs

Books have referenced other books for thousands of years. But a human has to enact each reference by fetching the other book and turning pages until the referenced text is found. The dream that the World Wide Web (WWW, or simply "the Web") has fulfilled is to delegate to the machine the responsibility of resolving the reference.

The moment that inert text like "the discussion of cookies in Chapter 9" becomes underlined and clickable on a computer screen so that a click takes you to the text that it is referencing, it becomes a *hyperlink*. Full documents whose text can contain embedded hyperlinks are called *hypertext* documents. When images, sound, and video are added to the mix, the user is experiencing *hypermedia*.

In each case, the prefix *hyper-* indicates that the medium itself understands the ways that documents mutually reference each other and can enact those links for a user. The phrase "see page 103" in a printed book does not, itself, have the power to carry you to the destination that it describes. The browser displaying a hyperlink, by contrast, does have this power.

To power hypermedia, the uniform resource locator (URL) was invented. It offers a uniform scheme by which not only modern hypertext documents but also even old FTP files and Telnet servers can be referenced. You have seen many such examples in the address bar of your web browser.

```
# Some sample URLs

https://www.python.org/
http://en.wikipedia.org/wiki/Python_(programming_language)
http://localhost:8000/headers
ftp://ssd.jpl.nasa.gov/pub/eph/planets/README.txt
telnet://rainmaker.wunderground.com
```

The initial label like `https` or `http` is the *scheme*, which names the protocol by which a document can be retrieved. Following the colon and two slashes `://` comes the hostname and optional port number. Finally, a *path* selects one particular document out of all the documents that might be available on a service.

This syntax can be used for more general purposes than describing material to be fetched from a network. The more general concept of a uniform resource identifier (URI) can be used either to identify physical network-accessible documents or as a generic unique identifier used to give computer-readable names to conceptual entities, that is, labels that are called uniform resource names (URNs). Everything in this book will specifically be a URL.

The pronunciation of *URL*, by the way, is *you-are-ell*. An "earl" is a member of the British aristocracy whose rank is not quite that of a marquis but who does rank above a viscount—so an earl is the equivalent of a count over on the Continent (not, in other words, a network document address).

When a document is automatically generated based on parameters specified by the user, the URL is extended with a *query string* that starts with a question mark (?) and then uses the ampersand character (&) to delimit each further parameter. Each parameter consists of a name, an equals sign, and a value.

```
https://www.google.com/search?q=apod&btnI=yes
```

Finally, a URL can be suffixed with a *fragment* that names the particular location on a page to which the link is referring.

```
http://tools.ietf.org/html/rfc2324#section-2.3.2
```

The fragment is different from the other components of a URL. Because a web browser presumes that it needs to fetch the entire page named by the path in order to find the element named by the fragment, it does not actually transmit the fragment in its HTTP request! All that the server can learn from the browser when it fetches an HTTP URL is the hostname, the path, and the query. The hostname, you will recall from Chapter 9, is delivered as the Host header, and the path and query are concatenated together to produce the full path that follows the HTTP method on the first line of the request.

If you study RFC 3986, you will discover a few additional features that are only rarely in use. It is the authoritative resource to consult when you run across rare features that you want to learn more about, like the possibility of including a user@password authentication string right in the URL itself.

Parsing and Building URLs

The urllib.parse module that comes built in to the Python Standard Library provides the tools that you'll need both to interpret and to build URLs. Splitting a URL into its component pieces is a single function call. It returns what in earlier versions of Python was simply a tuple, and you can still view the result that way and use integer indexing—or tuple unpacking in an assignment statement—to access its items.

```
>>> from urllib.parse import urlsplit
>>> u = urlsplit('https://www.google.com/search?q=apod&btnI=yes')
>>> tuple(u)
('https', 'www.google.com', '/search', 'q=apod&btnI=yes', '')
```

But the tuple also supports named attribute access to its items to help make your code more readable when you are inspecting a URL.

```
>>> u.scheme
'https'
>>> u.netloc
'www.google.com'
>>> u.path
'/search'
>>> u.query
'q=apod&btnI=yes'
>>> u.fragment
''
```

The "network location" `netloc` can have several subordinate pieces, but they are uncommon enough that `urlsplit()` does not break them out as separate items in its tuple. Instead, they are available only as attributes of its result.

```
>>> u = urlsplit('https://brandon:atigdng@localhost:8000/')
>>> u.netloc
'brandon:atigdng@localhost:8000'
>>> u.username
'brandon'
>>> u.password
'atigdng'
>>> u.hostname
'localhost'
>>> u.port
8000
```

Reducing a URL to pieces is only half of the process of parsing. The path and query components can both include characters that had to be escaped before becoming part of the URL. For example, & and # cannot appear literally because they delimit the URL itself. And the character / needs to be escaped if it occurs inside a particular a path component because the slash serves to separate path components.

The query portion of a URL has encoding rules all its own. Query values often contain spaces—think of all of the searches you type into Google that include a space—and so the plus sign + is designated as an alternative way of encoding spaces in queries. The query string would otherwise only have the option of encoding spaces the way the rest of the URL does, as a %20 hexadecimal escape code.

The only correct way to parse a URL that is accessing the "Q&A" section of your site in order to access the "TCP/IP" section and do a search there for information about "packet loss" is as follows:

```
>>> from urllib.parse import parse_qs, parse_qsl, unquote
>>> u = urlsplit('http://example.com/Q%26A/TCP%2FIP?q=packet+loss')
>>> path = [unquote(s) for s in u.path.split('/')]
>>> query = parse_qsl(u.query)
>>> path
['', 'Q&A', 'TCP/IP']
>>> query
[('q', 'packet loss')]
```

Note that my splitting of the path using `split()` returns an initial empty string because this particular path is an absolute path that begins with a slash.

The query is given as a list of tuples, and not a simple dictionary, because a URL query string allows a query parameter to be specified multiple times. If you are writing code that does not care about this possibility, you can pass the list of tuples to `dict()` and you will only see the last value given for each parameter. If you want a dictionary back but also want to let a parameter be specified multiple times, you can switch from `parse_qsl()` to `parse_qs()` and get back a dictionary whose values are lists.

```
>>> parse_qs(u.query)
{'q': ['packet loss']}
```

The Standard Library provides all of the necessary routines to go back in the other direction. Given the `path` and query shown previously, Python can reconstruct the URL from its parts by quoting each path component, joining them back together with slashes, encoding the query, and presenting the result to the "unsplit" routine that is the opposite of the `urlsplit()` function called earlier.

```
>>> from urllib.parse import quote, urlencode, urlunsplit
>>> urlunsplit(('http', 'example.com',
...             '/'.join(quote(p, safe='') for p in path),
...             urlencode(query), ''))
'http://example.com/Q%26A/TCP%2FIP?q=packet+loss'
```

If you carefully defer all URL parsing to these Standard Library routines, you should find that all of the tiny details of the full specification are taken care of for you.

The code in the previous examples is so utterly correct that some programmers might even describe it as fussy, or even overwrought. How often, really, do path components themselves have slashes in them? Most web sites are careful to design path elements, called *slugs* by developers, so that they never require ugly escaping to appear in a URL. If a site only allows URL slugs to include letters, numbers, dashes, and the underscore, then the fear that a slug could itself include a slash is obviously misplaced.

If you are sure that you are dealing with paths that never have escaped slashes inside individual path components, then you can simply expose the whole path to quote() and unquote() without the bother of splitting it first.

```
>>> quote('Q&A/TCP IP')
'Q%26A/TCP%20IP'
>>> unquote('Q%26A/TCP%20IP')
'Q&A/TCP IP'
```

In fact, the quote() routine expects this to be the common case, and so its parameter default is safe='/', which will normally leave slashes untouched. That is what was overridden by safe='' in the fussy version of the code.

The Standard Library urllib.parse module has several more specialized routines than the general ones outlined previously, including urldefrag() for splitting the URL apart from its fragment at the # character. Read the documentation to learn about this and the other functions that can make a few special cases more convenient.

Relative URLs

Your filesystem command line supports a "change working directory" command that establishes the location where the system will start searching *relative* paths, which lack a leading slash. Paths that do start with a slash are explicitly declaring that they begin their search at the root of the filesystem. They are *absolute* paths, which always name the same location regardless of your working directory.

```
$ wc -l /var/log/dmesg
977 dmesg
$ wc -l dmesg
wc: dmesg: No such file or directory
$ cd /var/log
$ wc -l dmesg
977 dmesg
```

Hypertext has the same concept. If all the links in a document are absolute URLs, like the ones in the previous section, then there is no question about the resource to which each of them links. However, if the document includes relative URLs, then the document's own location will have to be taken into account.

Python provides a urljoin() routine that understands the entire standard in all of its nuance. Given a URL that you have recovered from inside a hypertext document that might be either relative or absolute, you can pass it to urljoin() to have any missing information filled in. If the URL was absolute to begin with, no problem; it will be returned unchanged.

The argument order of `urljoin()` is the same as that of `os.path.join()`. First provide the base URL of the document that you are examining and then provide the URL that you have found inside of it. There are several different ways that a relative URL can rewrite parts of its base.

```
>>> from urllib.parse import urljoin
>>> base = 'http://tools.ietf.org/html/rfc3986'
>>> urljoin(base, 'rfc7320')
'http://tools.ietf.org/html/rfc7320'
>>> urljoin(base, '.')
'http://tools.ietf.org/html/'
>>> urljoin(base, '..')
'http://tools.ietf.org/'
>>> urljoin(base, '/dailydose/')
'http://tools.ietf.org/dailydose/'
>>> urljoin(base, '?version=1.0')
'http://tools.ietf.org/html/rfc3986?version=1.0'
>>> urljoin(base, '#section-5.4')
'http://tools.ietf.org/html/rfc3986#section-5.4'
```

Again, it is perfectly safe to provide an absolute URL to `urljoin()` because it will detect the fact that it is entirely self-contained and return it without any modifications from the base URL.

```
>>> urljoin(base, 'https://www.google.com/search?q=apod&btnI=yes')
'https://www.google.com/search?q=apod&btnI=yes'
```

Relative URLs make it easy, even on static parts of a page, to write web pages that are agnostic about whether they are served by HTTP or HTTPS because a relative URL can omit the scheme but specify everything else. In that case, only the scheme is copied from the base URL.

```
>>> urljoin(base, '//www.google.com/search?q=apod')
'http://www.google.com/search?q=apod'
```

If your site is going to use relative URLs, then it is critical that you be strict about whether pages carry a trailing slash or not because a relative URL means two different things depending on whether the trailing slash is present.

```
>>> urljoin('http://tools.ietf.org/html/rfc3986', 'rfc7320')
'http://tools.ietf.org/html/rfc7320'
>>> urljoin('http://tools.ietf.org/html/rfc3986/', 'rfc7320')
'http://tools.ietf.org/html/rfc3986/rfc7320'
```

What might look to the naked eye as a slight difference between these two base URLs is crucial for the meaning of any relative links! The first URL can be thought of as visiting the `html` directory in order to display the `rfc3986` file that it finds there, which leaves the "current working directory" as the `html` directory. The second URL instead treats `rfc3986` itself as the directory that it is visiting, because only directories can take a trailing slash in a real filesystem. So, the relative link built atop the second URL starts building at the `rfc3986` component instead of at its parent `html` component.

Always design your site so that a user arriving at a URL that is written the wrong way gets immediately redirected to the correct path. For example, if you were to try visiting the second URL from the previous example, then the IETF web server will detect the erroneous trailing slash and declare a Location: header with the correct URL in its response.

This is a lesson if you ever write a web client: relative URLs are *not* necessarily relative to the path that you provided in your HTTP request! If the site chooses to respond with a Location header, then relative URLs should be constructed relative to that alternative location.

The Hypertext Markup Language

There are shelves of books about the core document formats that power the Web. There are also the active standards that describe the hypertext document format itself, the mechanisms available for styling them with Cascading Style Sheets (CSS), and the API through which a browser-embedded language such as JavaScript (JS) can make live changes to a document as the user interacts with it or as more information is retrieved from the server. The core standards and resources are as follows:

```
http://www.w3.org/TR/html5/
http://www.w3.org/TR/CSS/
https://developer.mozilla.org/en-US/docs/Web/JavaScript
https://developer.mozilla.org/en-US/docs/Web/API/Document_Object_Model
```

As this is a network-programming book, I will limit my attention to the way that these technologies involve the network.

The *Hypertext Markup Language* (HTML) is a scheme for taking plain text and decorating it using almost unreasonable numbers of angle brackets—that is, the less-than and greater-than signs ⟨...⟩ reimaged as opening and closing brackets. Each pair of angle brackets creates a *tag* that either opens a new *element* in the document or indicates with an initial slash that it closes an element that was previously opened. A simple paragraph with a word in bold and another in italics might appear as follows:

```
<p>This is a paragraph with <b>bold</b> and <i>italic</i> words.</p>
```

Some tags are self-contained instead of requiring a corresponding closing tag to appear later—most famously, the <br> tag that creates a mid-paragraph line break. More scrupulous authors type this as the self-closing tag
instead, a habit they learn from the Extensible Markup Language (XML), but HTML makes this optional.

In fact, HTML makes many things optional, including proper closing tags. When an <ul> unordered list element ends, a conforming parser will also understand that the particular list element <li> that it has been reading is also now closed and finished, whether or not an actual </li> tag was encountered.

The example paragraph given previously makes it clear that HTML is concentric. A designer can put elements inside of elements inside of yet other elements as they build up a complete web page out of boxes. As the designer builds, they almost inevitably wind up reusing elements from the limited set that HTML defines for several different purposes on the page. Even though the new HTML5 standard allows new elements to be created on the fly in mid-page, designers tend to stick with the standard ones.

A large page might use a generic tag like <div> (which is the most generic kind of box) or <span> (the most generic way to mark running text) for a dozen different purposes each. How can CSS style each element appropriately, and JavaScript let the user interact with them differently, when all <div> elements are exactly the same tag?

The answer is that the HTML author can specify a *class* for each element that provides a more specific label by which it can be addressed. There are two general approaches to using classes.

The blanket approach is for the designer to attach a unique class to every single HTML element in their design.

```
<div class="weather">
  <h5 class="city">Provo</h5>
  <p class="temperature">61°F</p>
</div>
```

Their CSS and JavaScript could then refer to these elements with selectors like .city and .temperature or, if they want to be more specific, h5.city and p.temperature. The simplest form of CSS selector provides a tag name and then a period-prefixed class name, either of which is optional.

Or the designer might reason that there is only one purpose that an <h5> could have inside of one of their weather emblems, and also only one purpose that a paragraph would serve, and so choose to decorate only the outer element with a class.

```
<div class="weather"><h5>Provo</h5><p>61°F</p></div>
```

They would now need more complex patterns to specify that they want the <h5> and the <p> that live inside a <div> with the class that makes its kind of <div> unique. Patterns are built up by whitespace-concatenating the pattern that matches the outer tag with the pattern for the inner tag.

```
.weather h5
.weather p
```

Consult the CSS standard or an introduction to CSS to learn all of the options that are available beyond these simple possibilities. You can also read an introduction to JavaScript or a powerful document manipulation library like jQuery if you want to learn how selectors can be used to target elements from live code running in the browser.

You can investigate how your favorite web sites package up information through two features of a modern browser like Google Chrome or Firefox. They will show you the HTML code—syntax highlighted, no less—for the page you are looking at if you press Ctrl+U. You can right-click any element and select Inspect Element to bring up debugging tools that let you investigate how each document element relates to the content that you are seeing on the page, as shown in Figure 11-1.

Figure 11-1. *The Inspect tab in Google Chrome*

And while in the inspector, you can switch to a Network tab that will show you all of the other resources that were downloaded and displayed as the result of visiting the page.

Note that the Network pane, shown in Figure 11-2, normally comes up empty. Click Reload once you have it up to see it fill with information.

Figure 11-2. *The Google Chrome Network tab showing the resources downloaded to render python.org*

Beware that the live document that you investigate with Inspect Element might bear little or no resemblance to the HTML that was initially delivered as the page's source, depending on whether JavaScript has gone to work and added or removed elements from the page subsequent to the initial page load. If you see an element that interests you in the inspector but cannot find it in the original source, you will probably have to visit the debugger's Network tab to figure out which extra resources JavaScript is fetching that it might have used to build those additional page elements.

As you now begin to experiment with small web applications in the subsequent program listings, you will want to use your browser's Inspect Element feature whenever possible to examine the pages that the applications return.

Reading and Writing to a Database

Imagine a simple bank application that wants to allow account holders to send each other payments using a web application. At the very least, such an application will need a table of payments, a way of inserting a new payment, and a way of fetching all of the payments that have involved the account of the currently logged-in user so that they can be displayed.

Listing 11-1 presents a simple library demonstrating all three of these features, and it is backed by the SQLite database that comes built-in to the Python Standard Library. So, the listing should work anywhere that you have Python installed!

Listing 11-1. A Routine for Building and Talking to a Database

```
#!/usr/bin/env python3
# Foundations of Python Network Programming, Third Edition
# https://github.com/brandon-rhodes/fopnp/blob/m/py3/chapter11/bank.py
# A small library of database routines to power a payments application.

import os, pprint, sqlite3
from collections import namedtuple

def open_database(path='bank.db'):
    new = not os.path.exists(path)
    db = sqlite3.connect(path)
    if new:
        c = db.cursor()
        c.execute('CREATE TABLE payment (id INTEGER PRIMARY KEY,'
                  ' debit TEXT, credit TEXT, dollars INTEGER, memo TEXT)')
        add_payment(db, 'brandon', 'psf', 125, 'Registration for PyCon')
        add_payment(db, 'brandon', 'liz', 200, 'Payment for writing that code')
        add_payment(db, 'sam', 'brandon', 25, 'Gas money-thanks for the ride!')
        db.commit()
    return db

def add_payment(db, debit, credit, dollars, memo):
    db.cursor().execute('INSERT INTO payment (debit, credit, dollars, memo)'
                        ' VALUES (?, ?, ?, ?)', (debit, credit, dollars, memo))

def get_payments_of(db, account):
    c = db.cursor()
    c.execute('SELECT * FROM payment WHERE credit = ? or debit = ?'
              ' ORDER BY id', (account, account))
    Row = namedtuple('Row', [tup[0] for tup in c.description])
    return [Row(*row) for row in c.fetchall()]

if __name__ == '__main__':
    db = open_database()
    pprint.pprint(get_payments_of(db, 'brandon'))
```

The SQLite engine fits each database inside a single file on disk, so the open_database() function can check for the existence of the file to determine whether the database is being created or merely reopened. When creating the database, it builds a single payment table and adds three example payments so that your web application will have something to display besides an empty list of payments.

The schema is overly simple—the bare minimum needed to get this application running. In real life, there would need to be a users' table for usernames and secure password hashes, and an official table of bank accounts where money could come from and be saved to. Instead of being realistic, this app allows the user to create example account names as they type.

One key operation to study in this example is that all of the arguments to its SQL calls are properly escaped. A major source of security flaws today is programmer failure to escape special characters properly when submitting them to an interpreted language like SQL. What if a malicious user of your web front end thinks of a way to type the memo field so that it includes special SQL code? The best protection is to rely on the database itself—and not your own logic—to quote data properly.

Listing 11-1 does this correctly by giving SQLite a question mark (?) everywhere that the code wants a value interpolated, instead of trying to do any escaping or interpolation of its own.

The other key operation is to mix down the raw database rows into something more semantic. The `fetchall()` method is not unique to sqlite3 but is part of the DB-API 2.0 that all modern Python database connectors support for interoperability. Moreover, it does not return an object, or even a dictionary, for each row that comes back from the database. It returns a tuple for each returned row.

```
(1, 'brandon', 'psf', 125, 'Registration for PyCon')
```

The result of handling these raw tuples could be unfortunate. Ideas in your code like "the account credited" or "the number of dollars paid" might appear as `row[2]` or `row[3]` and be difficult to read. So, `bank.py` instead spins up a quick named-tuple class that will also respond to attribute names such as `row.credit` and `row.dollars`. Creating a new class each time `SELECT` is called is not optimal but provides the kind of semantics that web application code needs in one or two quick lines of code—letting you more quickly turn to web application code itself.

A Terrible Web Application (in Flask)

In addition to reading the program listings that follow, you can experiment with the sample web applications in the next several listings by checking out the source code repository for this chapter here:

```
https://github.com/brandon-rhodes/fopnp
```

You can browse the files specific to this chapter here:

```
https://github.com/brandon-rhodes/fopnp/tree/m/py3/chapter11
```

The first file you should study is `app_insecure.py`, which is shown in Listing 11-2. It is worth reading through the code carefully before facing these questions: Does it look like the kind of terrible and untrustworthy code that results in security compromises and public disgrace? Does it even look dangerous?

Listing 11-2. An Insecure Web Application (Not Flask's Fault!)

```python
#!/usr/bin/env python3
# Foundations of Python Network Programming, Third Edition
# https://github.com/brandon-rhodes/fopnp/blob/m/py3/chapter11/app_insecure.py
# A poorly-written and profoundly insecure payments application.
# (Not the fault of Flask, but of how we are choosing to use it!)

import bank
from flask import Flask, redirect, request, url_for
from jinja2 import Environment, PackageLoader
```

```python
app = Flask(__name__)
get = Environment(loader=PackageLoader(__name__, 'templates')).get_template

@app.route('/login', methods=['GET', 'POST'])
def login():
    username = request.form.get('username', '')
    password = request.form.get('password', '')
    if request.method == 'POST':
        if (username, password) in [('brandon', 'atigdng'), ('sam', 'xyzzy')]:
            response = redirect(url_for('index'))
            response.set_cookie('username', username)
            return response
    return get('login.html').render(username=username)

@app.route('/logout')
def logout():
    response = redirect(url_for('login'))
    response.set_cookie('username', '')
    return response

@app.route('/')
def index():
    username = request.cookies.get('username')
    if not username:
        return redirect(url_for('login'))
    payments = bank.get_payments_of(bank.open_database(), username)
    return get('index.html').render(payments=payments, username=username,
        flash_messages=request.args.getlist('flash'))

@app.route('/pay', methods=['GET', 'POST'])
def pay():
    username = request.cookies.get('username')
    if not username:
        return redirect(url_for('login'))
    account = request.form.get('account', '').strip()
    dollars = request.form.get('dollars', '').strip()
    memo = request.form.get('memo', '').strip()
    complaint = None
    if request.method == 'POST':
        if account and dollars and dollars.isdigit() and memo:
            db = bank.open_database()
            bank.add_payment(db, username, account, dollars, memo)
            db.commit()
            return redirect(url_for('index', flash='Payment successful'))
        complaint = ('Dollars must be an integer' if not dollars.isdigit()
                     else 'Please fill in all three fields')
    return get('pay.html').render(complaint=complaint, account=account,
                                  dollars=dollars, memo=memo)

if __name__ == '__main__':
    app.debug = True
    app.run()
```

Not only is the listing dangerous, but it is also vulnerable to many of the most important attack vectors active on the modern Web! By studying its shortcomings over the next few sections of this chapter, you will learn the minimum armor that an application needs to survive. These weaknesses are all mistakes in its data processing, and are separate from the question of whether the site has been properly protected with TLS against prying eyes in the first place. You can go ahead and imagine that it is indeed protected by encryption, perhaps by a reverse proxy sitting in front of the server (see Chapter 10), because I will be considering what an attacker could do even without being able to see data passing between a particular user and the application.

The application uses the Flask web framework to take care of the basics of operating as a Python web application: answering 404 for pages that the application does not define, parsing data from HTML forms (as you will learn in the following sections), and making it easy to compose correct HTTP responses containing either HTML text from one of its templates or a redirect to another URL. You can learn much more about Flask than will be mentioned in this chapter by visiting its documentation at the `http://flask.pocoo.org/` web site.

Imagine that programmers who are not familiar with the Web had put together this listing. They have heard of template languages that make it easy to add their own text to HTML, so they figured out how to get `Jinja2` loaded and running. Furthermore, they discovered that the Flask micro-framework is second only to Django in popularity and, liking the fact that a Flask application can fit in a single file, they have decided to try it.

Reading from top to bottom, you can see a `login()` page and a `logout()` page. Because this app has no real user database, the login page simply hard-codes two possible user accounts and passwords. You will learn more about form logic in a moment, but you can already see that the result of logging in and logging out is the creation and deletion of a cookie (see Chapter 9 and Chapter 10) that, when present in subsequent requests, marks them as belonging to a particular authenticated user.

The other two pages on the site protect themselves from unauthorized users both by looking for this cookie and by redirecting back to the login page if they are unhappy with the lack of a value. The `login()` view has only two lines of code (well, three because of line length) beyond the check for a logged-in user: it pulls the current user's payments from the database, and it puts them together with some other information to provide to the HTML page template. That the page might want to know the username makes sense, but why does the code check the URL parameters (which Flask makes available as a `request.args` dictionary) for a message named `'flash'`?

The answer is apparent if you read the `pay()` page. In the case of a successful payment, the user will be redirected to the index page but will probably want some indication that the form had its intended effect. This is provided by a *flash message*, as web frameworks call them, displayed at the top of the page. (The name has nothing to do with the old Adobe Flash system for writing ads, but it refers to the fact that the message is "flashed" in front of the user when a page is next viewed and then disappears). In this first draft of the web application, the flash message is simply carried as a query string in the URL.

```
http://example.com/?flash=Payment+successful
```

The rest of the `pay()` routine is a familiar dance to the readers of web applications: checking whether a form has been submitted successfully and performing some action if it has. Because the user or browser might have provided or omitted any of the form parameters, the code gingerly and cautiously looks for them with the `get()` method of the `request.form` dictionary that can return a default (here, the empty string `''`) if a key is missing.

If the request is satisfactory, then the payment is added permanently to the database. Otherwise, the form is presented to the user. If they have already done the work of typing in some information, then the code is careful not to throw that work away: instead of presenting them with a blank form and error message that discards their work, it passes the values they have typed back into the template so that they can be redisplayed.

Reviewing the three HTML templates mentioned in Listing 11-2 will be crucial to the next section's discussion of forms and methods. There are actually four templates, because the common design elements of the HTML have been factored out into a base template, which is the most common pattern used by designers building multipage sites.

The template in Listing 11-3 defines a page skeleton with insertion points where other templates can insert a page title and a page body. Note that the title can be used twice, once in the `<title>` element and once in the `<h1>` element, thanks to how well designed the Jinja2 template language is—written by Armin Ronacher, who also wrote Werkzeug (see Chapter 10) and Flask.

Listing 11-3. *The* `base.html` *Page Jinja2 Template*

```
<html>
  <head>
    <title>{% block title %}{% endblock %}</title>
    <link rel="stylesheet" type="text/css" href="/static/style.css">
  </head>
  <body>
    <h1>{{ self.title() }}</h1>
    {% block body %}{% endblock %}
  </body>
</html>
```

The Jinja2 template language is what decides, for example, that a double-brace syntax, as in {{ username }}, is how you ask for a value to be substituted into a template and that brace-percent maneuvers like {% for %} can be used to loop and repeatedly produce the same HTML pattern. See its documentation at `http://jinja.pocoo.org/` for more about its syntax and features.

The login page shown in Listing 11-4 consists of nothing but a title and the form itself. You can see for the first time a pattern that you will see again: a form element that provides an initial value="..." that should already appear in the editable element when it first appears on the screen.

Listing 11-4. *The* `login.html` *Jinja2 Template*

```
{% extends "base.html" %}
{% block title %}Please log in{% endblock %}
{% block body %}
<form method="post">
  <label>User: <input name="username" value="{{ username }}"></label>
  <label>Password: <input name="password" type="password"></label>
  <button type="submit">Log in</button>
</form>
{% endblock %}
```

By using this {{ username }} substitution into the value="...", this form will help the user avoid having to retype their username if they mistype the password and get the same form over again.

The index page that will live at / has much more going on in its template, as you can see from Listing 11-5. Any flash messages, if present, go right below the title. Then comes an unordered list (<ul>) of list items (<li>) that each describes a single payment made to or from the account of the logged-in user, which has the title "Your Payments" displayed above it. Finally, there are links to the new-payment page and the logout link.

Listing 11-5. *The* `index.html` *Jinja2 Template*

```
{% extends "base.html" %}
{% block title %}Welcome, {{ username }}{% endblock %}
{% block body %}
{% for message in flash_messages %}
  <div class="flash_message">{{ message }}<a href="/">&times;</a></div>
{% endfor %}
<p>Your Payments</p>
```

```
<ul>
  {% for p in payments %}
    {% set prep = 'from' if (p.credit == username) else 'to' %}
    {% set acct = p.debit if (p.credit == username) else p.credit %}
    <li class="{{ prep }}">${{ p.dollars }} {{ prep }} <b>{{ acct }}</b>
    for: <i>{{ p.memo }}</i></li>
  {% endfor %}
</ul>
<a href="/pay">Make payment</a> | <a href="/logout">Log out</a>
{% endblock %}
```

Note that the code is not interested in displaying the current user's account name over and over again as it loops to display their incoming and outgoing payments. So, it instead figures out, for each payment, whether the credit or debit account name is the one that matches the current user and then makes sure that it prints the other account name instead—using with the correct preposition so that the user can tell which way their money has flowed. This is possible thanks to Jinja2's {% set ... %} command, which makes quick little presentation calculations like this quite easy to do in-template when the designer realizes what they want.

There often seem to be dozens of ways that the user can fail to fill out a form correctly, and Listing 11-6 prepares itself by expecting to receive a complaint string for prominent display at the top of the form, if such a string is provided. Beyond this nicety, the code is mostly repetitive: three form fields that, if the form was filled out incorrectly and is being redisplayed, need to be prefilled with whatever text the user already had there when they tried submitting it.

Listing 11-6. The pay.html Jinja2 Template

```
{% extends "base.html" %}
{% block title %}Make a Payment{% endblock %}
{% block body %}
<form method="post" action="/pay">
  {% if complaint %}<span class="complaint">{{ complaint }}</span>{% endif %}
  <label>To account: <input name="account" value="{{ account }}"></label>
  <label>Dollars: <input name="dollars" value="{{ dollars }}"></label>
  <label>Memo: <input name="memo" value="{{ memo }}"></label>
  <button type="submit">Send money</button> | <a href="/">Cancel</a>
</form>
{% endblock %}
```

It is a best practice to have an escape route next to every submit button on a site. Experiments suggest that users make the fewest mistakes if, however, the escape route is obviously smaller and less significant than the default action of submitting the form—and it is especially important that the escape route *not* look like a button!

So, pay.html is careful to make its "Cancel" escape route a simple link, visually separated from the button by the conventional pipe symbol (|) that is currently popular in this visual context.

If you want to try this application, you can check out the source code, enter the chapter11 directory that contains bank.py, app_insecure.py, and the associated templates/ directory, and type the following:

```
$ pip install flask
$ python3 app_insecure.py
```

The result should be an announcement that it is up and running at a URL that it will print to your screen.

```
* Running on http://127.0.0.1:5000/
* Restarting with reloader
```

With debug mode turned on (see the second-to-last line of Listing 11-2), Flask will even restart itself and reload your application if you edit one of the listings, which makes it easy to explore the effects of small changes to the code quickly.

There is one small detail missing here. If `base.html` in Listing 11-3 mentions `style.css`, where is it? It is sitting inside of the `static/` directory that you can find right next to the application in the source repository. You will want to review it if you find that you are interested not only in network programming but in the idea of web design.

The Dance of Forms and HTTP Methods

An HTML form has the default action of GET, and it can be as simple as a single input field.

```
<form action="/search">
  <label>Search: <input name="q"></label>
  <button type="submit">Go</button>
</form>
```

There is no space in this book to discuss form design—a huge subject fraught with technical decisions. There are a dozen kinds of input to consider, besides text fields like the one here. And even text fields have many options surrounding them. Are you going to use CSS3 to add some sample text to the input field that disappears as the user starts typing? Should some in-browser JavaScript code perhaps gray out the submit button until the user has entered a search term? Should you put instructions, or a few example search terms, below the input field to suggest ideas to the user? Should a submit button ever actually say "Submit" or instead state what happens once the form is submitted to the server? Will a minimalist designer ask you to omit the Go button altogether, simplifying the site but requiring the user to know that they can hit Return to submit their search?

But these questions are covered at length in books and sites about web design. This book can focus only on what forms mean for the network.

A form that performs a GET places the input fields directly in the URL and thus in the path transmitted with the HTTP request.

```
GET /search?q=python+network+programming HTTP/1.1
Host: example.com
```

Think of what this means. The parameters of a GET become part of your browser history, and it will be visible to anyone looking over your shoulder at the browser's address bar. This means that a GET can never be used to deliver sensitive information like a password or credential. When you fill out a GET form, you are stating, "Where I would like to go next?" and you are essentially helping the browser compose a handcrafted URL for a page that you want the server to invent so that you can visit it. Filling out the previous search form with three different phrases will result in the creation of three separate pages, three entries in your browser history that you can return to later, and three URLs that can be shared with friends if you want them to see the same page of results.

A form that performs a GET request is how you ask to go somewhere, merely by describing your destination.

This is in stark contrast to the opposite kind of HTML form, where the method is POST or PUT or DELETE. For these forms, absolutely no information from the form makes it into the URL and thenceforth to the path in the HTTP request.

```
<form method="post" action="/donate">
  <label>Charity: <input name="name"></label>
  <label>Amount: <input name="dollars"></label>
  <button type="submit">Donate</button>
</form>
```

When this HTML form is submitted, the browser places the data into the body of the request in its entirety, leaving the path completely alone.

```
POST /donate HTTP/1.1
Host: example.com
Content-Type: application/x-www-form-urlencoded
Content-Length: 39

name=PyCon%20scholarships&dollars=35
```

Here you are not passively asking to go visit a "$35 for PyCon scholarships" page because you are interested in looking at it. On the contrary. You are committing to an action—an action that will be twice as expensive and have twice the impact if you decide to perform the POST twice instead of just once. The form parameters are not placed in the URL because "$35 for PyCon scholarships" is not the name of a place you want to go visit. It is what the late philosopher J.L. Austin would call a *speech act*, that is, words that cause a new state of affairs in the world.

There is, by the way, an alternative form encoding *multipart/forms* based on the MIME standard (Chapter 12) that browsers can use for uploading large payloads like entire files. However, either way, the semantics of the POST form are the same.

Web browsers are extremely cautious about POST precisely because they understand it to be an action. If the user tries to click Reload while looking at a page returned from POST, the browser will interrupt them with a dialog box. You can see one if you bring up the web application from Listing 11-2, visit its /pay form, and then submit the form without typing anything so that it comes back immediately with the complaint "Dollars must be an integer." When I then click Reload in Google Chrome, a dialog box pops up.

Confirm Form Resubmission

The page that you're looking for used information that you entered. Returning to the page might cause any action you took to be repeated. Do you want to continue?

You should see a similar warning in your own browser. While looking at the form with human eyes, you can see clearly that the form submit does not seem to have taken effect; but the browser has no way of knowing that the POST failed to have an effect. It sent a POST, it received a page, and for all it knows the page says something like "Thank you for donating $1,000," and the effect of submitting it again could be disastrous.

There are two techniques that web sites can use to avoid stranding the user on a page that is the result of a POST and that therefore will cause endless trouble for both the Reload and the Forward and Back buttons in the user's browser.

- Use JavaScript, or HTML5 form input constraints, to try to prevent the user from submitting invalid values in the first place. If the submit button does not light up until the form is ready for submission or if the entire form round-trip can be handled in JavaScript without the page being reloaded, then an invalid submission—such as the empty form that you submitted a moment ago—will not strand the user at a POST result.

- When a form is finally submitted correctly and its action succeeds, the web application should resist the temptation to respond directly with a 200 OK page that describes the completed action. Instead, respond with a 303 See Other redirect to another URL specified in the Location header. This will force the browser to follow up the successful POST with an immediate GET that lands the user somewhere else. The user can now hit Reload, Forward, and Back to their heart's content, resulting only in safe repeated GETs of the results page, instead of repeated attempts to submit the form.

While the simple application in Listing 11-2 is too primitive to shield the user from seeing a POST result in the case that the form is invalid, it does at least perform a successful 303 See Also powered by the Flask redirect() constructor when either the /login form or the /pay form succeeds. This is a best practice for which you should find support in all web frameworks.

When Forms Use Wrong Methods

Web applications that misuse HTTP methods cause problems with automated tools, user expectations, and the browser.

I remember a friend whose small-business web page was stored within a local hosting company's home-grown PHP content management system. An admin screen presented him with links to the images that were used on his site. We highlighted the page and asked a browser to download all of the links so that he would have his own backup of the images. Minutes later he received a text from a friend: why were all of the images disappearing from his web site?

It turns out that the Delete button next to each image was not, alas, a real button that launched a POST operation. Instead, each Delete was merely a link to a plain old URL, which had the nasty side effect of deleting an image if you visited it! His browser was willing to GET the hundred links on the page because a GET should always, under all circumstances, be a safe operation. His hosting company had betrayed that trust, and the result was that his web site had to be restored from their backups.

The opposite error—performing "read" operations with POST—has less dire effects. It merely destroys usability rather than deleting all of your files.

I once had the displeasure of using a homegrown search engine internal to a large institution. After several searches, I had a page of results in front of me that my supervisor needed to see, so I highlighted the URL and prepared to paste it into an e-mail.

Then I read the URL and was dismayed. Even without knowing how the server worked, I was sure that /search.pl was not by itself going to bring this page of results back up when my supervisor visited it!

The query was invisible to my browser's location bar because the search form was incorrectly designed to use POST. This made the URL of every single search look exactly the same, meaning that searches could neither be shared nor bookmarked. And when I tried to navigate through a series of searches with my browser's Forward and Back buttons, I got a sequence of pop-up windows asking if I really wanted to resubmit each search! As far as the browser knew, any of those POSTs could have had side effects.

Using GET for places and POST for actions is crucial not merely for the sake of the protocol but for a productive user experience.

Safe and Unsafe Cookies

The web application in Listing 11-2 attempts to provide privacy to its users. It requires a successful login before it divulges the user's list of payments in response to a GET of the / page. It also requires the user to have logged in before it will accept a POST to the /pay form that lets the user transfer money.

Unfortunately, it is quite easy to exploit the application and make payments on behalf of another user!

Consider the steps that a malicious user who gains access to the site might take, perhaps by opening their own account on the site to investigate how it works. They will open the debugging tools in Firefox or Google Chrome and then log on to the site, watching the outgoing and incoming headers in the Network pane to see how the site works. And what will they see coming back in response to their username and password?

```
HTTP/1.0 302 FOUND
...
Set-Cookie: username=badguy; Path=/
...
```

How interesting! Their successful login has delivered a cookie named username to their browser, with their own username badguy as the value. Apparently, the site is blithely trusting that subsequent requests with this cookie must necessarily indicate that they have typed their username and password correctly.

But surely the caller can give this cookie any value they want?

They can attempt to forge the cookie by clicking through the correct privacy menus in their browser, or they can attempt to access the site from Python. Using Requests, they might first see whether they can fetch the front page. An unauthenticated request gets forwarded to the /login page, as one would expect.

```
>>> import requests
>>> r = requests.get('http://localhost:5000/')
>>> print(r.url)
http://localhost:5000/login
```

But what if the bad guy inserts a cookie that makes it look like the brandon user has already logged on?

```
>>> r = requests.get('http://localhost:5000/', cookies={'username': 'brandon'})
>>> print(r.url)
http://localhost:5000/
```

Success! Because the site trusts that it set the value of this cookie, it is now responding to HTTP requests as though they came from another user. All that the bad guy has to know is the username of another user of the payment system, and they can forge a request to send money anywhere they want.

```
>>> r = requests.post('http://localhost:5000/pay',
...     {'account': 'hacker', 'dollars': 100, 'memo': 'Auto-pay'},
...     cookies={'username': 'brandon'})
>>> print(r.url)
http://localhost:5000/?flash=Payment+successful
```

It worked—$100 has now been paid from the brandon account to one under their control.

The lesson is that cookies should never be designed so that a user, on their own, could construct one. Assume that your users are clever and will eventually catch on if all you are doing is obscuring their username with base-64 encoding, or swapping the letters around or performing a simple exclusive-or of the value with a constant mask. There are three safe approaches to creating nonforgeable cookies.

- You can leave the cookie readable but sign it with a digital signature. This leaves attackers frustrated. They can see that the cookie has their username in it and will wish that they could just rewrite the username with that of an account they want to hijack. But because they cannot forge the digital signature to sign this new version of the cookie, they cannot convince your site that the rewritten cookie is legitimate.

- You can completely encrypt the cookie so that the user cannot even interpret its value. It will appear as an opaque value that they cannot parse or understand.

- You can create a purely random string for the cookie that has no inherent meaning, perhaps using a standard UUID library, and save it in your own database so that you recognize the cookie as belonging to the user when they make their next request. This persistent session storage will need to be accessible to all of your front-end web machines if several successive HTTP requests from the same user might wind up being forwarded to your different servers. Some applications put sessions in their main database, while others use a Redis instance or other shorter-term storage to prevent increasing the query load to their main persistent data store.

For this sample application, you can take advantage of Flask's built-in ability to digitally sign cookies so that they cannot be forged. On a real production server, you would want to keep the signing key safely separated from your source code, but for this example it can go near the top of the source file. Not only does including the key within the source code for a production system reveal the key to anyone with access to your version control system, but it is also likely to expose the credential to your developer laptops and your continuous integration process.

```
app.secret_key = 'saiGeij8AiS2ahleahMo5dahveixuV3J'
```

Flask will then use the secret key every time you set a cookie using its special `session` object, as during login.

```
session['username'] = username
session['csrf_token'] = uuid.uuid4().hex
```

And Flask will again use the key before trusting any cookie values that it pulls back out of the incoming request. A cookie whose signature is not correct is assumed to be forged and treated as though it is simply not present in the request at all.

```
username = session.get('username')
```

You will see these improvements in action in Listing 11-8.

Another worry with cookies is that they should never be passed over an unencrypted HTTP channel because they will then be visible to everyone else on the same coffee shop wireless network. Many sites carefully set their cookies using an HTTP-secured login page, only to expose them completely as the browser then pulls all of the CSS, JavaScript, and images that are fetched over plain HTTP from the same hostname.

To prevent cookie exposure, find out how to make your web framework set the `Secure` parameter on every cookie that you send to the browser. It will then be careful never to include it in unencrypted requests for resources that everyone is allowed access to anyway.

Nonpersistent Cross-Site Scripting

If an opponent cannot steal or forge a cookie that will let their browser (or Python program) perform actions on behalf of another user, then they can shift gears. If they can figure out how to take control of another user's browser that is logged in, then they will never even have to see the cookie. By performing actions with that browser, the cookie will automatically be included in each request.

There are at least three well-known approaches to this kind of attack. The server in Listing 11-2 is vulnerable to all three, and you are now going to learn about each of them in turn.

The first type is the *nonpersistent* version of *cross-site scripting* (XSS), where an attacker figures out how to make a web site—like the example payment system—present attacker-written content as though it came from the site. Imagine that the attacker wanted to send $110 to an account that they controlled. They might craft the JavaScript shown in Listing 11-7.

Listing 11-7. Script `attack.js` for Making Payments

```
<script>
var x = new XMLHttpRequest();
x.open('POST', 'http://localhost:5000/pay');
x.setRequestHeader('Content-Type', 'application/x-www-form-urlencoded');
x.send('account=hacker&dollars=110&memo=Theft');
</script>
```

If this code is merely present on the page when the user was logged into the payments application, then the POST request it describes will fire off and make the payment, automatically, on behalf of the innocent user. Because the code inside `<script>` tags is invisible when viewing a rendered web page, the user will not even see that anything is amiss unless they hit Ctrl+U to View Source—and even then, they would have to recognize the `<script>` element as something unusual that is not normally part of the page.

But how could an attacker make this HTML appear?

The answer is that the attacker can simply inject this HTML through the `flash` parameter that the code is inserting, raw, into the page template of the / page! Because the author of Listing 11-2 has not read enough documentation, they do not realize that Jinja2 in its raw form does not automatically escape special characters like `<` and `>` because it does not know—unless it is told—that you are using it to compose HTML.

The attacker can build a URL whose `flash` parameter includes their script.

```
>>> with open('/home/brandon/fopnp/py3/chapter11/attack.js') as f:
...     query = {'flash': f.read().strip().replace('\n', ' ')}
>>> print('http://localhost:5000/?' + urlencode(query))
http://localhost:5000/?flash=%3Cscript%3E+var+x+%3D+new+XMLHttpRequest%28%29%3B+x.open%28%27
POST%27%2C+%27http%3A%2F%2Flocalhost%3A5000%2Fpay%27%29%3B+x.setRequestHeader%28%27Content-
Type%27%2C+%27application%2Fx-www-form-urlencoded%27%29%3B+x.send%28%27account%3Dhacker%26dollars%3D
110%26memo%3DTheft%27%29%3B+%3C%2Fscript%3E
```

Finally, the attacker needs to concoct a way to entice the user to see and follow the link.

This can be difficult when targeting one specific user. The attacker might need to forge what looks like an e-mail from one of the user's real friends with the link hidden behind text that the user will want to click. Research is required, and the failure modes are many. The attacker might log on to an IRC channel where the user is chatting and say that the link is "an article" about a topic on which the user has just expressed an opinion. In the latter case, the attacker will often share a shortened link that expands to the XSS link only once the user has clicked it—because seeing the full link shown previously is likely to make the user suspicious.

However, when targeting no specific user and a large site, such as a payment processing system used by millions of people, the attacker can often be less specific. The poisonous link, embedded in an enticing spam e-mail sent to millions of people, might generate a few clicks from people logged on to the payment system and thus generate income for the attacker.

Try generating the link, using the Requests code given previously. Then click it, both when you are logged in to the payments site and when you are not.

When you are logged in, you should find—each time you reload the main page—that another payment appears, automatically performed on your behalf by the link itself that you have visited. Press Ctrl+U in Firefox or Google Chrome to see that the JavaScript and surrounding `<script>` tags have made it intact into the page.

If you find that the attack is not working, open the JavaScript console in your browser. My version of Chrome is sophisticated enough that it detected and cancelled the attack: "The XSS Auditor refused to execute a script...because its source code was found within the request." Only if this protection is turned off or if the attacker finds a more nefarious way to exploit the flash message can a good modern browser be fooled by the primitive version of the attack that is being launched here.

Even if the attack works, the fact that a blank green message box appears with no message inside might strike the user as suspicious. As an exercise, try to fix this flaw in the previous URL: outside of the script tag, see whether you can provide a bit of real text like "Welcome back" that will make the green message area look more acceptable.

The defense against the attack that will be undertaken in Listing 11-8 is to remove the flash message—this bit of contextual information about what the /pay form just accomplished, that the app wants to display on the next page that the user visits—from the URL entirely. Instead, you can keep the flash message on the server side until the next request comes in. Like most frameworks, Flask already provides a mechanism for this in its pair of functions `flash()` and `get_flashed_messages()`.

Persistent Cross-Site Scripting

Without the ability to set the flash message through a long and ugly URL, the attacker will have to shift to injecting their JavaScript through some other mechanism. Scanning the main page, their eyes might fall on the Memo field of the displayed payments. What characters can they type into the memo?

Getting a memo to appear on your page is, of course, a more difficult business than providing it in a URL that they can give you anonymously. The attacker is going to have to register with the site using fake credentials or compromise the account of another user in order to send you a payment whose Memo field includes the `<script>` element and JavaScript from Listing 11-7.

You can inject such code yourself. Using the password that you can see in Listing 11-2, log in to the application as sam and then try sending me a payment. Include a nice little note about how you enjoyed this book and are tipping me extra. That way, I will hopefully not be suspicious about your payment. Once you have appended the script element but before you click "Send money," the fields will look something like this:

```
To account: brandon
Dollars:    1
Memo:       A small thank-you.<script>...</script>
```

Now press the submit button. Then log out, log back in as brandon, and start hitting Reload. Every time the brandon user visits the front page, yet another payment will be made from his account!

This *persistent* version of a cross-site scripting attack is, as you can see, quite powerful. Whereas the link created earlier worked only when the user clicked it, the persistent version—where the JavaScript now appears invisibly and runs every time they visit the site—will happen over and over again until the data on the server is cleaned or deleted. When XSS attacks have been launched through public form messages on vulnerable sites, they have affected hundreds and thousands of users until finally being repaired.

The reason that Listing 11-2 is vulnerable to this problem is that its author has used Jinja2 templates without really understanding them. Their documentation makes it clear that they do no escaping automatically. Only if you know to turn on its escaping will Jinja2 protect characters like < and > that are special in HTML.

Listing 11-8 will protect against all XSS attacks by calling Jinja2 through the Flask render_template() function, which will turn on HTML escaping automatically when it sees that the template filenames end with the extension html. By relying on a common pattern of the web framework instead of doing things yourself, you can be opted in to patterns that can protect you from incautious design decisions.

Cross-Site Request Forgery

With all content now being properly escaped on your site, XSS attacks should no longer be an issue. But the attacker has one more trick up their sleeve: attempting to submit the form from a completely different site because they really have no reason to launch the form from your site. They can predict ahead of time what all of the field values need to be, so they are free to launch a request to /pay from any other web page you might visit.

All they have to do is invite you to visit a page where they have hidden the JavaScript or embed it in a comment if they find a forum thread in which you are involved on a site that does not properly escape or remove script tags from forum comments.

You might think that the attacker will need to build a form that is ready to send them money and then make its button a tempting target for your mouse.

```
<form method="post" action="http://localhost:5000/pay">
  <input type="hidden" name="account" value="sam">
  <input type="hidden" name="dollars" value="220">
  <input type="hidden" name="message" value="Someone won big">
  <button type="submit">Reply</button>
</form>
```

However, thanks to the fact that JavaScript is probably turned on in your browser, they probably can simply insert the `<script>` element from Listing 11-7 into the page, forum post, or comment on the page you are going to load and then sit back and wait for a payment to appear in their account.

This is a classic *cross-site request forgery* (CSRF) attack, and it does not require that the attacker figure out how to compromise the payments system. All that is needed is payment forms that are easy to compose combined with any web site—anywhere in the world—where the attacker can add JavaScript and where you are likely to visit. Every web site you visit would need to be secure to protect against the possibility of this injection.

So, applications need to protect against it.

How can applications prevent CSRF attacks? By making forms difficult to fill out and submit. Instead of making simple forms with the minimum number of fields necessary to make a payment, they need an extra field that contains a secret that only the legitimate user of the form will ever see or that their browser will ever see; it need not be visible to the user reading and using the form through their browser. Because the attacker will not know the hidden value that any particular user has hidden in every /pay form they submit, the attacker cannot forge a POST to that address that the server will find convincing.

Again, Listing 11-8 will use Flask's ability to put secrets safely in the cookie to assign a secret random string to each user every time they log in. This example requires you to imagine, of course, that a payments site would be protected in real life with HTTPS so that having the secret delivered in a web page or cookie is safe and cannot be observed in transit.

Having chosen a per-session random secret, the payments site can add it invisibly to every /pay form presented to the user. Hidden form fields are a built-in feature of HTML for reasons like CSRF protection. The following field is added to the form in pay2.html, the replacement for Listing 11-6 that will be used by Listing 11-8:

```
<input name="csrf_token" type="hidden" value="{{ csrf_token }}">
```

An extra check is then made every time the form is posted to make sure the CSRF value from the form matches what was delivered in the HTML version of the form to the user. If they do not match, then the site assumes that an attacker is attempting to submit the form on the user's behalf and rejects the attempt with 403 Forbidden.

The CSRF protection in Listing 11-8 is done manually so that you can see the moving parts and understand how the randomly chosen extra field makes it impossible for an attacker to guess how to build a valid form. In real life, you should expect to find CSRF protection built into any web framework you choose, or at least to be available as a standard plug-in. The Flask community suggests several approaches, including one that comes built in to the popular Flask-WTF library for building and parsing HTML forms.

The Improved Application

The name of Listing 11-8 is app_improved.py and not "perfect" or "secure" because, frankly, it is difficult to prove that any particular example program is really completely free of possible vulnerabilities.

Listing 11-8. The app_improved.py Payments Application

```
#!/usr/bin/env python3
# Foundations of Python Network Programming, Third Edition
# https://github.com/brandon-rhodes/fopnp/blob/m/py3/chapter11/app_improved.py
# A payments application with basic security improvements added.

import bank, uuid
from flask import (Flask, abort, flash, get_flashed_messages,
                   redirect, render_template, request, session, url_for)

app = Flask(__name__)
app.secret_key = 'saiGeij8AiS2ahleahMo5dahveixuV3J'
```

```python
@app.route('/login', methods=['GET', 'POST'])
def login():
    username = request.form.get('username', '')
    password = request.form.get('password', '')
    if request.method == 'POST':
        if (username, password) in [('brandon', 'atigdng'), ('sam', 'xyzzy')]:
            session['username'] = username
            session['csrf_token'] = uuid.uuid4().hex
            return redirect(url_for('index'))
    return render_template('login.html', username=username)

@app.route('/logout')
def logout():
    session.pop('username', None)
    return redirect(url_for('login'))

@app.route('/')
def index():
    username = session.get('username')
    if not username:
        return redirect(url_for('login'))
    payments = bank.get_payments_of(bank.open_database(), username)
    return render_template('index.html', payments=payments, username=username,
                           flash_messages=get_flashed_messages())

@app.route('/pay', methods=['GET', 'POST'])
def pay():
    username = session.get('username')
    if not username:
        return redirect(url_for('login'))
    account = request.form.get('account', '').strip()
    dollars = request.form.get('dollars', '').strip()
    memo = request.form.get('memo', '').strip()
    complaint = None
    if request.method == 'POST':
        if request.form.get('csrf_token') != session['csrf_token']:
            abort(403)
        if account and dollars and dollars.isdigit() and memo:
            db = bank.open_database()
            bank.add_payment(db, username, account, dollars, memo)
            db.commit()
            flash('Payment successful')
            return redirect(url_for('index'))
        complaint = ('Dollars must be an integer' if not dollars.isdigit()
                     else 'Please fill in all three fields')
    return render_template('pay2.html', complaint=complaint, account=account,
                           dollars=dollars, memo=memo,
                           csrf_token=session['csrf_token'])

if __name__ == '__main__':
    app.debug = True
    app.run()
```

As I write this, the Shellshock vulnerability has just been announced: for the past 22 years, without anyone noticing, the widely used Bash shell has been willing to run any code presented to it as specially formatted environment variables—like those that the old CGI mechanism will happily set based on incoming untrusted HTTP headers. If major production software can be vulnerable to unexpected features and interactions after more than two decades, it is hard to make promises about the absolute security of a demonstration web application that I wrote solely for this chapter.

But here is the listing. Its templates do proper escaping, it uses internal storage for flash messages instead of sending them round-trip through the user's browser, and a hidden random UUID in each form it presents to the user makes them impossible to forge.

Note that two of the major improvements—switching to internally stored flash messages and asking Jinja2 to do proper escaping of characters before adding them to the HTML—have come about by using standard mechanisms already built into Flask instead of relying on my own code.

This illustrates an important point. Not only will your applications often be shorter, more concise, and more convenient to write if you read framework documentation thoroughly and lean on as many of its features as you can, but it will often be more secure because you will be using patterns written by a professional and carefully improved by the web framework's entire community. In many cases, these conveniences will address security or performance problems of which you might not even be aware.

The application is now fairly well automated when it comes to its interaction with the network. But there are still many seams showing when it comes to the handling of views and forms.

The code has to check manually whether the user is logged in. Each form field needs to be copied manually from the request into the HTML so that the user does not need to retype it. And the conversation with the database is disappointingly low-level; you must open database sessions yourself and then remember to commit if you want the payment to be recorded permanently by SQLite.

There are good best practices and third-party tools in the Flask community to which you could turn to address these common patterns. But instead, for variety, the last example will be the same application written in a framework that takes more of these responsibilities away from you from day 1.

The Payments Application in Django

The Django web framework is probably the most popular among Python programmers today because it is a "full-stack" web framework that comes with everything built in that a novice programmer needs. Not only does Django have a templates system and URL routing framework, but it can also talk to the database for you, render the results as Python objects, and even compose and interpret forms without needing a single third-party library. In a world where many people programming for the Web have little training, a framework that establishes coherent and safe patterns can be more valuable than a more flexible tool that sends the programmer hunting for their own ORM and forms library, when they might not even have a clear idea about how those pieces fit together.

You can find the Django application in its entirety at the source code repository for this book. Again, here is the URL for this chapter:

```
https://github.com/brandon-rhodes/fopnp/tree/m/py3/chapter11
```

There are several files of boilerplate that are not worth quoting in full here in the pages of this book.

- `manage.py`: This is an executable script sitting in the chapter11/ directory that lets you run Django commands to set up and start the application in development mode, as you will see in a moment.

- `djbank/__init__.py`: This is an empty file that tells Python that the directory is a Python package from which modules can be loaded.

- `djbank/admin.py`: This contains three lines of code that make the Payment model appear in the Admin interface, as described in the "Choosing a Web Framework" section that follows.

- djbank/settings.py: This contains the plug-ins and configuration that govern how the application loads and runs. The only change I made to the defaults written by Django 1.7 is a last line that points Django at the static/ files directory sitting in the main chapter11/ directory so that the Django application can share the same style.css file that was used by Listing 11-2 and Listing 11-8.

- djbank/templates/*.html: The page templates are a bit more primitive than the Jinja2 templates shown in Listings 11-3 through 11-6 because the Django template language is less convenient and less powerful. But, because the basic syntax is the same, the differences are not worth discussion in this book. Consult the documentation of both template systems if you want to learn the details.

- djbank/wgsi.py: This offers a WSGI callable that a WSGI-compliant web server, whether Gunicorn or Apache (see Chapter 10), can call to get the payments application up and running.

The remaining four files are interesting for the way in which the framework, without needing any extensions, already supports many common patterns of which Python code can take advantage.

Thanks to its built-in object-relational mapper (ORM), Django absolves the application of having to know how to write any SQL queries of its own. The entire issue of proper quoting of SQL values disappears with it. Listing 11-9 describes the database table by listing its fields in a declarative Python class, which will be used to represent the table rows when they are returned. Django lets you attach complicated validation logic to a class like this, if your data restrictions go beyond those that can be expressed by the field types alone.

Listing 11-9. The models.py for the Django App

```
#!/usr/bin/env python3
# Foundations of Python Network Programming, Third Edition
# https://github.com/brandon-rhodes/fopnp/blob/m/py3/chapter11/djbank/models.py
# Model definitions for our Django application.

from django.db import models
from django.forms import ModelForm

class Payment(models.Model):
    debit = models.CharField(max_length=200)
    credit = models.CharField(max_length=200, verbose_name='To account')
    dollars = models.PositiveIntegerField()
    memo = models.CharField(max_length=200)

class PaymentForm(ModelForm):
    class Meta:
        model = Payment
        fields = ['credit', 'dollars', 'memo']
```

The bottom class declaration tells Django to prepare a form for creating and editing database rows. It will ask the user only about the three fields listed, leaving the debit field for you to fill in from the currently logged-in username. This class, as you will see, is able to face in both directions in the web app's conversation with the user: it can render the form as a series of HTML <input> fields, and then it can turn around and parse the HTTP POST data that comes back once the form is submitted in order to build or modify a Payment database row.

When you are using a micro-framework such as Flask, you will have to choose an outside library to support operations like this. SQLAlchemy, for example, is a renowned ORM, and many programmers choose not to work with Django specifically so that they can enjoy SQLAlchemy's power and elegance.

But SQLAlchemy itself does not know about HTML forms, so the programmer using a microframework will need to find yet another third-party library to do the other half of what the previous models.py file does for the Django programmer.

Instead of having the programmer attach URL paths to Python view functions using a Flask-style decorator, Django has the application writer create a urls.py file like that shown in Listing 11-10. While this gives each individual view a bit less context when read on its own, it makes them each position-independent and works to centralize control of the URL space.

Listing 11-10. The urls.py for the Django App

```python
#!/usr/bin/env python3
# Foundations of Python Network Programming, Third Edition
# https://github.com/brandon-rhodes/fopnp/blob/m/py3/chapter11/djbank/urls.py
# URL patterns for our Django application.

from django.conf.urls import patterns, include, url
from django.contrib import admin
from django.contrib.auth.views import login

urlpatterns = patterns('',
    url(r'^admin/', include(admin.site.urls)),
    url(r'^accounts/login/$', login),
    url(r'^$', 'djbank.views.index_view', name='index'),
    url(r'^pay/$', 'djbank.views.pay_view', name='pay'),
    url(r'^logout/$', 'djbank.views.logout_view'),
    )
```

Django makes the quirky decision to use regular expression matching to match URLs, which can lead to difficult-to-read patterns when a URL includes several variable portions. They can also—and I speak from experience—be quite difficult to debug.

These patterns establish essentially the same URL space as in the earlier Flask applications, except that the path to the login page is where the Django authentication module expects it to be. Instead of writing up your own login page—and hoping you write it correctly and without some subtle security flaw—this code relies on the standard Django login page to have gotten things right.

The views that finally tie this Django application together in Listing 11-11 are at once both simpler and more complicated than the corresponding views in the Flask version of the app.

Listing 11-11. The views.py for the Django App

```python
#!/usr/bin/env python3
# Foundations of Python Network Programming, Third Edition
# https://github.com/brandon-rhodes/fopnp/blob/m/py3/chapter11/djbank/views.py
# A function for each view in our Django application.

from django.contrib import messages
from django.contrib.auth.decorators import login_required
from django.contrib.auth import logout
from django.db.models import Q
from django.shortcuts import redirect, render
from django.views.decorators.http import require_http_methods, require_safe
from .models import Payment, PaymentForm
```

```
def make_payment_views(payments, username):
    for p in payments:
        yield {'dollars': p.dollars, 'memo': p.memo,
               'prep': 'to' if (p.debit == username) else 'from',
               'account': p.credit if (p.debit == username) else p.debit}

@require_http_methods(['GET'])
@login_required
def index_view(request):
    username = request.user.username
    payments = Payment.objects.filter(Q(credit=username) | Q(debit=username))
    payment_views = make_payment_views(payments, username)
    return render(request, 'index.html', {'payments': payment_views})

@require_http_methods(['GET', 'POST'])
@login_required
def pay_view(request):
    form = PaymentForm(request.POST or None)
    if form.is_valid():
        payment = form.save(commit=False)
        payment.debit = request.user.username
        payment.save()
        messages.add_message(request, messages.INFO, 'Payment successful.')
        return redirect('/')
    return render(request, 'pay.html', {'form': form})

@require_http_methods(['GET'])
def logout_view(request):
    logout(request)
    return redirect('/')
```

The big question you should ask is, where is the cross-site scripting protection? The answer is that it was automatically added to settings.py and turned on when I asked Django to build the skeleton for this application with the manage.py startapp command!

Without your even having to know that CSRF protection exists, your forms will refuse to work unless you remember to add {% csrf_token %} to your form template. And if you forget, the Django error message displayed by its runserver development mode explains the requirement. This is an extremely powerful pattern for new web developers who do not understand the issues at stake: the Django default will generally keep them safe from the most common catastrophic errors with forms and fields, in a way that microframeworks rarely match.

The views in this application are conceptually simpler than their equivalents in the Flask-powered listings because this code leans on built-in Django features for almost everything, instead of having to implement things such as login and session manipulation. The login page does not even appear because urls.py simply uses Django's. The logout page can just call logout() and not worry about how it works. Views can be marked with @login_required and skip having to worry about whether the user is logged in.

The only helper that corresponds directly to a similar feature in our Flask application is the @require_http_methods() decorator, which is giving you the same protection against invalid or unsupported HTTP methods that Flask gave you built in to its own view decorators.

Working with the database is now beautifully simple. The bank.py module with its SQL has disappeared entirely. Django has already chosen to set up a SQLite database—that is one of the defaults already present in settings.py—and it is ready to open a session to the database the moment that the code queries the model class from the models.py file. It is also calling COMMIT automatically when the code calls save() on a new Payment because the code has not asked Django to open an extended database transaction for you.

The fields of the payment form, because the form gets written out as HTML and then pulled back in from the POST parameters, are simply gone. As requested, it has left the debit field unspecified so that the code can fill it in with the current username. But the Django forms library is taking care of everything else for you.

The one awkwardness is that a bit of logic that really belongs in the template—the choice of words and presentation surrounding the display of payments on the main page—has now had to move into the Python code because the Django template system did not make the logic as easy to express. But Python makes the alternative fairly easy for you: the index() view calls a generator that produces a dict of information about each payment, converting the raw object into the values in which the template will be interested.

Some programmers chafe at such an underpowered template system. Others learn how to write Django "template tags" that let them invoke bits of their own logic from deep within a template. Still other developers argue that code like Listing 11-11 is best in the long run anyway because it is easier to write tests for a routine such as make_payment_views() than for logic stranded inside a template.

To run this Django application, check out the Chapter 11 source code from the link given earlier, install Django 1.7 under Python 3, and run these three commands:

```
$ python manage.py syncdb
$ python manage.py loaddata start
$ python manage.py runserver
```

With the last command up and running, you can visit http://localhost:8000/ and see how Django has let you construct much the same application that was built with Flask earlier in this chapter.

Choosing a Web Framework

The web framework landscape is always innovating in a strong and healthy community like the Python programming language. Although it will probably make this book look dated in just a few short years, here is a quick survey of the most popular frameworks in order to give you a flavor for the choices facing a typical developer:

- *Django*: A good framework for the first-time web programmer. Features such as CSRF protection are built in. Its ORM and template language are built in. Not only does this relieve the amateur from having to choose separate libraries of their own, but it means that all third-party Django tools can assume a common set of interfaces for dealing with both HTML and the database. Django is famous for its admin interface—try visiting the /admin page after running Listing 11-11 to see an example of how administrators can interact directly with the database through autogenerated create, edit, and delete forms!

- *Tornado*: A web framework like none of the others listed here because it uses the asynchronous callback pattern from Chapter 9 to allow many dozens or hundreds of client connections to be supported per operating system thread, instead of just one client per thread. It also stands out because it is not tied to supporting WSGI—it has direct support for WebSockets (described in the next section). The cost is that many libraries have difficulty working with its callback pattern, so the programmer has to find async alternatives to the usual ORM or database connector that they would choose.

- *Flask*: The most popular of the microframeworks, built atop solid tools and supporting many modern features (if the programmer knows to look for and take advantage of them). Often combined with SQLAlchemy or a nonrelational database back end.

- *Bottle*: An alternative to Flask that fits in a single file bottle.py instead of requiring several separate packages to be installed. Especially attractive to developers who have not yet worked the pip install tool into their workflow. Its template language is particularly well designed.

- *Pyramid*: A remarkable and high-performance synthesis of the lessons learned by community members in the old Zope and Pylons communities and the go-to framework for developers working in fluid URL spaces like those created when you author a *content management system* (CMS) that lets users create subfolders and additional web pages through a mere click of their mouse. While it can support predefined URL structures as well as any of the previous frameworks, it can go further by supporting object traversal where the framework itself understands that your URL components are naming containers, content, and views that the URL is visiting, in the same way that a filesystem path visits directories before arriving at a file.

You might be tempted to choose a web framework by its reputation—based perhaps on the previous paragraphs, plus a close read of their web sites and what you see on social media sites or Stack Overflow.

But I will suggest an even more important direction: if you have co-workers or friends at your local Python meetup who are already partisans of a framework and can offer you regular help through e-mail or IRC, you might want to choose that framework over a comparable one whose web site or feature list you like a little more. Having the live help of someone who has already been through the typical error messages and misunderstandings can often trump whether a particular feature of the framework is slightly more or less difficult to use.

WebSockets

Web sites powered by JavaScript often want to support live updates of their content. If someone tweets, then Twitter wants to update the page you are looking at without the expense of the browser polling every second to ask whether anything new has appeared. The *Websocket Protocol* (RFC 6455) is the most powerful and turbocharged of the possible solutions to this "long polling problem."

Earlier work-arounds were possible, like the famous genre of Comet techniques. One Comet technique is for the client to make an HTTP request to a path; in response, the server hangs, leaving the socket open, and waits to respond until an actual event (such as a new incoming tweet) finally happens and can be delivered in the response.

Because WSGI supports only traditional HTTP, you will have to move outside the realm of both standard web frameworks and the full slate of WSGI-compatible web servers such as Gunicorn, Apache, and nginx in order to support WebSockets.

The fact that WSGI cannot do WebSockets is one major reason for the popularity of the stand-alone Tornado server-framework.

Whereas HTTP operates lockstep where the client speaks first with a single request and then waits for the server to complete its response before following up with another request, a socket that has switched into WebSockets mode supports messages traveling in either direction at any moment without waiting for each other. The client can send live updates to the server as the user moves around the screen interacting with the web page, while the server is simultaneously sending down updates that are arriving from other sources.

On the wire, a WebSocket conversation starts with what looks like an HTTP request and response but which, in their headers and status code, are negotiating a switch away from HTTP on the socket. Once the switch is complete, a new system of framing data takes over that is detailed in the RFC.

WebSocket programming typically involves heavy coordination between a front-end JavaScript library and the code running on the server, which is not covered in this book. A simple starting point would be the documentation for the `tornado.websocket` module, which includes a snippet of Python and JavaScript code that can talk to each other through a pair of symmetric callbacks. Check out any good reference on asynchronous front-end browser programming for ideas on how you can use such a mechanism to power live updates to web pages.

Web Scraping

The number of programmers who start their web programming careers by trying to scrape a web site is probably much larger than the number who start by writing their own example site. After all, how many beginning programmers have access to great stacks of data waiting to be displayed on the Web compared to the number who can easily think of data already on the Web that they would like to copy?

A first piece of advice about web scraping: avoid it, always, if at all possible!

There are often many ways to get data besides raw scraping. Using such data sources is less expensive not only for you, the programmer, but also for the site itself. The Internet Movie Database will let you download movie data from www.imdb.com/interfaces so that you can run statistics across Hollywood films without forcing the main site to render hundreds of thousands of extra pages, which then forces you to parse them! Many sites such as Google and Yahoo provide APIs for their core services that can help you avoid getting back raw HTML.

If Google searches for the data you want but is not turning up any download or API alternatives, there are a few rules of the road to keep in mind. Search for whether the site you are targeting has a "Terms of Service" page. Also check for a /robots.txt file that will tell you which URLs are designed for downloading by search engines and which should be avoided. This can help you avoid getting several copies of the same article but with different ads, while also helping the site control the load it faces.

Obeying the Terms of Service and robots.txt can also make it less likely that your IP will be blocked for offering an excessive traffic load.

Scraping a web site will, in the most general case, require everything you have learned in Chapter 9, Chapter 10, and this chapter about HTTP and the way that it is used by web browsers.

- The GET and POST methods and how a method, path, and headers combine to form an HTTP request

- The status codes and structure of an HTTP response, including the difference between a success, a redirect, a temporary failure, and a permanent failure

- Basic HTTP authentication—both how it is demanded by a server response and then provided in a client request

- Form-based authentication and how it sets cookies that then need to be present in your subsequent requests for them to be judged authentic

- JavaScript-based authentication, where the login form performs a direct POST back to the web server without letting the browser itself get involved in submitting the form

- The way that hidden form fields, and even new cookies, can be supplied in HTTP responses as you are browsing to protect the site from CSRF attacks

- The difference between a query or action that appends data to the URL and performs a GET for that location versus an action that does a direct POST of data to the server that is carried as the request body instead

- The contrast between POST URLs designed for form-encoded data arriving from the browser and URLs designed for direct interaction with front-end JavaScript code and therefore likely to expect and return data in JSON or another programmer-friendly format

Scraping a complicated site will often require hours of experimentation, tweaking, and long sessions of clicking around in your browser's web developer tools to learn what is going on. Three tabs are essential, and all three should be available in either Firefox or Google Chrome once you have right-clicked a page and selected Inspect Element. The Elements tab (refer to Figure 11-1) shows you the live document, even if JavaScript has been adding and removing things so that you can learn which elements live inside of which other ones. The Network tab (refer to Figure 11-2) lets you hit Reload and see the HTTP request and responses—even those kicked off by JavaScript—that together have delivered a complete page. And the Console lets you see any errors that the page is encountering, including ones that might not be signaled to you as a user.

There are two general flavors of automation that programmers tackle.

The first is where you are casting a wide net because there is a large amount of data you want to download. Aside from the possibility of an initial login step to get the cookies that you need, this kind of task tends to involve repeated GET operations that might fuel even further GETs as you read links from the pages that you are downloading. This pattern is the same pattern undertaken by the "spider" programs that web search engines use to learn the pages that exist on each web site.

The term *spider* for these programs comes from the early days when the term *web* still made people think of spider webs.

The other flavor is when you perform a specific and targeted action at only one or two pages, instead of wanting a whole section of a web site. This might be because you need the data only from a specific page—maybe you want your shell prompt to print the temperature from a specific weather page—or because you are trying to automate an action that would normally require a browser such as actions like paying a customer or listing yesterday's credit card transactions so that you can look for fraud. This often involves far more caution regarding clicks and forms and authentication, and it often requires a full-fledged browser running the show instead of Python by itself because the bank uses in-page JavaScript to discourage automated attempts to gain unauthorized access to accounts.

Remember to check terms-of-service conditions and a site's robots.txt files before even considering unleashing an automated program against it. And expect to be blocked if your program's behavior—even when it gets stuck in edge cases that you did not anticipate—becomes noticeably more demanding than a normal human user clicking through the page that they are stopping to scan or read.

I am not even going to talk about OAuth and other maneuvers that make it even more difficult for programmers to run programs that accomplish what the programmer would otherwise need a browser to do. When unfamiliar maneuvers or protocols seem to be involved, look for as much help from third-party libraries as possible and watch your outgoing headers carefully to try to make them match exactly what you see emitted when you post a form or visit a page successfully with your browser. Even the user-agent field can matter, depending on how opinionated the site is!

Fetching Pages

There are three board approaches to fetching pages from the Web so that you can examine their content in a Python program.

- Making direct GET or POST requests using a Python library. Use the Requests library as your go-to solution, and ask it for a `Session` object so that it can keep up with cookies and do connection pooling for you. An alternative for low-complexity situations is `urllib.request` if you want to stay within the Standard Library.

- There was once a middle ground of tools that could act enough like a primitive web browser that they could find `<form>` elements and help you build an HTTP request using the same rules that a browser would use to deliver the form inputs back to the server. Mechanize was the most famous, but I cannot find that it has been maintained—probably because so many sites are now complicated enough that JavaScript is nearly a requirement for browsing the modern Web.

- You can use a real web browser. You will control Firefox with the Selenium Webdriver library in the examples that follow, but experiments are also ongoing with "headless" tools that would act like browsers without having to bring up a full window. They typically work by creating a WebKit instance that is not connected to a real window. PhantomJS has made this approach popular in the JavaScript community, and `Ghost.py` is one current experiment in bringing the capability to Python.

If you already know which URLs you want to visit, your algorithm can be quite simple. Take the list of URLs, run an HTTP request against each one, and save or examine its content. Things get complicated only if you do not know the list of URLs up front and need to learn them as you go. You will then need to keep up with where you have been so that you do not visit a URL twice and go in loops forever.

Listing 11-12 shows a modest example of a closely targeted scraper. It is designed to log in to the payments application and report on the income the user has earned. Before running it, start up a copy of the payment program in one window.

```
$ python app_improved.py
```

Listing 11-12. Logging In to the Payments System and Adding Up Income

```python
#!/usr/bin/env python3
# Foundations of Python Network Programming, Third Edition
# https://github.com/brandon-rhodes/fopnp/blob/m/py3/chapter11/mscrape.py
# Manual scraping, that navigates to a particular page and grabs data.

import argparse, bs4, lxml.html, requests
from selenium import webdriver
from urllib.parse import urljoin

ROW = '{:>12}  {}'

def download_page_with_requests(base):
    session = requests.Session()
    response = session.post(urljoin(base, '/login'),
                            {'username': 'brandon', 'password': 'atigdng'})
    assert response.url == urljoin(base, '/')
    return response.text

def download_page_with_selenium(base):
    browser = webdriver.Firefox()
    browser.get(base)
    assert browser.current_url == urljoin(base, '/login')
    css = browser.find_element_by_css_selector
    css('input[name="username"]').send_keys('brandon')
    css('input[name="password"]').send_keys('atigdng')
    css('input[name="password"]').submit()
    assert browser.current_url == urljoin(base, '/')
    return browser.page_source

def scrape_with_soup(text):
    soup = bs4.BeautifulSoup(text)
    total = 0
    for li in soup.find_all('li', 'to'):
        dollars = int(li.get_text().split()[0].lstrip('$'))
        memo = li.find('i').get_text()
        total += dollars
        print(ROW.format(dollars, memo))
    print(ROW.format('-' * 8, '-' * 30))
    print(ROW.format(total, 'Total payments made'))
```

```
def scrape_with_lxml(text):
    root = lxml.html.document_fromstring(text)
    total = 0
    for li in root.cssselect('li.to'):
        dollars = int(li.text_content().split()[0].lstrip('$'))
        memo = li.cssselect('i')[0].text_content()
        total += dollars
        print(ROW.format(dollars, memo))
    print(ROW.format('-' * 8, '-' * 30))
    print(ROW.format(total, 'Total payments made'))

def main():
    parser = argparse.ArgumentParser(description='Scrape our payments site.')
    parser.add_argument('url', help='the URL at which to begin')
    parser.add_argument('-l', action='store_true', help='scrape using lxml')
    parser.add_argument('-s', action='store_true', help='get with selenium')
    args = parser.parse_args()
    if args.s:
        text = download_page_with_selenium(args.url)
    else:
        text = download_page_with_requests(args.url)
    if args.l:
        scrape_with_lxml(text)
    else:
        scrape_with_soup(text)

if __name__ == '__main__':
    main()
```

Once this Flask application is running on port 5000, you are ready to kick off mscrape.py in another terminal window. Install the Beautiful Soup third-party library first, if it is not available on your system, and you will also need Requests.

```
$ pip install beautifulsoup4
$ pip install requests
$ python mscrape.py http://127.0.0.1:5000/
       125  Registration for PyCon
       200  Payment for writing that code
    --------  ------------------------------
       325  Total payments made
```

Running in its default mode like this, mscrape.py first uses the Requests library to log in to the site using the login form. This is what will provide the Session object with the cookie that it needs then to fetch the front page successfully. The script then parses the page, fetches the list-item elements marked with the class to, and adds up those outgoing payments as it displays them with a few print() calls.

By providing the -s option, you can switch mscrape.py so that it does something rather more exciting: running a full version of Firefox, if it finds it installed on your system, to visit the web site instead! You will need the Selenium package installed for this mode to work.

```
$ pip install selenium
$ python mscrape.py -s http://127.0.0.1:5000/
        125   Registration for PyCon
        200   Payment for writing that code
     --------  -----------------------------
        325   Total payments made
```

You can press Ctrl+W to dismiss Firefox once the script has printed its output. While you can write Selenium scripts so that they close Firefox automatically, I prefer to leave it open when writing and debugging so that I can see what went wrong in the browser if the program hits an error.

The difference between these two approaches deserves to be stressed. To write the code that uses Requests, you need to open the site yourself, study the login form, and copy the information you find there into the data that the post() method uses to log in. Once you have done so, your code has no way to know whether the login form changes in the future or not. It will simply keep using the hard-coded input names 'username' and 'password' whether they are still relevant or not.

So, the Requests approach is, at least when written this way, really nothing like a browser. It is at no point opening the login page and seeing a form there. It is, rather, assuming the existence of the login page and doing an end-run around it to POST the form that is its result. Obviously, this approach will break if the login form is ever given, say, a secret token to prevent mass attempts to guess user passwords. In that case, you would need to add a first GET of the /login page itself to grab the secret token that would need to be combined with your username and password to make a valid POST.

The Selenium-based code in mscape.py takes the opposite approach. Like a user sitting down at the browser, it acts as though it simply sees a form and selects its elements and starts typing. Then it reaches over and clicks the button to submit the form. As long as its CSS selectors continue to identify the form fields correctly, the code will succeed in logging in regardless of any secret tokens or special JavaScript code to sign or automate the form post because Selenium is simply doing in Firefox exactly what you would do to log on.

Selenium is, of course, much slower than Requests, especially when you first kick it off and have to wait for Firefox to start. But it can quickly perform actions that might otherwise take you hours of experimentation to get working in Python. An interesting approach to a difficult scraping job can be a hybrid approach: could you use Selenium to log in and gain the necessary cookies and then tell Requests about them so that your mass fetch of further pages does not need to wait on the browser?

Scraping Pages

When a site returns data in CSV, JSON, or some other recognized data format, you will of course use the corresponding module in the Standard Library or a third-party library to get it parsed so that you can process it. But what if the information you need is hidden in user-facing HTML?

Reading raw HTML after pressing Ctrl+U in Google Chrome or Firefox can be quite wearisome, depending on how the site has chosen to format it. It is often more pleasant to right-click, select Inspect Element, and then happily browse the collapsible document tree of elements that the browser sees—assuming that the HTML is properly formatted and that a mistake in the markup has not hidden the data you need from the browser! The problem with the live element inspector, as you have already seen, is that by the time you see the document, any JavaScript programs that run in the web page might already have edited it out of all recognition.

There are at least two easy tricks to looking at such pages. The first is to turn JavaScript off in your browser and click Reload for the page you are reading. It should now re-appear in the element inspector but without any changes being made: you should see exactly what your Python code will see when it downloads the same document.

The other trick is to use some kind of "tidy" program, like that distributed by the W3C and available as the `tidy` package on Debian and Ubuntu. It turns out that both of the parsing libraries that were used in Listing 11-12 have such routines built in. Once the `soup` object exists, you can display its elements to the screen with helpful indentation with the following:

```
print(soup.prettify())
```

An lxml document tree requires a little more work to display.

```
from lxml import etree
print(etree.tostring(root, pretty_print=True).decode('ascii'))
```

Either way, the result is likely to be far easier to read than the raw HTML if the site that is delivering it is not putting elements on separate lines and indenting them to make their document structure clear—steps that, of course, can be inconvenient and would increase the bandwidth needs of any site serving HTML.

Examining HTML involves the following three steps:

1. Ask your library of choice to parse the HTML. This can be difficult for the library because much HTML on the Web contains errors and broken markup. But designers often never notice this because browsers always try to recover and understand the markup anyway. After all, what browser vendor would want their browser to be the only one that returns an error for some popular web site when all of the other browsers display it just fine? Both of the libraries used in Listing 11-12 have a reputation for being robust HTML parsers.

2. Dive into the document using *selectors*, which are text patterns that will automatically find the elements you want. While you can instead make the dive yourself, slowly iterating over each element's children and looking for the tags and attributes that interest you, it is generally much faster to use selectors. They also usually result in cleaner Python code that is easier to read.

3. Ask each element object for the text and attribute values you need. You are then back in the world of normal Python strings and can use all of the normal string methods to postprocess the data.

This three-stage process is enacted twice in Listing 11-12 using two separate libraries.

The `scrape_with_soup()` function uses the venerable BeautifulSoup library that is a go-to resource for programmers the world over. Its API is quirky and unique because it was the first library to make document parsing so convenient in Python, but it does get the job done.

All "soup" objects, whether the one representing the whole document or a subordinate one that represents a single element, offer a `find_all()` method that will search for subordinate elements that match a given tag name and, optionally, HTML class name. The `get_text()` method can be used when you finally reach the bottom element you want and are ready to read its content. With these two methods alone, the code is able to get data from this simple web site, and even complicated web sites can often be scraped with only a half-dozen or a dozen separate steps.

The full BeautifulSoup documentation is available online at `www.crummy.com/software/BeautifulSoup/`.

The `scrape_with_lxml()` function instead uses the modern and fast lxml library that is built atop libxml2 and libxslt. It can be difficult to install if you are on a legacy operating system that does not come with compilers installed—or if you have not installed the `python-dev` or `python-devel` package with which your operating system might support compiled Python packages. Debian-derived operating systems will already have the library compiled against the system Python as a package, often simply named python-lxml.

A modern Python distribution such as Anaconda will have lxml already compiled and ready to install, even on Mac OS X and Windows: `http://continuum.io/downloads`.

If you are able to get it installed, Listing 11-12 can use the library to parse the HTML instead.

```
$ pip install lxml
$ python mscrape.py -l http://127.0.0.1:5000/
        125  Registration for PyCon
        200  Payment for writing that code
        --------  -----------------------------
        325  Total payments made
```

Again, the same basic steps are in operation as with BeautifulSoup. You start at the top of the document, use a find or search method—in this case `cssselect()`—to zero in on the elements that interest you, and then use further searches either to grab subordinate elements or, in the end, to ask elements for the text that they contain so that you can parse and display it.

lxml is not only faster than BeautifulSoup, but it also presents many options for how you can select elements.

- It supports CSS patterns with `cssselect()`. This is especially important when looking for elements by class because an element is considered to be in the class x whether its class attribute is written as `class="x"` or `class="x y"` or `class="w x"`.

- It supports XPath expressions with its `xpath()` method, beloved by XML aficionados. They look like `'.//p'` to find all paragraphs, for example. One fun aspect of an XPath expression is that you can end it with `'.../text()'` and simply get back the text inside each element, instead of getting back Python objects, of which you then have to request the text inside of them.

- It natively supports a fast subset of XPath operations through its `find()` and `findall()` methods.

Note that, in both of these cases, the scraper had to do a bit of work because the payment description field is its own `<i>` element but the dollar amount at the beginning of each line was not placed inside its own element by the site designer. This is a quite typical problem; some things that you want from a page will be sitting conveniently in an element by themselves, while others will be in the middle of other text and will need you to use traditional Python string methods such as `split()` and `strip()` to rescue them from their context.

Recursive Scraping

The source code repository for this book includes a small static web site that makes it deliberately difficult for a web scraper to reach all of its pages. You can view it online here:

```
https://github.com/brandon-rhodes/fopnp/tree/m/py3/chapter11/tinysite/
```

If you have checked out the source code repository, you can serve it on your own machine by using Python's built-in web server.

```
$ cd py3/chapter11/tinysite
$ python -m http.server
Serving HTTP on 0.0.0.0 port 8000 ...
```

If you view the page source and then look around using the web debugging tools of your browser, you will see that not all of the links on the front page at http://127.0.0.1:8000/ are delivered at the same moment. Only two, in fact ("page1" and "page2") are present in the raw HTML of the page as real anchor tags with `href=""` attributes.

The next two pages are behind a form with a Search submit button, and they will not be accessible unless the button is clicked.

The two final links ("page5" and "page6") appear at the bottom of the screen as the result of a short snippet of dynamic JavaScript code. This simulates the behavior of web sites that show you the skeleton of a page quickly but then do another round-trip to the server before the data in which you are interested appears.

At this point—where you want to do a full-fledged recursive search of all of the URLs on a web site or even just within part of it—you might want to go looking for a web-scraping engine that could help you. In the same way that web frameworks factor common patterns out of web applications, like needing to return 404 for nonexistent pages, scraping frameworks know all about keeping up with pages that have been visited already and which ones still need to be visited.

The most popular web scraper at the moment is Scrapy (http://scrapy.org/) whose documentation you can study if you want to try describing a scraping task in a way that will fit into its model.

In Listing 11-13 you can look behind the scenes to see what a real—if simple—scraper looks like underneath. This one requires lxml, so install that third-party library, as described in the previous section, if you can.

Listing 11-13. Simple Recursive Web Scraper That Does GET

```python
#!/usr/bin/env python3
# Foundations of Python Network Programming, Third Edition
# https://github.com/brandon-rhodes/fopnp/blob/m/py3/chapter11/rscrape1.py
# Recursive scraper built using the Requests library.

import argparse, requests
from urllib.parse import urljoin, urlsplit
from lxml import etree

def GET(url):
    response = requests.get(url)
    if response.headers.get('Content-Type', '').split(';')[0] != 'text/html':
        return
    text = response.text
    try:
        html = etree.HTML(text)
    except Exception as e:
        print('    {}: {}'.format(e.__class__.__name__, e))
        return
    links = html.findall('.//a[@href]')
    for link in links:
        yield GET, urljoin(url, link.attrib['href'])

def scrape(start, url_filter):
    further_work = {start}
    already_seen = {start}
    while further_work:
        call_tuple = further_work.pop()
        function, url, *etc = call_tuple
        print(function.__name__, url, *etc)
        for call_tuple in function(url, *etc):
            if call_tuple in already_seen:
                continue
            already_seen.add(call_tuple)
            function, url, *etc = call_tuple
            if not url_filter(url):
                continue
            further_work.add(call_tuple)
```

```
def main(GET):
    parser = argparse.ArgumentParser(description='Scrape a simple site.')
    parser.add_argument('url', help='the URL at which to begin')
    start_url = parser.parse_args().url
    starting_netloc = urlsplit(start_url).netloc
    url_filter = (lambda url: urlsplit(url).netloc == starting_netloc)
    scrape((GET, start_url), url_filter)

if __name__ == '__main__':
    main(GET)
```

Beyond the task of starting up and reading its command-line arguments, Listing 11-13 has only two moving parts. The simplest is its GET() function, which attempts to download a URL and attempts to parse it if its type is HTML; only if those steps succeed does it pull the href="" attributes of all the anchor tags (<a>) to learn the additional pages to which the current page has links. Because any of these links might be relative URLs, it calls urljoin() on every one of them to supply any base components that they might lack.

For each URL that the GET() function discovers in the text of the page, it returns a tuple stating that it would like the scraping engine to call itself on the URL it has discovered, unless the engine knows that it has done so already.

The engine itself merely needs to keep up with which combinations of functions and URLs it has already invoked so that a URL that appears again and again on the web site gets visited only once. It keeps a set of URLs it has seen before and another of URLs that have not yet been visited, and it continues looping until the latter set is finally empty.

You can run this scraper against a big public web site, like httpbin.

```
$ python rscrape1.py http://httpbin.org/
```

Or you can run it against the small static site whose web server you started up a few paragraphs ago—and, alas, this scraper will find only the two links that appear literally in the HTML as first delivered by the HTTP response.

```
$ python rscrape1.py http://127.0.0.1:8000/
GET http://127.0.0.1:8000/
GET http://127.0.0.1:8000/page1.html
GET http://127.0.0.1:8000/page2.html
```

Two ingredients are needed if the scraper is to see more.

First, you will need to load the HTML in a real browser so that the JavaScript can run and load the rest of the page.

Second, you will need to have a second operation besides GET() that takes a deep breath and clicks the Search button to see what lies behind it.

This is the sort of operation that should never, under any circumstances, be part of an automated scraper designed to pull general content from a public web site because, as you have learned at length by this point, form submission is expressly designed for user actions, especially if backed by a POST operation. (In this case, the form does a GET and is thus at least a little safer.) However, in this case, you have studied this small site and have concluded that clicking the button should be safe.

Note that Listing 11-14 can simply reuse the engine from the previous scraper because the engine was not tightly coupled to any particular opinion of what functions it should call. It will call any functions that are submitted to it as work.

Listing 11-14. Recursively Scraping a Web Site with Selenium

```
#!/usr/bin/env python3
# Foundations of Python Network Programming, Third Edition
# https://github.com/brandon-rhodes/fopnp/blob/m/py3/chapter11/rscrape2.py
# Recursive scraper built using the Selenium Webdriver.

from urllib.parse import urljoin
from rscrape1 import main
from selenium import webdriver

class WebdriverVisitor:
    def __init__(self):
        self.browser = webdriver.Firefox()

    def GET(self, url):
        self.browser.get(url)
        yield from self.parse()
        if self.browser.find_elements_by_xpath('.//form'):
            yield self.submit_form, url

    def parse(self):
        # (Could also parse page.source with lxml yourself, as in scraper1.py)
        url = self.browser.current_url
        links = self.browser.find_elements_by_xpath('.//a[@href]')
        for link in links:
            yield self.GET, urljoin(url, link.get_attribute('href'))

    def submit_form(self, url):
        self.browser.get(url)
        self.browser.find_element_by_xpath('.//form').submit()
        yield from self.parse()

if __name__ == '__main__':
    main(WebdriverVisitor().GET)
```

Because Selenium instances are expensive to create—they have to start up a copy of Firefox, after all—you dare not call the Firefox() method every time you need to fetch a URL. Instead, the GET() routine is written as a method here, instead of a bare function, so that the browser attribute can survive from one GET() call to the next and also be available when you are ready to call submit_form().

The submit_form() method is where this listing really diverges from the previous one. When the GET() method sees the search form sitting on the page, it sends an additional tuple back to the engine. In addition to yielding one tuple for every link that it sees on a page, it will yield a tuple that will load the page up and click the big Search button. That is what lets this scraper reach deeper into this site than the previous one.

```
$ python rscrape2.py http://127.0.0.1:8000/
GET http://127.0.0.1:8000/
GET http://127.0.0.1:8000/page1.html
GET http://127.0.0.1:8000/page2.html
submit_form http://127.0.0.1:8000/
GET http://127.0.0.1:8000/page5.html
GET http://127.0.0.1:8000/page6.html
GET http://127.0.0.1:8000/page4.html
GET http://127.0.0.1:8000/page3.html
```

The scraper is thus able to find every single page on the site despite that some links are loaded dynamically through JavaScript and others are reached only through a form post. Through powerful techniques like this, you should find that your interactions with any web site could be automated through Python.

Summary

HTTP was designed to deliver the World Wide Web: a collection of documents interconnected with hyperlinks that each name the URL of a further page, or section of a page, that can be visited simply by clicking the text of the hyperlink. The Python Standard Library has helpful routines for parsing and building URLs and for turning partial "relative URLs" into absolute URLs by filling in any incomplete components with information from the base URL of the page where they appeared.

Web applications typically connect some persistent data store, like a database, with code that responds to incoming HTTP requests and builds HTML pages in response. It is crucial to let the database do its own quoting when you try to insert untrusted information from out on the Web, and both the DB-API 2.0 and any ORM you might use in Python will be careful to do this quoting correctly.

Web frameworks range from simple to full stack. With a simple framework, you will make your own choice of both a template language and an ORM or other persistence layer. A full-stack framework will instead offer its own versions of these tools. In either case, some means of connecting URLs to your own code will be available that supports both static URLs and also URLs such as /person/123/ that have path components that can vary. Quick ways to render and return templates, as well as to return redirects or HTTP errors, will also be provided.

The vast danger that faces every site author is that the many ways that components interact in a complicated system like the Web can allow users either to subvert your own intentions or each other's. The possibility of cross-site scripting attacks, cross-site request forgery, and attacks on your user's privacy must all be kept in mind at the interface between the outside world and your own code. These dangers should be thoroughly understood before you ever write code that accepts data from a URL path, a URL query string, or a POST or file upload.

The trade-off between frameworks is often the choice between a full-stack solution like Django, which encourages you to stay within its tool set but tends to choose good defaults for you (such as having CSRF protection turned on automatically in your forms), or a solution such as Flask or Bottle, which feels sleeker and lighter and lets you assemble your own solution, but that requires you to know up front all of the pieces you need. If you write an app in Flask simply not knowing that you need CSRF protection, you will go without it.

The Tornado framework stands out for its async approach that allows many clients to be served from a single operating-system-level thread of control. With the emergence of asyncio in Python 3, approaches like Tornado can be expected to move toward a common set of idioms like those that WSGI already provides for threaded web frameworks today.

Turning around and scraping a web page involves a thorough knowledge of how web sites normally work so that what would normally be user interactions can instead be scripted—including such complexities as logging on or filling out and submitting a form. Several approaches are available in Python both for fetching pages and for parsing them. Requests or Selenium for fetching and BeautifulSoup or lxml for parsing are among the favorites at this point.

And thus with a study of web application writing and scraping, this book completes its coverage of HTTP and the World Wide Web. The next chapter begins a tour of several less well-known protocols supported in the Python Standard Library by turning to the subject of e-mail messages and how they are formatted.

CHAPTER 12

Building and Parsing E-Mail

This is the first of four chapters on the important topic of e-mail. This particular chapter does not discuss network communication. Instead, it sets the stage for the next three:

- This chapter describes how e-mail messages are formatted, with a particular focus on the correct inclusion of multimedia and internationalization. This establishes the payload format for the protocols outlined in the subsequent three chapters.

- Chapter 13 explains the Simple Mail Transport Protocol (SMTP), which is used to transport e-mail messages from the machine on which they are composed to the server that holds the message, making them ready for reading by a particular recipient.

- Chapter 14 describes the old, poorly designed Post Office Protocol (POP) by which someone who is ready to read their e-mail can download and view new messages that are waiting in their in box on their e-mail server.

- Chapter 15 covers the Internet Message Access Protocol (IMAP), which is a better and more modern option for locally viewing e-mail that is being hosted for you on your e-mail server. Not only does IMAP support fetching and viewing, but it also lets you mark messages as read and store them in different folders on the server itself.

These four chapters, as you can see, are in an order that suggests the natural lifespan of an e-mail. First, an e-mail is composed from various pieces of text, multimedia, and metadata, such as its sender and recipient. Then SMTP carries it from its place of origin to its destination server. Finally, a protocol like POP or IMAP is used by the recipient's e-mail client—commonly Mozilla Thunderbird or Microsoft Outlook—to pull a copy of the message to their desktop, laptop, or tablet for viewing. Be aware, however, that this last step is becoming less common: many people today read their e-mail through *webmail* services, which allow them to log on with a web browser and view their e-mails rendered as HTML without the e-mails ever leaving the e-mail server. Hotmail was once very popular, while Gmail is perhaps the largest such service today.

Remember, whatever happens to an e-mail later—whether you use SMTP, POP, or IMAP—the rules about how e-mail is formatted and represented are exactly the same. Those rules are the subject of this chapter.

E-Mail Message Format

The famous RFC 822 of 1982 reigned for almost 20 years as the definition of e-mail until finally requiring an update. This update was provided by RFC 2822 in 2001 before being itself superseded in 2008 with the issuing of RFC 5322. You will want to refer to these standards when you are tasked with writing very serious or high-profile code for dealing with e-mail messages. For the purposes here, only a few facts about e-mail formatting need immediate attention.

- E-mail is represented as plain ASCII text, using character codes 1 through 127.

- The end-of-line marker is the two-character sequence carriage-return-plus-linefeed (CRLF), which is the same pair of codes used to advance to the next line on an old teletype machine and that is still the standard line-ending sequence in Internet protocols today.

- An e-mail consists of headers, a blank line, and then the body.

- Each header is formatted as a case-insensitive name, a colon, and a value, which can stretch to several lines if the second and subsequent lines of the header are indented with whitespace.

- Because neither Unicode characters nor binary payloads are allowed in plain text, other standards, which I will explain later in this chapter, provide encodings by which richer information can be mixed down to plain ASCII text for transmission and storage.

You can read an actual e-mail message, as it arrived in my in box, in Listing 12-1.

Listing 12-1. Real-World E-Mail Message After Delivery Is Complete

```
X-From-Line: rms@gnu.org  Fri Dec  3 04:00:59 1999
Return-Path: <rms@gnu.org>
Delivered-To: brandon@europa.gtri.gatech.edu
Received: from pele.santafe.edu (pele.santafe.edu [192.12.12.119])
        by europa.gtri.gatech.edu (Postfix) with ESMTP id 6C4774809
        for <brandon@rhodesmill.org>; Fri,  3 Dec 1999 04:00:58 -0500 (EST)
Received: from aztec.santafe.edu (aztec [192.12.12.49])
        by pele.santafe.edu (8.9.1/8.9.1) with ESMTP id CAA27250
        for <brandon@rhodesmill.org>; Fri, 3 Dec 1999 02:00:57 -0700 (MST)
Received: (from rms@localhost)
        by aztec.santafe.edu (8.9.1b+Sun/8.9.1) id CAA29939;
        Fri, 3 Dec 1999 02:00:56 -0700 (MST)
Date: Fri, 3 Dec 1999 02:00:56 -0700 (MST)
Message-Id: <199912030900.CAA29939@aztec.santafe.edu>
X-Authentication-Warning: aztec.santafe.edu: rms set sender to rms@gnu.org using -f
From: Richard Stallman <rms@gnu.org>
To: brandon@rhodesmill.org
In-reply-to: <m3k8my7x1k.fsf@europa.gtri.gatech.edu> (message from Brandon
        Craig Rhodes on 02 Dec 1999 00:04:55 -0500)
Subject: Re: Please proofread this license
Reply-To: rms@gnu.org
References: <199911280547.WAA21685@aztec.santafe.edu> <m3k8my7x1k.fsf@europa.gtri.gatech.edu>
Xref: 38-74.clients.speedfactory.net scrapbook:11
Lines: 1

Thanks.
```

Even though only one line of text body was actually delivered with this message, you can see that it accumulated quite a bit of additional information during its transmission over the Internet.

Although all of the headers from the From line down might well have been present when the e-mail was composed, many of the headers above it were probably added at various stages in its transmission history. Each client and server that handles an e-mail message reserves the right to add additional headers. This means that each e-mail message accumulates a personal history as it wings its way across the network, which can typically be read by starting with the last headers and reading upward until you get to the first.

In this case, the e-mail seems to have originated in Santa Fe on a machine named aztec, where its author was connected directly over the local host internal interface. The aztec machine then used SMTP to forward the message to pele, which probably performed e-mail transmission either for a department or for the entire campus. Finally, pele made an SMTP connection to the europa machine on my desk at Georgia Tech, which wrote the message to disk so that I could read it later.

I will pause to introduce a few specific e-mail headers at this point; see the standards for a complete list.

- *From* names the author of the e-mail message. Like the headers that follow, it supports both an actual name as well as that person's e-mail address inside angle brackets.

- *Reply-to* specifies where replies should be destined, if not to the author listed in the *From* header.

- *To* is a list of one or more primary recipients.

- *Cc* lists one or more recipients who should receive "carbon copies" of the e-mail, but who are not directly addressed by the communication.

- *Bcc* lists recipients who should be given secret carbon copies of the e-mail but without any of the other recipients knowing this. Careful e-mail clients therefore strip *Bcc* off before actually transmitting an e-mail.

- *Subject* is a human-readable summary of the message contents written by the message author.

- *Date* specifies when the message was sent or received. Typically, if the sender's e-mail client includes a date, then the receiving e-mail server and reader will not overwrite it. But if the sender does not include a date, then it might be added later for completeness when the e-mail is received.

- *Message-Id* is a unique string for identifying the e-mail.

- *In-Reply-To* are the unique Message-Id's of the previous messages to which this message is a reply. These can be very useful if you are asked to build a threaded display that places reply messages beneath the e-mails to which they are replies.

- *Received* is added each time the e-mail arrives at another "hop" on its way across the Internet via SMTP. E-mail server administrators often pore through these tree rings in order to determine why a message was or was not delivered correctly.

You can see that the plain-text limitation on e-mail has repercussions for both the headers and the body: both of them are limited to being ASCII in a simple example like this. In the sections that follow, I will explain both the standards that govern how a header can include international characters and the standards that set how the e-mail body can include international or binary data.

Building an E-Mail Message

The primary interface in Python for building e-mail messages is the EmailMessage class, which will be used in every program listing in this chapter. It is the result of hard work by Python email module guru R. David Murray, whom I want to thank for his guidance and advice as I put together the scripts in this chapter. The simplest example is shown in Listing 12-2.

Listing 12-2. Generating a Simple Text E-Mail Message

```
#!/usr/bin/env python3
# Foundations of Python Network Programming, Third Edition
# https://github.com/brandon-rhodes/fopnp/blob/m/py3/chapter12/build_basic_email.py

import email.message, email.policy, email.utils, sys
```

```
text = """Hello,
This is a basic message from Chapter 12.
 - Anonymous"""

def main():
    message = email.message.EmailMessage(email.policy.SMTP)
    message['To'] = 'recipient@example.com'
    message['From'] = 'Test Sender <sender@example.com>'
    message['Subject'] = 'Test Message, Chapter 12'
    message['Date'] = email.utils.formatdate(localtime=True)
    message['Message-ID'] = email.utils.make_msgid()
    message.set_content(text)
    sys.stdout.buffer.write(message.as_bytes())

if __name__ == '__main__':
    main()
```

▨ **Caution**   The code in this chapter specifically targets Python 3.4 and later, the version of Python that introduced the `EmailMessage` class to the old e-mail module. If you need to target older versions of Python 3 and cannot upgrade, study the older scripts at `https://github.com/brandon-rhodes/fopnp/tree/m/py3/old-chapter12`.

You can generate even simpler e-mail messages by omitting the headers shown here, but this is the minimal set that you should generally consider on the modern Internet.

The API of `EmailMessage` lets your code reflect the text of your e-mail message very closely. Although you are free to set headers and provide the content in any order that makes the best sense of your code, setting the headers first and then setting the body last provides a pleasing symmetry with the way the message will appear both on the wire and also when viewed in an e-mail client.

Note that I am setting two headers here that you should always include, but whose values will not be set for you automatically. I am providing the Date in the special format required by the e-mail standards by taking advantage of the `formatdate()` function that is already built in to the standard set of e-mail utilities in Python. The Message-Id is also carefully constructed from random information to make it (hopefully) unique among all of the e-mail messages that have ever been written in the past or that will ever be written in the future.

The resulting script simply prints the e-mail on its standard output, which makes it very easy to experiment with and immediately shows the results of any edits or modifications you made.

```
To: recipient@example.com
From: Test Sender <sender@example.com>
Subject: Test Message, Chapter 12
Date: Fri, 28 Mar 2014 16:54:17 -0400
Message-ID: <20140328205417.5927.96806@guinness>
Content-Type: text/plain; charset="utf-8"
Content-Transfer-Encoding: 7bit
MIME-Version: 1.0

Hello,
This is a basic message from Chapter 12.
 - Anonymous
```

If you were to build an e-mail message using the old `Message` class instead of `EmailMessage`, you would see that several of these headers would be missing. Instead of specifying a transfer encoding, Multipurpose Internet Mail Extensions (MIME) version, and content type, old-fashioned e-mail messages like the one in Listing 12-1 simply omit these headers and trust that e-mail clients will assume the traditional defaults. But the modern `EmailMessage` builder is more careful to specify explicit values to ensure the highest level of interoperability possible with modern tools.

Header names, as stated before, are case insensitive. So conforming e-mail clients will make no distinction between the meaning of `Message-Id` in Listing 12-1 and `Message-ID` (with a capital D instead) in the generated e-mail.

You can give the `formatdate()` function a specific Python `datetime` to display if you do not want it to use the current date and time, and you can also choose to have it use Greenwich Mean Time (GMT) instead of the local time zone. See Python's documentation for details.

Be warned that the unique `Message-ID` is constructed from several pieces of information that you might not want disclosed if you are in a very high-security situation: the exact time and date and millisecond of your call to `make_msgid()`, the process ID of this invocation of your Python script, and even your current hostname if you fail to provide an alternative with the optional `domain=` keyword. Implement an alternative unique-id solution (perhaps calling upon an industrial-strength universally unique identifier [UUID] algorithm) if you want to avoid disclosing any of these pieces of information.

Finally, note that even though the text is not officially in conformance with transmission as an email—the triple-quoted string constant has no terminal line ending in order to save vertical space in the script—the combination of `set_content()` and `as_bytes()` ensured that the e-mail message was properly terminated with a newline.

Adding HTML and Multimedia

Many ad-hoc mechanisms were invented in the early days to carry binary data across the 7-bit ASCII world of e-mail, but it was the MIME standard that established an interoperable and extensible mechanism for non-ASCII payloads. MIME allows the Content-Type e-mail header to specify a *boundary* string that splits the e-mail into smaller message *parts* whenever it appears on a line with two hyphens in front of it. Each part can have its own headers and therefore its own content type and encoding. If a part goes so far as to specify its own boundary string, then parts can even be made up of further subparts, creating a hierarchy.

The Python `email` module does provide low-level support for building a MIME message out of whatever parts and subparts you wish. Simply build several `email.message.MIMEPart` objects—each one can be given headers and a body, using the same interface as an `EmailMessage`—then `attach()` them to their parent part or message:

```
my_message.attach(part1)
my_message.attach(part2)
...
```

However, you should only resort to manual assembly if you are working to reproduce some particular message structure exactly, which is demanded by your application or project specifications. In most situations, you can simply create an `EmailMessage` (as in Listing 12-2) and call, in order, the following four methods to build your result:

- `set_content()` should be called first to install the main message body.

- `add_related()` can then be called zero or more times to supplement the main content with other resources it will need to render. Most often, you will use this when your main content is HTML and needs images, CSS style sheets, and JavaScript files to render correctly in an e-mail client that supports rich content. Each related resource should have a Content-Id (`cid`) by which the main HTML document can reference it in hyperlinks.

- add_alternative() can then be called zero or more times to provide other renderings of your e-mail message. If the body is HTML, for example, you might provide a plain-text alternative rendering for less-capable e-mail clients.

- add_attachment() can be called zero or more times to supply any attachments like PDF documents, images, or spreadsheets that should accompany the message. Each attachment traditionally specifies a default file name for use if the recipient asks their e-mail client to save the attachment.

Looking back, you can see that Listing 12-2 followed the above procedure exactly—it called set_content() as its first step, then simply elected to call each of the other three methods zero times. The result was the simplest possible e-mail structure, presenting a unified body with no subparts.

But how does e-mail look when things get more complicated? Listing 12-3 has been designed to give the answer.

Listing 12-3. Building a MIME-Powered E-Mail with HTML, an Inline Image, and Attachments

```
#!/usr/bin/env python3
# Foundations of Python Network Programming, Third Edition
# https://github.com/brandon-rhodes/fopnp/blob/m/py3/chapter12/build_mime_email.py

import argparse, email.message, email.policy, email.utils, mimetypes, sys

plain = """Hello,
This is a MIME message from Chapter 12.
- Anonymous"""

html = """<p>Hello,</p>
<p>This is a <b>test message</b> from Chapter 12.</p>
<p>- <i>Anonymous</i></p>"""

img = """<p>This is the smallest possible blue GIF:</p>
<img src="cid:{}" height="80" width="80">"""

# Tiny example GIF from http://www.perlmonks.org/?node_id=7974
blue_dot = (b'GIF89a1010\x900000\xff000,000010100\x02\x02\x0410;'
            .replace(b'0', b'\x00').replace(b'1', b'\x01'))

def main(args):
    message = email.message.EmailMessage(email.policy.SMTP)
    message['To'] = 'Test Recipient <recipient@example.com>'
    message['From'] = 'Test Sender <sender@example.com>'
    message['Subject'] = 'Foundations of Python Network Programming'
    message['Date'] = email.utils.formatdate(localtime=True)
    message['Message-ID'] = email.utils.make_msgid()

    if not args.i:
        message.set_content(html, subtype='html')
        message.add_alternative(plain)
    else:
        cid = email.utils.make_msgid()  # RFC 2392: must be globally unique!
        message.set_content(html + img.format(cid.strip('<>')), subtype='html')
```

```
        message.add_related(blue_dot, 'image', 'gif', cid=cid,
                            filename='blue-dot.gif')
        message.add_alternative(plain)

    for filename in args.filename:
        mime_type, encoding = mimetypes.guess_type(filename)
        if encoding or (mime_type is None):
            mime_type = 'application/octet-stream'
        main, sub = mime_type.split('/')
        if main == 'text':
            with open(filename, encoding='utf-8') as f:
                text = f.read()
            message.add_attachment(text, sub, filename=filename)
        else:
            with open(filename, 'rb') as f:
                data = f.read()
            message.add_attachment(data, main, sub, filename=filename)

    sys.stdout.buffer.write(message.as_bytes())

if __name__ == '__main__':
    parser = argparse.ArgumentParser(description='Build, print a MIME email')
    parser.add_argument('-i', action='store_true', help='Include GIF image')
    parser.add_argument('filename', nargs='*', help='Attachment filename')
    main(parser.parse_args())
```

There are four different ways you can call the script in Listing 12-3. In order of increasing complexity, they are:

- `python3 build_mime_email.py`

- `python3 build_mime_email.py attachment.txt attachment.gz`

- `python3 build_mime_email.py -i`

- `python3 build_mime_email.py -i attachment.txt attachment.gz`

To save space, I will only display the output of the first and last of these four command lines here, but you should download build_mime_email.py yourself and try out the others if you want to see how the MIME standard supports gradually increasing levels of complexity depending on the needs of the caller. Although two sample files—attachment.txt (plain text) and attachment.gz (binary)—are included in the book's source repository next to the script, feel free to list any attachments on the command line that you wish. Doing so will let you see how different binary payloads get encoded by the Python email module.

Calling build_mime_email.py without any options or attachments produces the simplest-possible MIME structure for providing two alternative versions of an e-mail: HTML and plain text. The results of this are shown here.

```
To: Test Recipient <recipient@example.com>
From: Test Sender <sender@example.com>
Subject: Foundations of Python Network Programming
Date: Tue, 25 Mar 2014 17:14:01 -0400
Message-ID: <20140325232008.15748.50494@guinness>
MIME-Version: 1.0
Content-Type: multipart/alternative; boundary="===============1627694678=="

--===============1627694678==
Content-Type: text/html; charset="utf-8"
Content-Transfer-Encoding: 7bit

<p>Hello,</p>
<p>This is a <b>test message</b> from Chapter 12.</p>
<p>- <i>Anonymous</i></p>

--===============1627694678==
Content-Type: text/plain; charset="utf-8"
Content-Transfer-Encoding: 7bit
MIME-Version: 1.0

Hello,
This is a MIME message from Chapter 12.
- Anonymous

--===============1627694678==--
```

At its top level, the above e-mail follows the old standard format: headers, blank line, and body. But now the body is suddenly more interesting. In order to carry two payloads, plain text and HTML, the headers specify a boundary that splits the body into several smaller parts. Each part is itself in the traditional format: headers, blank line, and body. There is only one (rather obvious) restriction on the contents of a part: a part cannot contain a copy of either its own boundary line or the boundary line of any of the enclosing messages.

The multipart/alternative content type is one example of a whole family of multipart/* content types, all of which follow exactly the same rules regarding the establishment of a boundary line and its use in delimiting the MIME subparts beneath it. Its role is to carry several versions of a message, any one of which can be displayed to the user and thereby communicate the message's whole meaning. In this case, the user can be shown either the HTML or the plain text, but the user will see essentially the same e-mail either way. Most clients will opt for HTML if they are capable of displaying it. Although most e-mail clients will hide the fact than an alternative was even offered, some do offer a button or drop-down menu that will let the user see an alternative version if they wish.

Note that the MIME-Version header only gets specified at the top level of the message, but the email module has handled this without the sender having to know that detail of the standard.

The rules about multipart sections are as follows:

- If you call add_related() at least once, then the body you specified with set_content() will get grouped together with all of the related content inside a single multipart/related section.

- If you call add_alternative() at least once, then a multipart/alternative container is created to hold the original body together with the alternative part(s) you add.

- Finally, if you call add_attachment() at least once, then an outer multipart/mixed container is generated to hold the content next to all of the attachments you add.

You can see all of these mechanisms in play together by examining the following output, which is from the most complicated of the four command lines given above. It asks for both an inline-related image to accompany the HTML with –i and also for attachments to be included after the body.

```
To: Test Recipient <recipient@example.com>
From: Test Sender <sender@example.com>
Subject: Foundations of Python Network Programming
Date: Tue, 25 Mar 2014 17:14:01 -0400
Message-ID: <20140325232008.15748.50494@guinness>
MIME-Version: 1.0
Content-Type: multipart/mixed; boundary="===============0086939546=="


--===============0086939546==
Content-Type: multipart/alternative; boundary="===============0903170602=="


--===============0903170602==
Content-Type: multipart/related; boundary="===============1911784257=="


--===============1911784257==
Content-Type: text/html; charset="utf-8"
Content-Transfer-Encoding: 7bit

<p>Hello,</p>
<p>This is a <b>test message</b> from Chapter 12.</p>
<p>- <i>Anonymous</i></p><p>This is the smallest possible blue GIF:</p>
<img src="cid:20140325232008.15748.99346@guinness" height="80" width="80">


--===============1911784257==
Content-Type: image/gif
Content-Transfer-Encoding: base64
Content-Disposition: attachment; filename="blue-dot.gif"
Content-ID: <20140325232008.15748.99346@guinness>
MIME-Version: 1.0

R0lGODlhAQABAJAAAAAA/wAAACwAAAAAAQABAAACAgQBADs=


--===============1911784257==--


--===============0903170602==
Content-Type: text/plain; charset="utf-8"
Content-Transfer-Encoding: 7bit
MIME-Version: 1.0

Hello,
This is a MIME message from Chapter 12.
- Anonymous


--===============0903170602==--
```

```
--===============0086939546==
Content-Type: text/plain; charset="utf-8"
Content-Transfer-Encoding: 7bit
Content-Disposition: attachment; filename="attachment.txt"
MIME-Version: 1.0

This is a test

--===============0086939546==
Content-Type: application/octet-stream
Content-Transfer-Encoding: base64
Content-Disposition: attachment; filename="attachment.gz"
MIME-Version: 1.0

H4sIAP3o2D8AAwvJyCxWAKJEhZLU4hIuAIwtwPoPAAAA

--===============0086939546==---
```

This e-mail is concentric, with three levels of multipart content inside one another! As before, you can see that all of the details have been handled for us. Each level has its own randomly generated boundary that does not conflict with the boundary of either of the other levels. The proper kind of multipart container has been chosen in each case for the kind of content that is included inside it.

Finally, proper encodings have been specified. Plain text has been permitted to travel literally inside the body of the e-mail, while Base64 encoding has been used for binary data-like images that are not 7-bit safe. Note that in both of these generation scripts, the e-mail object was asked to render itself explicitly as bytes, instead of asking for text that would then have to be encoded before being saved or transmitted.

Adding Content

All four of the methods used to add content in Listing 12-3 share the same calling convention. Consult the Python documentation to learn every possible combination that is supported in the particular version of Python 3 that you are using. Here are some common combinations for the methods set_content(), add_related(), add_alternative(), or add_attachment():

- *method*('string data of type str')
  method('string data of type str', subtype='html')

  These create parts that are some flavor of text. The content type will be text/plain unless you provide a custom subtype—the second example call, for instance, results in a content type of text/html.

- *method*(b'raw binary payload of type bytes', type='image', subtype='jpeg')

  If you provide raw binary data, then Python will not try to guess what the type should be. You have to provide both the MIME type and subtype yourself, which will be combined with a slash in the output. Note that Listing 12-3 uses a mechanism outside the email module itself, the mimetypes module, to try to guess an appropriate type for each attachment file you specify on the command line.

- *method(..., cte='quoted-printable')*

  All of these methods seem to default to one of only two content transfer encodings. Safe 7-bit information is included verbatim in the e-mail using bare and readable ASCII encoding, while anything more dangerous gets encoded using Base64. If you are ever in a situation where you are frequently inspecting incoming or outgoing e-mails manually, you might find the latter option unfortunate—it means, for example, that a text part with one single Unicode character inside it will get turned into completely unreadable Base64 rubbish. You can override the choice of encoding with the cte keyword. In particular, you might find the quoted-printable encoding attractive: ASCII characters are preserved verbatim in the encoded e-mail, and escape sequences are used for any bytes that have their eighth bit set.

- add_related(..., cid='<Content ID>')

  Usually, you will want each related part to be identified by a custom content ID so that your HTML can link to it. The content ID should always be surrounded by angle brackets in your call, but have them removed when you actually form the cid: link in your HTML. It is notable that content IDs are supposed to be globally unique—every content ID you ever include in a document is supposed to be unique among all content IDs ever included in an e-mail in the entire history of the world! Listing 12-3 uses make_msgid() because the email module provides no specific facility for building unique content IDs.

- add_attachment(..., filename='data.csv')

  When adding attachments, most e-mail clients (as well as their users) will expect at least a suggested file name, though of course the e-mail recipient can override this default when they select "Save" if they choose to.

There are, again, other more complicated versions of these calls for special cases that you can learn about in the official Python documentation, but these should carry you through the most common situations in building MIME e-mails.

Parsing E-Mail Messages

There are two basic approaches to reading an e-mail message once you have parsed it using one of the functions in the email module. The simple approach is to assume that the message offers a body and attachments through standard and customary use of MIME and lets the convenience methods built into EmailMessage help you find them. The more complex approach is to visit all of the parts and subparts of the message manually and then decide on your own what they mean and how they might be saved or displayed.

Listing 12-4 illustrates the simple approach. As with saving e-mail messages, it is important to be careful to read input as bytes and then to hand those bytes to the email module without attempting any decoding step of your own.

Listing 12-4. Asking EmailMessage for the Body and Attachments

```
#!/usr/bin/env python3
# Foundations of Python Network Programming, Third Edition
# https://github.com/brandon-rhodes/fopnp/blob/m/py3/chapter12/display_email.py

import argparse, email.policy, sys

def main(binary_file):
    policy = email.policy.SMTP
    message = email.message_from_binary_file(binary_file, policy=policy)
    for header in ['From', 'To', 'Date', 'Subject']:
        print(header + ':', message.get(header, '(none)'))
    print()
```

```
    try:
        body = message.get_body(preferencelist=('plain', 'html'))
    except KeyError:
        print('<This message lacks a printable text or HTML body>')
    else:
        print(body.get_content())

    for part in message.walk():
        cd = part['Content-Disposition']
        is_attachment = cd and cd.split(';')[0].lower() == 'attachment'
        if not is_attachment:
            continue
        content = part.get_content()
        print('* {} attachment named {!r}: {} object of length {}'.format(
            part.get_content_type(), part.get_filename(),
            type(content).__name__, len(content)))

if __name__ == '__main__':
    parser = argparse.ArgumentParser(description='Parse and print an email')
    parser.add_argument('filename', nargs='?', help='File containing an email')
    args = parser.parse_args()
    if args.filename is None:
        main(sys.stdin.buffer)
    else:
        with open(args.filename, 'rb') as f:
            main(f)
```

The script falls quite naturally into two parts once its command-line arguments have been parsed and the message itself has been read and turned into an EmailMessage. Because you want the email module to have access to the message's exact binary representation on disk, you either open its file in binary mode 'rb' or use the binary buffer attribute of Python's standard input object, which will return raw bytes.

The first crucial step is the call to the get_body() method, which sends Python on a search deeper and deeper into the message's MIME structure looking for the part best qualified to serve as the body. The preferencelist that you specify should be ordered with the formats that you prefer preceding the formats that you are less likely to want to display. Here HTML content is preferred over a plain-text version of the body, but either can be accepted. If a suitable body cannot be found, then KeyError is raised.

Note that the default preferencelist, used if you fail to specify one of your own, has three elements because it puts multipart/related as its first preference ahead of both HTML and plain text. This default is suitable if you are writing a sophisticated e-mail client—perhaps a webmail service or an application with a built-in WebKit pane—that can not only format HTML correctly but can also display inline images and supports style sheets. The object you get back will be the related-content MIME part itself, and you will then have to look inside it to find both the HTML and all of the multimedia that it needs. Because the small script here is simply printing the resulting body to the standard output, however, I have skipped this possibility.

Having displayed the best body that can be found, it is then time to search for any attachments the user might want displayed or saved. Note that the example script asks for all of the essential information that MIME specifies for an attachment: its content type, file name, and then the data itself. In a real application, you would probably open a file for writing and save these data instead of just printing its length and type to the screen.

Note that because of a bug in Python 3.4, this display script is forced to make its own decision about which message parts are attachments and which are not. In a future version of Python, you will be able to replace this manual iteration of the tree and test every single part's content disposition with a simple call to the iter_attachments() method of your message instead.

The script that follows will work on any of the MIME messages generated by the earlier scripts, no matter how complicated. Given the simplest message, it simply displays the "interesting" headers and body.

```
$ python3 build_basic_email.py > email.txt
$ python3 display_email.py email.txt
From: Test Sender <sender@example.com>
To: recipient@example.com
Date: Tue, 25 Mar 2014 17:14:01 -0400
Subject: Test Message, Chapter 12

Hello,
This is a basic message from Chapter 12.
 - Anonymous
```

But even the most complicated message is not too much for it. The get_body() logic successfully dives inside the mixed multipart outer layer, into the alternative multipart middle, and finally even down into the related multipart innards of the message before reemerging with the HTML version of the e-mail body. Moreover, each of the attachments that were included are inspected as well.

```
$ python3 build_mime_email.py -i attachment.txt attachment.gz > email.txt
$ python3 display_email.py email.txt
From: Test Sender <sender@example.com>
To: Test Recipient <recipient@example.com>
Date: Tue, 25 Mar 2014 17:14:01 -0400
Subject: Foundations of Python Network Programming

Hello,
This is a MIME message from Chapter 12.
- Anonymous

* image/gif attachment named 'blue-dot.gif': bytes object of length 35
* text/plain attachment named 'attachment.txt': str object of length 15
* application/octet-stream attachment named 'attachment.gz': bytes object of length 33
```

Walking MIME Parts

If the logic in Listing 12-4 ever winds up not being sufficient for your application—if it cannot find the body text of a particular e-mail that your project needs to be able to parse, or if certain poorly specified attachments are being skipped to which your customers need access—then you will need to fall back to visiting every part of an e-mail message yourself and implementing your own algorithm for which parts to display, which to save as attachments, and which to ignore or throw away.

There are three basic rules to keep in mind when dismembering a MIME e-mail.

- Your first call when examining a section should be to the is_multipart() method to determine whether the MIME part you are inspecting is a container for further MIME subparts. You can also call get_content_type() if you want the fully qualified type with a slash between the main type and subtype, and either get_content_maintype() or get_content_subtype() if you only care about one half or the other.

- When confronted with a multipart, use the iter_parts() method to loop over or fetch the parts immediately beneath it so you can in turn discover which of the subparts are themselves multipart and which instead simply contain content.

- When examining a normal part, the Content-Disposition header will tell you whether it is intended as an attachment (look for the word *attachment* preceding any semicolon in the header's value).

- Calling the get_content() method decodes and returns the data itself from inside a MIME part as either a text str or a binary bytes object depending on whether the main content type is text or not.

The code in Listing 12-5 uses a recursive generator to visit every part of a multipart message. The generator's operation is similar to that of the build-in walk() method, except that this generator keeps up with the index of each subpart in case it needs to be fetched later.

Listing 12-5. Visiting Every Part of a Multipart Method Manually

```
#!/usr/bin/env python3
# Foundations of Python Network Programming, Third Edition
# https://github.com/brandon-rhodes/fopnp/blob/m/py3/chapter12/display_structure.py

import argparse, email.policy, sys

def walk(part, prefix=''):
    yield prefix, part
    for i, subpart in enumerate(part.iter_parts()):
        yield from walk(subpart, prefix + '.{}'.format(i))

def main(binary_file):
    policy = email.policy.SMTP
    message = email.message_from_binary_file(binary_file, policy=policy)
    for prefix, part in walk(message):
        line = '{} type={}'.format(prefix, part.get_content_type())
        if not part.is_multipart():
            content = part.get_content()
            line += ' {} len={}'.format(type(content).__name__, len(content))
            cd = part['Content-Disposition']
            is_attachment = cd and cd.split(';')[0].lower() == 'attachment'
            if is_attachment:
                line += ' attachment'
            filename = part.get_filename()
            if filename is not None:
                line += ' filename={!r}'.format(filename)
        print(line)

if __name__ == '__main__':
    parser = argparse.ArgumentParser(description='Display MIME structure')
    parser.add_argument('filename', nargs='?', help='File containing an email')
    args = parser.parse_args()
    if args.filename is None:
        main(sys.stdin.buffer)
    else:
        with open(args.filename, 'rb') as f:
            main(f)
```

You can exercise this script against any of the e-mail messages that the earlier scripts can generate. (Or, of course, you could try feeding it a real-life e-mail of your own.) Running it against the most complex message that can be generated using the above scripts produces the following results.

```
$ python3 build_mime_email.py -i attachment.txt attachment.gz > email.txt
$ python3 display_structure.py email.txt
 type=multipart/mixed
.0 type=multipart/alternative
.0.0 type=multipart/related
.0.0.0 type=text/html str len=215
.0.0.1 type=image/gif bytes len=35 attachment filename='blue-dot.gif'
.0.1 type=text/plain str len=59
.1 type=text/plain str len=15 attachment filename='attachment.txt'
.2 type=application/octet-stream bytes len=33 attachment filename='attachment.gz'
```

The part numbers that introduce each line of output can be used in further code that you write in order to dive directly into the message to fetch the particular part in which you are interested by providing each integer index to the get_payload() method. For example, if you wanted to fetch the blue dot GIF image from inside this message, you would call:

```
part = message.get_payload(0).get_payload(0).get_payload(1)
```

Note again that only multipart parts are allowed to have further MIME subparts inside. Every part with a nonmultipart content type is a leaf node in the tree above, containing simple content with no further e-mail-relevant structure beneath.

Header Encodings

The parsing scripts above, thanks to the email module, will correctly handle internationalized headers that encode special characters using the conventions of RFC 2047 without any modification. Listing 12-6 generates such an e-mail with which you can perform tests. Note that because Python 3 source code is UTF-8 encoded by default, you can include international characters without needing a -*- coding: utf-8 -*- declaration at the top, as was necessary with Python 2.

Listing 12-6. Generate an Internationalized E-Mail to Test the Parsing Script

```
#!/usr/bin/env python3
# Foundations of Python Network Programming, Third Edition
# https://github.com/brandon-rhodes/fopnp/blob/m/py3/chapter12/build_unicode_email.py

import email.message, email.policy, sys

text = """\
Hwær cwom mearg? Hwær cwom mago?
Hwær cwom maþþumgyfa?
Hwær cwom symbla gesetu?
Hwær sindon seledreamas?"""
```

```
def main():
    message = email.message.EmailMessage(email.policy.SMTP)
    message['To'] = 'Böðvarr <recipient@example.com>'
    message['From'] = 'Eardstapa <sender@example.com>'
    message['Subject'] = 'Four lines from The Wanderer'
    message['Date'] = email.utils.formatdate(localtime=True)
    message.set_content(text, cte='quoted-printable')
    sys.stdout.buffer.write(message.as_bytes())

if __name__ == '__main__':
    main()
```

The output e-mail uses a special ASCII encoding of binary data for the To: header because of the special characters inside it. Furthermore, following on from advice given earlier, note that by specifying a quoted-printable content encoding for the body, you avoid generating a block of Base64 data and instead represent most of the characters by their straight ASCII codes, as shown in the following results.

```
To: =?utf-8?b?QsO2w7B2YXJy?= <recipient@example.com>
From: Eardstapa <sender@example.com>
Subject: Four lines from The Wanderer
Date: Fri, 28 Mar 2014 22:11:48 -0400
Content-Type: text/plain; charset="utf 8"
Content-Transfer-Encoding: quoted-printable
MIME-Version: 1.0

Hw=C3=A6r cwom mearg? Hw=C3=A6r cwom mago?
Hw=C3=A6r cwom ma=C3=BE=C3=BEumgyfa?
Hw=C3=A6r cwom symbla gesetu?
Hw=C3=A6r sindon seledreamas?
```

The display script successfully untangles all of this, since the email module does all of the decoding and processing for us.

```
$ python3 build_unicode_email.py > email.txt
$ python3 display_email.py email.txt
From: Eardstapa <sender@example.com>
To: Böðvarr <recipient@example.com>
Date: Tue, 25 Mar 2014 17:14:01 -0400
Subject: Four lines from The Wanderer

Hwær cwom mearg? Hwær cwom mago?
Hwær cwom maþþumgyfa?
Hwær cwom symbla gesetu?
Hwær sindon seledreamas?
```

If you ever want to investigate e-mail header encoding further, read the Python documentation for the lower-level email.header module and, in particular, its Header class.

Parsing Dates

Standards-compliant dates were used in the scripts above through the `formatdate()` function in `email.utils`, which uses the current date and time by default. But they can also be provided with a low-level Unix timestamp. If you are doing higher-level date manipulation and have generated a `datetime` object, simply use the `format_datetime()` function instead to do the same kind of formatting.

When parsing an e-mail, you can perform the inverse operation through three other methods inside `email.utils`.

- Both `parsedate()` and `parsedate_tz()` return time tuples of the sort that Python supports at a low level through its `time` module following the old C-language conventions for doing date arithmetic and representation.

- The modern `parsedate_to_datetime()` function instead returns a full `datetime` object, and it is probably the call you will want to make in most production code.

Note that many e-mail programs fail to follow exactly the relevant standards when writing Date headers, and although these routines try to be forgiving, there may be circumstances in which they cannot produce a valid date value and return None instead. You will want to check for this value before assuming that you have been given back a date. A few example calls follow.

```
>>> from email import utils
>>> utils.parsedate('Tue, 25 Mar 2014 17:14:01 -0400')
(2014, 3, 25, 17, 14, 1, 0, 1, -1)
>>> utils.parsedate_tz('Tue, 25 Mar 2014 17:14:01 -0400')
(2014, 3, 25, 17, 14, 1, 0, 1, -1, -14400)
>>> utils.parsedate_to_datetime('Tue, 25 Mar 2014 17:14:01 -0400')
datetime.datetime(2014, 3, 25, 17, 14, 1,
                  tzinfo=datetime.timezone(datetime.timedelta(-1, 72000)))
```

If you are going to be doing any arithmetic with dates, I strongly suggest that you investigate the third-party `pytz` module, which has become a community best practice around date manipulation.

Summary

The powerful `email.message.EmailMessage` class introduced into Python 3.4 by R. David Murray makes both the generation and consumption of MIME messages much more convenient than in previous versions of Python. As usual, the only caution is to pay close attention to the distinction between bytes and strings. Try to do your entire socket or file I/O as bytes, and let the `email` module do all of its own encoding so that every step is done correctly.

An e-mail is typically generated by instantiating `EmailMessage` and then specifying headers and content. Headers are set by treating the message as a dictionary with case-insensitive string keys, where the string values are stored that will be properly encoded upon output if any of their characters are non-ASCII. Content is set through a cascade of four methods—`set_content()`, `add_related()`, `add_alternative()`, and `add_attachment()`—that handle both text and bytes payloads correctly in all cases.

An e-mail message can be read back in and examined as an `EmailMessage` object by running any of the email module's parsing functions (`message_from_binary_file()` is the approach used in the listings in this chapter) with a policy argument turning on all of the modern features of the `EmailMessage` class. Each resulting object will either be a multipart with further subparts inside of it or a bare piece of content that Python returns as a string or as bytes data.

Headers are automatically internationalized and decoded on output and input. The special Date header's format is supported by methods in `email.utils` that let your code both read and write its value using instances of the modern Python `datetime` object.

The next chapter will look specifically at the use of the SMTP protocol for e-mail transmission.

## CHAPTER 13

SMTP

As outlined at the beginning of Chapter 12, the actual movement of e-mail between systems is accomplished through SMTP, the Simple Mail Transport Protocol. It was first defined in 1982 in RFC 821; the most recent RFC defining of SMTP is RFC 5321. The protocol typically serves two roles:

1. When a user types an e-mail message on a laptop or desktop machine, the e-mail client uses SMTP to submit the e-mail to a server that can send it along to its destination.

2. E-mail servers themselves use SMTP to *deliver* messages, sending each message across the Internet from one server to another until it reaches the server in charge of the recipient's e-mail address's *domain* (the part of the e-mail address after the @ sign).

There are several differences between how SMTP is used for submission and delivery. Before discussing them, however, I will quickly outline the difference between users who check e-mail with a local e-mail *client* and those who use a *webmail* service instead.

E-mail Clients vs. Webmail Services

The role of SMTP in message *submission*, where the user clicks Send and expects a message to go winging its way across the Internet, will probably be least confusing if I trace the history of how users have historically worked with Internet e-mail.

The key concept to understand is that users have *never* been asked to sit around and wait for an e-mail message actually to be delivered. This process can often take quite a bit of time—and up to several dozen repeated attempts—before an e-mail message is actually delivered to its destination. Any number of things could cause delays: a message could have to wait because other messages are already being transmitted across a link of limited bandwidth, the destination server might be down for a few hours, or its network might not be currently accessible because of a glitch. If the e-mail is destined for a large organization, such as a university, it might have to make several different "hops" as it arrives at the big university server, then is directed to a smaller e-mail machine for one particular college within the larger university, and finally is delivered to a departmental e-mail server.

Thus understanding what happens when the user clicks Send is, essentially, comprehending how the finished e-mail message gets submitted to the first of possibly several e-mail *queues* in which it can languish until the circumstances are just right for its delivery to occur. (This will be discussed in the next section on e-mail delivery.)

In the Beginning Was the Command Line

The first generation of e-mail users were given usernames and passwords by their business or university, which provided them with command-line access to the large mainframes where user files and general-purpose programs were kept. Each large machine typically ran an e-mail daemon that maintained an outgoing queue; right on the same box where the users were busily typing messages using small command-line e-mail programs. Several such programs each had their heyday; mail was followed by the fancier mailx, which was then eclipsed by the far prettier interfaces—with greater capabilities—of elm, pine, and finally mutt.

THE SMTP PROTOCOL

Purpose: deliver e-mail to a server

Standard: RFC 2821

Runs atop: TCP or TLS

Port number: 53

Libraries: smtplib

But for all of these early users, the network was not even involved in the simple task of e-mail submission; after all, the e-mail client and the server were on the same machine! The actual means of bridging this small gap and performing e-mail submission was a mere implementation detail, usually hidden behind a command-line client program that came with the server software that knew exactly how to communicate with it. The first widespread e-mail daemon, sendmail, came with a program for submitting e-mail called /usr/lib/sendmail.

Because the first-generation client programs for reading and writing e-mail were designed to interact with sendmail, the e-mail daemons that have subsequently risen to popularity, like qmail, postfix, and exim, generally followed suit by providing a sendmail binary of their own (its official home is now /usr/sbin, thanks to recent file system standards) that, when invoked by the user's e-mail program, follows that specific e-mail daemon's own peculiar procedure for getting a message moved into the queue.

When an e-mail arrived, it was typically deposited into a file belonging to the user to whom the message had been addressed. The e-mail client running on the command line could simply open this file and parse it to see the messages that were waiting for the user to read. This book does not cover these *mailbox formats*, because its focus is on how e-mail uses the network. If you are curious, however, you can check out the mailbox package in the Python Standard Library, which supports all of the strange and curious ways in which various e-mail programs have read and written messages to disk over the years.

The Rise of Clients

The next generation of users to begin using the Internet was often not familiar with the idea of a command line. Users were skilled in the use of the graphical interface of the Apple Macintosh—or, when it arrived later, the Microsoft Windows operating system—and they expected to accomplish things by clicking an icon and running a graphical program. Thus a number of different e-mail clients were written that brought this Internet service to the desktop. Mozilla Thunderbird and Microsoft Outlook are only two of the most popular of these clients still in use today.

The problems with this approach are obvious. First, reading incoming e-mail was transformed from a simple task for your e-mail program—which had previously been able to open a local file and read it—to being an operation that now required a network connection. When you opened your graphical e-mail program, it somehow had to reach across the Internet to a full-time server that had been receiving e-mail on your behalf while you were away, and bring the e-mail down to the local machine.

Second, users are notorious for not properly backing up their desktop and laptop file systems, and clients that downloaded and stored messages locally thereby made those messages vulnerable to obliteration when the laptop or desktop hard drive crashed. By contrast, university and industrial servers—despite their clunky command lines—usually had small armies of people specifically tasked with keeping their data archived, duplicated, and safe.

Third, laptop and desktop machines are usually not suitable environments for an e-mail server and its queue of outgoing messages. Users, after all, often turn their machines off when they are done using them, disconnect from the Internet, or leave the Internet café and lose their wireless signal. Outgoing messages generally need more than a few moments online to finish their retries and final transmission, so completed e-mails need some way to be *submitted* back to a full-time server for queuing and delivery.

But programmers are clever people, and they came up with a series of solutions to these problems. First, new protocols were invented—first the Post Office Protocol (POP), which I'll discuss in Chapter 14, and then the Internet Message Access Protocol (IMAP), which is covered in Chapter 15—that let a user's e-mail client authenticate with a password and download e-mail from the full-time server that had been storing it. Passwords were necessary to stop other people from connecting to your Internet service provider's servers and reading your e-mail! This solved the first problem.

But what about the second problem, persistence; that is, avoiding the loss of e-mail when desktop and laptop hard drives crash? This inspired two sets of advances. First, people using POP often learned to turn off its default mode in which the e-mail on the server is deleted once is has been downloaded, and they learned to leave copies of important e-mails on the server, from which they could fetch e-mail again later if they had to reinstall their computer and start from scratch. Second, they started moving to IMAP, if their e-mail server indeed chose to support this more advanced protocol. Using IMAP meant they could not only leave incoming e-mail messages on the server for safekeeping, but they could also arrange the messages in folders right there on the server! This let them use their e-mail client program as a mere window through which to browse e-mail, which itself remained stored on the server rather than having to manage an e-mail storage area on their laptop or desktop itself.

Finally, how does e-mail make it back to the server when the user finishes writing an e-mail message and clicks Send? This task—again, officially called e-mail submission, brings me back to the subject of this chapter; that is, e-mail submission takes place using the SMTP protocol. But, as I'll explain, there are usually two differences between SMTP as it is spoken between servers on the Internet and the way that it is spoken during client e-mail submission, and both differences are driven by the modern need to combat spam. First, most ISPs block outgoing TCP connections to port 25 from laptops and desktops so that these small machines cannot be hijacked by viruses and used as e-mail servers. Instead, e-mail submission is usually directed to port 587. Second, to prevent spammers from connecting to your ISP and claiming they want to send a message purportedly from you, e-mail clients use *authenticated SMTP* that includes the user's username and password.

Through these mechanisms, e-mail has been brought to the desktop—both in large organizations, like universities and businesses, and also in ISPs catering to users at home. It is still common to provide instructions to each user that tells them to:

- Install an e-mail client like Thunderbird or Outlook.

- Enter the hostname and protocol from which e-mail can be fetched.

- Configure the outgoing server's name and SMTP port number.

- Assign a username and password with which connections to both services can be authenticated.

Although e-mail clients can be cumbersome to configure and the servers can be difficult maintain, they were originally the only way that e-mail could be offered, using a familiar graphical interface, to the new breed of users staring at large colorful displays. Nowadays, they allow users an enviable freedom of choice: their ISP simply decides whether to support POP, IMAP, or both and the user (or, at least, the nonenterprise user!) is then free to try the various e-mail clients and settle on the one they like best.

The Move to Webmail

Finally, yet another generational shift has occurred on the Internet. Users once had to download and install a plethora of clients in order to experience all that the Internet had to offer. Many seasoned readers will remember having Windows or Mac machines on which they eventually installed client programs for such diverse protocols as Telnet, FTP, the Gopher directory service, Usenet newsgroups, and, when it came along, the World Wide Web. (Unix users typically found clients for each basic protocol already installed when they first logged in to a well-configured machine, though they might have chosen to install more advanced replacements for some of the programs, like ncftp in place of the clunky default FTP client.)

But, no longer! The average Internet user today knows only a single client: their web browser. Thanks to the fact that web pages can now use JavaScript to respond and redraw themselves as the user clicks and types on their keyboard, the Web is not only replacing all traditional Internet protocols—users browse and fetch files on web pages, not through FTP; they read message boards, rather than connecting to the Usenet—but it is also obviating the need for many traditional desktop clients. Why convince thousands of users to download and install a new e-mail client, clicking through several warnings about how your software might harm their computer, if your application is one that could be offered through an interactive web page?

In fact, the web browser has become so preeminent that many Internet users are not even aware that they *have* a web browser. They therefore use the words "Internet" and "Web" interchangeably, and they think that both terms refer to "all those documents and links that give me Facebook, YouTube, and Wikipedia." This obliviousness to the fact that they are viewing the Web's glory through some particular client program with a name and identity—say, through the pane of Internet Explorer—is a constant frustration to evangelists for alternatives like Firefox, Google Chrome, and Opera, who find it difficult to convince people to change from a program that they are not even aware they are using!

Obviously, if such users are to read e-mail, it must be presented to them on a web page, where they read incoming e-mail, sort it into folders, and compose and send replies. Thus there are many web sites offering e-mail services through the browser—Gmail and Yahoo! Mail being among the most popular—as well as server software, like the popular SquirrelMail, that system administrators can install if they want to offer webmail to users at their school or business.

What does this transition mean for e-mail protocols and the network? Interestingly enough, the webmail phenomenon essentially moves us *back* in time to the simpler days when e-mail submission and e-mail reading were private affairs, confined to a single mainframe server and usually not an experience that involved using public protocols at all. Of course, these modern services, especially the ones run by large ISPs, and companies like Google and Yahoo!, must be gargantuan affairs, involving hundreds of servers at locations around the world; so, certainly, network protocols are doubtlessly involved at every level of e-mail storage and retrieval.

But the point is that these are now *private* transactions, internal to the organization running the webmail service. You browse e-mail in your web browser; you write e-mail using the same interface; and when you click Send, well, who knows what protocol Google or Yahoo! uses internally to pass the new message from the web server receiving your HTTP POST to a mail queue from which it can be delivered? It could be SMTP; it could be an in-house RPC protocol; or it could even be an operation on common file systems to which the web and e-mail servers are both connected.

For the purposes of this book, the important thing is that, unless you are an engineer working at such an organization, you will never see whether POP, IMAP, or something else is at work behind the webmail interface you use to manipulate your messages.

E-mail browsing and submission, therefore, become a black box: your browser interacts with a web API and, on the other end, you will see plain old SMTP connections originating from and going to the large organization as e-mail is delivered in each direction. But in the world of webmail, client protocols are removed from the equation, taking us back to the old days of pure server-to-server unauthenticated SMTP.

How SMTP Is Used

The foregoing narrative has hopefully helped you structure your thinking about Internet e-mail protocols. With any luck, it has also helped you realize how they fit together in the bigger picture of getting messages to and from users.

The subject of this chapter, however, is a narrower one—the Simple Mail Transport Protocol. I'll start by stating the basics in the terms you learned in Part 1 of this book:

- SMTP is a TCP/IP-based protocol.
- Connections can be authenticated or not.
- Connections can be encrypted or not.

Most e-mail connections across the Internet these days seem to lack any attempt at encryption, which means that whoever owns the Internet backbone routers are theoretically in a position to read staggering amounts of other people's e-mail. What are the two ways, given the discussion in the previous section, that SMTP is used?

First, SMTP can be used for e-mail *submission* between a client e-mail program like Thunderbird or Outlook and a server at an organization that has given the user an e-mail address. These connections generally use authentication so that spammers cannot connect and send millions of messages on a user's behalf without their password. Once a message is received, the server puts it in a queue for delivery so that the e-mail client can forget about the message and assume that the server will keep trying to deliver it.

Second, SMTP is used *between* Internet e-mail servers as they move e-mail from its origin to its destination. This typically involves no authentication; after all, big organizations like Google, Yahoo!, and Microsoft do not know the passwords of each other's users, so when Yahoo! receives an e-mail from Google claiming that it was sent from an @gmail.com user, Yahoo! just has to believe them (or not—sometimes organizations blacklist each other if too much spam is making it through their servers. This happened to a friend of mine when Hotmail's e-mail server stopped accepting his e-mail newsletters from GoDaddy's servers because of alleged problems with spam).

Thus typically no authentication takes place between servers talking SMTP to each other—and even encryption against snooping routers seems to be used only rarely.

Because of the problem of spammers connecting to e-mail servers and claiming to be delivering e-mail from another organization's users, there has been an attempt made to lock down which specific servers can send e-mail on an organization's behalf. Though controversial, some e-mail servers consult the Sender Policy Framework (SPF), defined in RFC 4408, to see whether the server to which they are talking really has the authority to deliver the e-mails it is transmitting.

Let's turn to the technical question of how you will actually use SMTP from your Python programs. Figure 13-1 provides an example of a Python-driven SMTP session.

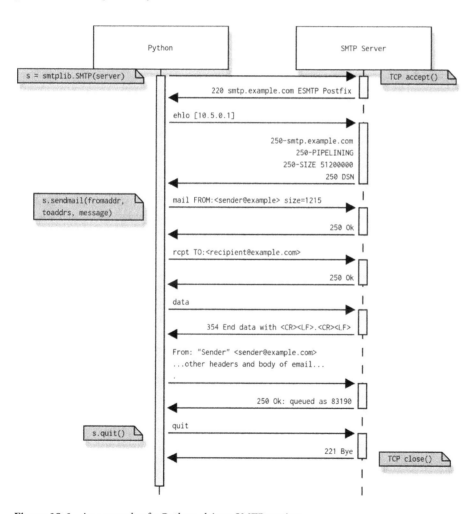

Figure 13-1. *An example of a Python-driven SMTP session*

Sending E-Mail

Before sharing the nitty-gritty details of the SMTP protocol, a warning is in order: if you are writing an interactive program, daemon, or web site that needs to send e-mail, then your site or system administrator (in cases where that is not you) might have an opinion about how your program sends e-mail, and they might save you *a lot* of work by doing so!

As noted previously, successfully sending e-mail generally requires a queue where a message can sit for seconds, minutes, or even days until it can be successfully transmitted toward its destination. Thus, you typically do *not* want your front-end programs using Python's smtplib to send e-mail directly to a message's destination, because if your first transmission attempt fails, then you will be stuck with the job of writing a full mail transfer agent (MTA), as the RFCs call an e-mail server, and giving it a full standards-compliant retry queue. This is not only a big job, but it is also one that has already been done well several times, and you will be wise to take advantage of one of the existing MTAs (look at postfix, exim, and qmail) before trying to write something on your own.

Only rarely will you be making SMTP connections out into the world from Python. More often, your system administrator will tell you one of two things:

- That you should make an authenticated SMTP connection to a e-mail server that already exists within your organization, using a username and password that will belong to your application.

- That you should run a local binary on the system—like the sendmail program—that the system administrator has already gone to the trouble of configuring so that local programs can send e-mail.

The Python Library FAQ has sample code for invoking a sendmail compatible program. Take a look at the section "How do I send mail from a Python script?" found at http://docs.python.org/faq/library.html.

Because this book is about networking, I won't cover this possibility in detail. However, remember to do raw SMTP yourself *only* when no simpler mechanism exists on your machine for sending e-mail.

Headers and the Envelope Recipient

The key concept involved in SMTP that consistently confuses beginners is that the addressee headers you are so familiar with—To, Cc (carbon copy), and Bcc (blind carbon copy)—are *not* consulted by the SMTP protocol to decide where your e-mail goes! This surprises many users. After all, almost every e-mail program in existence asks you to fill in those addressee fields, and when you click Send, the message wings it way toward those mailboxes. What could be more natural? But it turns out that this is a feature of the e-mail client itself, not of the SMTP protocol: the protocol knows only that each message has an "envelope" around it naming a sender and some recipients. SMTP itself does not care whether those names are ones that it can find in the headers of the message.

That e-mail must work this way will actually be quite obvious if you think for a moment about the Bcc blind carbon-copy header. Unlike the To and Cc headers, which make it to the e-mail's destination and let each recipient see who else was sent that e-mail, the Bcc header names people whom you want to receive the e-mail *without* any of the other recipients knowing. Blind copies let you quietly bring a message to someone's attention without alerting the other recipients of the e-mail.

The existence of a header like Bcc, which can be present when you compose a message but does not actually get included in the outgoing message, raises two points:

- Your e-mail client edits your message's headers before sending it. Besides removing the Bcc header so that none of the e-mail's recipients gets a copy of it, the client typically adds headers as well, such as a unique message ID and perhaps the name of the e-mail client itself (an e-mail I just received on my desktop, for example, identifies the X-Mailer that sent it as YahooMailClassic).

- An e-mail can pass across SMTP toward a destination address that is not mentioned *anywhere* in the e-mail headers or text itself—and it can do this for the most legitimate of reasons.

This mechanism also helps support e-mailing lists, so that an e-mail whose To line says advocacy@python.org can actually be delivered, without rewritten headers, to the dozens or hundreds of people who subscribe to that list without exposing all of their e-mail addresses to every reader of the list.

So, as you read the following descriptions of SMTP, keep reminding yourself that the headers-plus-body that make up the e-mail message itself are separate from the "envelope sender" and "envelope recipient" that will be mentioned in the protocol descriptions. Yes, it is true that your e-mail client, whether you are using /usr/sbin/sendmail or Thunderbird or Google Mail, probably asked you for the recipient's e-mail address only once; but it then proceeded to use it in *two* different places: once in the To header at the top of the message itself and then again "outside" of the message when it spoke SMTP in order to send the e-mail on its way.

Multiple Hops

Once upon a time, e-mail often traveled over only one SMTP "hop" between the mainframe on which it was composed to the machine on whose disk the recipient's in box was stored. These days, messages often travel through a half-dozen servers or more before reaching their destination. This means that the SMTP envelope recipient, described in the previous section, repeatedly changes as the message nears its destination.

An example should make this clear. Several of the following details are fictitious, but they should give you a good idea of how messages actually traverse the Internet.

Imagine a worker in the central IT organization at Georgia Tech who tells his friend that his e-mail address is brandon@gatech.edu. When the friend later sends him a message, the friend's e-mail provider will look up the domain gatech.edu in the Domain Name Service (DNS; see Chapter 4), receive a series of MX records in reply, and connects to one of those IP address to deliver the message. Simple enough, right?

But the server for gatech.edu serves an entire campus! To find out where brandon is, it consults a table, finds his department, and learns that his official e-mail address is actually:

brandon.rhodes@oit.gatech.edu

So the gatech.edu server in turn does a DNS lookup of oit.gatech.edu and then uses SMTP—the message's second SMTP hop, if you are counting—to send the message to the e-mail server for OIT, the Office of Information Technology.

But OIT long ago abandoned their single-server solution that used to keep all of their e-mail on a single Unix server. Instead, they now run a sophisticated e-mail solution that users can access through webmail, POP, and IMAP. Incoming e-mail arriving at oit.gatech.edu is first sent randomly to one of several spam-filtering servers (third hop), say the server named spam3.oit.gatech.edu. Then, if it survives the spam check and is not discarded, it is handed off randomly to one of eight redundant e-mail servers, and so after the fourth hop, the message is in the queue on mail7.oit.gatech.edu.

The routing servers, like mail7, can then query a central directory service to determine which back-end mail stores, connected to large disk arrays, host which users' mailboxes. So mail7 does an LDAP lookup for brandon.rhodes, concludes that his e-mail lives on the anvil.oit.gatech.edu server, and in a fifth and final SMTP hop, the e-mail is delivered to anvil and is written to its redundant disk array.

That is why e-mail often takes at least a few seconds to traverse the Internet: large organizations and big ISPs tend to have several levels of servers that a message must negotiate before its delivery.

How can you investigate an e-mail's route? It was emphasized previously that the SMTP protocol does not *read* e-mail headers, but it has its own idea about where a message should be going—which, as you have just seen, can change with every hop that a message takes toward its destination. But it turns out that e-mail servers are encouraged to *add* new headers, precisely to keep track of a message's circuitous route from its origin to its destination.

These headers are called Received headers, and they are a gold mine for confused system administrators trying to debug problems with their e-mail systems. Take a look at any e-mail message and ask your e-mail client to display all of the headers. You should be able to see every step that the message took toward its destination. (Spammers often write several fictitious Received headers at the top of their messages to make it look like the message originated from a reputable organization.) Finally, there is probably a Delivered-to header that is written when the last server in the chain is finally able to write the message triumphantly to physical storage in someone's mailbox.

Because each server tends to add its Received header to the *top* of the e-mail message, this saves time and prevents each server from having to search to the bottom of the Received headers that have been written so far. You should read them backward: the oldest Received header will be the one listed last, so as you read up the screen toward the top, you will be following the e-mail from its origin to its destination. Try it: bring up a recent e-mail message that you have received, select its View All Message Headers or Show Original option, and look for the received headers near the top. Did the message require more, or fewer, steps to reach your in box than you would have expected?

Introducing the SMTP Library

Python's built-in SMTP implementation is in the Python Standard Library module smtplib, which makes it easy to do simple tasks with SMTP.

In the examples that follow, the programs are designed to take several command-line arguments: the name of an SMTP server, a sender address, and one or more recipient addresses. Please use them cautiously; name only an SMTP server that you yourself run or that you know will be happy to receive your test messages, lest you wind up getting your IP address banned for sending spam!

If you don't know where to find an SMTP server, you might try running an e-mail daemon like postfix or exim locally and then pointing these example programs at localhost. Some UNIX, Linux, and Mac OS X systems have an SMTP server like one of these already listening for connections from the local machine.

Otherwise, consult your network administrator or Internet provider to obtain a proper hostname and port. Note that you usually cannot just pick an e-mail server at random; many store or forward e-mail only from certain authorized clients.

With that addressed, you are ready to move on to Listing 13-1, which illustrates a very simple SMTP program.

Listing 13-1. Sending E-mail with smtplib.sendmail()

```
#!/usr/bin/env python3
# Foundations of Python Network Programming, Third Edition
# https://github.com/brandon-rhodes/fopnp/blob/m/py3/chapter13/simple.py

import sys, smtplib

message_template = """To: {}
From: {}
Subject: Test Message from simple.py

Hello,

This is a test message sent to you from the simple.py program
in Foundations of Python Network Programming.
"""

def main():
    if len(sys.argv) < 4:
        name = sys.argv[0]
        print("usage: {} server fromaddr toaddr [toaddr...]".format(name))
        sys.exit(2)

    server, fromaddr, toaddrs = sys.argv[1], sys.argv[2], sys.argv[3:]
    message = message_template.format(', '.join(toaddrs), fromaddr)
```

```
connection = smtplib.SMTP(server)
connection.sendmail(fromaddr, toaddrs, message)
connection.quit()

s = '' if len(toaddrs) == 1 else 's'
print("Message sent to {} recipient{}".format(len(toaddrs), s))

if __name__ == '__main__':
    main()
```

This program is quite simple because it uses a very powerful and general function from inside the Python Standard Library. It starts by generating a simple message from the user's command-line arguments (for details on generating fancier messages that contain elements beyond simple plain text, see Chapter 12). Then it creates an smtplib.SMTP object that connects to the specified server. Finally, all that's required is a call to sendmail(). If that returns successfully, then you know that the e-mail server accepted the message without error.

As mentioned previously in this chapter, you can see that the idea of who receives the message—the "envelope recipient"—is, down at this level, separate from the actual text of the message. This particular program writes a To header that happens to contain the same addresses to which it is sending the message; but the To header is just a piece of text, and it could instead say anything else. (Whether that "anything else" would be willingly displayed by the recipient's e-mail client or cause a server along the way to discard the message as spam is another question!)

If you run the program from inside of the book's network playground, it should successfully be able to connect like this:

```
$ python3 simple.py mail.example.com sender@example.com recipient@example.com
Message successfully sent to 1 recipient
```

Thanks to the hard work that the authors of the Python Standard Library have put into the sendmail() method, it might be the only SMTP call you ever need! But to understand the steps that it is taking under the hood to get your message delivered, let's delve into more detail about how SMTP works.

Error Handling and Conversation Debugging

There are several different exceptions that might be raised while you're programming with smtplib. They are:

- socket.gaierror for errors looking up address information
- socket.error for general network and communication problems
- socket.herror for other addressing errors
- smtplib.SMTPException or a subclass of it for SMTP conversation problems

The first three errors were covered in more detail in Chapter 3; they are raised in the operating system's TCP stack, detected and raised as exceptions by Python's networking code, and passed straight through the smtplib module and up to your program. However, as long as the underlying TCP socket works, all problems that actually involve the SMTP e-mail conversation will result in an smtplib.SMTPException.

The smtplib module also provides a way to get a series of detailed messages about the steps it takes to send an e-mail. To enable that level of detail, you can call the following option:

```
connection.set_debuglevel(1)
```

With this option, you should be able to track down any problems. Take a look at Listing 13-2 for a sample program that provides basic error handling and debugging.

Listing 13-2. A More Cautious SMTP Client

```python
#!/usr/bin/env python3
# Foundations of Python Network Programming, Third Edition
# https://github.com/brandon-rhodes/fopnp/blob/m/py3/chapter13/debug.py

import sys, smtplib, socket

message_template = """To: {}
From: {}
Subject: Test Message from simple.py

Hello,

This is a test message sent to you from the debug.py program
in Foundations of Python Network Programming.
"""

def main():
    if len(sys.argv) < 4:
        name = sys.argv[0]
        print("usage: {} server fromaddr toaddr [toaddr...]".format(name))
        sys.exit(2)

    server, fromaddr, toaddrs = sys.argv[1], sys.argv[2], sys.argv[3:]
    message = message_template.format(', '.join(toaddrs), fromaddr)

    try:
        connection = smtplib.SMTP(server)
        connection.set_debuglevel(1)
        connection.sendmail(fromaddr, toaddrs, message)
    except (socket.gaierror, socket.error, socket.herror,
            smtplib.SMTPException) as e:
        print("Your message may not have been sent!")
        print(e)
        sys.exit(1)
    else:
        s = '' if len(toaddrs) == 1 else 's'
        print("Message sent to {} recipient{}".format(len(toaddrs), s))
        connection.quit()

if __name__ == '__main__':
    main()
```

This program looks similar to the previous one; however, the output will be very different. Take a look at Listing 13-3 for an example.

Listing 13-3. Debugging Output from `smtplib`

```
$ python3 debug.py mail.example.com sender@example.com recipient@example.com
send: 'ehlo [127.0.1.1]\r\n'
reply: b'250-guinness\r\n'
reply: b'250-SIZE 33554432\r\n'
```

```
reply: b'250 HELP\r\n'
reply: retcode (250); Msg: b'guinness\nSIZE 33554432\nHELP'
send: 'mail FROM:<sender@example.com> size=212\r\n'
reply: b'250 OK\r\n'
reply: retcode (250); Msg: b'OK'
send: 'rcpt TO:<recipient@example.com>\r\n'
reply: b'250 OK\r\n'
reply: retcode (250); Msg: b'OK'
send: 'data\r\n'
reply: b'354 End data with <CR><LF>.<CR><LF>\r\n'
reply: retcode (354); Msg: b'End data with <CR><LF>.<CR><LF>'
data: (354, b'End data with <CR><LF>.<CR><LF>')
send: b'To: recipient@example.com\r\nFrom: sender@example.com\r\nSubject: Test Message from
simple.py\r\n\r\nHello,\r\n\r\nThis is a test message sent to you from the debug.py program\r\nin
Foundations of Python Network Programming.\r\n.\r\n'
reply: b'250 OK\r\n'
reply: retcode (250); Msg: b'OK'
data: (250, b'OK')
send: 'quit\r\n'
reply: b'221 Bye\r\n'
reply: retcode (221); Msg: b'Bye'
Message sent to 1 recipient
```

From this example, you can see the conversation that smtplib is having with the SMTP server over the network. As you implement code that uses more advanced SMTP features, the details shown here will be more important, so let's look at what's happening.

First, the client (the smtplib library) sends an EHLO command (an "extended" successor to a more ancient command that was named, more readably, HELO) with your hostname in it. The remote server responds with its own hostname, and it lists any optional SMTP features that it supports.

Next, the client sends the mail from command, which states the "envelope sender" e-mail address and the size of the message. The server at this moment has the opportunity to reject the message (for example, because it thinks you are a spammer); but in this case it responds with 250 Ok. (Note that in this case, the code 250 is what matters; the remaining text is just a human-readable comment and varies from server to server.)

Then the client sends a rcpt to command, with the "envelope recipient," which I discussed previously in this chapter. You can finally see that, indeed, it is transmitted separately from the text of the message itself when using the SMTP protocol. If you were sending the message to more than one recipient, they would each be listed on the rcpt to line.

Finally, the client sends a data command, transmits the actual message (using verbose carriage-return-linefeed line endings, you will note, per the Internet e-mail standard), and finishes the conversation.

The smtplib module is doing all of this automatically for you in this example. In the rest of the chapter, I'll explain how to take more control of the process to take advantage of some more advanced features.

▓ **Caution** Don't get a false sense of confidence that because no error was detected during this first hop, you're convinced that the message is now guaranteed to be delivered. In many cases, an e-mail server may accept a message, only to have delivery fail at a later time. Reread the "Multiple Hops" section and imagine how many possibilities of failure there are before that sample message reaches its destination!

Getting Information from *EHLO*

Sometimes it is nice to know what kind of messages a remote SMTP server will accept. For instance, most SMTP servers have a limit on what size message they permit, and if you fail to check first, then you may transmit a very large message only to have it rejected when you have completed transmission.

In the original version of SMTP, a client would send an HELO command as the initial greeting to the server. A set of extensions to SMTP, called ESMTP, has been developed to allow more powerful conversations. ESMTP-aware clients will begin the conversation with EHLO, which signals an ESMTP-aware server that it can reply to with extended information. This extended information includes the maximum message size, along with any optional SMTP features that the server supports.

However, you must be careful to check the return code. Some servers do not support ESMTP. On those servers, EHLO will just return an error. In that case, you must send an HELO command instead.

In the previous examples, I used sendmail() immediately after creating the SMTP object, so smtplib automatically sent its own "hello" message to the server to get the conversation started for you. But if it sees you attempt to send the EHLO or HELO command on your own, then the Python sendmail() method will not attempt to send a hello command itself.

Listing 13-4 shows a program that gets the maximum size from the server and returns an error before sending if a message would be too large.

Listing 13-4. Checking Message Size Restrictions

```
#!/usr/bin/env python3
# Foundations of Python Network Programming, Third Edition
# https://github.com/brandon-rhodes/fopnp/blob/m/py3/chapter13/ehlo.py

import smtplib, socket, sys

message_template = """To: {}
From: {}
Subject: Test Message from simple.py

Hello,

This is a test message sent to you from the ehlo.py program
in Foundations of Python Network Programming.
"""

def main():
    if len(sys.argv) < 4:
        name = sys.argv[0]
        print("usage: {} server fromaddr toaddr [toaddr...]".format(name))
        sys.exit(2)

    server, fromaddr, toaddrs = sys.argv[1], sys.argv[2], sys.argv[3:]
    message = message_template.format(', '.join(toaddrs), fromaddr)
```

```
try:
    connection = smtplib.SMTP(server)
    report_on_message_size(connection, fromaddr, toaddrs, message)
except (socket.gaierror, socket.error, socket.herror,
        smtplib.SMTPException) as e:
    print("Your message may not have been sent!")
    print(e)
    sys.exit(1)
else:
    s = '' if len(toaddrs) == 1 else 's'
    print("Message sent to {} recipient{}".format(len(toaddrs), s))
    connection.quit()

def report_on_message_size(connection, fromaddr, toaddrs, message):
    code = connection.ehlo()[0]
    uses_esmtp = (200 <= code <= 299)
    if not uses_esmtp:
        code = connection.helo()[0]
        if not (200 <= code <= 299):
            print("Remote server refused HELO; code:", code)
            sys.exit(1)

    if uses_esmtp and connection.has_extn('size'):
        print("Maximum message size is", connection.esmtp_features['size'])
        if len(message) > int(connection.esmtp_features['size']):
            print("Message too large; aborting.")
            sys.exit(1)

    connection.sendmail(fromaddr, toaddrs, message)

if __name__ == '__main__':
    main()
```

If you run this program, and the remote server provides its maximum message size, then the program will display the size on your screen and verify that its message does not exceed that size before sending. (For a tiny message like this, the check is rather silly, but the listing illustrates the pattern you can use successfully with much larger messages.)

Here is what running this program might look like:

```
$ python3 ehlo.py mail.example.com sender@example.com recipient@example.com
Maximum message size is 33554432
Message successfully sent to 1 recipient
```

Take a look at the part of the code that verifies the result from a call to ehlo() or helo(). Those two functions return a list; the first item in the list is a numeric result code from the remote SMTP server. Results between 200 and 299, inclusive, indicate success; everything else indicates a failure. Therefore, if the result is within that range, you know that the server processed the message properly.

▪ **Caution** The same caution as before applies here. The fact that the first SMTP server accepts the message does not mean that it will actually be delivered; a later server may have a more restrictive maximum size.

Besides message size, other ESMTP information is available as well. For instance, some servers may accept data in raw 8-bit mode if they provide the 8BITMIME capability. Others may support encryption, as described in the next section. For more on ESMTP and its capabilities, which may vary from server to server, consult RFC 1869 or your own server's documentation.

Using Secure Sockets Layer and Transport Layer Security

As discussed previously, e-mails sent in plain text over SMTP can be read by anyone with access to an Internet gateway or router across which the packets happen to pass, including the wireless network at the coffee shop from which your e-mail client might be trying to send. The best solution to this problem is to encrypt each e-mail with a public key whose private key is possessed only by the person to whom you are sending the e-mail; there are freely available systems like the GNU Privacy Guard for doing exactly this. But regardless of whether the messages themselves are protected, individual SMTP conversations between particular pairs of machines can be encrypted and authenticated using SSL/TLS, as introduced in Chapter 6. In this section, you will learn about how SSL/TLS fits in with SMTP conversations.

Keep in mind that TLS protects only the SMTP "hops" that choose to use it—even if you carefully use TLS to send an e-mail to a server, you have no control over whether that server uses TLS again if it has to forward your e-mail across another hop toward its destination.

The general procedure for using TLS in SMTP is as follows:

1. Create the SMTP object, as usual.

2. Send the EHLO command. If the remote server does not support EHLO, then it will not support TLS.

3. Check s.has_extn() to see if starttls is present. If not, then the remote server does not support TLS and the message can only be sent normally, in the clear.

4. Build an SSL context object to verify the server's identity for you.

5. Call starttls() to initiate the encrypted channel.

6. Call ehlo() a second time; this time, it's encrypted.

7. Finally, send your message.

The first question you have to ask yourself when working with TLS is whether you should return an error if TLS is not available. Depending on your application, you might want to raise an error for any of the following conditions:

- There is no support for TLS on the remote side.

- The remote side fails to establish a TLS session properly.

- The remote server presents a certificate that cannot be validated.

Let's step through each of these scenarios and see when they may deserve an error message.

First, it is sometimes appropriate to treat a lack of support for TLS altogether as an error. This could be the case if you are writing an application that speaks to only a limited set of e-mail servers—perhaps e-mail servers run by your company that you know should support TLS or e-mail servers run by an institution that you know supports TLS.

Because only a minority of e-mail servers on the Internet today supports TLS, an e-mail program should not, in general, treat its absence as an error. Many TLS-aware SMTP clients will use TLS if available but will fall back on standard, unsecured transmission otherwise. This is known as *opportunistic encryption*, and it is less secure than forcing all communications to be encrypted, but it protects messages when the capability is present.

Second, sometimes a remote server claims to be TLS aware but then fails to properly establish a TLS connection. This is often due to a misconfiguration on the server's end. To be as robust as possible, you may wish to retry a failed encrypted transmission to such a server over a new connection that you do not even try to encrypt.

Third, there is the situation where you cannot completely authenticate the remote server. Again, for a complete discussion of peer validation, see Chapter 6. If your security policy dictates that you must exchange e-mail only with trusted servers, then lack of authentication is clearly a problem warranting an error message.

Listing 13-5 acts as a TLS-capable, general-purpose client. It will connect to a server and use TLS if it can; otherwise, it will fall back and send the message as usual. It *will* die with an error if the attempt to start TLS fails while talking to an ostensibly capable server.

Listing 13-5. Using TLS Opportunistically

```
#!/usr/bin/env python3
# Foundations of Python Network Programming, Third Edition
# https://github.com/brandon-rhodes/fopnp/blob/m/py3/chapter13/tls.py

import sys, smtplib, socket, ssl

message_template = """To: {}
From: {}
Subject: Test Message from simple.py

Hello,

This is a test message sent to you from the tls.py program
in Foundations of Python Network Programming.
"""

def main():
    if len(sys.argv) < 4:
        name = sys.argv[0]
        print("Syntax: {} server fromaddr toaddr [toaddr...]".format(name))
        sys.exit(2)

    server, fromaddr, toaddrs = sys.argv[1], sys.argv[2], sys.argv[3:]
    message = message_template.format(', '.join(toaddrs), fromaddr)

    try:
        connection = smtplib.SMTP(server)
        send_message_securely(connection, fromaddr, toaddrs, message)
    except (socket.gaierror, socket.error, socket.herror,
            smtplib.SMTPException) as e:
        print("Your message may not have been sent!")
        print(e)
        sys.exit(1)
    else:
        s = '' if len(toaddrs) == 1 else 's'
        print("Message sent to {} recipient{}".format(len(toaddrs), s))
        connection.quit()
```

```
def send_message_securely(connection, fromaddr, toaddrs, message):
    code = connection.ehlo()[0]
    uses_esmtp = (200 <= code <= 299)
    if not uses_esmtp:
        code = connection.helo()[0]
        if not (200 <= code <= 299):
            print("Remove server refused HELO; code:", code)
            sys.exit(1)

    if uses_esmtp and connection.has_extn('starttls'):
        print("Negotiating TLS....")
        context = ssl.SSLContext(ssl.PROTOCOL_SSLv23)
        context.set_default_verify_paths()
        context.verify_mode = ssl.CERT_REQUIRED
        connection.starttls(context=context)
        code = connection.ehlo()[0]
        if not (200 <= code <= 299):
            print("Couldn't EHLO after STARTTLS")
            sys.exit(5)
        print("Using TLS connection.")
    else:
        print("Server does not support TLS; using normal connection.")

    connection.sendmail(fromaddr, toaddrs, message)

if __name__ == '__main__':
    main()
```

Notice that the call to sendmail() in the last few listings is the same, regardless of whether TLS is used. Once TLS is started, the system hides that layer of complexity from you, so you do not need to worry about it.

Authenticated SMTP

Finally, there is the topic of authenticated SMTP, where your ISP, university, or company e-mail server needs you to log in with a username and password, to prove that you are not a spammer, before they allow you to send e-mail.

For maximum security, TLS should be used in conjunction with authentication; otherwise your password (and username, for that matter) will be visible to anyone observing the connection. The proper way to do this is to establish the TLS connection first and then send your authentication information only over the encrypted communications channel.

Authentication itself is simple; smtplib provides a login() function that takes a username and a password. Listing 13-6 shows an example. To avoid repeating code already shown in previous listings, this listing does *not* take the advice provided in the previous paragraph, and it sends the username and password over an unauthenticated connection that will send them in the clear.

Listing 13-6. Authenticating over SMTP

```python
#!/usr/bin/env python3
# Foundations of Python Network Programming, Third Edition
# https://github.com/brandon-rhodes/fopnp/blob/m/py3/chapter13/login.py

import sys, smtplib, socket
from getpass import getpass

message_template = """To: {}
From: {}
Subject: Test Message from simple.py

Hello,

This is a test message sent to you from the login.py program
in Foundations of Python Network Programming.
"""

def main():
    if len(sys.argv) < 4:
        name = sys.argv[0]
        print("Syntax: {} server fromaddr toaddr [toaddr...]".format(name))
        sys.exit(2)

    server, fromaddr, toaddrs = sys.argv[1], sys.argv[2], sys.argv[3:]
    message = message_template.format(', '.join(toaddrs), fromaddr)

    username = input("Enter username: ")
    password = getpass("Enter password: ")

    try:
        connection = smtplib.SMTP(server)
        try:
            connection.login(username, password)
        except smtplib.SMTPException as e:
            print("Authentication failed:", e)
            sys.exit(1)
        connection.sendmail(fromaddr, toaddrs, message)
    except (socket.gaierror, socket.error, socket.herror,
            smtplib.SMTPException) as e:
        print("Your message may not have been sent!")
        print(e)
        sys.exit(1)
    else:
        s = '' if len(toaddrs) == 1 else 's'
        print("Message sent to {} recipient{}".format(len(toaddrs), s))
        connection.quit()

if __name__ == '__main__':
    main()
```

Most outgoing e-mail servers on the Internet do not support authentication. If you are using a server that does not support authentication, you will receive an *Authentication failed* error message from the login() attempt. You can prevent that by checking connection.has_extn('auth') after calling connection.ehlo() provided that the remote server supports ESMTP.

You can run this program just like the previous examples. If you run it with a server that does support authentication, you will be prompted for a username and password. If they are accepted, then the program will proceed to transmit your message.

SMTP Tips

Here are some tips to help you implement SMTP clients:

- There is no way to guarantee that a message was delivered. Sometimes you'll know immediately that your attempt failed, but the lack of an error does not mean that something else will not go wrong before the message is safely delivered to the recipient.

- The sendmail() function raises an exception if *any* of the recipients failed, though the message may still have been sent to other recipients. Check the exception you get back for more details. If it is very important for you to know specifics of which addresses failed—say because you will want to try retransmitting later without producing duplicate copies for the people who have already received the message—you may need to call sendmail() individually for each recipient. Note, however, that this more naïve approach will cause the message body to be transmitted multiple times, once for each recipient.

- SSL/TLS is insecure without certificate validation: until validation happens, you could be talking to any old server that has temporarily gotten control of the normal server's IP address. To support certificate verification, remember to create an SSL context object, as shown in the TLS previous example, and provide it as the sole argument to starttls().

- Python's smtplib is not meant to be a general-purpose e-mail relay. Rather, you should use it to send messages to an SMTP server close to you that will handle the actual delivery of e-mail.

Summary

SMTP is used to transmit e-mail messages to e-mail servers. Python provides the smtplib module for SMTP clients to use. By calling the sendmail() method of SMTP objects, you can transmit messages. The sole means of specifying the actual recipients of a message is with parameters to sendmail(); the To, Cc, and Bcc message headers in the text of the message itself are separate from the actual list of recipients.

Several different exceptions could be raised during an SMTP conversation. Interactive programs should check for and handle them appropriately.

ESMTP is an extension to SMTP. It allows you to discover the maximum message size supported by a remote SMTP server prior to transmitting a message. ESMTP also permits TLS, which is a way to encrypt your conversation with a remote server. Fundamentals of TLS were covered in Chapter 6.

Some SMTP servers require authentication. You can authenticate with the login() method. SMTP does *not* provide functions for downloading messages from a mailbox to your own computer. To accomplish that, you will need the protocols discussed in the next two chapters. POP, discussed in Chapter 14, is a simple way to download messages. IMAP, discussed in Chapter 15, is a more capable and powerful protocol.

CHAPTER 14

POP

POP, the Post Office Protocol, is a simple protocol for downloading e-mail from a server. It is typically used through an e-mail client like Thunderbird or Outlook. You can reread the first few sections of Chapter 13 if you want the big picture of where e-mail clients and protocols like POP fit into the history of Internet e-mail.

If you are tempted to use POP, then you should consider using IMAP instead; Chapter 15 will explain the features that IMAP provides that make it a far more solid foundation for remote e-mail access than the primitive operations supported by POP.

The most common implementation of POP is version 3, commonly referred to as POP3. Because version 3 is so dominant, the terms POP and POP3 are practically interchangeable today.

POP's chief benefit—and also its biggest weakness—is its simplicity. If you simply need to access a remote mailbox, download any new e-mail that has appeared, and have the choice of deleting the e-mail after the download, then POP will be perfect for you. You will be able to accomplish this task quickly and without complex code.

But download and delete are pretty much all that POP is good for. It does not support multiple mailboxes on the remote side nor does it provide any reliable, persistent message identification. This means that you cannot use POP as a protocol for e-mail synchronization, where you leave the original copy of each e-mail message on the server while making a copy to read locally, because when you return to the server later, you cannot easily tell which messages you have already downloaded. If you need this feature, you should check out IMAP, which will be covered in Chapter 15.

The Python Standard Library provides the poplib module, which provides a convenient interface for using POP. This chapter will explain how to use poplib to connect to a POP server, gather summary information about a mailbox, download messages, and delete the originals from the server. Once you know how to complete these four tasks, you will have covered all of the standard POP features!

Note that the Python Standard Library does not provide the ability to act as a POP server, but only as a client. If you need to implement a server, you will need to find a third-party Python package that provides POP server functionality.

POP Server Compatibility

POP servers are notoriously bad at following standards. Standards also simply do not exist for some POP behaviors, leaving the details up to the authors of server software. So while basic operations will generally work fine, certain behaviors do vary from server to server.

For instance, some servers will mark all of your messages as read whenever you connect to the server—whether you download any of them or not! Other servers will mark a message as read only when it is downloaded. Some servers never mark any messages as read at all. The standard itself seems to assume the latter behavior, but is not clear either way. Keep these differences in mind as you read this chapter.

Figure 14-1 illustrates a very simple POP conversation driven from Python.

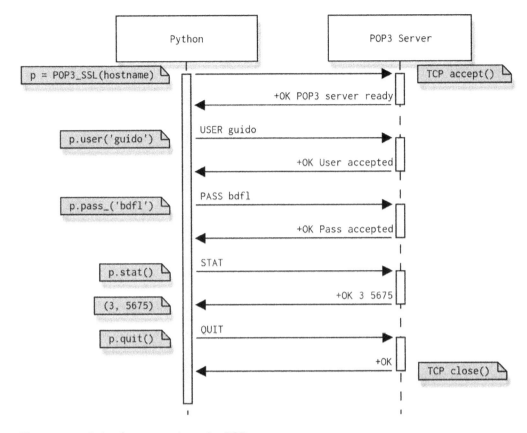

Figure 14-1. *A simple conversation using POP*

Connecting and Authenticating

POP supports several authentication methods. The two most common are basic username-password authentication and APOP, which is an optional extension to POP that helps protect passwords from being sent in plain text if you are using an ancient POP server that does not support SSL.

The process of connecting and authenticating to a remote server looks like this in Python:

1. Create a POP3_SSL or just a plain POP3 object, and pass the remote hostname and port to it.

2. Call user() and pass_() to send the username and password. Note the underscore in pass_()! It is present because pass is a keyword in Python and cannot be used for a method name.

3. If the exception poplib.error_proto is raised, it means that the login has failed and the string value of the exception contains the error explanation sent by the server.

The choice between POP3 and POP3_SSL is governed by whether your e-mail provider offers—or, in this day and age, even requires—that you connect over an encrypted connection. Consult Chapter 6 for more information about SSL, but the general rule should be to use SSL whenever it is at all feasible to do so.

Listing 14-1 uses the foregoing steps to log in to a remote POP server. Once connected, it calls stat(), which returns a simple tuple giving the number of messages in the mailbox and the messages' total size. Finally, the program calls quit(), which closes the POP connection.

THE POP-3 PROTOCOL

Purpose: Allow download of e-mail from inbox

Standard: RFC 1939 (May 1996)

Runs atop: TCP/IP

Default port: 110 (cleartext), 995 (SSL)

Libraries: poplib

Listing 14-1. A Very Simple POP Session

```python
#!/usr/bin/env python3
# Foundations of Python Network Programming, Third Edition
# https://github.com/brandon-rhodes/fopnp/blob/m/py3/chapter14/popconn.py

import getpass, poplib, sys

def main():
    if len(sys.argv) != 3:
        print('usage: %s hostname username' % sys.argv[0])
        exit(2)

    hostname, username = sys.argv[1:]
    passwd = getpass.getpass()

    p = poplib.POP3_SSL(hostname)  # or "POP3" if SSL is not supported
    try:
        p.user(username)
        p.pass_(passwd)
    except poplib.error_proto as e:
        print("Login failed:", e)
    else:
        status = p.stat()
        print("You have %d messages totaling %d bytes" % status)
    finally:
        p.quit()

if __name__ == '__main__':
    main()
```

■ **Caution** Although this program does not alter any messages, some POP servers will nonetheless alter mailbox flags simply because you connected. Running the examples in this chapter against a live mailbox could cause you to lose information about which messages are read, unread, new, or old. Unfortunately, that behavior is server dependent and beyond the control of POP clients. I strongly recommend running these examples against a test mailbox rather than your live mailbox!

This program takes two command-line arguments: the hostname of your POP server, and your username. If you do not know this information, contact your Internet provider or network administrator. Note that on some services, your username will be a plain string (like guido), whereas on others it will be your full e-mail address (guido@example.com).

The program will then prompt you for your password. Finally, it will display the mailbox status, without touching or altering any of your mail.

Here is how you might run the program inside of the Mininet playground, which you can download from the book's source repository (see Chapter 1):

```
$ python3 popconn.py mail.example.com brandon
Password: abc123
You have 3 messages totaling 5675 bytes
```

If you see output like this, then your first POP conversation has taken place successfully!

When POP servers do not support SSL to protect your connection from snooping, they sometimes at least support an alternate authentication protocol called APOP, which uses a challenge–response scheme to ensure that your password is not sent in the clear. (However, all of your e-mail will still be visible to any third party watching the packets go by!) The Python Standard Library makes this very easy to attempt: just call the apop() method, then fall back to basic authentication if the POP server to which you are talking does not understand.

To use APOP but fall back to plain authentication, you could use a stanza like the one shown in Listing 14-2 inside your POP program (like Listing 14-1).

Listing 14-2. Attempting APOP and Falling Back

```
print("Attempting APOP authentication...")
try:
    p.apop(user, passwd)
except poplib.error_proto:
    print("Attempting standard authentication...")
    try:
        p.user(user)
        p.pass_(passwd)
    except poplib.error_proto as e:
        print("Login failed:", e)
        sys.exit(1)
```

■ **Caution**   As soon as a login succeeds by whatever method, some older POP servers will lock the mailbox. Locking might mean that no alterations to the mailbox may be made, or even that no more e-mail may be delivered until the lock is gone. The problem is that some POP servers do not properly detect errors, and they will keep a box locked indefinitely if your connection gets hung up without your calling quit(). At one time, the world's most popular POP server fell into this category! Thus it is vital to always call quit() in your Python programs when finishing up a POP session. You will note that all of the program listings shown here are always careful to quit() down in a finally block that Python is guaranteed to execute last.

Obtaining Mailbox Information

The preceding example showed you stat(), which returns the number of messages in the mailbox and their total size. Another useful POP command is list(), which returns more detailed information about each message.

The most interesting part is the message number, which is required to retrieve messages later. Note that there may be gaps in message numbers: at a given moment a mailbox may, for example, contain only message numbers 1, 2, 5, 6, and 9. Also, the number assigned to a particular message may be different on each connection that you make to the POP server.

Listing 14-3 shows how to use the list() command to display information about each message.

Listing 14-3. Using the POP list() Command

```python
#!/usr/bin/env python3
# Foundations of Python Network Programming, Third Edition
# https://github.com/brandon-rhodes/fopnp/blob/m/py3/chapter14/mailbox.py

import getpass, poplib, sys

def main():
    if len(sys.argv) != 3:
        print('usage: %s hostname username' % sys.argv[0])
        exit(2)

    hostname, username = sys.argv[1:]
    passwd = getpass.getpass()

    p = poplib.POP3_SSL(hostname)
    try:
        p.user(username)
        p.pass_(passwd)
    except poplib.error_proto as e:
        print("Login failed:", e)
    else:
        response, listings, octet_count = p.list()
        if not listings:
            print("No messages")
        for listing in listings:
            number, size = listing.decode('ascii').split()
            print("Message %s has %s bytes" % (number, size))
    finally:
        p.quit()

if __name__ == '__main__':
    main()
```

The list() function returns a tuple containing three items. You should generally pay attention to the second item. Here is the raw output for one of my POP mailboxes at the moment, which has three messages in it:

```
('+OK 3 messages (5675 bytes)', ['1 2395', '2 1626', '3 1654'], 24)
```

The three strings inside the second item give the message number and size for each of the three messages in my inbox. The simple parsing performed by Listing 14-3 lets it present the output in a prettier format. Here is how you might run it against the POP server deployed inside of the book's network playground (see Chapter 1):

```
$ python3 mailbox.py mail.example.com brandon
Password: abc123
Message 1 has 354 bytes
Message 2 has 442 bytes
Message 3 has 1173 bytes
```

Downloading and Deleting Messages

You should now be getting the hang of POP: when using poplib, you issue small atomic commands that always return a tuple, inside of which are various strings and lists of strings that show you the results. You are now actually ready to manipulate messages! The three relevant methods, which all identify messages using the same integer identifiers that are returned by list(), are as follows:

- retr(num): This method downloads a single message and returns a tuple containing a result code and the message itself, delivered as a list of lines. This will cause most POP servers to set the "seen" flag for the message to "true," barring you from ever seeing it from POP again (unless you have another way into your mailbox that lets you set messages back to "Unread").

- top(num, body_lines): This method returns its result in the same format as retr() without marking the message as "seen." But instead of returning the whole message, it just returns the headers plus however many lines of the body you ask for in body_lines. This is useful for previewing messages if you want to let the user decide which ones to download.

- dele(num): This method marks the message for deletion from the POP server, to take place when you quit this POP session. Typically, you would do this only if the user directly requests irrevocable destruction of the message or if you have stored the message to redundant storage (and perhaps backed it up) and have used something like fsync() to ensure that the data have really been written, because you will never again be able to retrieve the message from the server.

To put everything together, take a look at Listing 14-4, which is a fairly functional e-mail client that speaks POP! It checks your in box to determine how many messages there are and to learn their numbers; then it uses top() to offer a preview of each one; and, at the user's option, it can retrieve the whole message and delete it from the mailbox.

Listing 14-4. A Simple POP E-mail Reader

```
#!/usr/bin/env python3
# Foundations of Python Network Programming, Third Edition
# https://github.com/brandon-rhodes/fopnp/blob/m/py3/chapter14/download-and-delete.py

import email, getpass, poplib, sys

def main():
    if len(sys.argv) != 3:
        print('usage: %s hostname username' % sys.argv[0])
        exit(2)
```

```
        hostname, username = sys.argv[1:]
        passwd = getpass.getpass()

        p = poplib.POP3_SSL(hostname)
        try:
            p.user(username)
            p.pass_(passwd)
        except poplib.error_proto as e:
            print("Login failed:", e)
        else:
            visit_all_listings(p)
        finally:
            p.quit()

def visit_all_listings(p):
    response, listings, octets = p.list()
    for listing in listings:
        visit_listing(p, listing)

def visit_listing(p, listing):
    number, size = listing.decode('ascii').split()
    print('Message', number, '(size is', size, 'bytes):')
    print()
    response, lines, octets = p.top(number, 0)
    document = '\n'.join( line.decode('ascii') for line in lines )
    message = email.message_from_string(document)
    for header in 'From', 'To', 'Subject', 'Date':
        if header in message:
            print(header + ':', message[header])
    print()
    print('Read this message [ny]?')
    answer = input()
    if answer.lower().startswith('y'):
        response, lines, octets = p.retr(number)
        document = '\n'.join( line.decode('ascii') for line in lines )
        message = email.message_from_string(document)
        print('-' * 72)
        for part in message.walk():
            if part.get_content_type() == 'text/plain':
                print(part.get_payload())
                print('-' * 72)
    print()
    print('Delete this message [ny]?')
    answer = input()
    if answer.lower().startswith('y'):
        p.dele(number)
        print('Deleted.')

if __name__ == '__main__':
    main()
```

You will note that the listing uses the email module, introduced in Chapter 12, to great advantage, because even fancy modern MIME e-mails with HTML and images usually have a text/plain section that the email module can extract on behalf of a simple program like this for printing to the screen.

If you run this program in the book's network playground (see Chapter 1), you'll see output similar to the following:

```
$ python3 download-and-delete.py mail.example.com brandon
password: abc123
Message 1 (size is 354 bytes):

From: Administrator <admin@mail.example.com>
To: Brandon <brandon@mail.example.com>
Subject: Welcome to example.com!

Read this message [ny]? y
---------------------------------------------------------------------
We are happy that you have chosen to use example.com's industry-leading
Internet e-mail service and we hope that you experience is a pleasant
one.  If you ever need your password reset, simply contact our staff!

- example.com
---------------------------------------------------------------------

Delete this message [ny]? y
Deleted.
```

Summary

POP provides a simple way to download e-mail messages stored on a remote server. With Python's poplib interface, you can obtain information about the number of messages in a mailbox and the size of each message. You can also retrieve or delete individual messages by number.

Connecting to a POP server may lock a mailbox. Therefore, it's important to try to keep POP sessions as brief as possible and always call quit() when done.

POP should be used with SSL whenever possible to protect your passwords and e-mail messages' contents. In the absence of SSL, try to at least use APOP; send your password in the clear only in dire circumstances where you desperately need to use POP and none of the fancier options work.

Although POP is a simple and widely deployed protocol, it has a number of drawbacks that make it unsuitable for some applications. For instance, it can access only one folder, and it does not provide persistent tracking of individual messages.

The next chapter discusses IMAP, a protocol that provides the features of POP with a number of new features as well.

CHAPTER 15

IMAP

At first glance, the Internet Message Access Protocol (IMAP) resembles the POP protocol described in Chapter 14. Plus, if you read the first sections of Chapter 13, which provide the entire picture of how e-mail travels across the Internet, you will already know that the two protocols fill a quite similar role: POP and IMAP are two ways that a laptop or desktop computer can connect to a remote Internet server to view and manipulate a user's e-mail.

And that's where the resemblance ends. Whereas the capabilities of POP are rather anemic—users can download new messages to their personal computers—the IMAP protocol offers such a full array of capabilities that many users sort and archive their e-mail permanently on the server, keeping it safe from a laptop or desktop hard drive crash. Among the advantages that IMAP has over POP are:

- Mail can be sorted into several folders, rather than having to arrive in a single in box.

- Flags are supported for each message, like "read," "replied," "seen," and "deleted."

- Messages can be searched for text strings right on the server, without having to download each one.

- A locally stored message can be uploaded directly to one of the remote folders.

- Persistent unique message numbers are maintained, making robust synchronization possible between a local message store and the messages kept on the server.

- Folders can be shared with other users or marked read-only.

- Some IMAP servers can present nonmail sources, like Usenet newsgroups, as though they were e-mail folders.

- An IMAP client can selectively download one part of a message, for example, grabbing a particular attachment or only the message headers, without having to wait to download the rest of the message.

Taken together, these features mean that IMAP can be used for many more operations than the simple download-and-delete spasm that POP supports. Many e-mail readers, like Thunderbird and Outlook, can present IMAP folders so that they operate with the same capabilities of locally stored folders. When a user clicks a message, the e-mail reader downloads it from the IMAP server and displays it, instead of having to download all of the messages in advance; the reader can also set the message's "read" flag at the same time.

THE IMAP PROTOCOL

Purpose: Read, arrange, and delete E-mail from E-mail folders

Standard: RFC 3501 (2003)

Runs atop: TCP/IP

Default port: 143 (cleartext), 993 (SSL)

Library: imaplib, IMAPClient

```
Exceptions: socket.error, socket.gaierror, IMAP4.error,
    IMAP4.abort, IMAP4.readonly
```

IMAP clients can also synchronize themselves with an IMAP server. Someone about to leave on a business trip might download an IMAP folder to a laptop. Then, on the road, e-mail might be read, deleted, or replied to, and the user's e-mail program would record these actions. When the laptop finally reconnects to the network, their e-mail client can mark the messages on the server with the same "read" or "replied" flags already set locally, and it can go ahead and delete the messages from the server that were already deleted locally so that the user does not see them twice.

The result is one of IMAP's biggest advantages over POP: users can see the same e-mail, in the same state, from all of their laptop and desktop machines. POP users can only see the same e-mail multiple times (if they tell their e-mail clients to leave e-mail on the server), or each message will be downloaded only once to the machine on which they happen to read it (if the e-mail clients delete the mail), which means that their e-mail winds up scattered across all of the machines from which they check it. IMAP users avoid this dilemma.

Of course, IMAP can also be used in exactly the same manner as POP—to download mail, store it locally, and delete the messages immediately from the server—for those who do not want or need its advanced features.

There are several versions of the IMAP protocol available. The most recent, and by far the most popular, is known as IMAP4rev1. In fact, the term "IMAP" is today generally synonymous with IMAP4rev1. This chapter assumes that all IMAP servers are IMAP4rev1 servers. Very old IMAP servers, which are quite uncommon, may not support all of the features discussed in this chapter.

You can also access a good how-to tutorial about writing an IMAP client at the following links:

www.dovecot.org/imap-client-coding-howto.html
www.imapwiki.org/ClientImplementation

If you are doing anything beyond simply writing a small, single-purpose client to summarize the messages in your in box or automatically download attachments, then you should read the information at the foregoing resources thoroughly—or read a book on IMAP, if you want a more thorough reference—so that you can correctly handle all of the situations you might run into with different servers and their implementations of IMAP. This chapter will teach just the basics, with a focus on how best to connect from Python.

Understanding IMAP in Python

The Python Standard Library contains an IMAP client interface, named imaplib, which offers rudimentary access to the protocol. Unfortunately, it limits itself to knowing how to send requests and deliver their responses back to your code. It makes no actual attempt to implement the detailed rules in the IMAP specification for parsing the returned data. As an example of how values returned from imaplib are usually too raw to be useful in a program, take a look at Listing 15-1. It is a simple script that uses imaplib to connect to an IMAP account, list the "capabilities" that the server advertises, and then display the status code and data returned by the LIST command.

Listing 15-1. Connecting to IMAP and Listing Folders

```python
#!/usr/bin/env python3
# Foundations of Python Network Programming, Third Edition
# https://github.com/brandon-rhodes/fopnp/blob/m/py3/chapter15/open_imaplib.py
# Opening an IMAP connection with the pitiful Python Standard Library

import getpass, imaplib, sys

def main():
    if len(sys.argv) != 3:
        print('usage: %s hostname username' % sys.argv[0])
        sys.exit(2)

    hostname, username = sys.argv[1:]
    m = imaplib.IMAP4_SSL(hostname)
    m.login(username, getpass.getpass())
    try:
        print('Capabilities:', m.capabilities)
        print('Listing mailboxes ')
        status, data = m.list()
        print('Status:', repr(status))
        print('Data:')
        for datum in data:
            print(repr(datum))
    finally:
        m.logout()

if __name__ == '__main__':
    main()
```

If you run this script with the appropriate arguments, it will start by asking for your password; IMAP authentication is almost always accomplished through a username and password:

```
$ python open_imaplib.py imap.example.com brandon@example.com
Password:
```

If your password is correct, it will then display a response that looks something like the results shown in Listing 15-2. As promised, you'll see first the "capabilities," which lists the IMAP features that this server supports. And, I must admit, the type of this list is very Pythonic: whatever form the list had on the wire has been turned into a pleasant tuple of strings.

Listing 15-2. Example Output of the Previous Listing

```
Capabilities: ('IMAP4REV1', 'UNSELECT', 'IDLE', 'NAMESPACE', 'QUOTA',
 'XLIST', 'CHILDREN', 'XYZZY', 'SASL-IR', 'AUTH=XOAUTH')
Listing mailboxes
Status: 'OK'
Data:
b'(\\HasNoChildren) "/" "INBOX"'
b'(\\HasNoChildren) "/" "Personal"'
b'(\\HasNoChildren) "/" "Receipts"'
```

```
b'(\\HasNoChildren) "/" "Travel"'
b'(\\HasNoChildren) "/" "Work"'
b'(\\Noselect \\HasChildren) "/" "[Gmail]"'
b'(\\HasChildren \\HasNoChildren) "/" "[Gmail]/All Mail"'
b'(\\HasNoChildren) "/" "[Gmail]/Drafts"'
b'(\\HasChildren \\HasNoChildren) "/" "[Gmail]/Sent Mail"'
b'(\\HasNoChildren) "/" "[Gmail]/Spam"'
b'(\\HasNoChildren) "/" "[Gmail]/Starred"'
b'(\\HasChildren \\HasNoChildren) "/" "[Gmail]/Trash"'
```

But things fall apart when you turn to the results of the list() method. First, you will be returned its status code as the plain string 'OK', so code that uses imaplib has to check incessantly on whether the code is 'OK' or whether it indicates an error. This is not terribly Pythonic, because Python programs can usually run without doing error checking and be secure in the knowledge that an exception will be thrown if anything goes wrong.

Second, imaplib provides no help in interpreting the results! The list of e-mail folders in this IMAP account uses all sorts of protocol-specific quoting: each item in the list names the flags set on each folder, then it designates the character used to separate folders and subfolders (the slash character, in this case), and finally it supplies the quoted name of the folder. But all of this is returned to raw data, requiring you to interpret strings like the following:

```
(\HasChildren \HasNoChildren) "/" "[Gmail]/Sent Mail"
```

Third, the output is a mix of different sequences: the flags are still uninterpreted byte strings, while each delimiter and folder name has been decoded to a real Unicode string.

So, unless you want to implement several details of the protocol yourself, you will want a more capable IMAP client library.

IMAPClient

Fortunately, a popular and battle-tested IMAP library for Python does exist, and it is available for easy installation from the Python Package Index. Menno Smits, a friendly Python programmer, wrote the IMAPClient package, and it in fact uses the Python Standard Library imaplib behind the scenes to do its work.

If you want to try out IMAPClient, try installing it in a "virtualenv," as described in Chapter 1. Once installed, you can use the python interpreter in the virtual environment to run the program, as shown in Listing 15-3.

Listing 15-3. Listing IMAP Folders with IMAPClient

```
#!/usr/bin/env python3
# Foundations of Python Network Programming, Third Edition
# https://github.com/brandon-rhodes/fopnp/blob/m/py3/chapter15/open_imap.py
# Opening an IMAP connection with the powerful IMAPClient

import getpass, sys
from imapclient import IMAPClient

def main():
    if len(sys.argv) != 3:
        print('usage: %s hostname username' % sys.argv[0])
        sys.exit(2)
```

```
hostname, username = sys.argv[1:]
c = IMAPClient(hostname, ssl=True)
try:
    c.login(username, getpass.getpass())
except c.Error as e:
    print('Could not log in:', e)
else:
    print('Capabilities:', c.capabilities())
    print('Listing mailboxes:')
    data = c.list_folders()
    for flags, delimiter, folder_name in data:
        print('  %-30s%s %s' % (' '.join(flags), delimiter, folder_name))
finally:
    c.logout()

if __name__ == '__main__':
    main()
```

You can see immediately from the code that more details of the protocol exchange are now being handled on your behalf. For example, you no longer get a status code back that you have to check every time you run a command; instead, the library is doing that check for you and will raise an exception to stop you in your tracks if anything goes wrong. Figure 15-1 provides a sample conversation between Python and an IMAP server.

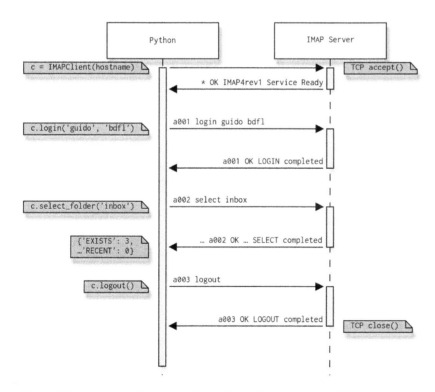

Figure 15-1. *An example conversation between Python and an IMAP server*

Second, you can see that each result from the LIST command—which in this library is offered as the list_folders() method instead of the list() method offered by imaplib—has already been parsed into Python data types. Each line of data comes back as a tuple, giving you the folder flags, folder name delimiter, and folder name, and the flags themselves are a sequence of strings.

Look at Listing 15-4 to see what the output of this second script looks like.

Listing 15-4. Properly Parsed Flags and Folder Names

```
Capabilities: ('IMAP4REV1', 'UNSELECT', 'IDLE', 'NAMESPACE', 'QUOTA', 'XLIST', 'CHILDREN', 'XYZZY',
'SASL-IR', 'AUTH=XOAUTH')
Listing mailboxes:
  \HasNoChildren              / INBOX
  \HasNoChildren              / Personal
  \HasNoChildren              / Receipts
  \HasNoChildren              / Travel
  \HasNoChildren              / Work
  \Noselect \HasChildren      / [Gmail]
  \HasChildren \HasNoChildren / [Gmail]/All Mail
  \HasNoChildren              / [Gmail]/Drafts
  \HasChildren \HasNoChildren / [Gmail]/Sent Mail
  \HasNoChildren              / [Gmail]/Spam
  \HasNoChildren              / [Gmail]/Starred
  \HasChildren \HasNoChildren / [Gmail]/Trash
```

The standard flags listed for each folder may be zero or more of the following:

- \Noinferiors: This means that the folder does not contain any subfolders and that it is impossible for it to contain subfolders in the future. Your IMAP client will receive an error if it tries to create a subfolder within this folder.

- \Noselect: This means that it is not possible to run select_folder() on this folder; that is, this folder does not and cannot contain any messages. (Perhaps it exists just to allow subfolders beneath it, as one possibility.)

- \Marked: This means that the server considers this box to be interesting in some way. Generally, this indicates that new messages have been delivered since the last time the folder was selected. However, the absence of \Marked does *not* guarantee that the folder does not contain new messages; some servers simply do not implement \Marked at all.

- \Unmarked: This guarantees that the folder doesn't contain new messages.

Some servers return additional flags not covered in the standard. Your code must be able to accept and ignore those additional flags.

Examining Folders

Before you can actually download, search, or modify any messages, you must "select" a particular folder to look at. This means that the IMAP protocol is stateful: it remembers which folder you are currently looking at, and its commands operate on the current folder without making you repeat its name over and over again. Only when your connection is closed and you reconnect are you starting fresh with a clean slate. This can make interaction more pleasant, but it also means that your program has to be careful that it always knows what folder is selected, or it might wind up doing something to the wrong folder.

So when you select a folder, you tell the IMAP server that all of the commands that follow—until you change folders or exit the current one—will apply to the selected folder.

When selecting, you have the option to select the folder "read-only," instead of selecting it in full read/write mode, by supplying a `readonly=True` argument. This causes any operations that would delete or modify messages to return an error message should you attempt them. Besides preventing you from making any mistakes when you want to leave all of the messages intact, the fact that you are just reading can be used by the server to optimize access to the folder. (For example, it might read-lock, but not write-lock, the actual folder storage on disk while you have it selected.)

Message Numbers vs. UIDs

IMAP provides two different ways to refer to a specific message within a folder: by a temporary message number (which typically goes 1, 2, 3, and so forth) or by a unique identifier (UID). The difference between the two lies in their persistence. Message numbers are assigned at the moment you select a folder over a particular connection. This means they can be pretty and sequential, but it also means that if you revisit the same folder later, a given message might then have a different number. For programs such as live e-mail readers or simple download scripts, this behavior (which is the same as POP) is fine; you won't care that the numbers might be different the next time you connect.

But a UID, by contrast, is designed to remain the same, even if you close your connection to the server and do not reconnect again. If a message had UID 1053 today, then the same message will have UID 1053 tomorrow, and no other message in that folder will ever have UID 1053. If you are writing a synchronization tool, this behavior is quite useful! It will allow you to verify with 100 percent certainty that actions are being taken against the correct message. This is one of the things that makes IMAP so much more fun to use than POP.

Note that if you return to an IMAP account and the user has, without telling you, deleted a folder and then created a new one with the same name, then it might look to your program as though the same folder is present but that the UID numbers are conflicting and no longer agree. Even a folder rename, if you fail to notice it, might make you lose track of which messages in the IMAP account correspond to which messages you have already downloaded. But it turns out that IMAP is prepared to protect you against this, and (as I'll explain soon) provides a `UIDVALIDITY` folder attribute that you can compare from one session to the next to see whether UIDs in the folder will really correspond to the UIDs that the same messages had when you last connected.

Most IMAP commands that work with specific messages can take either message numbers or UIDs. Normally, IMAPClient always uses UIDs and ignores the temporary message numbers assigned by IMAP. But if you want to see the temporary numbers instead, simply instantiate IMAPClient with a `use_uid=False` argument, or you can even set the value of the class's `use_uid` attribute to `False` and `True` on the fly during your IMAP session.

Message Ranges

Most IMAP commands that work with messages can work with one or more messages. This can make processing far faster if you need a whole group of messages. Instead of issuing separate commands and receiving separate responses for each individual message, you can operate on a group of messages as a whole. This is often faster because you no longer have to deal with a network roundtrip for every single command.

Where you would usually supply a message number, you can instead supply a comma-separated list of message numbers. Also, if you want all messages whose numbers are in a range but you do not want to have to list all of their numbers (or if you do not even know their numbers—maybe you want "everything starting with message one" without having to fetch their numbers first), you can use a colon to separate the start and end message numbers. An asterisk means "and all of the rest of the messages." Here is an example specification:

```
2,4:6,20:*
```

It means "message 2, messages 4 through 6, and message 20 through the end of the mail folder."

Summary Information

When you first select a folder, the IMAP server provides some summary information about it—about the folder itself and also about its messages.

The summary is returned by IMAPClient as a dictionary. Here are the keys that most IMAP servers will return when you run select_folder():

- EXISTS: An integer giving the number of messages in the folder.

- FLAGS: A list of the flags that can be set on messages in this folder.

- RECENT: Specifies the server's estimate of the number of messages that have appeared in the folder since the last time an IMAP client ran select_folder() on it.

- PERMANENTFLAGS: Specifies the list of custom flags that can be set on messages; this is usually empty.

- UIDNEXT: The server's guess about the UID that will be assigned to the next incoming (or uploaded) message.

- UIDVALIDITY: A string that can be used by clients to verify that the UID numbering has not changed. If you come back to a folder and this is a different value than the last time you connected, then the UID number has started over and your stored UID values are no longer valid.

- UNSEEN: Specifies the message number of the first unseen message (the one without the \Seen flag) in the folder.

Of these flags, servers are only required to return FLAGS, EXISTS, and RECENT, though most will include at least UIDVALIDITY as well. Listing 15-5 shows a sample program that reads and displays the summary information of my INBOX e-mail folder.

Listing 15-5. Displaying Folder Summary Information

```
#!/usr/bin/env python3
# Foundations of Python Network Programming, Third Edition
# https://github.com/brandon-rhodes/fopnp/blob/m/py3/chapter15/folder_info.py
# Opening an IMAP connection with IMAPClient and listing folder information.

import getpass, sys
from imapclient import IMAPClient

def main():
    if len(sys.argv) != 4:
        print('usage: %s hostname username foldername' % sys.argv[0])
        sys.exit(2)

    hostname, username, foldername = sys.argv[1:]
    c = IMAPClient(hostname, ssl=True)
    try:
        c.login(username, getpass.getpass())
    except c.Error as e:
        print('Could not log in:', e)
    else:
        select_dict = c.select_folder(foldername, readonly=True)
        for k, v in sorted(select_dict.items()):
            print('%s: %r' % (k, v))
    finally:
        c.logout()
```

```
if __name__ == '__main__':
    main()
```

When run, this program displays results such as this:

```
$ ./folder_info.py imap.example.com brandon@example.com
Password:
EXISTS: 3
PERMANENTFLAGS: ('\\Answered', '\\Flagged', '\\Draft', '\\Deleted',
                 '\\Seen', '\\*')
READ-WRITE: True
UIDNEXT: 2626
FLAGS: ('\\Answered', '\\Flagged', '\\Draft', '\\Deleted', '\\Seen')
UIDVALIDITY: 1
RECENT: 0
```

This shows that my INBOX folder contains three messages, none of which have arrived since I last checked. If your program is interested in using UIDs that it stored during previous sessions, remember to compare the UIDVALIDITY to a stored value from a previous session.

Downloading an Entire Mailbox

With IMAP, the FETCH command is used to download mail, which an IMAPClient exposes as its fetch() method.

The simplest way to fetch involves downloading all messages at once in a single big gulp. Although this is the simplest and requires the least network traffic (because you do not have to issue repeated commands and receive multiple responses), it does mean that all of the returned messages will need to sit in memory together as your program examines them. For very large mailboxes whose messages have lots of attachments, this is obviously not practical!

Listing 15-6 downloads all of the messages from the INBOX folder into your computer's memory in a Python data structure, and then displays a bit of summary information about each one.

Listing 15-6. Downloading All Messages in a Folder

```
#!/usr/bin/env python3
# Foundations of Python Network Programming, Third Edition
# https://github.com/brandon-rhodes/fopnp/blob/m/py3/chapter15/folder_summary.py
# Opening an IMAP connection with IMAPClient and retrieving mailbox messages.

import email, getpass, sys
from imapclient import IMAPClient

def main():
    if len(sys.argv) != 4:
        print('usage: %s hostname username foldername' % sys.argv[0])
        sys.exit(2)

    hostname, username, foldername = sys.argv[1:]
    c = IMAPClient(hostname, ssl=True)
    try:
        c.login(username, getpass.getpass())
    except c.Error as e:
        print('Could not log in:', e)
```

```
        else:
            print_summary(c, foldername)
    finally:
        c.logout()

def print_summary(c, foldername):
    c.select_folder(foldername, readonly=True)
    msgdict = c.fetch('1:*', ['BODY.PEEK[]'])
    for message_id, message in list(msgdict.items()):
        e = email.message_from_string(message['BODY[]'])
        print(message_id, e['From'])
        payload = e.get_payload()
        if isinstance(payload, list):
            part_content_types = [ part.get_content_type() for part in payload ]
            print('  Parts:', ' '.join(part_content_types))
        else:
            print('  ', ' '.join(payload[:60].split()), '...')

if __name__ == '__main__':
    main()
```

Remember that IMAP is stateful: first you use select_folder() to put yourself "inside" the given folder, and then you can run fetch() to ask for message content. (You can later run close_folder() if you want to leave and not be inside a given folder any more.) The range '1:*' means "the first message through the end of the mail folder," because message IDs—whether temporary or UIDs—are always positive integers.

The perhaps odd-looking string 'BODY.PEEK[]' is the way to ask IMAP for the "whole body" of the message. The string 'BODY[]' means "the whole message"; inside the square brackets, as you will see, you can instead ask for just specific parts of a message.

And PEEK indicates that you are just looking inside the message to build a summary, and that you do *not* want the server to set the \Seen flag automatically on all of these messages for you and thus ruin its memory about which messages the user has read. (This seemed to be a nice feature for me to add to a little script like this that you might run against a real mailbox—I would not want to mark all of your messages as read!)

The dictionary that is returned maps message UIDs to dictionaries giving information about each message. As you iterate across its keys and values, you look in each message dictionary for the 'BODY[]' key that IMAP has filled in with the information about the message for which you asked: its full text, returned as a large string.

Using the email module that I discussed in Chapter 12, the script asks Python to grab the From: line and a bit of the message's content and print them to the screen as a summary. Of course, if you wanted to extend this script so that you save the messages in a file or database instead, you could just omit the email parsing step and instead treat the message body as a single string to be deposited in storage and parsed later.

Here is what the results look like when you run this script:

```
$ ./mailbox_summary.py imap.example.com brandon INBOX
Password:
2590 "Amazon.com" <order-update@amazon.com>
   Dear Brandon, Portable Power Systems, Inc. shipped the follo ...
2469 Meetup Reminder <info@meetup.com>
   Parts: text/plain text/html
2470 billing@linode.com
   Thank you. Please note that charges will appear as "Linode.c ...
```

Of course, if the messages contained large attachments, it could be ruinous to download them in their entirety just to print a summary; but because this is the simplest message-fetching operation, I thought that it would be reasonable to start with it!

Downloading Messages Individually

E-mail messages can be quite large, and so can e-mail folders—many e-mail systems permit users to have hundreds or thousands of messages, each of which can be 10MB or more. That kind of mailbox can easily exceed the RAM on the client machine if its contents are all downloaded at once, as was done in the previous example.

To help network-based e-mail clients that do not want to keep local copies of every message, IMAP supports several operations besides the big "fetch the whole message" command discussed in the previous section.

- An e-mail's headers can be downloaded as a block of text, separately from the message.

- Particular headers from a message can be requested and returned without downloading them all.

- The server can be asked to recursively explore and return an outline of the MIME structure of a message.

- The text of particular sections of the message can be returned.

This allows IMAP clients to perform very efficient queries that download only the information they need to display for the user, decreasing the load on the IMAP server and the network and allowing results to be displayed more quickly to the user.

For an example of how a simple IMAP client works, examine Listing 15-7, which puts together a number of ideas about browsing an IMAP account. This should provide more context than would be possible if these features were spread out over a half-dozen shorter program listings at this point in the chapter! You can see that the client consists of three concentric loops that each takes input from users as they view the list of e-mail folders, then the list of messages within a particular e-mail folder, and finally the sections of a specific message.

Listing 15-7. A Simple IMAP Client

```
#!/usr/bin/env python3
# Foundations of Python Network Programming, Third Edition
# https://github.com/brandon-rhodes/fopnp/blob/m/py3/chapter15/simple_client.py
# Letting a user browse folders, messages, and message parts.

import getpass, sys
from imapclient import IMAPClient

banner = '-' * 72

def main():
    if len(sys.argv) != 3:
        print('usage: %s hostname username' % sys.argv[0])
        sys.exit(2)

    hostname, username = sys.argv[1:]
    c = IMAPClient(hostname, ssl=True)
    try:
        c.login(username, getpass.getpass())
    except c.Error as e:
        print('Could not log in:', e)
```

```
    else:
        explore_account(c)
    finally:
        c.logout()

def explore_account(c):
    """Display the folders in this IMAP account and let the user choose one."""

    while True:

        print()
        folderflags = {}
        data = c.list_folders()
        for flags, delimiter, name in data:
            folderflags[name] = flags
        for name in sorted(folderflags.keys()):
            print('%-30s %s' % (name, ' '.join(folderflags[name])))
        print()

        reply = input('Type a folder name, or "q" to quit: ').strip()
        if reply.lower().startswith('q'):
            break
        if reply in folderflags:
            explore_folder(c, reply)
        else:
            print('Error: no folder named', repr(reply))

def explore_folder(c, name):
    """List the messages in folder `name` and let the user choose one."""

    while True:
        c.select_folder(name, readonly=True)
        msgdict = c.fetch('1:*', ['BODY.PEEK[HEADER.FIELDS (FROM SUBJECT)]',
                                  'FLAGS', 'INTERNALDATE', 'RFC822.SIZE'])
        print()
        for uid in sorted(msgdict):
            items = msgdict[uid]
            print('%6d  %20s  %6d bytes  %s' % (
                uid, items['INTERNALDATE'], items['RFC822.SIZE'],
                ' '.join(items['FLAGS'])))
            for i in items['BODY[HEADER.FIELDS (FROM SUBJECT)]'].splitlines():
                print(' ' * 6, i.strip())

        reply = input('Folder %s - type a message UID, or "q" to quit: '
                      % name).strip()
        if reply.lower().startswith('q'):
            break
        try:
            reply = int(reply)
        except ValueError:
            print('Please type an integer or "q" to quit')
```

```
        else:
            if reply in msgdict:
                explore_message(c, reply)

    c.close_folder()

def explore_message(c, uid):
    """Let the user view various parts of a given message."""

    msgdict = c.fetch(uid, ['BODYSTRUCTURE', 'FLAGS'])

    while True:
        print()
        print('Flags:', end=' ')
        flaglist = msgdict[uid]['FLAGS']
        if flaglist:
            print(' '.join(flaglist))
        else:
            print('none')
        print('Structure:')
        display_structure(msgdict[uid]['BODYSTRUCTURE'])
        print()
        reply = input('Message %s - type a part name, or "q" to quit: '
                      % uid).strip()
        print()
        if reply.lower().startswith('q'):
            break
        key = 'BODY[%s]' % reply
        try:
            msgdict2 = c.fetch(uid, [key])
        except c._imap.error:
            print('Error - cannot fetch section %r' % reply)
        else:
            content = msgdict2[uid][key]
            if content:
                print(banner)
                print(content.strip())
                print(banner)
            else:
                print('(No such section)')

def display_structure(structure, parentparts=[]):
    """Attractively display a given message structure."""

    # The whole body of the message is named 'TEXT'.
```

```
    if parentparts:
        name = '.'.join(parentparts)
    else:
        print('  HEADER')
        name = 'TEXT'

    # Print a simple, non-multipart MIME part.  Include its disposition,
    # if available.

    is_multipart = not isinstance(structure[0], str)

    if not is_multipart:
        parttype = ('%s/%s' % structure[:2]).lower()
        print('  %-9s' % name, parttype, end=' ')
        if structure[6]:
            print('size=%s' % structure[6], end=' ')
        if structure[9]:
            print('disposition=%s' % structure[9][0],
                  ' '.join('{}={}'.format(k, v) for k, v in structure[9][1:]),
                  end=' ')
        print()
        return

    # For a multipart part, print all of its subordinate parts.

    parttype = 'multipart/%s' % structure[1].lower()
    print('  %-9s' % name, parttype, end=' ')
    print()
    subparts = structure[0]
    for i in range(len(subparts)):
        display_structure(subparts[i], parentparts + [ str(i + 1) ])

if __name__ == '__main__':
    main()
```

You can see that the outer function uses a simple list_folders() call to present the users with a list of e-mail folders, like some of the program listings previously discussed. Each folder's IMAP flags are also displayed. This lets the program give users a choice between folders:

```
INBOX                       \HasNoChildren
Receipts                    \HasNoChildren
Travel                      \HasNoChildren
Work                        \HasNoChildren
Type a folder name, or "q" to quit:
```

Once a user has selected a folder, things become more interesting: a summary has to be printed for each message. Different e-mail clients make different choices about what information to present about each message in a folder. The code in Listing 15-7 chooses to select a few header fields together with the message's date and size. Note that it is careful to use BODY.PEEK instead of BODY to fetch these items, since the IMAP server would otherwise mark the messages as \Seen merely because they had been displayed in a summary!

The results of this fetch() call are printed to the screen once an e-mail folder has been selected:

```
2703   2010-09-28 21:32:13   19129 bytes   \Seen
       From: Brandon Craig Rhodes
       Subject: Digested Articles

2704   2010-09-28 23:03:45   15354 bytes
       Subject: Re: [venv] Building a virtual environment for offline testing
       From: "W. Craig Trader"

2705   2010-09-29 08:11:38   10694 bytes
       Subject: Re: [venv] Building a virtual environment for offline testing
       From: Hugo Lopes Tavares

Folder INBOX - type a message UID, or "q" to quit:
```

As you can see, the fact that several items of interest can be supplied to the IMAP fetch() command allows you to build fairly sophisticated message summaries with only a single roundtrip to the server!

Once the user has selected a particular message, a technique that I have not discussed so far is used: fetch() is asked to return the BODYSTRUCTURE of the message, which is the key to seeing a MIME message's parts without having to download its entire text. Instead of making you pull several megabytes over the network just to list a large message's attachments, BODYSTRUCTURE simply lists its MIME sections as a recursive data structure.

Simple MIME parts are returned as a tuple:

```
('TEXT', 'PLAIN', ('CHARSET', 'US-ASCII'), None, None, '7BIT', 2279, 48)
```

The elements of this tuple, which are detailed in section 7.4.2 of RFC 3501, are as follows (starting from item index zero, of course):

1. MIME type

2. MIME subtype

3. Body parameters, presented as a tuple (name, value, name, value, ...) where each parameter name is followed by its value

4. Content ID

5. Content description

6. Content encoding

7. Content size in bytes

8. For textual MIME types, this gives the content length in lines

When the IMAP server sees that a message is multipart, or when it examines one of the parts of the message that it discovers is itself multipart (see Chapter 12 for more information about how MIME messages can nest other MIME messages inside them), then the tuple it returns will begin with a list of substructures, which are each a tuple laid out just like the outer structure. Then it will finish with some information about the multipart container that bound those sections together:

```
([(...), (...)], "MIXED", ('BOUNDARY', '=-=-='), None, None)
```

The value "MIXED" indicates exactly what kind of multipart container is being represented—in this case, the full type is multipart/mixed. Other common "multipart" subtypes, besides "MIXED", are "ALTERNATIVE", "DIGEST", and "PARALLEL". The remaining items beyond the multipart type are optional, but if present, they provide a set of name-value parameters (here indicating what the MIME multipart boundary string was), the multipart's disposition, its language, and its location (typically given by a URL).

Given these rules, you can see how a recursive routine like display_structure() in Listing 15-7 is perfect for unwinding and displaying the hierarchy of parts in a message. When the IMAP server returns a BODYSTRUCTURE, the routine goes to work and prints out something like this for examination by the user:

```
Folder INBOX - type a message UID, or "q" to quit: 2701
Flags: \Seen
HEADER
TEXT       multipart/mixed
1          multipart/alternative
1.1        text/plain size=253
1.2        text/html size=508
2          application/octet-stream size=5448 ATTACHMENT FILENAME='test.py'
Message 2701 - type a part name, or "q" to quit:
```

You can see that the message whose structure is shown here is a quite typical modern e-mail, with a fancy rich-text HTML portion for users who view it in a browser or modern e-mail client, and a plain-text version of the same message for those using more traditional devices or applications. It also contains a file attachment, complete with a suggested file name in case the user wants to download it to the local file system. This sample program does not attempt to save anything to the hard drive, both for simplicity and safety; instead, the user can select any portion of the message—such as the special sections HEADER and TEXT, or one of the specific parts like 1.1—and its content will be printed to the screen.

If you examine the program listing, you will see that all of this is supported simply by calls to the IMAP fetch() method. Part names like HEADER and 1.1 are simply more options for what you can specify when you call fetch(), and they can be used right alongside other values like BODY.PEEK and FLAGS. The only difference is that the latter values work for all messages; whereas a part name like 2.1.3 would exist only for multipart messages whose structure included a part with that designation.

One oddity that you will note is that the IMAP protocol does *not* actually provide you with any of the multipart names that a particular message supports! Instead, you have to count the number of parts listed in the BODYSTRUCTURE starting with the index 1 in order to determine which part number you should request. You can see that the display_structure() routine here uses a simple loop to accomplish this counting.

One final note about the fetch() command: it not only lets you pull just the parts of a message that you need at any given moment, but it also truncates them if they are quite long and you just want to provide an excerpt from the beginning to tantalize the user! To use this feature, follow any part name with a slice in angle brackets that indicates the range of characters that you want—it works very much like Python's slice operation:

```
BODY[]<0.100>
```

This would return the first 100 bytes of the message body, from offset zero to offset one hundred. This can let you inspect both text and the beginning of an attachment to learn more about its content before letting the user decide whether to select or download it.

Flagging and Deleting Messages

You might have noticed, while trying out Listing 15-7 or reading its sample output, that IMAP marks messages with attributes called *flags*, which typically take the form of a backslash-prefixed word, such as \Seen as seen for one of the messages just cited. Several of these are standard, and they are defined in RFC 3501 for use on all IMAP servers. Here is what the most important ones mean:

- \Answered: The user has replied to the message.

- \Draft: The user has not finished composing the message.

- \Flagged: The message has somehow been singled out specially; the purpose and meaning of this flag vary between e-mail readers.

- \Recent: No IMAP client has seen this message before. This flag is unique in that the flag cannot be added or removed by normal commands; it is automatically removed after the mailbox is selected.

- \Seen: The message has been read.

As you can see, these flags correspond roughly to the information that many e-mail readers visually present about each message. Although the terminology may differ (many clients talk about "new" rather than "not seen" messages), almost all e-mail readers display these flags. Particular servers may also support other flags, and the code for those flags will not necessarily begin with a backslash. Also, the \Recent flag is not reliably supported by all servers, so general-purpose IMAP clients can treat it only as, at best, a hint.

The IMAPClient library supports several methods for working with flags. The simplest retrieves the flags as though you had done a fetch() asking for 'FLAGS', but it goes ahead and removes the dictionary around each answer:

```
>>> c.get_flags(2703)
{2703: ('\\Seen',)}
```

There are also calls to add and remove flags from a message:

```
c.remove_flags(2703, ['\\Seen'])
c.add_flags(2703, ['\\Answered'])
```

In case you want to change the set of flags for a particular message completely without figuring out the correct series of adds and removes, you can use set_flags() unilaterally to replace the whole list of message flags with a new one:

```
c.set_flags(2703, ['\\Seen', '\\Answered'])
```

Any of these operations can take a list of message UIDs instead of the single UID shown in these examples.

Deleting Messages

One last interesting use of flags is found in how IMAP supports message deletion. The process, for safety, takes two steps: first the client marks one or more messages with the \Delete flag; then it calls expunge() to perform the pending requested deletions as a single operation.

The IMAPClient library does not make you do this manually, however (though that will work); instead it hides the fact that flags are involved behind a simple delete_messages() routine that marks the messages for you. It still has to be followed by expunge() if you actually want the operation to take effect, however:

```
c.delete_messages([2703, 2704])
c.expunge()
```

Note that expunge() will reorder the temporary IDs of the messages in the mailbox, which is yet another reason for using UIDs instead.

Searching

Searching is another feature that is very important for a protocol designed to let you keep all of your e-mail on the e-mail server itself: without search, an e-mail client would have to download all of a user's e-mail anyway the first time they wanted to perform a full-text search to find an e-mail message.

The essence of search is simple: you call the `search()` method on an IMAP client instance, and you are returned the UIDs (assuming, of course, that you accept the IMAPClient default of `use_uid=True` for your client) of the messages that match your criteria:

```
>>> c.select_folder('INBOX')
>>> c.search('SINCE 13-Jul-2013 TEXT Apress')
[2590L, 2652L, 2653L, 2654L, 2655L, 2699L]
```

These UIDs can then be the subject of a `fetch()` command that retrieves the information about each message you need in order to present a summary of the search results to the user.

The query shown in the foregoing example combines two criteria: one requesting recent messages (those that have arrived since July 13, 2013, the date on which I am typing this) and the other asking that the message text have the word Apress somewhere inside, and the results will include only messages that satisfy the first criteria *and* the second criteria—that is the result of concatenating two criteria with a space so that they form a single string. If instead you wanted messages that match at least one of the criteria, but did not need to match both, you can join the criteria with an OR operator:

```
OR (SINCE 20-Aug-2010) (TEXT Apress)
```

There are many criteria that you can combine in order to form a query. Like the rest of IMAP, they are specified in RFC 3501. Some criteria are quite simple and refer to binary attributes like flags:

```
ALL: Every message in the mailbox
UID (id, ...): Messages with the given UIDs
LARGER n: Messages more than n octets in length
SMALLER m: Messages less than m octets in length
ANSWERED: Have the flag \Answered
DELETED: Have the flag \Deleted
DRAFT: Have the flag \Draft
FLAGGED: Have the flag \Flagged
KEYWORD flag: Have the given keyword flag set
NEW: Have the flag \Recent
OLD: Lack the flag \Recent
UNANSWERED: Lack the flag \Answered
UNDELETED: Lack the flag \Deleted
UNDRAFT: Lack the flag \Draft
UNFLAGGED: Lack the flag \Flagged
UNKEYWORD flag: Lack the given keyword flag
UNSEEN: Lack the flag \Seen
```

There are also a number of flags that match items in each message's headers. Each of them searches for a given string in the header of the same name, except for the "send" tests, which look at the Date header:

```
BCC string
CC string
FROM string
HEADER name string
SUBJECT string
TO string
```

An IMAP message has two dates: the internal Date header specified by the sender, which is called its *send date*, and the date at which it actually arrived at the IMAP server. (The former could obviously be a forgery; the latter is as reliable as the IMAP server and its clock.) So there are two sets of criteria for dates, depending on the date for which you want to query:

```
BEFORE 01-Jan-1970
ON 01-Jan-1970
SINCE 01-Jan-1970
SENTBEFORE 01-Jan-1970
SENTON 01-Jan-1970
SENTSINCE 01-Jan-1970
```

Finally, there are two search operations that refer to the text of the message itself—these are the big workhorses that support full-text searches of the kind your users probably expect when they type into a search field in an e-mail client:

```
BODY string: The message body must contain the string.
TEXT string: The entire message, either body or header, must contain the string somewhere.
```

See the documentation for the particular IMAP server you are using to learn whether it returns any "near miss" matches, like those supported by modern search engines, or only exact matches for the words that you provide.

If your strings contain any characters that IMAP might consider special, try surrounding them with double quotes, and then backslash quote any double quotes within the strings themselves:

```
>>> c.search(r'TEXT "Quoth the raven, \"Nevermore.\""')
[2652L]
```

Note that by using a raw Python r'...' string here, I avoided having to double up the backslashes to get single backslashes through to IMAP.

Manipulating Folders and Messages

Creating or deleting folders is performed quite simply in IMAP by providing the name of the folder:

```
c.create_folder('Personal')
c.delete_folder('Work')
```

Some IMAP servers or configurations may not permit these operations, or they may have restrictions on naming; be sure to have error checking in place when calling them.

There are two operations that can create new e-mail messages in your IMAP account besides the "normal" means of waiting for people to send them to you.

First, you can copy an existing message from its home folder into another folder. Start by using select_folder() to visit the folder where the messages live, and then run the copy method like this:

```
c.select_folder('INBOX')
c.copy([2653L, 2654L], 'TODO')
```

Finally, it is possible to add a message to a mailbox with IMAP. You do not need to send the message first with SMTP; IMAP is all that is needed. Adding a message is a simple process, although there are a couple of things about which you must be aware.

The primary concern is line endings. Many Unix machines use a single ASCII line feed character (0x0a, or '\n' in Python) to designate the end of a line of text. Windows machines use two characters: CR-LF, a manual return (0x0D, or '\r' in Python) followed by a line feed. Older Macs use just the manual return.

Like many Internet protocols (HTTP comes immediately to mind), IMAP internally uses CR-LF ('\r\n' in Python) to designate the end of a line. Some IMAP servers will have problems if you upload a message that uses any other character for the end of a line. Therefore, you must always be careful to have the correct line endings when you translate uploaded messages. This problem is more common than you might expect, because most local mailbox formats use only '\n' for the end of each line.

However, you must also be cautious in how you change the line endings, because some messages may use '\r\n' somewhere inside them despite using only '\n' for the first few dozen lines, and IMAP clients have been known to fail if a message uses both different line endings! The solution is a simple one, thanks to Python's powerful splitlines() string method that recognizes all three possible line endings; simply call the function on your message and then rejoin the lines with the standard line ending:

```
>>> 'one\rtwo\nthree\r\nfour'.splitlines()
['one', 'two', 'three', 'four']
>>> '\r\n'.join('one\rtwo\nthree\r\nfour'.splitlines())
'one\r\ntwo\r\nthree\r\nfour'
```

The actual act of appending a message, once you have the line endings correct, is arranged by calling the append() method on your IMAP client:

```
c.append('INBOX', my_message)
```

You can also supply a list of flags as a keyword argument, as well as a msg_time to be used as its arrival time, by passing a normal Python datetime object.

Asynchrony

Finally, a major admission needs be made about this chapter's approach toward IMAP: even though I have described IMAP as though the protocol were synchronous, it in fact supports clients that want to send dozens of requests down the socket to the server and then receive the answers back in whatever order the server can most efficiently fetch the e-mail from disk and respond.

The IMAPClient library hides this protocol flexibility by always sending one request, waiting for the response, and then returning that value. But other libraries, and in particular the IMAP capabilities provided inside Twisted Python, let you take advantage of its asynchronicity.

For most Python programmers who need to script mailbox interactions, the synchronous approach taken in this chapter should work just fine. And if you do branch out and switch to an asynchronous library, then you will at least already know all of the IMAP commands from their descriptions in this chapter, and you will only have to learn how to send those same commands through the asynchronous library's API.

Summary

IMAP is a robust protocol for accessing e-mail messages stored on a remote server. Many IMAP libraries exist for Python; `imaplib` is built into the Python Standard Library, but it requires you to do all sorts of low-level response parsing by yourself. A far better choice is IMAPClient by Menno Smits, which you can install from the Python Package Index.

On an IMAP server, your e-mail messages are grouped into folders, some of which will come predefined by your particular IMAP provider and some of which you can create yourself. An IMAP client can create folders, delete folders, insert new messages into a folder, and move existing messages between folders.

Once a folder has been selected, which is the rough IMAP equivalent of a "change directory" command on a file system, messages can be listed and fetched very flexibly. Instead of having to download every message in its entirety (though, of course, that is an option), the client can ask for particular information from a message, like a few headers and its message structure, in order to build a display or summary into which the user can click, pulling message parts and attachments down from the server on demand.

The client can also set flags on each message—some of which are also meaningful to the server—and it can delete messages by setting the \Delete flag and then performing an expunge operation.

Finally, IMAP offers sophisticated search functionality so that common user operations can be supported without requiring the e-mail data to be downloaded to the local machine.

In the next chapter we will leave the topic of e-mail and consider a quite different type of communication: delivering shell commands to a remote server and receiving their output in response.

CHAPTER 16

Telnet and SSH

If you have never read it, then you should brew some of your favorite coffee, sit down, and treat yourself to Neal Stephenson's essay "In the Beginning. . . Was the Command Line" (William Morrow Paperbacks, 1999). You can also download a copy from his web site in the form (appropriately enough) of a raw text file at www.cryptonomicon.com/beginning.html.

The command line is the topic of this chapter. It covers how you can access it over the network, together with enough discussion about its typical behavior to get you through any frustrating issues that you might encounter while trying to use it.

Happily enough, the old-fashioned idea of sending simple textual commands to another computer will, for many readers, be one of the most relevant topics of this book. The main network protocol discussed—the Secure Shell (SSH)—seems to be used everywhere to configure and maintain machines of all kinds.

When you get a new account at a web hosting company and you have finished using its fancy control panel to set up your domain names and list of web applications, the command line is then your primary means of installing and running the code behind your web sites.

Virtual servers, or physical servers from companies like Rackspace and Linode, are almost always administered through SSH connections.

If you build a cloud of dynamically allocated servers using an API-based virtual hosting service like Amazon AWS, you will find that Amazon gives you access to your new host by asking you for an SSH key and installing it so that you can log into your new instance immediately and without a password.

It is as if once early computers became able to receive text commands and return text output in response, they reached a kind of pinnacle of usefulness that has yet to be improved upon. Language is the most powerful means humans have for expressing meaning, and no amount of pointing, clicking, or dragging with a mouse has ever expressed even a fraction of what can be communicated when you type, even in the cramped and exacting language of the Unix shell.

Command-Line Automation

Before getting into the details of how the command line works and how you can access a remote command line over the network, note that there are more specific tools you might want to examine if your specific goal is to perform remote system administration. In order of increasing sophistication, here are three directions in which the Python community has taken remote automation:

1. *Fabric* lets you script actions to be performed over SSH connections to your servers, but besides making you operate at the fairly low level of specific commands, it supports only Python 2 at the moment (see www.fabfile.org/).

2. *Ansible* is a sleek and powerful system that lets you declare how dozens or hundreds of remote machines should be configured. It connects to each one of them with SSH, and it performs whatever checks or updates are necessary. Its speed and design have drawn attention not only from the Python community but from the system administration discipline at large (see http://docs.ansible.com/index.html).

3. *SaltStack* makes you install its own agent on each client machine instead of simply riding atop SSH. This allows the master to push new information to other machines much more quickly than would be possible over hundreds or thousands of simultaneous SSH connections. In return, it is blazingly fast, even for huge installations and large clusters (see www.saltstack.com/).

Finally, I should mention *pexpect*. While technically it is not a program that knows how to use the network, it is often used to control the system ssh or telnet command when a Python programmer wants to automate interactions with a remote prompt of some kind. This typically takes place in a situation where no API is available for a device and commands simply have to be typed each time the command-line prompt appears. Configuring simple network hardware often requires this kind of clunky step-by-step interaction. You can learn more about pexpect at http://pypi.python.org/pypi/pexpect.

Of course, it might be that no automated solution like these will quite suffice for your project, and you will actually have to roll up your sleeves and learn how to manipulate remote-shell protocols yourself. In that case, you have come to the right place. Keep reading!

Command-Line Expansion and Quoting

If you have ever typed commands at a Unix command prompt, you are aware that not every character you type is interpreted literally. For example, consider the following command. (Note that in this and all of the examples that follow in this chapter, I will be using the dollar sign, $, as the shell's *prompt*, which tells you "it is your turn to type.")

```
$ echo *
sftp.py shell.py ssh_commands.py ssh_simple.py ssh_simple.txt ssh_threads.py telnet_codes.py
telnet_login.py
```

The asterisk (*) in this command was not interpreted to mean "print an actual asterisk character to the screen." Instead, the shell thought I was trying to write a pattern to match all the file names in the current directory. To print a real asterisk, I have to use another special character, an *escape* character, because it lets me "escape" from the shell's normal meaning to tell it that I just mean the asterisk literally.

```
$ echo Here is a lone asterisk: \*
Here is a lone asterisk: *

$ echo And here are '*' two "*" more asterisks
And here are * two * more asterisks
```

Shells can run subprocesses whose output is then used in the text of yet another command—and they can even do math nowadays. To figure out how many words per line Neal Stephenson fits in the plain-text version of his "In the Beginning. . . Was the Command Line" essay, you can ask the ubiquitous bash Bourne-again shell—the standard shell on most Linux systems these days—to divide the number of words in the essay by the number of lines and produce a result.

```
$ echo $(( $(wc -w < command.txt) / $(wc -l < command.txt) )) words per line
44 words per line
```

As made obvious by this example, the rules by which modern shells interpret the special characters in your command line have become quite complex. The manual page for the bash shell currently runs a total of 5,375 lines, or 223 screens full of text in a standard 80×24 terminal window! Obviously, it would lead this chapter far astray if I were to explore even a fraction of the possible ways that a shell can mangle a command that you type.

Instead, to help you use the command line effectively, you will focus in the next sections on just two key points:

- Special characters are interpreted as special by the shell you are using, like bash. They do not mean anything special to the operating system itself.

- When passing commands to a shell either locally or, as will be more common in this chapter, across the network, you need to escape the special characters you use so that they are not expanded into unintended values on the remote system.

I will now tackle each of these points in their own section. Keep in mind that I am talking about common server operating systems like Linux and OS X, not more primitive ones like Windows, which I will discuss in its own section.

Unix Command Arguments Can Include (Almost) Any Character

The pure, low-level Unix command line has no special or reserved characters. This is an important fact for you to grasp. If you have used a shell like bash for any length of time, you may have come to view your system command line as being something like a minefield. On one hand, all of the special characters make it easy to, say, name all the files in the current directory as arguments to a command. However, on the other hand, it can be difficult to echo a message to the screen that does something as simple as mix single with double quotes, and it can be hard to learn which characters are safe and which are among the many that the shell considers special.

The simple lesson of this section is that the whole set of conventions regarding the special characters of the shell has nothing to do with your operating system. They are simply and entirely a behavior of the bash shell, or of whichever of the other popular (or arcane) shells you are using. It does not matter how familiar the rules seem or how difficult it is for you to imagine using a Unix-like system without them. If you take the shell away, then the phenomenon of special characters vanishes.

You can observe this quite simply by launching a process yourself and trying to throw some special characters at a familiar command.

```
>>> import subprocess
>>> args = ['echo', 'Sometimes', '*', 'is just an asterisk']
>>> subprocess.call(args)
Sometimes * is just an asterisk
```

Here you are opting to launch a new process with arguments without asking a shell to get involved. The process—in this case the echo command—is getting exactly those characters, instead of having the * turned into a list of file names first.

Though the asterisk wildcard character is used frequently, the shell's most common special character is one that you use all the time: the space character. Each space is interpreted as a delimiter separating arguments. This results in endless hours of entertainment when people include spaces in Unix file names and then try to move the file somewhere else.

```
$ mv Smith Contract.txt ~/Documents
mv: cannot stat `Smith': No such file or directory
mv: cannot stat `Contract.txt': No such file or directory
```

To make the shell understand that you are talking about one file with a space in its name, not two files, you have to contrive something like one of these possible command lines:

```
$ mv Smith\ Contract.txt ~/Documents
$ mv "Smith Contract.txt" ~/Documents
$ mv Smith*Contract.txt ~/Documents
```

The last possibility obviously means something different than the first two, since it will match *any* file name that happens to start with Smith and end with Contract.txt regardless of whether the text between them is a simple space character or a much longer sequence of text. I have often seen users resort to using a wildcard in frustration when they are still learning shell conventions and cannot remember how to type a literal space character.

If you want to convince yourself that none of the characters that the bash shell has taught you to be careful about is anything special, Listing 16-1 shows a simple shell written in Python that treats only the space character as special but passes everything else through literally to the command.

Listing 16-1. Shell Supporting Whitespace-Separated Arguments

```python
#!/usr/bin/env python3
# Foundations of Python Network Programming, Third Edition
# https://github.com/brandon-rhodes/fopnp/blob/m/py3/chapter16/shell.py
# A simple shell, so you can try running commands at a prompt where no
# characters are special (except that whitespace separates arguments).

import subprocess

def main():
    while True:
        args = input('] ').strip().split()
        if not args:
            pass
        elif args == ['exit']:
            break
        elif args[0] == 'show':
            print("Arguments:", args[1:])
        else:
            try:
                subprocess.call(args)
            except Exception as e:
                print(e)

if __name__ == '__main__':
    main()
```

Of course, the fact that this simple shell offers no special quoting characters means that you cannot use it to talk about files with spaces in their names because it always, without exception, thinks that a space means the end of one parameter and the beginning of the next.

By running this shell and trying all sorts of special characters of which you have been afraid to use, you can see that they mean absolutely nothing if passed directly to the common commands you do use. (The shell in Listing 16-2 uses a] prompt to make it easy to tell apart from your own shell.)

```
$ python shell.py
] echo Hi there!
Hi there!
] echo An asterisk * is not special.
An asterisk * is not special.
] echo The string $HOST is not special, nor are "double quotes".
The string $HOST is not special, nor are "double quotes".
] echo What? No *<>!$ special characters?
What? No *<>!$ special characters?
] show "The 'show' built-in lists its arguments."
Arguments: ['"The', "'show'", 'built-in', 'lists', 'its', 'arguments."']
] exit
```

You can see absolute evidence here that Unix commands—in this case, the /bin/echo command that you are calling over and over again—pay no attention to special characters in their arguments. The echo command happily accepts characters like double quotes, dollar signs, and asterisks inside its argument list and treats them all as literal characters. As the foregoing show command illustrates, Python is simply reducing your arguments to a list of strings for the operating system to use in creating a new process.

What if you fail to split your command into separate arguments and pass a command name and argument to the operating system as a single string?

```
>>> import subprocess
>>> subprocess.call(['echo hello'])
Traceback (most recent call last):
  ...
FileNotFoundError: [Errno 2] No such file or directory: 'echo hello'
```

Do you see what has happened? The operating system does not know that spaces should be special. Thus, the system thinks that it is being asked to run a command literally named echo[space]hello, and unless you have created such a file in the current directory, it fails to find it and raises an exception.

There is one single character that is, in fact, special to the system: the null character (the character having the Unicode and ASCII code zero). The null character is used in Unix-like systems to mark the end of each command-line argument in memory. Thus, if you try using a null character in an argument, Unix will think the argument has ended, and it will ignore the rest of its text. To prevent you from making this mistake, Python stops you in your tracks if you include a null character in a command-line argument.

```
>>> subprocess.call(['echo', 'Sentences can end\0 abruptly.'])
Traceback (most recent call last):
  ...
TypeError: embedded NUL character
```

Happily, since every command on the system is designed to live within this limitation, you will generally find that there is never any reason to put null characters into command-line arguments anyway. (Specifically, they cannot appear in file names for exactly the same reason they cannot appear in argument lists: the operating system is supplied with file names in null-terminated strings.)

Quoting Characters for Protection

In the previous section, you used routines in Python's subprocess module to invoke commands directly. This was great, and it let you pass characters that would have been special to a normal interactive shell. If you have a big list of file names with spaces and other special characters in them, it can be wonderful simply to pass them into a subprocess call and have the command on the receiving end understand you perfectly.

However, when you are using remote-shell protocols over the network, you are generally going to be talking to a shell like bash instead of getting to invoke commands directly as you do through the subprocess module. This means that remote-shell protocols will feel more like the system() routine from the os module, which invokes a shell to interpret your command and therefore involves you in all of the complexities of the Unix command line.

```
>>> import os
>>> os.system('echo *')
sftp.py shell.py ssh_commands.py ssh_simple.py ssh_simple.txt ssh_threads.py telnet_codes.py
telnet_login.py
```

The many varieties of system and embedded shells to which your network programs might connect offer all sorts of quoting and wildcard conventions. They can, in some cases, be quite arcane. Nevertheless, if the other end of a network connection is a standard Unix shell of the sh family, like bash or zsh, then you are in luck: the fairly obscure Python pipes module, which is normally used to build complex shell command lines, contains a helper function that is perfect for escaping arguments. It is called quote, and it can simply be passed a string.

```
>>> from pipes import quote
>>> print(quote("filename"))
filename
>>> print(quote("file with spaces"))
'file with spaces'
>>> print(quote("file 'single quoted' inside!"))
 'file '"'"'single quoted'"'"' inside!'
>>> print(quote("danger!; rm -r *"))
'danger!; rm -r *'
```

So, preparing a command line for remote execution can be as simple as running quote() on each argument and then pasting the result together with spaces.

Note that sending commands to a remote shell with Python does not typically involve you in the terrors of *two* levels of shell quoting, which you might have run into if you have ever tried to build a remote SSH command line that itself uses fancy quoting. The attempt to write shell commands that themselves pass arguments to a remote shell tends to generate a series of experiments like this:

```
$ echo $HOST
guinness
$ ssh asaph echo $HOST
guinness
$ ssh asaph echo \$HOST
asaph
$ ssh asaph echo \\$HOST
guinness
$ ssh asaph echo \\\$HOST
$HOST
$ ssh asaph echo \\\\$HOST
\guinness
```

Every one of these responses is reasonable, as you can demonstrate to yourself. First use echo to see what each command looks like when quoted by the local shell and then paste that text into a remote SSH command line to see how the processed text is handled there. However, these commands can be tricky to write, and even a practiced Unix shell scripter can guess wrong when trying to predict the output from the foregoing series of commands!

The Terrible Windows Command Line

Did you enjoy reading the previous sections on the Unix shell and how arguments are ultimately delivered to a process? Well, if you are going to be connecting to a Windows machine using a remote-shell protocol, then you can forget everything you have just read. Windows is amazingly primitive. Instead of delivering command-line arguments to a new process as separate strings, it simply hands over the text of the entire command line to the new process that is starting up and makes the process try to figure out itself how the user might have quoted file names with spaces in them!

Of course, merely to survive, people in the Windows world have adopted more or less consistent traditions about how commands will interpret their arguments. For example, you can put double quotes around a multiword file name and expect nearly all programs to recognize that you are naming one file, not several. Most commands also try to understand that asterisks in a file name are wildcards. But this is always a choice made by the program you are running, not by the command prompt.

As you will see, there exists a primitive network protocol—the ancient Telnet protocol—that also sends command lines simply as text, just as Windows does, so that your program will have to do some kind of escaping if it sends arguments with spaces or special characters in them. However, if you are using a modern remote protocol like SSH that lets you send arguments as a list of strings rather than as a single string, then be aware that on Windows systems all that SSH can do is paste your carefully constructed command line back together and hope that the Windows command can figure it out.

When sending commands to Windows, you might want to take advantage of the list2cmdline() routine offered by the Python subprocess module. It takes a list of arguments similar to what you would use for a Unix command and attempts to paste them together—using double quotes and backslashes when necessary—so that conventional Windows programs can parse the command line back into exactly the same arguments.

```
>>> from subprocess import list2cmdline
>>> args = ['rename', 'salary "Smith".xls', 'salary-smith.xls']
>>> print(list2cmdline(args))
rename "salary \"Smith\".xls" salary-smith.xls
```

Some quick experimentation with your network library and remote-shell protocol of choice should help you figure out what Windows needs in your situation. For the rest of this chapter, I will make the simplifying assumption that you are connecting to servers that use a modern Unix-like operating system that can keep discrete command-line arguments separate without extra quoting.

Things Are Different in a Terminal

You will probably talk to more programs than just a shell over your Python-powered remote connection. You will often want to watch the incoming data stream for the data and errors printed by the command you are running. Sometimes you will also want to send data back, either to provide the remote program with input or to respond to questions and prompts that the program presents.

When performing tasks such as these, at times you may be dismayed to find programs hanging indefinitely without ever sending the output on which you are waiting. Alternatively, data you send might not seem to be getting through. To help you through situations like this, a brief discussion of Unix terminals is in order.

A *terminal* is a device into which a user types text and on whose screen the computer's response can be displayed. If a Unix machine has physical serial ports that can host a physical terminal, then the device directory will contain entries such as /dev/ttyS1 with which programs can send and receive strings to that device. However, most terminals these days are, in reality, other programs: an xterm terminal, a Gnome or KDE terminal program, the Mac OS X iTerm or Terminal, or even a PuTTY client on a Windows machine that has connected via a remote-shell protocol of the kind discussed in this chapter.

Programs running inside a terminal on your computer will often try to autodetect whether they are talking to a person, and only if they are connected to a terminal device will they assume that their output should be formatted for humans. Therefore, the Unix operating system provides a set of "pseudo-terminal" devices (which might have less confusingly been named "virtual" terminals) with names like /dev/tty42 to which processes can be connected if you want them to be convinced that they are communicating with a real person. When someone brings up an xterm or connects through SSH, the xterm or SSH daemon grabs a fresh pseudo-terminal, configures it, and runs the user's shell attached to it. The shell examines its standard input, sees that it is a terminal, and presents a prompt since it believes that it is talking to a person.

▪ **Note**   Because the noisy TeleType machine was the earliest example of a computer terminal, Unix often uses TTY as the abbreviation for a terminal device. That is why the call to test whether your input is a terminal is named isatty().

This is a crucial distinction to understand: the shell presents a prompt because, and only because, it thinks it is connected to a terminal. If you start up a shell and give it a standard input that is not a terminal—like, say, a pipe from another command—then no prompt will be printed, but it will still respond to commands.

```
$ cat | bash
echo Here we are inside of bash, with no prompt
Here we are inside of bash, with no prompt
python3
print('Python has not printed a prompt, either.')
import sys
print('Is this a terminal?', sys.stdin.isatty())
```

Not only has bash not printed a prompt, neither has Python. In fact, Python is being unusually quiet. While bash at least responded to our echo command with a line of text, at this point you have typed three lines of input into Python without seeing any response. What is going on?

The answer is that since its input is not a terminal, Python thinks that it should just blindly read an entire Python script from standard input. After all, its input is a file, and files have whole scripts inside. To complete this potentially endless read-until-end-of-file that Python is performing, you will have to press Ctrl-D to send an "end-of-file" to cat, which will then close its own output and let the example finish.

Once you have closed its input, Python will interpret and run the three-line script you have provided (everything past the word python in the session just shown), and you will see the results on your terminal followed by the prompt of the shell that you started at.

```
Python has not printed a prompt, either.
Is this a terminal? False
```

Some programs auto-adjust their output format depending on whether they are talking to a terminal. The ps command will truncate each output line to your terminal width if used interactively but produce arbitrarily wide output if its output is a pipe or file. Also, the familiar column-based output of the ls command gets replaced with a file name on each line (which is, you must admit, an easier format for reading by another program).

```
$ ls
sftp.py    ssh_commands.py   ssh_simple.txt  telnet_codes.py
shell.py  ssh_simple.py      ssh_threads.py  telnet_login.py
$ ls | cat
sftp.py
shell.py
ssh_commands.py
ssh_simple.py
ssh_simple.txt
ssh_threads.py
telnet_codes.py
telnet_login.py
```

So, what does all of this have to do with network programming? Well, the two behaviors you have seen—the fact that programs tend to display prompts if connected to a terminal but omit them and run silently if they are reading from a file or from the output of another command—also occur at the remote end of the shell protocols that you are considering in this chapter.

A program running behind Telnet, for example, always thinks it is talking to a terminal. Thus, your scripts or programs must always expect to see a prompt each time the shell is ready for input, and so forth. However, when you make a connection over the more sophisticated SSH protocol, you will actually have your choice of whether the program thinks that its input is a terminal or just a plain pipe or file. You can test this easily from the command line if there is another computer to which you can connect.

```
$ ssh -t asaph
asaph$ echo "Here we are, at a prompt."
Here we are, at a prompt.
asaph$ exit
$ ssh -T asaph
echo "The shell here on asaph sees no terminal; so, no prompt."
The shell here on asaph sees no terminal; so, no prompt.
exit
$
```

Thus, when you spawn a command through a modern protocol like SSH, you need to consider whether you want the program on the remote end thinking that you are a person typing at it through a terminal or whether it had best think it is talking to raw data coming in through a file or pipe.

Programs are not actually required to act any differently when talking to a terminal. It is just for our convenience that they vary their behavior. They do so by calling the equivalent of the Python isatty() call ("Is this a teletype?") that you saw in the foregoing example session and then vary their behavior depending on what this call returns. Here are some common ways they behave differently:

- Programs that are often used interactively will present a human-readable prompt when they are talking to a terminal. However, when they think input is coming from a file, they avoid printing a prompt because otherwise your screen would become littered with hundreds of successive prompts as you ran a long shell script or Python program!

- Nowadays, sophisticated interactive programs usually turn on command-line editing when their input is a TTY. This makes many control characters special because they are used to accessing the command-line history and performing editing commands. When they are not under the control of a terminal, these same programs turn command-line editing off and absorb control characters as normal parts of their input stream.

- Many programs read only one line of input at a time when listening to a terminal because humans like to get an immediate response to every command they type. However, when reading from a pipe or file, these same programs will wait until thousands of characters have arrived before they try to interpret their first batch of input. As you just saw, `bash` stays in line-at-a-time mode even if its input is a file, but Python decided it wanted to read a whole Python script from its input before trying to execute even its first line.

- It is even more common for programs to adjust their output based on whether they are talking to a terminal. If a user might be watching, they want each line, or even each character, of output to appear immediately. But if they are talking to a mere file or pipe, they will wait and batch up large chunks of output and more efficiently send the whole chunk at one time.

Both of the last two issues, which involve buffering, cause all sorts of problems when you take a process that is usually done manually and try to automate it—because in doing so, you often move from terminal input to input provided through a file or pipe, and suddenly you find that the programs behave quite differently. They might even seem to be hanging because "print" statements are not producing immediate output but are instead saving up their results to push out all at once when their output buffer is full.

The foregoing problem is why many carefully written programs, both in Python and in other languages, frequently call `flush()` on their output to make sure that anything waiting in a buffer goes ahead and gets sent out, regardless of whether the output looks like a terminal.

These therefore are the basic problems with terminals and buffering: programs change their behavior, often in idiosyncratic ways, when talking to a terminal, and they often start heavily buffering their output if they think they are writing to a file or pipe instead of letting you see their output immediately.

Terminals Do Buffering

Beyond the program-specific behaviors just described, there is one further class of problems presented by terminal devices. What happens when you want a program to read its input one character at a time, but the Unix terminal device itself is buffering your keystrokes to deliver them as a whole line? This common problem happens because the Unix terminal defaults to "canonical" input processing where it lets the user enter a whole line—and even edit it by backspacing and retyping—before finally pressing Enter and letting the program see what they have typed.

If you want to turn off canonical processing so that a program can see every individual character as it is typed, you can use the `stty` "set the current TTY's settings" command to disable it.

```
$ stty -icanon
```

Another problem is that Unix terminals traditionally supported a pair of keystrokes originally designed so that users could pause the output and read a screen full of text before it scrolled off and was replaced by more text. Often, these were the characters Ctrl+S for "Stop" and Ctrl+Q for "Keep going," and it was a source of great annoyance if binary data worked its way into an automated Telnet connection because then the first Ctrl+S that happened to pass across the channel would pause the terminal and probably ruin the session.

Again, this setting can be turned off with `stty`.

```
$ stty -ixon -ixoff
```

Those are the two biggest problems that you will run into with terminals doing buffering, but there are plenty of less famous settings that can also cause you grief. Because there are so many—and because they vary between Unix implementations—the `stty` command actually supports two modes. The modes are `cooked` and `raw`, which turn dozens of settings like `icanon` and `ixon` on and off together.

```
$ stty raw
$ stty cooked
```

In case you make your terminal settings a hopeless mess after some experimentation, most Unix systems provide a command for resetting the terminal to reasonable, sane settings. (Note that if you have played with `stty` too severely, you might need to hit Ctrl+J to submit the reset command since your Return key, whose equivalent is Ctrl+M, actually functions only to submit commands because of a terminal setting called `icrnl`.)

```
$ reset
```

If instead of trying to get the terminal to behave across a Telnet or SSH session you happen to be talking to a terminal from your own Python script, check out the `termios` module that comes with the Standard Library. By puzzling through its example code and remembering how Boolean bitwise math works, you should be able to control all of the same settings that you just accessed through the `stty` command.

This book lacks the space to look at terminals in any further detail (since one or two chapters of examples could easily be inserted right here to cover just the more interesting techniques and cases), but there are lots of great resources for learning more about them—a classic is Chapter 19, "Pseudo Terminals," of W. Richard Stevens' *Advanced Programming in the UNIX Environment* (Addison-Wesley Professional, 1992).

Telnet

This brief section is all you will find in this book about the ancient Telnet protocol. Why? It is insecure: anyone watching your Telnet packets fly by will see your username, password, and everything you do on the remote system. It is clunky, and it has been completely abandoned for most systems administration.

■ THE TELNET PROTOCOL

Purpose: Remote shell access

Standard: RFC 854 (1989)

Runs atop: TCP/IP

Default port: 23

Library: telnetlib

Exceptions: socket.error, socket.gaierror, EOFError, select.error

---

The only time I ever find myself needing Telnet is when communicating with a small, embedded system, like a Linksys router or DSL modem or network switch deep inside a well-firewalled corporate network. In case you have to write a Python program that has to speak Telnet to one of these devices, here are a few pointers on using the Python `telnetlib`.

First, you have to realize that all Telnet does is to establish a channel—in fact, a fairly plain TCP socket (see Chapter 3)—and then copy information in both directions across that channel. Everything you type is sent out across the wire, and Telnet prints to the screen everything it receives. This means Telnet is ignorant of all sorts of things about which you might expect a remote-shell protocol to be aware.

For example, it is commonplace that when you Telnet to a Unix machine, you are presented with a `login:` prompt at which you type your username and then a `password:` prompt where you enter your password. The small, embedded devices that still use Telnet nowadays might follow a slightly simpler script, but they too often ask for some sort of password or authentication. Either way, Telnet itself knows nothing about this pattern of exchange! To your Telnet client, `password:` is just nine random characters that come flying across the TCP connection and that it must print to your screen. It has no idea that you are being prompted, that you are responding, or that, in a moment, the remote system will know who you are.

The fact that Telnet is ignorant of authentication has an important consequence: you cannot give any arguments to the Telnet command itself to be preauthenticated to the remote system, nor avoid the login and password prompts that will pop up when you first connect. If you are going to use plain Telnet, somehow you are going to have to watch the incoming text for those two prompts (or however many prompts the remote system supplies) and then respond by typing the correct replies.

Obviously, if systems vary in what username and password prompts they present, then you can hardly expect standardization in the error messages or responses that are printed when your password fails. That is why Telnet is so hard to script and program from a language like Python. Unless you know every single error message that the remote system could print in response to your login and password—which might not just be its "bad password" message but also things like "cannot spawn shell: out of memory," "home directory not mounted," and "quota exceeded: confining you to a restricted shell"—your script will sometimes run into situations where it is waiting to see either a command prompt or a particular error message, and it will instead simply wait forever without seeing anything in the inbound character stream that it recognizes.

Therefore, if you are using Telnet, you are playing a purely textual game. You watch for text to arrive and then try to reply with something intelligible to the remote system. To help you with this, the Python telnetlib provides not only basic methods for sending and receiving data but also a few routines that will watch and wait for a particular string to arrive from the remote system. In this respect, telnetlib is a little bit like the third-party Python pexpect library that I mentioned earlier in this chapter, and therefore it is a bit like the venerable Unix expect command. In fact, one of these telnetlib routines is, in honor of its predecessor, named expect().

Listing 16-2 connects to a host, automates the entire back-and-forth login conversation itself, and then runs a simple command so that you can see its output. This is what it looks like, minimally, to automate a Telnet conversation.

Listing 16-2. Logging Into a Remote Host Using Telnet

```python
#!/usr/bin/env python3
# Foundations of Python Network Programming, Third Edition
# https://github.com/brandon-rhodes/fopnp/blob/m/py3/chapter16/telnet_login.py
# Connect to localhost, watch for a login prompt, and try logging in

import argparse, getpass, telnetlib

def main(hostname, username, password):
    t = telnetlib.Telnet(hostname)
    # t.set_debuglevel(1)         # uncomment to get debug messages
    t.read_until(b'login:')
    t.write(username.encode('utf-8'))
    t.write(b'\r')
    t.read_until(b'assword:')     # first letter might be 'p' or 'P'
    t.write(password.encode('utf-8'))
    t.write(b'\r')
    n, match, previous_text = t.expect([br'Login incorrect', br'\$'], 10)
    if n == 0:
        print('Username and password failed - giving up')
    else:
        t.write(b'exec uptime\r')
        print(t.read_all().decode('utf-8'))  # read until socket closes

if __name__ == '__main__':
    parser = argparse.ArgumentParser(description='Use Telnet to log in')
    parser.add_argument('hostname', help='Remote host to telnet to')
    parser.add_argument('username', help='Remote username')
```

```
args = parser.parse_args()
password = getpass.getpass('Password: ')
main(args.hostname, args.username, password)
```

If the script is successful, it shows you what the simple uptime command prints on the remote system.

```
$ python telnet_login.py example.com brandon
Password: abc123
10:24:43 up 5 days, 12:13, 14 users, load average: 1.44, 0.91, 0.73
```

The listing shows you the general structure of a session powered by telnetlib. First, a connection is established that is represented in Python by an instance of the Telnet class. Here only the hostname is specified, though you can also provide a port number to connect to some other service port than standard Telnet.

You can call set_debuglevel(1) if you want your Telnet object to print out all of the strings that it sends and receives during the session. This actually turned out to be important for writing even the very simple script shown in the listing, because in two different cases the script hung and I had to rerun it with debugging messages turned on so that I could see the actual output and fix the script. (Once I failed to match the exact text that was coming back, and the other time I forgot the '\r' at the end of the uptime command.) I generally turn off debugging only once a program is working perfectly and then turn it back on whenever I want to do more work on the script.

Note that Telnet does not disguise the fact that its service is backed by a TCP socket, and it will pass through to your program any socket.error or socket.gaierror exceptions that are raised.

Once the Telnet session is established, interaction generally falls into a receive-and-send pattern, where you wait for a prompt or response from the remote end and then send your next piece of information. The listing illustrates two methods of waiting for text to arrive:

- The simple read_until() method watches for a literal string to arrive, and then it returns a string that provides all the text that it received from the moment it started listing until the moment it finally saw the string you were waiting for.

- The more powerful and sophisticated expect() method takes a list of Python regular expressions. Once the text arriving from the remote end finally adds up to something that matches one of the regular expressions, expect() returns three items: the index in your list of the pattern that matched, the regular expression SRE_Match object itself, and the text that was received leading up to the matching text. For more information on what you can do with a SRE_Match, including finding the values of any subexpressions in your pattern, read the Standard Library documentation for the re module.

Regular expressions, as always, have to be written carefully. When I first wrote this script, I used '$' as the expect() pattern that watched for the shell prompt to appear—which, alas, is a special character in a regular expression! So, the corrected script shown in the listing escapes the $ so that expect() actually waits until it sees a dollar sign arrive from the remote end.

If the script sees an error message because of an incorrect password and does not get stuck waiting forever for a login or password prompt that never arrives or that looks different from it was expecting, it exits.

```
$ python telnet_login.py example.com brandon
Password: wrongpass
Username and password failed - giving up
```

If you wind up writing a Python script that has to use Telnet, it will simply be a larger or more complicated version of the same simple pattern shown here.

Both read_until() and expect() take an optional second argument named timeout that places a maximum limit on how long in seconds the call will watch for the text pattern before giving up and returning control to your Python script. If they quit and give up because of the timeout, they do not raise an error; instead (awkwardly enough), they just return the text they have seen so far and leave it to you to figure out whether that text contains the pattern!

There are a few odds and ends in the Telnet object that I need not cover here. You will find them in the telnetlib Standard Library documentation, including an interact() method that lets the user "talk" directly over your Telnet connection using the terminal! This kind of call was popular back in the old days when you wanted to automate login but then take control and issue normal commands yourself.

The Telnet protocol does have a convention for embedding control information, and telnetlib follows these protocol rules carefully to keep your data separate from any control codes that appear. Thus, you can use a Telnet object to send and receive all of the binary data you want and ignore the fact that control codes might be arriving as well. However, if you are doing a sophisticated Telnet-based project, then you might need to process options.

Normally, each time a Telnet server sends an option request, telnetlib flatly refuses to send or receive that option. However, you can provide a Telnet object with your own callback function for processing options. A modest example is shown in Listing 16-3. For most options, it simply reimplements the default telnetlib behavior and refuses to handle any options. (Always remember to respond to each option one way or another; failing to do so will often hang the Telnet session as the server waits forever for your reply.) If the server expresses interest in the "terminal type" option, then this client sends a reply of mypython, which the shell command it runs after logging in then sees as its $TERM environment variable.

Listing 16-3. How to Process Telnet Option Codes

```
#!/usr/bin/env python3
# Foundations of Python Network Programming, Third Edition
# https://github.com/brandon-rhodes/fopnp/blob/m/py3/chapter16/telnet_codes.py
# How your code might look if you intercept Telnet options yourself

import argparse, getpass
from telnetlib import Telnet, IAC, DO, DONT, WILL, WONT, SB, SE, TTYPE

def process_option(tsocket, command, option):
    if command == DO and option == TTYPE:
        tsocket.sendall(IAC + WILL + TTYPE)
        print('Sending terminal type "mypython"')
        tsocket.sendall(IAC + SB + TTYPE + b'\0' + b'mypython' + IAC + SE)
    elif command in (DO, DONT):
        print('Will not', ord(option))
        tsocket.sendall(IAC + WONT + option)
    elif command in (WILL, WONT):
        print('Do not', ord(option))
        tsocket.sendall(IAC + DONT + option)

def main(hostname, username, password):
    t = Telnet(hostname)
    # t.set_debuglevel(1)        # uncomment to get debug messages
    t.set_option_negotiation_callback(process_option)
    t.read_until(b'login:', 10)
    t.write(username.encode('utf-8') + b'\r')
    t.read_until(b'password:', 10)    # first letter might be 'p' or 'P'
    t.write(password.encode('utf-8') + b'\r')
    n, match, previous_text = t.expect([br'Login incorrect', br'\$'], 10)
    if n == 0:
        print("Username and password failed - giving up")
    else:
        t.write(b'exec echo My terminal type is $TERM\n')
        print(t.read_all().decode('ascii'))
```

```
if __name__ == '__main__':
    parser = argparse.ArgumentParser(description='Use Telnet to log in')
    parser.add_argument('hostname', help='Remote host to telnet to')
    parser.add_argument('username', help='Remote username')
    args = parser.parse_args()
    password = getpass.getpass('Password: ')
    main(args.hostname, args.username, password)
```

For more details about how Telnet options work, again you can consult the relevant RFCs. In the next section, I will leave behind the ancient insecure Telnet protocol and begin discussing a modern and safe approach to running remote commands.

SSH: The Secure Shell

The SSH protocol is one of the best-known examples of a secure, encrypted protocol (HTTPS is probably the best known).

■ THE SSH PROTOCOL

Purpose: Secure remote shell, file transfer, port forwarding

Standard: RFC 4250–4256 (2006)

Runs atop: TCP/IP

Default port: 22

Library: paramiko

Exceptions: socket.error, socket.gaierror, paramiko.SSHException

---

SSH is descended from an earlier protocol that supported "remote login," "remote shell," and "remote file copy" commands named rlogin, rsh, and rcp, which in their time tended to become much more popular than Telnet at sites that supported them. You cannot imagine what a revelation rcp was, in particular, unless you have spent hours trying to transfer a binary file between computers armed with only Telnet and a script that tries to type your password for you, only to discover that your file contains a byte that looks like a control character to Telnet or the remote terminal, causing the whole thing to hang until you add a layer of escaping (or figure out how to disable both the Telnet escape key and all interpretation taking place on the remote terminal).

However, the best feature of the rlogin family members was that they did not just echo username and password prompts without actually knowing the meaning of what was going on. Instead, they stayed involved throughout the process of authentication, and you could even create a file in your home directory that told them "When someone named brandon tries to connect from the asaph machine, just let them in without a password." Suddenly, system administrators and Unix users alike received back hours each month that would have otherwise been spent typing their password. Moreover, suddenly you could rcp copy ten files from one machine to another nearly as easily as you could have copied them into a local folder.

SSH has preserved all of these great features of the early remote-shell protocol while bringing about security and hard encryption that is trusted worldwide for administering critical servers. This chapter will focus on the third-party paramiko Python package that can speak the SSH protocol and does it so successfully that it has actually been ported to Java as well because people in the Java world wanted to be able to use SSH as easily as we do when using Python.

An Overview of SSH

The first section of this book talked a lot about multiplexing—about how UDP (Chapter 2) and TCP (Chapter 3) take the underlying IP protocol, which has no concept that there might actually be several users or applications on a single computer that need to communicate, and add the concept of UDP and TCP port numbers so that several different conversations between a pair of IP addresses can take place at the same time.

Once that basic level of multiplexing was established, we more or less left the topic behind. Through more than a dozen chapters now, we have studied protocols that take a UDP or TCP connection and then happily use it for exactly one thing—downloading a web page or transmitting an e-mail—never trying to do several things at the same time over a single socket.

Now as we arrive at SSH, we find a protocol so sophisticated that it actually implements its own multiplexing. Several "channels" of information can all share the same SSH socket. Every block of information SSH sends across its socket is labeled with a "channel" identifier so that several conversations can share the socket.

There are at least two reasons that subchannels make sense. First, even though the channel ID takes up a bit of bandwidth for every single block of information transmitted, the additional data is small compared to how much extra information SSH has to transmit to negotiate and maintain encryption anyway. Second, channels make sense because the real expense of an SSH connection is setting it up. Host key negotiation and authentication can together take up several seconds of real time, and once the connection is established, you want to be able to use it for as many operations as possible. Thanks to the SSH notion of a channel, you can amortize the high cost of connecting by performing many operations before you let the connection close.

Once connected, you can create several kinds of channels:

- An interactive shell session, like that supported by Telnet

- The individual execution of a single command

- A file transfer session letting you browse the remote filesystem

- A port forward that intercepts TCP connections

You will learn about all of these kinds of channels in the following sections.

SSH Host Keys

When an SSH client first connects to a remote host, the two exchange temporary public keys that let them encrypt the rest of their conversation without revealing any information to any watching third parties. Then, before the client is willing to divulge any further information, it demands proof of the remote server's identity. This makes good sense as a first step: if you were really talking to a hacker's software that has temporarily managed to grab the remote server's IP, you do not want SSH to divulge even your username—much less your password!

As you saw in Chapter 6, one answer to the problem of machine identity on the Internet is to build a public-key infrastructure. First you designate a set of organizations called *certificate authorities* that can issue certs. Then you install a list of their public keys in all of the web browsers and other SSL clients in existence. Then those organizations charge you money to verify that you really are google.com (or whoever you are) and that you deserve to have your google.com SSL certificate signed. Finally, you can install the certificate on your web server, and everyone will trust your identity.

There are many problems with this system from the point of view of SSH. While it is true that you can build a public-key infrastructure internal to an organization where you distribute your own signing authority's certificates to your web browsers or other applications and then can sign your own server certificates without paying a third party, a public-key infrastructure would still be quite a cumbersome process for something like SSH. Server administrators want to set up, use, and tear down servers all the time without having to talk to a central authority first.

So, SSH has the idea that each server, when installed, creates its own random public-private key pair that is not signed by anybody. Instead, one of two approaches is taken to key distribution.

- A system administrator writes a script that gathers up all the host public keys in an organization, creates an ssh_known_hosts listing them all, and places this file in the /etc/sshd directory on every system in the organization. They might also make it available to any desktop clients, like the PuTTY command under Windows. Now every SSH client will know about every SSH host key before they even connect for the first time.

- Alternatively, the administrator can simply abandon the idea of knowing host keys ahead of time and instead have each SSH client memorize them at the moment of first connection. Users of the SSH command line will be familiar with this: the client says it does not recognize the host to which you are connecting, you reflexively answer "yes," and its key gets stored in your ~/.ssh/known_hosts file. You actually have no guarantee on this first encounter that you are really talking to the host you think it is. Nevertheless, at least you will be guaranteed that every subsequent connection you ever make to that machine is going to the right place and not to other servers that someone is swapping into place at the same IP address (unless, of course, someone has stolen that host's keys).

The familiar prompt from the SSH command line when it sees an unfamiliar host looks like this:

```
$ ssh asaph.rhodesmill.org
The authenticity of host 'asaph.rhodesmill.org (74.207.234.78)' can't be established.
RSA key fingerprint is 85:8f:32:4e:ac:1f:e9:bc:35:58:c1:d4:25:e3:c7:8c.
Are you sure you want to continue connecting (yes/no)? yes
Warning: Permanently added 'asaph.rhodesmill.org,74.207.234.78' (RSA) to the list of known hosts.
```

That yes answer buried deep on the next-to-last full line is the answer that I typed giving SSH the go-ahead to make the connection and remember the key for next time. If SSH ever connects to a host and sees a different key, its reaction is quite severe.

```
$ ssh asaph.rhodesmill.org
@@@@@@@@@@@@@@@@@@@@@@@@@@@@@@@@@@@@@@@@@@@@@@@@@@@@
@ WARNING: REMOTE HOST IDENTIFICATION HAS CHANGED! @
@@@@@@@@@@@@@@@@@@@@@@@@@@@@@@@@@@@@@@@@@@@@@@@@@@@@
IT IS POSSIBLE THAT SOMEONE IS DOING SOMETHING NASTY!
Someone could be eavesdropping on you right now (man-in-the-middle attack)!
```

This message will be familiar to anyone who has ever had to rebuild a server from scratch and forgets to save its old SSH keys. Without them, the newly rebuilt host will now use new keys generated by the reinstall. It can be painful to go around to all of your SSH clients and remove the offending old key so that they will quietly learn the new one upon reconnection.

The paramiko library has full support for all of the normal SSH tactics surrounding host keys. However, its default behavior is rather spare. It loads no host key files by default, and it must therefore raise an exception for the first host to which you connect because it will not be able to verify its key.

```
>>> import paramiko
>>> client = paramiko.SSHClient()
>>> client.connect('example.com', username='test')
Traceback (most recent call last):
  ...
paramiko.ssh_exception.SSHException: Server 'example.com' not found in known_hosts
```

To behave like the normal SSH command, load both the system and the current user's known host keys before making the connection.

```
>>> client.load_system_host_keys()
>>> client.load_host_keys('/home/brandon/.ssh/known_hosts')
>>> client.connect('example.com', username='test')
```

The paramiko library also lets you choose how you handle unknown hosts. Once you have a client object created, you can provide it with a decision-making class that is asked what to do if a host key is not recognized. You can build these classes yourself by inheriting from the MissingHostKeyPolicy class.

```
>>> class AllowAnythingPolicy(paramiko.MissingHostKeyPolicy):
...     def missing_host_key(self, client, hostname, key):
...         return
...
>>> client.set_missing_host_key_policy(AllowAnythingPolicy())
>>> client.connect('example.com', username='test')
```

Note that through the arguments to the missing_host_key() method, you receive several pieces of information on which to base your decision. You could, for example, allow connections to machines on your own server subnet without a host key but disallow all others.

Inside paramiko there are also several decision-making classes that already implement several basic host key options.

- paramiko.AutoAddPolicy: Host keys are automatically added to your user host key store (the file ~/.ssh/known_hosts on Unix systems) when first encountered, but any change in the host key from then on will raise a fatal exception.

- paramiko.RejectPolicy: Connecting to hosts with unknown keys simply raises an exception.

- paramiko.WarningPolicy: An unknown host causes a warning to be logged, but the connection is allowed to proceed.

When writing a script that will be doing SSH, I always start by connecting to the remote host "by hand" with the normal ssh command-line tool so that I can answer "yes" to its prompt and get the remote host's key in my host keys file. This way, my programs should never have to worry about handling the case of a missing key and can die with an error if they encounter one.

However, if you like doing things less by hand than I do, then the AutoAddPolicy might be your best bet. It never needs human interaction, but it will at least assure you on subsequent encounters that you are still talking to the same machine as before. Therefore, even if the machine is a Trojan horse that is logging all of your interactions with it and secretly recording your password (if you are using one), it at least must prove to you that it holds the same secret key every time you connect.

SSH Authentication

The whole subject of SSH authentication is the topic of a large amount of good documentation, as well as articles and blog posts, all available on the Web. Information abounds about configuring common SSH clients, setting up an SSH server on a Unix or Windows host, and using public keys to authenticate yourself so that you do not have to keep typing your password all the time. Since this chapter is primarily about how to "speak SSH" from Python, I will just briefly outline how authentication works.

There are generally three ways to prove your identity to a remote server you are contacting through SSH.

- You can provide a username and password.

- You can provide a username and then have your client successfully perform a public-key challenge-response. This clever operation manages to prove that you are in possession of a secret "identity" key without actually exposing its contents to the remote system.

- You can perform Kerberos authentication. If the remote system is set up to allow Kerberos (which seems extremely rare these days) and if you have run the `kinit` command-line tool to prove your identity to one of the master Kerberos servers in the SSH server's authentication domain, then you should be allowed in without a password.

Since the third option is rare, we will concentrate on the first two.

Using a username and password with paramiko is easy—you simply provide them in your call to the `connect()` method.

```
>>> client.connect('example.com', username='brandon', password=mypass)
```

Public-key authentication where you use `ssh-keygen` to create an "identity" key pair (which is typically stored in your `~/.ssh` directory) that can be used to authenticate you without a password makes the Python code even easier!

```
>>> client.connect('my.example.com')
```

If your identity key file is stored somewhere other than in the normal `~/.ssh/id_rsa` file, then you can provide its file name—or a whole Python list of file names—to the `connect()` method manually.

```
>>> client.connect('my.example.com', key_filename='/home/brandon/.ssh/id_sysadmin')
```

Of course, per the normal rules of SSH, providing a public-key identity like this will work only if you have appended the public key in the `id_sysadmin.pub` file to your "authorized hosts" file on the remote end, typically named something like this:

```
/home/brandon/.ssh/authorized_keys
```

If you have trouble getting public-key authentication to work, always check the file permissions on both your remote `.ssh` directory and the files inside. Some versions of the SSH server will get upset if they see that these files are group-readable or group-writable. Using mode 0700 for the `.ssh` directory and 0600 for the files inside will often make SSH happiest. The task of copying SSH keys to other accounts has actually been automated in recent versions through a small command that will make sure that the file permissions get set correctly for you.

```
ssh-copy-id -i ~/.ssh/id_rsa.pub myaccount@example.com
```

Once the `connect()` method has succeeded, you are now ready to start performing remote operations, all of which will be forwarded over the same physical socket without requiring renegotiation of the host key, your identity, or the encryption that protects the SSH socket itself.

Shell Sessions and Individual Commands

Once you have a connected SSH client, the entire world of SSH operations is open to you. Simply by asking, you can access remote-shell sessions, run individual commands, commence file-transfer sessions, and set up port forwarding. You will look at each of these operations in turn.

First, SSH can set up a raw shell session for you, running on the remote end inside a pseudoterminal so that programs act like they normally do when they are interacting with the user at a terminal. This kind of connection behaves very much like a Telnet connection. Take a look at Listing 16-4 for an example that pushes a simple echo command at the remote shell and then asks it to exit.

Listing 16-4. Running an Interactive Shell Under SSH

```
#!/usr/bin/env python3
# Foundations of Python Network Programming, Third Edition
# https://github.com/brandon-rhodes/fopnp/blob/m/py3/chapter16/ssh_simple.py
# Using SSH like Telnet: connecting and running two commands

import argparse, paramiko, sys

class AllowAnythingPolicy(paramiko.MissingHostKeyPolicy):
    def missing_host_key(self, client, hostname, key):
        return

def main(hostname, username):
    client = paramiko.SSHClient()
    client.set_missing_host_key_policy(AllowAnythingPolicy())
    client.connect(hostname, username=username)  # password='')

    channel = client.invoke_shell()
    stdin = channel.makefile('wb')
    stdout = channel.makefile('rb')

    stdin.write(b'echo Hello, world\rexit\r')
    output = stdout.read()
    client.close()

    sys.stdout.buffer.write(output)

if __name__ == '__main__':
    parser = argparse.ArgumentParser(description='Connect over SSH')
    parser.add_argument('hostname', help='Remote machine name')
    parser.add_argument('username', help='Username on the remote machine')
    args = parser.parse_args()
    main(args.hostname, args.username)
```

You can see that this script bears the scars of a program operating over a terminal. Instead of being able to encapsulate neatly each of the two commands it is issuing and separate their arguments, it has to use spaces and carriage returns and trust the remote shell to divide things up properly. Note that this script is written under the assumption that you have an identity file and a remote authorized-keys file and, therefore, do not have to type a password. If you do, then you can edit the script to provide one using the commented-out password parameter. To avoid typing the password into your Python file, you can have it call getpass(), as you did in the Telnet example.

Also, if you run this command, you will see that the commands you type are actually echoed to you twice and that there is no obvious way to separate these command echoes from the actual command output.

```
Welcome to Ubuntu 13.10 (GNU/Linux 3.11.0-19-generic x86_64)
Last login: Wed Apr 23 15:06:03 2014 from localhost

echo Hello, world
exit
test@guinness:~$ echo Hello, world
Hello, world
test@guinness:~$ exit
logout
```

Can you guess what has happened?

Because you did not pause and wait patiently for a shell prompt before issuing the echo and exit commands (which would have required a loop doing repeated read() calls), the command text was delivered to the remote host while it was still in the middle of issuing its welcome messages. Because the Unix terminal is in a "cooked" state by default where it echoes the user's keystrokes, the commands got printed, just beneath the "Last login" line.

Then the actual bash shell started up, set the terminal to raw mode because it likes to offer its own command-line editing interface, and then started reading the commands character by character. Because it assumes you want to see what you are typing (even though you actually finished typing and it is just reading the characters from a buffer that is several milliseconds old), it echoes each command back to the screen a second time.

Of course, without a good bit of parsing and intelligence, you would have a hard time writing a Python routine that could pick out the actual command output (the words Hello, world) from the rest of the output you are receiving over the SSH connection.

Because of all of these quirky, terminal-dependent behaviors, you should generally avoid ever using invoke_shell() unless you are actually writing an interactive terminal program where you let a live user type commands.

A much better option for running remote commands is to use exec_command() that, instead of starting up a whole shell session, just runs a single command. It gives you control of that command's standard input, output, and error streams just as though you had run that command locally using the subprocess module in the Standard Library. Listing 16-5 shows a script demonstrating its use. The difference between exec_command() and a local subprocess (besides, of course, the fact that the command runs over on the remote machine!) is that you do not get the chance to pass command-line arguments to the remote server as separate strings. Instead, you have to pass a whole command line for interpretation by the shell on the remote end.

Listing 16-5. Running Individual SSH Commands

```python
#!/usr/bin/env python3
# Foundations of Python Network Programming, Third Edition
# https://github.com/brandon-rhodes/fopnp/blob/m/py3/chapter16/ssh_commands.py
# Running three separate commands, and reading three separate outputs

import argparse, paramiko

class AllowAnythingPolicy(paramiko.MissingHostKeyPolicy):
    def missing_host_key(self, client, hostname, key):
        return

def main(hostname, username):
    client = paramiko.SSHClient()
    client.set_missing_host_key_policy(AllowAnythingPolicy())
    client.connect(hostname, username=username)  # password='')
```

```
    for command in 'echo "Hello, world!"', 'uname', 'uptime':
        stdin, stdout, stderr = client.exec_command(command)
        stdin.close()
        print(repr(stdout.read()))
        stdout.close()
        stderr.close()

    client.close()

if __name__ == '__main__':
    parser = argparse.ArgumentParser(description='Connect over SSH')
    parser.add_argument('hostname', help='Remote machine name')
    parser.add_argument('username', help='Username on the remote machine')
    args = parser.parse_args()
    main(args.hostname, args.username)
```

Unlike all of our earlier Telnet and SSH conversations, this script will receive the output of these three commands as completely separate streams of data. There is no chance of confusing the output of one of the commands with any of the others.

```
$ python3 ssh_commands.py localhost brandon
'Hello, world!\n'
'Linux\n'
'15:29:17 up 5 days, 22:55,  5 users,  load average: 0.78, 0.83, 0.71\n'
```

Besides its security, this is the great advance that SSH provides: the ability to execute semantically separate tasks on the remote machine without having to make separate connections to the remote machine.

As mentioned in the "Telnet" section earlier, you might find quotes() from the Python pipes module to be helpful when building command lines for the exec_command() function if you need to quote command-line arguments so that spaces containing file names and special characters are interpreted correctly by the remote shell.

Every time you start a new SSH shell session with invoke_shell() and every time you kick off a command with exec_command(), a new SSH "channel" is created behind the scenes to provide the filelike Python objects that let you talk to the remote command's standard input, output, and error streams. These channels run in parallel, and SSH will cleverly interleave their data on your single SSH connection so that all of the conversations happen simultaneously without ever becoming confused.

Take a look at Listing 16-6 for a simple example of what is possible. Here two command lines are kicked off remotely, which are each a simple shell script with some echo commands interspersed with sleep pauses. If you want, you can pretend that these are really filesystem commands that return data as they walk the filesystem or that they are CPU-intensive operations that only slowly generate and return their results. The difference does not matter at all to SSH. What matters is that the channels are sitting idle for several seconds at a time and then coming alive again as more data becomes available.

Listing 16-6. SSH Channels Run in Parallel

```
#!/usr/bin/env python3
# Foundations of Python Network Programming, Third Edition
# https://github.com/brandon-rhodes/fopnp/blob/m/py3/chapter16/ssh_threads.py
# Running two remote commands simultaneously in different channels

import argparse, paramiko, threading
```

```
class AllowAnythingPolicy(paramiko.MissingHostKeyPolicy):
    def missing_host_key(self, client, hostname, key):
        return

def main(hostname, username):
    client = paramiko.SSHClient()
    client.set_missing_host_key_policy(AllowAnythingPolicy())
    client.connect(hostname, username=username)  # password='')

    def read_until_EOF(fileobj):
        s = fileobj.readline()
        while s:
            print(s.strip())
            s = fileobj.readline()

    ioe1 = client.exec_command('echo One;sleep 2;echo Two;sleep 1;echo Three')
    ioe2 = client.exec_command('echo A;sleep 1;echo B;sleep 2;echo C')
    thread1 = threading.Thread(target=read_until_EOF, args=(ioe1[1],))
    thread2 = threading.Thread(target=read_until_EOF, args=(ioe2[1],))
    thread1.start()
    thread2.start()
    thread1.join()
    thread2.join()

    client.close()

if __name__ == '__main__':
    parser = argparse.ArgumentParser(description='Connect over SSH')
    parser.add_argument('hostname', help='Remote machine name')
    parser.add_argument('username', help='Username on the remote machine')
    args = parser.parse_args()
    main(args.hostname, args.username)
```

To be able to process these two streams of data simultaneously, you are kicking off two threads and are handing each of them one of the channels from which to read. Both print each line of new information as soon as it arrives and finally exit when the readline() command indicates end-of-file by returning an empty string. When run, this script should return something like this:

```
$ python3 ssh_threads.py localhost brandon
One
A
B
Two
Three
C
```

As you can see, SSH channels over the same TCP connection are completely independent, can each receive (and send) data at their own pace, and can close independently when the particular command to which they are talking finally terminates. The same is true of the features you are about to look at—file transfer and port forwarding.

SFTP: File Transfer Over SSH

Version 2 of the SSH protocol includes a subprotocol called the SSH File Transfer Protocol (SFTP) that lets you walk the remote directory tree, create and delete directories and files, and copy files back and forth from the local to the remote machine. The capabilities of SFTP are so complex and complete, in fact, that not only do they support simple file-copy operations, but they can also power graphical file browsers and can even let the remote filesystem be mounted locally! (Google the sshfs system for details.)

The SFTP protocol is an incredible boon to those of us who once had to copy files using brittle scripts that tried to send data across Telnet via a careful escaping of binary data. Instead of making you power up its own sftp command line each time you want to move files, SSH follows the tradition of RSH by providing an scp command-line tool that acts just like the traditional cp command, but it lets you prefix any file name with hostname: to indicate that it exists on the remote machine. This means remote copy commands stay in your command-line history, just like your other shell commands, rather than being lost to the separate history buffer of a separate command prompt that you have to invoke and then quit (which was a great annoyance of traditional FTP clients).

Furthermore, the great and crowning achievement of SFTP and the sftp and scp commands is that they not only support password authentication but also let you copy files using the same public-key mechanism that lets you avoid typing your password over and over again when running remote commands with the ssh command.

If you briefly scan Chapter 17 on the old FTP system, you will get a good idea of the sorts of operations that SFTP supports. In fact, most of the SFTP commands have the same names as the local commands you already run to manipulate files on your Unix shell account, like chmod and mkdir, or have the same names as Unix system calls with which you might already be familiar through the Python os module, like lstat and unlink. Because these operations are so familiar, I never need any other support in writing SFTP commands than is provided by the bare paramiko documentation for the Python SFTP client at www.lag.net/paramiko/docs/paramiko.SFTPClient-class.

Here are the main things to remember when doing SFTP:

- The SFTP protocol is stateful, just like FTP and just like your normal shell account. Therefore, you can either pass all file and directory names as absolute paths that start at the root of the filesystem or use getcwd() and chdir() to move around the filesystem and then use paths that are relative to the directory in which you have arrived.

- You can open a file using either the file() or open() method (just like Python has a built-in callable that lives under both names), and you get back a filelike object connected to an SSH channel that runs independently of your SFTP channel. That is, you can keep issuing SFTP commands and then move around the filesystem and copy or open further files, and the original channel will still be connected to its file and ready for reading or writing.

- Because each open remote file gets an independent channel, file transfers can happen asynchronously. You can open many remote files at once and have them all streaming down to your disk drive or open new files and be sending data the other way. Be careful that you recognize this, or you might open so many channels at once that each one slows to a crawl.

- Finally, keep in mind that no shell expansion is done on any of the file names you pass across SFTP. If you try using a file name like * or one that has spaces or special characters, they are simply interpreted as part of the file name. No shell is involved when using SFTP. You are getting to talk right to the remote filesystem thanks to the support inside the SSH server itself. This means any support for pattern matching that you want to provide to the user has to be through fetching the directory contents yourself and then checking their pattern against each one, using a routine like those provided in fnmatch in the Python Standard Library.

Listing 16-7 shows a modest example SFTP session. It does something simple that system administrators might often need (but, of course, that they could just as easily accomplish with an scp command): it connects to the remote system and copies message log files out of the /var/log directory, perhaps for scanning or analysis on the local machine.

Listing 16-7. Listing a Directory and Fetching Files with SFTP

```
#!/usr/bin/env python3
# Foundations of Python Network Programming, Third Edition
# https://github.com/brandon-rhodes/fopnp/blob/m/py3/chapter16/sftp_get.py
# Fetching files with SFTP

import argparse, functools, paramiko

class AllowAnythingPolicy(paramiko.MissingHostKeyPolicy):
    def missing_host_key(self, client, hostname, key):
        return

def main(hostname, username, filenames):
    client = paramiko.SSHClient()
    client.set_missing_host_key_policy(AllowAnythingPolicy())
    client.connect(hostname, username=username)  # password='')

    def print_status(filename, bytes_so_far, bytes_total):
        percent = 100. * bytes_so_far / bytes_total
        print('Transfer of %r is at %d/%d bytes (%.1f%%)' % (
            filename, bytes_so_far, bytes_total, percent))

    sftp = client.open_sftp()
    for filename in filenames:
        if filename.endswith('.copy'):
            continue
        callback = functools.partial(print_status, filename)
        sftp.get(filename, filename + '.copy', callback=callback)
    client.close()

if __name__ == '__main__':
    parser = argparse.ArgumentParser(description='Copy files over SSH')
    parser.add_argument('hostname', help='Remote machine name')
    parser.add_argument('username', help='Username on the remote machine')
    parser.add_argument('filename', nargs='+', help='Filenames to fetch')
    args = parser.parse_args()
    main(args.hostname, args.username, args.filename)
```

Note that although I made a big deal of talking about how each file that you open with SFTP uses its own independent channel, the simple get() and put() convenience functions provided by paramiko, which are really lightweight wrappers for an open() followed by a loop that reads and writes, do not attempt any asynchrony; instead, they just block and wait until each whole file has arrived. This means that the foregoing script calmly transfers one file at a time, producing output that looks something like this:

```
$ python sftp.py guinness brandon W-2.pdf miles.png
Transfer of 'W-2.pdf' is at 32768/115065 bytes (28.5%)
Transfer of 'W-2.pdf' is at 65536/115065 bytes (57.0%)
Transfer of 'W-2.pdf' is at 98304/115065 bytes (85.4%)
Transfer of 'W-2.pdf' is at 115065/115065 bytes (100.0%)
Transfer of 'W-2.pdf' is at 115065/115065 bytes (100.0%)
Transfer of 'miles.png' is at 15577/15577 bytes (100.0%)
Transfer of 'miles.png' is at 15577/15577 bytes (100.0%)
```

Again, consult the excellent paramiko documentation at the URL just mentioned to see the simple but complete set of file operations that SFTP supports.

Other Features

I have just covered, in the past few sections, all of the SSH operations that are supported by methods on the basic SSHClient object. The more obscure features with which you might be familiar, like remote X11 sessions and port forwarding, require that you go one level deeper in the paramiko interface and talk directly to the client's "transport" object.

The transport is the class that actually knows the low-level operations that get combined to power an SSH connection. You can ask a client for its transport easily.

```
>>> transport = client.get_transport()
```

Though I lack the room to cover additional SSH features here, the understanding of SSH that you have gained 0in this chapter should help you understand them given the paramiko documentation combined with example code—whether from the demos directory of the paramiko project itself or from blogs, Stack Overflow, or other materials about paramiko that you might find online.

One feature I should mention explicitly is *port forwarding*, where SSH opens a port on either the local or remote host—at least making the port available to connections from localhost and possibly also accepting connections from other machines on the Internet—and "forwards" these connections across the SSH channel where it connects to some other host and port on the remote end, passing data back and forth.

Port forwarding can be useful. For example, I sometimes find myself developing a web application that I cannot run easily on my laptop because it needs access to a database and other resources that are available only on a server farm. But I might not want the hassle of running the application on a public port, where I might have to adjust firewall rules to open it, and then getting HTTPS running so that third parties cannot see my work-in-progress.

An easy solution is to run the under-development web application on the remote development machine the way I would locally—listening on localhost:8080 so that it cannot be contacted from another computer—and then tell SSH that I want connections to my local port 8080, made on my laptop, to be forwarded out so that they really connect to port 8080 on that local machine.

```
$ ssh -L 8080:localhost:8080 devel.example.com
```

If you need to create port forwards when running an SSH connection with paramiko, then I have bad news and good news. The bad news is that the top-level SSHClient does not, alas, provide an easy way to create a forward because it supports more common operations such as shell sessions. Instead, you will have to create the forward by talking directly to the "transport" object and then writing loops that copy data in both directions over the forward yourself.

But the good news is that paramiko comes with example scripts showing exactly how to write port-forwarding loops. These two scripts, from the main paramiko trunk, should get you started:

```
http://github.com/paramiko/paramiko/blob/master/demos/forward.py
http://github.com/paramiko/paramiko/blob/master/demos/rforward.py
```

Of course, since the port-forward data is passed back and forth across channels inside the SSH connection, you do not have to worry if they are raw, unprotected HTTP or other traffic that is normally visible to third parties; since they are now embedded inside SSH, they are protected by its own encryption from being intercepted.

Summary

Remote-shell protocols let you connect to remote machines, run shell commands, and see their output, just as though the commands were running inside a local terminal window. Sometimes you use these protocols to connect to an actual Unix shell and sometimes to small, embedded shells in routers or other networking hardware that needs configuring.

As always, when talking to Unix commands, you need to be aware of output buffering, special shell characters, and terminal input buffering as issues that can make your life difficult by munging your data or even hanging your shell connection.

The Python Standard Library natively supports the Telnet protocol through its `telnetlib` module. Although Telnet is ancient, is insecure, and can be difficult to script, it may often be the only protocol supported by simple devices to which you want to connect.

The Secure Shell protocol is the current state of the art, not only for connecting to the command line of a remote host but for copying files and forwarding TCP/IP ports as well. Python has quite excellent SSH support thanks to the third-party paramiko package. When making an SSH connection, you need to remember three things.

- Paramiko will need to verify (or be told explicitly to ignore) the identity of the remote machine, which is defined as the host key that it present when the connection is made.

- Authentication will typically be accomplished through a password or through the use of a public-private key pair whose public half you have put in your `authorized_keys` file on the remote server.

- Once you are authenticated, you can start all sorts of SSH services—remote shells, individual commands, and file-transfer sessions—and they can all run at once without your having to open new SSH connections, thanks to the fact that they will all get their own "channel" within the master SSH connection.

The next chapter will examine an older and less capable protocol for file transfer that dates back to the early days of the Internet: the File Transfer Protocol on which SFTP was based.

CHAPTER 17

FTP

File Transfer Protocol (FTP) was once among the most widely used protocols on the Internet, invoked whenever a user wanted to transfer files between Internet-connected computers. Alas, the protocol has seen better days, and today a better alternative exists for every one of its major roles.

There were four primary activities that FTP once powered. The first and major use of FTP was for file downloads. Lists of "anonymous" FTP servers that allowed public access were circulated, and users connected to retrieve documents, the source code to new programs, and media like images or movies. (You logged in to them with the username "anonymous" or "ftp," and then—out of politeness, so they would know who was using their bandwidth— you typed your e-mail address as the password.) FTP was always the protocol of choice when files needed to be moved between computer accounts, because trying to transfer large files with Telnet clients was often a dicey proposition.

Second, FTP was often jury-rigged to provide for anonymous upload. Many organizations wanted outsiders to be able to submit documents or files, and their solution was to set up FTP servers that allowed files to be written into a directory whose contents could not, then, be listed back again. That way, users could not see (and hopefully could not guess!) the names of the files that other users had just submitted and get to them before the site administrators did.

Third, the protocol was often in use to support the synchronization of entire trees of files between computer accounts. By using a client that provided for recursive FTP operations, users could push entire directory trees from one of their accounts to another, and server administrators could clone or install new services without having to rebuild them from scratch on a new machine. When using FTP like this, users were generally not aware of how the actual protocol worked or of the many separate commands needed to transfer so many different files: instead, they clicked a button and a large batch operation would run and then complete the process.

Fourth, and finally, FTP was used for its original purpose: interactive, full-fledged file management. The early FTP clients presented a command-line prompt that felt something like a Unix shell account itself, and—as I will explain— the protocol borrows from shell accounts both the idea of a "current working directory" and of a cd command to move from one directory to another. Later clients mimicked the idea of a Mac-like interface, with folders and files drawn on the computer screen. But in either case, in the activity of file-system browsing, the full capabilities of FTP finally came into play: it supported not only the operations of listing directories and uploading and downloading files, but also of creating and deleting directories, adjusting file permissions, and renaming files.

What to Use Instead of FTP

Today, there are better alternatives than the FTP protocol for pretty much anything you could want to do with it. Occasionally, you will still see URLs that start with ftp://, but they are becoming quite rare. This chapter will be useful if you have a legacy system and you need to speak FTP from your Python program or because you want to learn more about file transfer protocols in general and FTP is a good, historical place to start.

The biggest problem with the protocol is its lack of security: not only files, but usernames and passwords are sent completely in the clear and can be viewed by anyone observing network traffic.

A second issue is that an FTP user tends to make a connection, choose a working directory, and do several operations all over the same network connection. Modern Internet services, with millions of users, prefer protocols like HTTP (see Chapter 9) that consist of short, completely self-contained requests, instead of long-running FTP connections that require the server to remember things like a current working directory.

A final big issue is file-system security. Instead of showing users just a sliver of the host file system that the owner wanted exposed, early FTP servers tended simply to expose the entire file system, letting users cd to / and snoop around to see how the system was configured. True, you could run the server under a separate ftp user and try to deny that user access to as many files as possible; but many areas of the Unix file system need to be publicly readable purely so that normal users can use the programs there.

So what are the alternatives?

- For file download, HTTP (see Chapter 9) is the standard protocol on today's Internet, protected with SSL when necessary for security. Instead of exposing system-specific file name conventions as FTP does, HTTP supports system-independent URLs.

- Anonymous upload is a bit less standard, but the general tendency is to use a form on a web page that instructs the browser to use an HTTP POST operation to transmit the file that the user selects.

- File synchronization has improved immeasurably since the days when a recursive FTP file copy was the only common way to get files to another computer. Instead of wastefully copying every file, modern commands like rsync or rdist efficiently compare files at both ends of the connection and copy only the ones that are new or that have changed. (These commands are not covered in this book; try Googling them.) Nonprogrammers are most likely to use the Python-powered Dropbox service or any of the competing "cloud drive" services, which large providers now offer.

- Full file-system access is actually the one area where FTP can still commonly be found on today's Internet: thousands of cut-rate ISPs continue to support FTP, despite its lack of security, as the means by which users can copy their media and (typically) PHP source code into their web account. A much better alternative today is for service providers to support SFTP instead (see Chapter 16).

Note The FTP standard is RFC 959, available at www.faqs.org/rfcs/rfc959.html.

Communication Channels

FTP is unusual because, by default, it actually uses *two* TCP connections during operation. One connection is the control channel, which carries commands and the resulting acknowledgments or error codes. The second connection is the data channel, which is used solely for transmitting file data or other blocks of information, such as directory listings. Technically, the data channel is fully duplex, meaning that it allows files to be transmitted in both directions simultaneously. However, in actual practice, this capability is rarely used.

In traditional operations, the process of downloading a file from an FTP server runs like this:

1. First, the FTP client establishes a command connection by connecting to the FTP port on the server.

2. The client authenticates itself, usually with username and password.

3. The client changes directory on the server to where it wants to deposit or retrieve files.

4. The client begins listening on a new port for the data connection, and then it informs the server about that port.

5. The server connects to the port that the client has opened.

6. The file is transmitted.

7. The data connection is closed.

This idea that the server should connect back to the client worked well in the early days of the Internet; back then, almost every machine that could run an FTP client had a public IP address, and firewalls were relatively rare. Today, however, the picture is more complicated. Firewalls blocking incoming connections to desktop and laptop machines are now quite common, and many wireless, DSL, and in-house business networks do not offer client machines real public IP addresses anyway.

To accommodate this situation, FTP also supports what is known as *passive mode*. In this scenario, the data connection is made backward: the server opens an extra port, and it tells the client to make the second connection. Other than that, everything behaves the same way.

Today, passive mode is the default with most FTP clients, including Python's ftplib module, which I'll explain in this chapter.

Using FTP in Python

The Python module ftplib is the primary interface to FTP for Python programmers. It handles the details of establishing the various connections for you, and it provides convenient ways to automate common commands.

■ **Tip**   If you are interested only in downloading files, the urllib2 module introduced in Chapter 1 supports FTP, and it may be easier to use for simple downloading tasks; just run it with an ftp:// URL. In this chapter, I describe ftplib because it provides FTP-specific features that are not available with urllib2.

Listing 17-1 shows a very basic ftplib example. The program connects to a remote server, displays the welcome message, and prints the current working directory.

Listing 17-1. Making a Simple FTP Connection

```
#!/usr/bin/env python3
# Foundations of Python Network Programming, Third Edition
# https://github.com/brandon-rhodes/fopnp/blob/m/py3/chapter17/connect.py

from ftplib import FTP

def main():
    ftp = FTP('ftp.ibiblio.org')
    print("Welcome:", ftp.getwelcome())
    ftp.login()
    print("Current working directory:", ftp.pwd())
    ftp.quit()

if __name__ == '__main__':
    main()
```

The welcome message will generally have no information that could be usefully parsed by your program, but you might want to display it if a user is calling your client interactively. The login() function can take several parameters, including a username, password, and a third, rarely used, authentication token that FTP calls an "account." Here it was called without parameters, making the user log in as "anonymous" with a generic value for the password.

Recall that an FTP session can visit different directories, just like a shell prompt can move between locations with cd. Here, the pwd() function returns the current working directory on the remote site of the connection. Finally, the quit() function logs out and closes the connection.

Here is what the program outputs when run:

```
$ ./connect.py
Welcome: 220 ProFTPD Server (Bring it on...)
Current working directory: /
```

ASCII and Binary Files

When making an FTP transfer, you have to decide whether you want the file treated as a monolithic block of binary data or whether you want it parsed as a text file so that your local machine can paste its lines back together using whatever end-of-line character is native to your platform.

As you might predict, Python 3 faithfully expects and returns plain strings when you ask it to operate in text mode, but it requires byte strings if you are handling binary file data.

A file transferred in so-called ASCII mode is delivered one line at a time and, awkwardly enough, is delivered to your program without line endings, so that you have to glue the lines back together yourself. Take a look at Listing 17-2 for a Python program that downloads a well-known text file and saves it in your local directory.

Listing 17-2. Downloading an ASCII File

```python
#!/usr/bin/env python3
# Foundations of Python Network Programming, Third Edition
# https://github.com/brandon-rhodes/fopnp/blob/m/py3/chapter17/asciidl.py
# Downloads README from remote and writes it to disk.

import os
from ftplib import FTP

def main():
    if os.path.exists('README'):
        raise IOError('refusing to overwrite your README file')

    ftp = FTP('ftp.kernel.org')
    ftp.login()
    ftp.cwd('/pub/linux/kernel')

    with open('README', 'w') as f:
        def writeline(data):
            f.write(data)
            f.write(os.linesep)
```

```
        ftp.retrlines('RETR README', writeline)

    ftp.quit()

if __name__ == '__main__':
    main()
```

In the listing, the cwd() function selects a new working directory on the remote system. Then the retrlines() function begins the transfer. Its first parameter specifies a command to run on the remote system, usually RETR, followed by a file name. Its second parameter is a function that is called, over and over again, as each line of the text file is retrieved; if omitted, the data are simply printed to standard output. The lines are passed with the end-of-line character stripped, so the homemade writeline() function simply appends your system's standard line ending to each line as it is written out.

Try running this program; there should be a file in your current directory named README after the program is done.

Basic binary file transfers work in much the same way as text-file transfers. Listing 17-3 shows an example of this.

Listing 17-3. Downloading a Binary File

```
#!/usr/bin/env python3
# Foundations of Python Network Programming, Third Edition
# https://github.com/brandon-rhodes/fopnp/blob/m/py3/chapter17/binarydl.py

import os
from ftplib import FTP

def main():
    if os.path.exists('patch8.gz'):
        raise IOError('refusing to overwrite your patch8.gz file')

    ftp = FTP('ftp.kernel.org')
    ftp.login()
    ftp.cwd('/pub/linux/kernel/v1.0')

    with open('patch8.gz', 'wb') as f:
        ftp.retrbinary('RETR patch8.gz', f.write)

    ftp.quit()

if __name__ == '__main__':
    main()
```

When run, this program deposits a file named patch8.gz into your current working directory. The retrbinary() function simply passes blocks of data to the specified function. This is convenient, because a file object's write() function expects data, so in this case, no custom function is necessary.

Advanced Binary Downloading

The ftplib module provides a second function that can be used for binary downloading: ntransfercmd(). This command provides a lower-level interface, but it can be useful if you want to know a little bit more about what's going on during the download. In particular, this more advanced command lets you keep track of the number of bytes transferred, and you can use that information to display status updates for the user. Listing 17-4 shows a sample program that uses ntransfercmd().

Listing 17-4. Binary Download with Status Updates

```python
#!/usr/bin/env python3
# Foundations of Python Network Programming, Third Edition
# https://github.com/brandon-rhodes/fopnp/blob/m/py3/chapter17/advbinarydl.py

import os, sys
from ftplib import FTP

def main():
    if os.path.exists('linux-1.0.tar.gz'):
        raise IOError('refusing to overwrite your linux-1.0.tar.gz file')

    ftp = FTP('ftp.kernel.org')
    ftp.login()
    ftp.cwd('/pub/linux/kernel/v1.0')
    ftp.voidcmd("TYPE I")

    socket, size = ftp.ntransfercmd("RETR linux-1.0.tar.gz")
    nbytes = 0

    f = open('linux-1.0.tar.gz', 'wb')

    while True:
        data = socket.recv(2048)
        if not data:
            break
        f.write(data)
        nbytes += len(data)
        print("\rReceived", nbytes, end=' ')
        if size:
            print("of %d total bytes (%.1f%%)"
                    % (size, 100 * nbytes / float(size)), end=' ')
        else:
            print("bytes", end=' ')
        sys.stdout.flush()

    print()
    f.close()
    socket.close()
    ftp.voidresp()
    ftp.quit()

if __name__ == '__main__':
    main()
```

There are a few new things to note here. First is the call to voidcmd(). This passes an FTP command directly to the server and checks for an error, but returns nothing. In this case, the raw command is TYPE I. This sets the transfer mode to "image," which is how FTP refers internally to binary files. In the previous example, retrbinary() automatically ran this command behind the scenes, but the lower-level ntransfercmd() does not.

Next, note that ntransfercmd() returns a tuple consisting of a data socket and an estimated size. *Always* bear in mind that the size is merely an *estimate*, and it should not be considered authoritative; the file may end sooner, or it might go on much longer than this value. Also, if a size estimate from the FTP server is simply not available, then the estimated size returned will be None.

The object datasock is, in fact, a plain TCP socket, which has all of the behaviors described in Part 1 of this book (see Chapter 3 in particular). In this example, a simple loop calls recv() until it has read all of the data from the socket, writing it out to disk along the way and printing out status updates to the screen.

Tip Notice two things about the status updates printed to the screen by Listing 17-4. First, rather than printing a scrolling list of lines that disappear out of the top of the terminal, each line begins with a carriage return '\r', which moves the cursor back to your terminal's left edge so that each status line overwrites the previous one and creates the illusion of an increasing, animated percentage. Second, because you are telling each print statement to end the line with a space instead of a new line, you never actually let it finish a line of output, so you have to flush() the standard output to make sure that the status updates immediately reach the screen.

After receiving the data, it is important to close the data socket and call voidresp(), which reads the command response code from the server, raising an exception if there was any error during transmission. Even if you do not care about detecting errors, failing to call voidresp() will make future commands likely to fail because the server's output socket will be blocked waiting for you to read the results.

Here is an example of the output of running this program:

```
$ ./advbinarydl.py
Received 1259161 of 1259161 bytes (100.0%)
```

Uploading Data

File data can also be uploaded through FTP. As with downloading, there are two basic functions for uploading: storbinary() and storlines(). Both take a command to run and a file-like object to transmit. The storbinary() function will call the read() method repeatedly on that object until its content is exhausted, while storlines(), by contrast, calls the readline() method.

Unlike the corresponding download functions, these methods do not require you to provide a callable function of your own. (But you could, of course, pass a file-like object of your own crafting whose read() or readline() method computes the outgoing data as the transmission proceeds!)

Listing 17-5 shows you how to upload a file in binary mode.

Listing 17-5. Binary Upload

```
#!/usr/bin/env python3
# Foundations of Python Network Programming, Third Edition
# https://github.com/brandon-rhodes/fopnp/blob/m/py3/chapter17/binaryul.py

from ftplib import FTP
import sys, getpass, os.path
```

```
def main():
    if len(sys.argv) != 5:
        print("usage:", sys.argv[0],
                "<host> <username> <localfile> <remotedir>")
        exit(2)

    host, username, localfile, remotedir = sys.argv[1:]
    prompt = "Enter password for {} on {}: ".format(username, host)
    password = getpass.getpass(prompt)

    ftp = FTP(host)
    ftp.login(username, password)
    ftp.cwd(remotedir)
    with open(localfile, 'rb') as f:
        ftp.storbinary('STOR %s' % os.path.basename(localfile), f)
    ftp.quit()

if __name__ == '__main__':
    main()
```

This program looks quite similar to the earlier efforts. Because most anonymous FTP sites do not permit file uploading, you will have to find a server somewhere to test it against; I simply installed the old, venerable ftpd on my laptop for a few minutes and ran the test like this:

```
$ python binaryul.py localhost brandon test.txt /tmp
```

I entered my password at the prompt (brandon is my username on this machine). When the program finished, I checked and, sure enough, a copy of the test.txt file was now sitting in /tmp. Remember *not* to try this over a network to another machine, because FTP does not encrypt or protect your password!

You can modify this program to upload a file in ASCII mode by simply changing storbinary() to storlines().

Advanced Binary Uploading

Just as the download process had a complicated raw version, it is also possible to upload files manually using ntransfercmd(), as shown in Listing 17-6.

Listing 17-6. Uploading Files a Block at a Time

```
#!/usr/bin/env python3
# Foundations of Python Network Programming, Third Edition
# https://github.com/brandon-rhodes/fopnp/blob/m/py3/chapter17/advbinarydl.py

import os, sys
from ftplib import FTP

def main():
    if os.path.exists('linux-1.0.tar.gz'):
        raise IOError('refusing to overwrite your linux-1.0.tar.gz file')
```

```
ftp = FTP('ftp.kernel.org')
ftp.login()
ftp.cwd('/pub/linux/kernel/v1.0')
ftp.voidcmd("TYPE I")

socket, size = ftp.ntransfercmd("RETR linux-1.0.tar.gz")
nbytes = 0

f = open('linux-1.0.tar.gz', 'wb')

while True:
    data = socket.recv(2048)
    if not data:
        break
    f.write(data)
    nbytes += len(data)
    print("\rReceived", nbytes, end=' ')
    if size:
        print("of %d total bytes (%.1f%%)"
                % (size, 100 * nbytes / float(size)), end=' ')
    else:
        print("bytes", end=' ')
    sys.stdout.flush()

print()
f.close()
socket.close()
ftp.voidresp()
ftp.quit()

if __name__ == '__main__':
    main()
```

Note that the first thing you do when finished with the transfer is to call datasock.close(). When uploading data, closing the socket is the signal to the server that the upload is complete! If you fail to close the data socket after uploading all of your data, the server will keep waiting for the rest of the data to arrive.

Now you can perform an upload that continuously displays its status as it progresses:

```
$ python binaryul.py localhost brandon patch8.gz /tmp
Enter password for brandon on localhost:
Sent 6408 of 6408 bytes (100.0%)
```

Handling Errors

Like most Python modules, ftplib will raise an exception when an error occurs. It defines several exceptions of its own, and it can also raise socket.error and IOError. As a convenience, it offers a tuple, named ftplib.all_errors, which lists all of the exceptions that can possibly be raised by ftplib. This is often a useful shortcut for writing a try...except clause.

One of the problems with the basic retrbinary() function is that, in order to use it easily, you will usually wind up opening the file on the local end before beginning the transfer on the remote side. If your command aimed at the remote side retorts that the file does not exist, or if the RETR command otherwise fails, then you will have to close and delete the local file you have just created (or else wind up littering the file system with zero-length files).

With the ntransfercmd() method, by contrast, you can check for a problem prior to opening a local file. Listing 17-6 already follows these guidelines: if ntransfercmd() fails, the exception will cause the program to terminate before the local file is opened.

Scanning Directories

FTP provides two ways to discover information about server files and directories. These are implemented in ftplib as the nlst() and dir() methods.

The nlst() method returns a list of entries in a given directory—all of the files and directories are inside. However, the bare names are all that is returned. There is no other information about which particular entries are files or are directories, on the sizes of the files present, or anything else.

The more powerful dir() function returns a directory listing from the remote. This listing is in a system-defined format, but it typically contains a file name, size, modification date, and file type. On Unix servers, it is typically the output of one of these two shell commands:

```
$ ls -l
$ ls -la
```

Windows servers may use the output of dir. Although the output may be useful to an end user, it is difficult for a program to use, due to the varying output formats. Some clients that need these data implement parsers for the many different formats that ls and dir produce across machines and operating system versions; others can only parse the one format in use in a particular situation.

Listing 17-7 shows an example of using nlst() to get directory information.

Listing 17-7. Getting a Bare Directory Listing

```python
#!/usr/bin/env python3
# Foundations of Python Network Programming, Third Edition
# https://github.com/brandon-rhodes/fopnp/blob/m/py3/chapter17/nlst.py

from ftplib import FTP

def main():
    ftp = FTP('ftp.ibiblio.org')
    ftp.login()
    ftp.cwd('/pub/academic/astronomy/')
    entries = ftp.nlst()
    ftp.quit()

    print(len(entries), "entries:")
    for entry in sorted(entries):
        print(entry)

if __name__ == '__main__':
    main()
```

When you run this program, you will see output like this:

```
$ python nlst.py
13 entries:
INDEX
README
ephem_4.28.tar.Z
hawaii_scope
incoming
jupitor-moons.shar.Z
lunar.c.Z
lunisolar.shar.Z
moon.shar.Z
planetary
sat-track.tar.Z
stars.tar.Z
xephem.tar.Z
```

If you were to use an FTP client to log in to the server manually, you would see the same files listed. The result will be different when you try another file listing command, as shown in Listing 17-8.

Listing 17-8. Getting a Fancy Directory Listing

```python
#!/usr/bin/env python3
# Foundations of Python Network Programming, Third Edition
# https://github.com/brandon-rhodes/fopnp/blob/m/py3/chapter17/dir.py

from ftplib import FTP

def main():
    ftp = FTP('ftp.ibiblio.org')
    ftp.login()
    ftp.cwd('/pub/academic/astronomy/')
    entries = []
    ftp.dir(entries.append)
    ftp.quit()

    print(len(entries), "entries:")
    for entry in entries:
        print(entry)

if __name__ == '__main__':
    main()
```

Notice that the file names are in a convenient format for automated processing—a bare list of file names—but there is no extra information. Contrast the bare list of file names that you saw earlier with the output from Listing 17-8, which uses dir():

```
$ python dir.py
13 entries:
-rw-r--r--  1 (?) »   (?) »    »      750 Feb 14  1994 INDEX
-rw-r--r--  1 root »  bin »    »      135 Feb 11  1999 README
-rw-r--r--  1 (?) »   (?) »        341303 Oct  2  1992 ephem_4.28.tar.Z
drwxr-xr-x  2 (?) »   (?) »    »     4096 Feb 11  1999 hawaii_scope
drwxr-xr-x  2 (?) »   (?) »    »     4096 Feb 11  1999 incoming
-rw-r--r--  1 (?) »   (?) »    »     5983 Oct  2  1992 jupitor-moons.shar.Z
-rw-r--r--  1 (?) »   (?) »    »     1751 Oct  2  1992 lunar.c.Z
-rw-r--r--  1 (?) »   (?) »    »     8078 Oct  2  1992 lunisolar.shar.Z
-rw-r--r--  1 (?) »   (?) »    »    64209 Oct  2  1992 moon.shar.Z
drwxr-xr-x  2 (?) »   (?) »    »     4096 Jan  6  1993 planetary
-rw-r--r--  1 (?) »   (?) »       129969 Oct  2  1992 sat-track.tar.Z
-rw-r--r--  1 (?) »   (?) »    »   16504 Oct  2  1992 stars.tar.Z
-rw-r--r--  1 (?) »   (?) »       410650 Oct  2  1992 xephem.tar.Z
```

The dir() method takes a function that it calls for each line, delivering the directory listing in pieces just like retrlines() delivers the contents of particular files. Here, you simply supply the append() method of the plain old Python entries list.

Detecting Directories and Recursive Download

If you cannot guarantee what information an FTP server might choose to return from its dir() command, how are you going to tell directories from normal files—an essential step when downloading entire trees of files from the server?

The only sure answer, shown in Listing 17-9, is simply to try adding a cwd() into every name that nlst() returns and, if you succeed, conclude that the entity is a directory! This sample program does not do any actual downloading; instead, to keep things simple (and not to flood your disk with sample data), it prints out the directories it visits to the screen.

Listing 17-9. Trying to Recurse into Directories

```
#!/usr/bin/env python3
# Foundations of Python Network Programming, Third Edition
# https://github.com/brandon-rhodes/fopnp/blob/m/py3/chapter17/recursedl.py

from ftplib import FTP, error_perm

def walk_dir(ftp, dirpath):
    original_dir = ftp.pwd()
```

```
    try:
        ftp.cwd(dirpath)
    except error_perm:
        return   # ignore non-directores and ones we cannot enter
    print(dirpath)
    names = sorted(ftp.nlst())
    for name in names:
        walk_dir(ftp, dirpath + '/' + name)
    ftp.cwd(original_dir)   # return to cwd of our caller

def main():
    ftp = FTP('ftp.kernel.org')
    ftp.login()
    walk_dir(ftp, '/pub/linux/kernel/Historic/old-versions')
    ftp.quit()

if __name__ == '__main__':
    main()
```

This sample program will run a bit slow—there are, as it turns out, quite a few files in the old version's directory on the Linux kernel archive—but within a few dozen seconds, you should see the resulting directory tree displayed on the screen:

```
$ python recursedl.py
/pub/linux/kernel/Historic/old-versions
/pub/linux/kernel/Historic/old-versions/impure
/pub/linux/kernel/Historic/old-versions/old
/pub/linux/kernel/Historic/old-versions/old/corrupt
/pub/linux/kernel/Historic/old-versions/tytso
```

By adding a few print statements, you could supplement this list of directories by displaying every one of the files that the recursive process is (slowly) discovering. Moreover, by adding another few lines of code, you could be downloading the files themselves to corresponding directories that you create locally. However, the only really essential logic for a recursive download is already operating in the code in Listing 17-9: but the only foolproof way to know if an entry is a directory that you are allowed to enter is to try running cwd() against it.

Creating Directories, Deleting Things

Finally, FTP supports file deletion, and it supports both the creation and deletion of directories. These more obscure calls are all described in the ftplib documentation:

- delete(filename) will delete a file from the server.

- mkd(dirname) attempts to create a new directory.

- rmd(dirname) will delete a directory; note that most systems require the directory to be empty first.

- rename(oldname, newname) works, essentially, like the Unix command mv: if both names are in the same directory, the file is essentially renamed; but if the destination specifies a name in a different directory, then the file is actually moved.

Note that these commands, like all other FTP operations, are performed more or less as though you were really logged on to the remote server command line with the same username with which you logged in to the FTP. It is because of these last few commands that FTP can be used to back file browser applications that let users drag and drop files and directories seamlessly between their local system and the remote host.

Doing FTP Securely

Though I noted at the beginning of this chapter that there are far better protocols to adopt than FTP for pretty much anything you could use FTP to accomplish, in particular the robust and secure SFTP extension to SSH (see Chapter 16), I should be fair and note that a few FTP servers support TLS encryption (see Chapter 6) and that Python's ftplib does provide this protection if you want to take advantage of it.

To use TLS, create your FTP connection with the FTP_TLS class instead of the plain FTP class. Simply by doing this, your username and password and, in fact, the entire FTP command channel will be protected from prying eyes. If you then additionally run the class's prot_p() method (it takes no arguments), then the FTP data connection will be protected as well. Should you, for some reason, want to return to using an unencrypted data connection during the session, there is a prot_c() method that returns the data stream to normal. Again, your commands will continue to be protected as long as you are using the FTP_TLS class.

Check the Python Standard Library documentation for more details (they include a small code sample) if you wind up needing this extension to FTP: http://docs.python.org/3/library/ftplib.html.

Summary

FTP lets you transfer files between a client running on your machine and a remote FTP server. Though the protocol is not secure and is outdated when compared with better choices like SFTP, you might still find services and machines that require you to use it. In Python, the ftplib library is used to talk to FTP servers.

FTP supports binary and ASCII transfers. ASCII transfers are usually used for text files, and they permit line endings to be adjusted as the file is transferred. Binary transfers are used for everything else. The retrlines() function is used to download a file in ASCII mode, while retrbinary() downloads a file in binary mode.

You can also upload files to a remote server. The storlines() function uploads a file in ASCII mode, and storbinary() uploads a file in binary mode.

The ntransfercmd() function can be used for binary uploads and downloads. It gives you more control over the transfer process, and it is often used to support a progress bar for the user.

The ftplib module raises exceptions on errors. The special tuple ftplib.all_errors can be used to catch any error that it might raise.

You can use cwd() to change to a particular directory on the remote end. The nlst() command returns a simple list of all entries (files or directories) in a given directory. The dir() command returns a more detailed list, but in server-specific format. Even with only nlst(), you can usually detect whether an entry is a file or directory by attempting to use cwd() to change to it and noting whether you get an error.

In the next chapter, we turn from the simple action of file transfer to the more generic action of invoking a remote procedure on another server and getting typed data, instead of bare strings, back in response.

CHAPTER 18

RPC

Remote Procedure Call (RPC) systems let you call a function in another process or on a remote server using the same syntax you would use when calling a routine in a local API or library. This tends to be useful in two situations:

- Your program has a lot of work to do, and you want to spread it across several machines by making calls across the network, but without having to change the code that is making the call, which is now remote.

- You need data or information that is only available on another hard drive or network, and an RPC interface lets you easily send queries to another system to get back an answer.

The first remote procedure systems tended to be written for low-level languages like C. They placed bytes on the network that looked very much like the bytes already being written onto the processor stack every time one C function called another. And just as a C program could not safely call a library function without a header file that told it exactly how to lay out the function's arguments in memory (any errors often resulted in a crash), RPC calls could not be made without knowing ahead of time how the data would be serialized. In fact, each RPC payload looked exactly like a block of binary data as formatted by the Python `struct` module discussed in Chapter 5.

Today our machines and networks are fast enough, though, so we often exchange some memory and speed for protocols that are more robust and require less coordination between two pieces of code that are in conversation. Older RPC protocols would have sent a stream of bytes like the following:

```
0, 0, 0, 1, 64, 36, 0, 0, 0, 0, 0, 0
```

It would have been up to the receiver to know that the function's parameters are a 32-bit integer and a 64-bit floating point number, and then to decode the 12 bytes to the pair of values "integer 1" and "float 10.0." More modern RPC protocols use self-documenting formats like XML, however, which are written in a way that makes it all but impossible to interpret the arguments as anything other than an integer and a floating-point number:

```
<params>
  <param><value><i4>41</i4></value></param>
  <param><value><double>10.</double></value></param>
</params>
```

An earlier generation of programmer would have been appalled that 12 bytes of actual binary data have bloated into 108 bytes of protocol that have to be generated by the sender and then parsed on the receiving end, consuming hundreds of CPU (Central Processing Unit) cycles. Nonetheless, the elimination of ambiguity in the protocols is generally considered worth the expense. Of course, the above pair of values can also be expressed with less verbosity by using a more modern payload format than XML, like JSON the JavaScript Object Notation:

```
[1, 10.0]
```

In both cases, however, you can see that unambiguous textual representation has become the order of the day, and it has replaced the older practice of sending raw binary data whose meaning had to be known in advance.

Of course, by this point you might be asking exactly what makes RPC protocols all that special. After all, the choices I am talking about here—choosing a data format, sending a request, and receiving a response in return—are not specific to procedure calls; but they are common to any meaningful network protocol! Both HTTP and SMTP, to take two examples from previous chapters, must serialize data and define message formats. So again, you might wonder: What makes RPC all that special? There are three features that mark a protocol as an example of RPC.

First, an RPC protocol is distinguished by its lack of strong semantics for the meaning of each call. Whereas HTTP is used for the retrieval documents and SMTP supports the delivery of messages, an RPC protocol does not assign any meaning to the data passed except to support basic data types like integers, floats, strings, and lists. It is instead up to each particular API that you fashion using an RPC protocol to define what its calls mean.

Second, RPC mechanisms are a way to invoke methods, but they do not define them. When you read the specification of a more single-purpose protocol like HTTP or SMTP, you will note that they define a finite number of basic operations, like GET and PUT in the case of HTTP or EHLO and MAIL when you are using SMTP. But RPC mechanisms leave it up to you to define the *verbs* or function calls that your server will support; they do not specify them in advance.

Third, when you use RPC, your client and server code should not look very different from any other code that uses function calls. Unless you know that an object represents a remote server, the only pattern you might notice in the code is a certain caution with respect to the objects that are passed—lots of numbers, strings, and lists, but typically not *live* objects like open files. However, while the kinds of arguments passed might be limited, the function calls will "look normal" and not require decoration or elaboration in order to pass over the network.

Features of RPC

Besides serving the essential purpose of letting you make what appear to be local function or method calls, which are in fact passing across the network to a different server, RPC protocols have several key features, and also some differences, that you should keep in mind when choosing and then deploying an RPC client or server.

First, every RPC mechanism has limits on the kind of data you can pass. In fact, the most general-purpose RPC mechanisms tend to be the most restrictive, because they are designed to work with many different programming languages and thus can only support lowest-common-denominator features that appear in almost all of them.

The most popular protocols, therefore, support only a few kinds of numbers and strings; one sequence or list data type; and then something like a struct or associative array. Many Python programmers are disappointed to learn that only positional arguments are typically supported, because so few other languages at this point support keyword arguments.

When an RPC mechanism is tied to a specific programming language, it is free to support a wider range of parameters. In some cases, even live objects can be passed if the protocol can figure out some way to rebuild them on the remote side. In this case, only objects backed by live operating system resources, like an open file, live socket, or area of shared memory, become impossible to pass over the network.

A second common feature is the ability of the server to signal that an exception occurred while it was running the remote function. In such cases, the client RPC library will typically raise an exception itself to tell the caller that something has gone wrong. Of course live stack frames of the sort that Python makes available to an exception handler typically cannot be passed back; each stack frame, after all, probably refers to modules that do not even exist in the client program. But at least some sort of proxy exception that gives the right error message must be raised on the client side of the RPC conversation when a call fails on the server.

Third, many RPC mechanisms provide introspection, which is a way for clients to list the calls that are supported by that particular RPC service, and perhaps to discover which arguments they take. Some heavyweight RPC protocols actually require the client and server to exchange large documents describing the library or API they support; others just allow the client to fetch the list of function names and argument types; and other RPC implementations support no introspection at all. Python tends to be a bit weak in supporting introspection because Python, unlike a statically typed language, does not know which argument types are intended by the programmer who has written each function.

Fourth, each RPC mechanism needs to support some addressing scheme whereby you can reach out and connect to a particular remote API. Some such mechanisms are quite complicated, and they might even have the ability to connect you automatically to the correct server on your network for performing a particular task, without your having to know its name beforehand. Other mechanisms are quite simple and just ask you for the IP address, port number, or URL of the service you want to access. These mechanisms expose the underlying network addressing scheme, rather than creating a scheme of their own.

Finally, some RPC mechanisms support authentication, access control, and even full impersonation of particular user accounts when RPC calls are made by several different client programs wielding different credentials. But features like these are not always available; and, in fact, simple and popular RPC mechanisms usually lack them entirely. Simple RPC schemes use an underlying protocol like HTTP that provides its own authentication, and they leave it up to you to configure whatever passwords, public keys, or firewall rules are necessary to secure the lower-level protocol if you want your RPC service protected from arbitrary access.

XML-RPC

Let's begin this brief tour of RPC mechanisms by looking at the facilities built into Python for speaking XML-RPC. This might seem like a poor choice for the first example. After all, XML is famously clunky and verbose, and the popularity of XML-RPC in new services has been declining for years.

But XML-RPC has native support in Python's Standard Library precisely because it was one of the first RPC protocols of the Internet age, operating natively over HTTP instead of insisting on its own on-the-wire protocol. This means that the examples presented here will not even require third-party modules. Although this makes the RPC server somewhat less capable than if a third-party library were used, this will also make the examples simple for this initial foray into RPC.

THE XML-RPC PROTOCOL

Purpose: Remote procedure calls

Standard: `www.xmlrpc.com/spec`

Runs atop: HTTP

Data types: `int`; `float`; `unicode`; `list`; `dict` with `unicode` keys; with nonstandard extensions, `datetime` and `None`

Libraries: `xmlrpclib`, `SimpleXMLRPCServer`, `DocXMLRPCServer`

If you have ever used raw XML, then you are familiar with the fact that it lacks any data-type semantics. It cannot represent numbers, for example, but only *elements* that contain other elements, text strings, and text-string attributes. Thus the XML-RPC specification has to build additional semantics on top of the plain XML document format in order to specify how things like numbers should look when converted into marked-up text.

The Python Standard Library makes it easy to write either an XML-RPC client or server. Listing 18-1 shows a basic server that starts a web server on port 7001 and then listens for incoming Internet connections.

Listing 18-1. An XML-RPC Server

```
#!/usr/bin/env python3
# Foundations of Python Network Programming, Third Edition
# https://github.com/brandon-rhodes/fopnp/blob/m/py3/chapter18/xmlrpc_server.py
# XML-RPC server
```

```
import operator, math
from xmlrpc.server import SimpleXMLRPCServer
from functools import reduce

def main():
    server = SimpleXMLRPCServer(('127.0.0.1', 7001))
    server.register_introspection_functions()
    server.register_multicall_functions()
    server.register_function(addtogether)
    server.register_function(quadratic)
    server.register_function(remote_repr)
    print("Server ready")
    server.serve_forever()

def addtogether(*things):
    """Add together everything in the list `things`."""
    return reduce(operator.add, things)

def quadratic(a, b, c):
    """Determine `x` values satisfying: `a` * x*x + `b` * x + c == 0"""
    b24ac = math.sqrt(b*b - 4.0*a*c)
    return list(set([ (-b-b24ac) / 2.0*a,
                      (-b+b24ac) / 2.0*a ]))

def remote_repr(arg):
    """Return the `repr()` rendering of the supplied `arg`."""
    return arg

if __name__ == '__main__':
    main()
```

An XML-RPC service lives at a single URL of a web site, so you do not actually have to dedicate an entire port to an RPC service like this. Instead, you can integrate it with a normal web application that offers all sorts of other pages, or even separate RPC services, at other URLs. But if you do have an entire port to spare, then the Python XML-RPC server offers an easy way to bring up a web server that does nothing but talk XML-RPC.

You can see that the three sample functions that the server offers over XML-RPC (the ones that are added to the RPC service through the register_function() calls) are quite typical Python functions. And that again is the whole point of XML-RPC—it lets you make routines available for invocation over the network without having to write them any differently than if they were normal functions offered inside your program.

The SimpleXMLRPCServer offered by the Python Standard Library is, as its name implies, quite simple; it cannot offer other web pages, it does not understand any kind of HTTP authentication, and you cannot ask it to offer TLS security without subclassing it yourself and adding more code. Nevertheless, it will serve the purposes here admirably, showing you some of the basic features and limits of RPC while also letting you get up and running in only a few lines of code.

Note that two additional configuration calls are made in addition to the three calls that register the functions. Each of them turns on an additional service that is optional but often provided by XML-RPC servers: an introspection routine that a client can use to ask which RPC calls are supported by a given server, and the ability to support a *multicall* function that lets several individual function calls be bundled together into a single network roundtrip.

This server will need to be running before you can try any of the next three program listings, so bring up a command window and get it started:

```
$ python xmlrpc_server.py
Server ready
```

The server is now waiting for connections on localhost port 7001. All of the normal addressing rules apply to this TCP server that you learned in Chapters 2 and 3, so unless you adjust the code to bind to an interface other than localhost, you will have to connect to it from another command prompt on the same system. Begin by opening another command window and get ready to try out the next three listings as I review them.

First, let's try the introspection capability you turned on in this particular server. Note that this ability is optional, and it may not be available on many other XML-RPC services that you use online or that you deploy yourself. Listing 18-2 shows how introspection happens from the client's point of view.

Listing 18-2. Asking an XML-RPC Server What Functions It Supports

```
#!/usr/bin/env python3
# Foundations of Python Network Programming, Third Edition
# github.com/brandon-rhodes/fopnp/blob/m/py3/chapter18/xmlrpc_introspect.py
# XML-RPC client

import xmlrpc.client

def main():
    proxy = xmlrpc.client.ServerProxy('http://127.0.0.1:7001')

    print('Here are the functions supported by this server:')
    for method_name in proxy.system.listMethods():

        if method_name.startswith('system.'):
            continue

        signatures = proxy.system.methodSignature(method_name)
        if isinstance(signatures, list) and signatures:
            for signature in signatures:
                print('%s(%s)' % (method_name, signature))
        else:
            print('%s(...)' % (method_name,))

        method_help = proxy.system.methodHelp(method_name)
        if method_help:
            print('   ', method_help)

if __name__ == '__main__':
    main()
```

The introspection mechanism is not just an optional extension, and it is not actually defined in the XML-RPC specification itself! It lets the client call a series of special methods that all begin with the string `system` to distinguish them from normal methods. These special methods give information about the other calls available. Let's start by calling `listMethods()`. If introspection is supported at all, then you will receive back a list of other method names. For this example listing, let's ignore the system methods and only proceed to print out information about the other ones.

For each method, you'll attempt to retrieve its *signature* to learn what arguments and data types it accepts. Because the server is written in Python, a language without type declarations, it does not actually know what data types the functions expect:

```
$ python xmlrpc_introspect.py
Here are the functions supported by this server:
concatenate(...)
    Add together everything in the list `things`.
quadratic(...)
    Determine `x` values satisfying: `a` * x*x + `b` * x + c == 0
remote_repr(...)
    Return the `repr()` rendering of the supplied `arg`.
```

However, you can see that, while parameter types are not given in this case, documentation strings are indeed provided. In fact, the SimpleXMLRPCServer has fetched the function's docstrings and returned them. There are two uses that you might find for introspection in a real-world client. First, if you are writing a program that uses a particular XML-RPC service, then its online documentation might provide human-readable help. Second, if you are writing a client that is hitting a series of similar XML-RPC services that vary in the methods they provide, then a listMethods() call might help you work out which servers offer which commands.

You will recall that the whole point of an RPC service is to make function calls in a target language look as natural as possible. Moreover, as you can see in Listing 18-3, the Standard Library's xmlrpclib gives you a *proxy* object for making function calls against the server. These calls look exactly like local method calls.

Listing 18-3. Making XML-RPC Calls

```python
#!/usr/bin/env python3
# -*- coding: utf-8 -*-
# Foundations of Python Network Programming, Third Edition
# https://github.com/brandon-rhodes/fopnp/blob/m/py3/chapter18/xmlrpc_client.py
# XML-RPC client

import xmlrpc.client

def main():
    proxy = xmlrpc.client.ServerProxy('http://127.0.0.1:7001')
    print(proxy.addtogether('x', 'ÿ', 'z'))
    print(proxy.addtogether(20, 30, 4, 1))
    print(proxy.quadratic(2, -4, 0))
    print(proxy.quadratic(1, 2, 1))
    print(proxy.remote_repr((1, 2.0, 'three')))
    print(proxy.remote_repr([1, 2.0, 'three']))
    print(proxy.remote_repr({'name': 'Arthur',
                             'data': {'age': 42, 'sex': 'M'}}))
    print(proxy.quadratic(1, 0, 1))

if __name__ == '__main__':
    main()
```

Running the preceding code against the example server produces output from which you can learn several things about XML-RPC in particular and RPC mechanisms in general. Note how almost all of the calls work without a hitch and how both of the calls in this listing and the functions themselves from Listing 18-1 look like completely normal Python; there is nothing about them that is specific to a network:

```
$ python xmlrpc_client.py
xÿz
55
[0.0, 8.0]
[-1.0]
[1, 2.0, 'three']
[1, 2.0, 'three']
{'data': {'age': [42], 'sex': 'M'}, 'name': 'Arthur'}
Traceback (most recent call last):
  ...
xmlrpclib.Fault: <Fault 1: "<type 'exceptions.ValueError'>:math domain error">
```

But there are several details to which you will want to pay attention. First, note that XML-RPC is not imposing any restrictions on the argument types you are supplying. You can call addtogether() with either strings or numbers, and you can supply any number of arguments. The protocol itself does not care; it has no preconceived notion of how many arguments a function should take or what its types should be. Of course, if you were making calls to a language that did care—or even to a Python function that did not support variable-length argument lists—then the remote language could raise an exception. But that would be the language complaining, not the XML-RPC protocol itself.

Second, note that XML-RPC function calls, like those of Python and many other languages in its lineage, can take several arguments, but they can only return a single result value. That value might be a complex data structure, but it will be returned as a single result. And the protocol does not care whether that result has a consistent shape or size; the list returned by quadratic() (yes, I was tired of all of the simple add() and subtract() math functions that tend to get used in XML-RPC examples!) varies in the number of elements returned without any complaint from the network logic.

Third, note that the rich variety of Python data types must be reduced to the smaller set that XML-RPC itself happens to support. In particular, XML-RPC only supports a single sequence type: the list. So when you supply remote_repr() with a tuple of three items, it is actually a list of three items that gets received at the server. This is a common feature of all RPC mechanisms when they are coupled with a particular language. Types they do not directly support either have to be mapped to a different data structure (as the tuple was here turned into a list) or an exception has to be raised complaining that a particular argument type cannot be transmitted.

Fourth, complex data structures in XML-RPC can be recursive. You are not restricted to arguments that have only one level of complex data type inside. Passing a dictionary with another dictionary as one of its values works just fine, as you can see.

Finally, note that, as promised earlier, an exception in the function on the server made it successfully back across the network and was represented locally on the client by an xmlrpclib.Fault instance. This instance provided the remote exception name and the error message associated with it. Whatever language was used to implement the server routines, you can always expect XML-RPC exceptions to have this structure. The traceback is not terribly informative; while it tells you which call in the code triggered the exception, the innermost levels of the stack are simply the code of the xmlrpclib itself.

Thus far I've covered the general features and restrictions of XML-RPC. If you consult the documentation for either the client or the server module in the Python Standard Library, you can learn about a few more features. In particular, you can learn how to use TLS and authentication by supplying more arguments to the ServerProxy class. But one feature is important enough to cover here: the ability to make several calls in a network roundtrip when the server supports it (it is another one of those optional extensions), as shown in Listing 18-4.

Listing 18-4. Using XML-RPC Multicall

```python
#!/usr/bin/env python3
# Foundations of Python Network Programming, Third Edition
#   github.com/brandon-rhodes/fopnp/blob/m/py3/chapter18/xmlrpc_multicall.py
# XML-RPC client performing a multicall

import xmlrpc.client

def main():
    proxy = xmlrpc.client.ServerProxy('http://127.0.0.1:7001')
    multicall = xmlrpc.client.MultiCall(proxy)
    multicall.addtogether('a', 'b', 'c')
    multicall.quadratic(2, -4, 0)
    multicall.remote_repr([1, 2.0, 'three'])
    for answer in multicall():
        print(answer)

if __name__ == '__main__':
    main()
```

When you run this script, you can watch the server's command window to confirm that only a single HTTP request is made in order to answer all three function calls that get made:

```
localhost - - [04/Oct/2010 00:16:19] "POST /RPC2 HTTP/1.0" 200 -
```

The ability to log messages like the preceding one can be turned off, by the way; such logging is controlled by one of the options in SimpleXMLRPCServer. Note that the default URL used by both the server and the client is the path /RPC2, unless you consult the documentation and configure the client and server differently.

Three final points are worth mentioning before I move on to examine another RPC mechanism:

- There are two additional data types that sometimes prove hard to live without, so many XML-RPC mechanisms support them: dates and the value that Python calls None (other languages call this null or nil). Python's client and server both support options that will enable the transmission and reception of these nonstandard values.

- Keyword arguments are, alas, not supported by XML-RPC because few languages are sophisticated enough to include them. Some services get around this by allowing a dictionary to be passed as a function's final argument—or by disposing of positional arguments altogether and using a single dictionary argument for every function that specifies all of its parameters by name.

- Finally, keep in mind that dictionaries can only be passed if all of their keys are strings, whether normal or Unicode. See the "Self-Documenting Data" section later in this chapter for more information on how to think about this restriction.

Although the entire point of an RPC protocol like XML-RPC is to let you forget about the details of network transmission and focus on normal programming, you should see what your calls will look like on the wire at least once! Here is the first call to quadratic() that the sample client program makes:

```xml
<?xml version='1.0'?>
<methodCall>
<methodName>quadratic</methodName>
```

```
<params>
<param>
<value><int>2</int></value>
</param>
<param>
<value><int>-4</int></value>
</param>
<param>
<value><int>0</int></value>
</param>
</params>
</methodCall>
```

The response to the preceding call looks like this:

```
<?xml version='1.0'?>
<methodResponse>
<params>
<param>
<value><array><data>
<value><double>0.0</double></value>
<value><double>8.0</double></value>
</data></array></value>
</param>
</params>
</methodResponse>
```

If this response looks a bit verbose for the amount of data that it is transmitting, then you will be happy to learn about the RPC mechanism that I'll tackle next, JSON-RPC.

JSON-RPC

The bright idea behind JSON is to serialize data structures to strings that use the syntax of the JavaScript programming language. This means that JSON strings could, in theory, be turned back into data in a web browser simply by using the eval() function. (However, doing so with untrusted data is generally unwise, so most programmers use a formal JSON parser instead of taking advantage of its compatibility with JavaScript.) By using a syntax specifically designed for data rather than adapting a verbose document markup language like XML, this remote procedure call mechanism can make your data much more compact while simultaneously simplifying your parsers and library code.

THE JSON-RPC PROTOCOL

Purpose: Remote procedure calls

Standard: http://json-rpc.org/wiki/specification

Runs atop: HTTP

Data types: int; float; unicode; list; dict with unicode keys; None

Libraries: many third-party, including jsonrpclib

JSON-RPC is not supported in the Python Standard Library, so you will have to choose one of the several third-party distributions available. You can find these distributions on the Python Package Index. One of the first to officially support Python 3 is jsonrpclib-pelix. If you install it in a virtual environment (see Chapter 1), then you can try out the server and client presented in Listings 18-5 and 18-6, respectively.

Listing 18-5. A JSON-RPC Server

```
#!/usr/bin/env python3
# Foundations of Python Network Programming, Third Edition
# github.com/brandon-rhodes/fopnp/blob/m/py3/chapter18/jsonrpc_server.py
# JSON-RPC server needing "pip install jsonrpclib-pelix"

from jsonrpclib.SimpleJSONRPCServer import SimpleJSONRPCServer

def lengths(*args):
    """Measure the length of each input argument.

    Given N arguments, this function returns a list of N smaller
    lists of the form [len(arg), arg] that each state the length of
    an input argument and also echo back the argument itself.

    """
    results = []
    for arg in args:
        try:
            arglen = len(arg)
        except TypeError:
            arglen = None
        results.append((arglen, arg))
    return results

def main():
    server = SimpleJSONRPCServer(('localhost', 7002))
    server.register_function(lengths)
    print("Starting server")
    server.serve_forever()

if __name__ == '__main__':
    main()
```

The server code is quite simple, as an RPC mechanism should be. As with XML-RPC, you merely need to name the functions you want offered over the network, and they become available for queries. (You can also pass an object, and its methods will be registered with the server all at once.)

Listing 18-6. JSON-RPC Client

```
#!/usr/bin/env python3
# Foundations of Python Network Programming, Third Edition
# github.com/brandon-rhodes/fopnp/blob/m/py3/chapter18/jsonrpc_client.py
# JSON-RPC client needing "pip install jsonrpclib-pelix"
```

```
from jsonrpclib import Server

def main():
    proxy = Server('http://localhost:7002')
    print(proxy.lengths((1,2,3), 27, {'Sirius': -1.46, 'Rigel': 0.12}))

if __name__ == '__main__':
    main()
```

Writing client code is also quite simple. Sending several objects whose lengths you want measured—and having those data structures echoed right back by the server—enables you to see several details about this particular protocol.

First, note that the protocol allows you to send as many arguments as you want; it was not bothered by the fact that it could not introspect a static method signature from the function. This is similar to XML-RPC, but it is very different from XML-RPC mechanisms built for traditional, statically typed languages.

Second, note that the None value in the server's reply passes back unhindered. This is because this value is supported natively by the protocol itself, without having to activate any nonstandard extensions:

```
$ python jsonrpc_server.py
Starting server

[In another command window:]
$ python jsonrpc_client.py
[[3, [1, 2, 3]], [None, 27], [2, {'Rigel': 0.12, 'Sirius': -1.46}]]
```

Third, note that there is only one kind of sequence supported by JSON-RPC, which means that the tuple sent by the client had to be coerced to a list to make it across.

Of course the biggest difference between JSON-RPC and XML-RPC—that the data payload in this case is a small, sleek JSON message that knows natively how to represent each of the data types—is not even visible here. This is because both mechanisms do such a good job of hiding the network from the code. When running Wireshark on my localhost interface while running this example client and server, I can see that the actual messages being passed are as follows:

```
{"version": "1.1",
 "params": [[1, 2, 3], 27, {"Rigel": 0.12, "Sirius": -1.46}],
 "method": "lengths"}
{"result": [[3, [1, 2, 3]], [null, 27],
            [2, {"Rigel": 0.12, "Sirius": -1.46}]]}
```

Note that the popularity of JSON-RPC version 1 has led to several competing attempts to extend and supplement the protocol with additional features. You can do research online if you want to explore the current state of the standard and the conversation around it. For most basic tasks, you can simply use a good third-party Python implementation and not worry about the debate over extensions to the standard.

It would be remiss of me to leave this topic without mentioning one important fact. Although the preceding example is synchronous—the client sends a request and then waits patiently to receive only a single response and does nothing useful in the meantime—the JSON-RPC protocol does support attaching id values to each request. This means that you can have several requests under way before receiving any matching responses back with the same id attached. I will not explore the idea any further here because asynchrony, strictly speaking, goes beyond the traditional role of an RPC mechanism. Function calls in traditional procedural languages are, after all, strictly synchronous events. However, if you find the idea interesting, you should read the standard and then explore which Python JSON-RPC libraries might support your need for asynchrony.

Self-Documenting Data

You have just seen that both XML-RPC and JSON-RPC appear to support a data structure very much like a Python dictionary, but with an annoying limitation. In XML-RPC, the data structure is called a *struct*, whereas JSON calls it an *object*. To the Python programmer, however, it looks like a dictionary, and your first reaction will probably be annoyance that its keys cannot be integers, floats, or tuples.

Let's look at a concrete example. Imagine that you have a dictionary of physical element symbols indexed by their atomic number:

```
{1: 'H', 2: 'He', 3: 'Li', 4: 'Be', 5: 'B', 6: 'C', 7: 'N', 8: 'O'}
```

If you need to transmit this dictionary over an RPC mechanism, your first instinct might be to change the numbers to strings so that the dictionary can pass as a struct or object. It turns out that, in most cases, this instinct is wrong.

Simply put, the struct and object RPC data structures are not designed to pair keys with values in containers of an arbitrary size. Instead, they are designed to associate a small set of predefined attribute names with the attribute values that they happen to carry for some particular object. If you try to use a struct to pair random keys and values, you might inadvertently make your service very difficult to use for people unfortunate enough to be using statically typed programming languages.

Instead, you should think of dictionaries being sent across RPCs as being like Python objects, which typically each have a small collection of attribute names that are well known to your code. In the same way, the dictionaries you send across RPC should associate a small number of predefined keys with their related values.

All of this means that the dictionary presented previously should actually be serialized as a list of explicitly labeled values if it is going to be used by a general-purpose RPC mechanism:

```
[{'number': 1, 'symbol': 'H'},
 {'number': 2, 'symbol': 'He'},
 {'number': 3, 'symbol': 'Li'},
 {'number': 4, 'symbol': 'Be'},
 {'number': 5, 'symbol': 'B'},
 {'number': 6, 'symbol': 'C'},
 {'number': 7, 'symbol': 'N'},
 {'number': 8, 'symbol': 'O'}]
```

Note that the preceding examples show the Python dictionary as you would pass it into your RPC call, not the way it would be represented on the wire.

The key difference in this approach (besides the fact that this dictionary is appallingly longer) is that the earlier data structure was meaningless unless you knew ahead of time what the keys and values meant. It relied on convention to give the data meaning. But here you are including names with the data, which makes it self-descriptive: someone looking at these data on the wire or in a program has a higher chance of guessing what they represent.

This is how both XML-RPC and JSON-RPC expect you to use their key-value types, and this is where the names *struct* and *object* came from. They are, respectively, the C-language and JavaScript terms for an entity that holds named attributes. Again, this makes them much closer to being like Python objects than Python dictionaries.

If you have a Python dictionary like the one being discussed here, you can turn it into an RPC-appropriate data structure and then change it back with code like this:

```
>>>elements = {1: 'H', 2: 'He'}
>>>t = [{'number': key, 'symbol': value} for key, value in elements.items()]
>>>t
[{'symbol': 'H', 'number': 1}, {'symbol': 'He', 'number': 2}]
>>> {obj['number']: obj['symbol']) for obj in t}
{1: 'H', 2: 'He'}
```

Using named tuples (as they exist in the most recent versions of Python) might be an even better way to marshal such values before sending them, if you find yourself creating and destroying too many dictionaries to make this transformation appealing.

Talking About Objects: Pyro and RPyC

If the idea of RPC was to make remote function calls look like local ones, then the two basic RPC mechanisms discussed previously actually fail pretty spectacularly. If the functions you were calling happened to only use basic data types in their arguments and return values, then XML-RPC and JSON-RPC work fine. But think of all of the occasions when you use more complex parameters and return values instead! What happens when you need to pass live objects? This is generally a very hard problem to solve for two reasons.

First, objects have different behaviors and semantics in different programming languages. Thus, mechanisms that support objects tend to either be restricted to one particular language or offer an anemic description of how an "object" can behave that is culled from the lowest common denominator of the languages it wants to support.

Second, it is often not clear how much state needs to travel with an object to make it useful on another computer. True, an RPC mechanism can just start recursively descending into an object's attributes and getting those values ready for transmission across the network. However, on systems of even moderate complexity, you can wind up walking most of the objects in memory by doing simple-minded recursion into attribute values. And having gathered up what might be megabytes of data for transmission, what are the chances that the remote end actually needs all of those data?

The alternative to sending the entire contents of every object passed as a parameter, or returned as a value, is to send only an object name that the remote end can use to ask questions about the object's attributes if it needs to. This means that just one item of a highly connected object graph can be quickly transmitted, and only those parts of the graph that the remote site actually needs wind up getting transmitted. However, both schemes often result in expensive and slow services, and they can make it very difficult to keep track of how one object is allowed to affect the answers provided by another service on the other end of the network.

In fact, the task that XML-RPC and JSON-RPC force upon you (i.e., breaking down the question you want to ask a remote service so simple data types can be easily transmitted) often winds up being, simply, the task of software architecture. The restriction placed on parameter and return value data types makes you think through your service to the point where you see exactly what the remote service needs and why. Therefore, I recommend against jumping to a more object-based RPC service simply to avoid having to design your remote services and figure out exactly which data they need to do their job.

There are several big-name RPC mechanisms like SOAP and CORBA that, to varying degrees, try to address the big questions of how to support objects that might live on one server while being passed to another server on behalf of a client program sending an RPC message from yet a third server. In general, Python programmers seem to avoid these RPC mechanisms like the plague, unless a contract or assignment specifically requires them to speak these protocols to another existing system. They are beyond the scope of this book; and, if you need to use them, you should be prepared to buy at least an entire book on each such technology, as they can be that complex!

However, when all you have are Python programs that need to talk to each other, there is at least one excellent reason to look for an RPC service that knows about Python objects and their ways. Python has a number of very powerful data types, so it can simply be unreasonable to try "talking down" to the dialect of limited data formats like XML-RPC and JSON-RPC. This is especially true when Python dictionaries, sets, and `datetime` objects would express exactly what you want to say.

There are two Python-native RPC systems that I should mention: *Pyro* and *RPyC*. The Pyro project can be found at `http://pythonhosted.org/Pyro4/`. This well-established RPC library is built on top of the Python `pickle` module, and it can send any kind of argument and response value that is inherently *pickle-able*. Basically, this means that if an object and its attributes can be reduced to its basic types, then it can be transmitted. However, if the values you want to send or receive are ones that the `pickle` module chokes on, then Pyro will not work for your situation. (Though you could also check out the `pickle` documentation in the Python Standard Library. This library includes instructions on making classes pickle-able if Python cannot figure out how to pickle them itself.)

An RPyC Example

The RPyC project can be found at http://rpyc.readthedocs.org/en/latest/. This project takes a much more sophisticated approach toward objects. Indeed, it is more like the approach available in CORBA, where what actually gets passed across the network is a reference to an object that can be used to call back and invoke more of its methods later if the receiver needs to. The most recent version also seems to have put more thought into security, which is important if you are letting other organizations use your RPC mechanism. After all, if you let someone give you some data to unpickle, you are essentially letting them run arbitrary code on your computer!

You can see an example client and server in Listings 18-7 and 18-8, respectively. If you want an example of the incredible kinds of things that a system like RPyC makes possible, you should study these listings closely.

Listing 18-7. An RPyC Client

```python
#!/usr/bin/env python3
# Foundations of Python Network Programming, Third Edition
# https://github.com/brandon-rhodes/fopnp/blob/m/py3/chapter18/rpyc_client.py
# RPyC client

import rpyc

def main():
    config = {'allow_public_attrs': True}
    proxy = rpyc.connect('localhost', 18861, config=config)
    fileobj = open('testfile.txt')
    linecount = proxy.root.line_counter(fileobj, noisy)
    print('The number of lines in the file was', linecount)

def noisy(string):
    print('Noisy:', repr(string))

if __name__ == '__main__':
    main()
```

Listing 18-8. An RPyC Server

```python
#!/usr/bin/env python3
# Foundations of Python Network Programming, Third Edition
# https://github.com/brandon-rhodes/fopnp/blob/m/py3/chapter18/rpyc_server.py
# RPyC server

import rpyc

def main():
    from rpyc.utils.server import ThreadedServer
    t = ThreadedServer(MyService, port = 18861)
    t.start()

class MyService(rpyc.Service):
    def exposed_line_counter(self, fileobj, function):
        print('Client has invoked exposed_line_counter()')
```

```
        for linenum, line in enumerate(fileobj.readlines()):
            function(line)
        return linenum + 1

if __name__ == '__main__':
    main()
```

At first, the client might look like a rather standard program using an RPC service. After all, it calls a generically named connect() function with a network address and then accesses methods of the returned proxy object as though the calls were being performed locally. However, if you look closer, you will see some startling differences! The first argument to the RPC function is actually a live file object that does not necessarily exist on the server. The other argument is a function; another live object instead of the kind of inert data structure that RPC mechanisms usually support.

The server exposes a single method that takes the proffered file object and callable function. It uses these exactly as you would in a normal Python program that was happening inside a single process. It calls the file object's readlines(), and it expects the return value to be an iterator over which a for loop can repeat. Finally, the server calls the function object that has been passed in without any regard for where the function actually lives (namely, in the client). Note that RPyC's new security model dictates that, absent any special permission, it will only allow clients to call methods that start with the special prefix exposed_.

It is especially instructive to look at the output generated by running the client, assuming that a small testfile.txt indeed exists in the current directory and that it has a few words of wisdom inside:

```
$ python rpyc_client.py
Noisy: 'Simple\n'
Noisy: 'is\n'
Noisy: 'better\n'
Noisy: 'than\n'
Noisy: 'complex.\n'
The number of lines in the file was 5
```

Equally startling here are two facts. First, the server was able to iterate over multiple results from readlines(), even though this required the repeated invocation of file–object logic that lived on the client. Second, the server didn't somehow copy the noisy() function's code object so that it could run the function directly; instead, it repeatedly invoked the function, with the correct argument each time, on the client side of the connection!

How is this happening? Quite simply, RPyC takes exactly the opposite approach from the other RPC mechanisms examined previously. Whereas all of the other techniques try to serialize and send as much information across the network as possible and then leave the remote code to either succeed or fail with no further information, the RPyC scheme only serializes completely immutable items, such as Python integers, floats, strings, and tuples. For everything else, it passes across a remote object identifier that lets the remote side reach back into the client to access attributes and invoke methods on those live objects.

This approach results in quite a bit of network traffic. It can also result in a significant delay if lots of object operations have to pass back and forth between the client and server before an operation is complete. Establishing proper security is also an issue. To give the server permission to call things like readlines() on the client's own objects, I chose to make the client connection with a blanket assertion of allow_public_attrs. But if you are not comfortable giving your server code such complete control, then you might have to spend a bit of time getting the permissions exactly right for your operations to work without exposing too much potentially dangerous functionality.

So the technique can be expensive, and security can be tricky if the client and server do not trust each other. But when you need it, there is really nothing like RPyC for letting Python objects on opposite sides of a network boundary cooperate with each other. You can even let more than two processes play the game; check out the RPyC documentation for more details!

The fact that RPyC works successfully like this against vanilla Python functions and objects, without any requirement that they inherit from or mix in any special network capabilities, is an incredible testament to the power that Python gives us to intercept operations performed on an object and handle those events in our own way—even by asking a question across the network!

RPC, Web Frameworks, and Message Queues

Be willing to explore alternative transmission mechanisms for your work with RPC services. The classes provided in the Python Standard Library for XML-RPC, for example, are not even used by many Python programmers who need to speak that protocol. After all, one often deploys an RPC service as part of a larger web site, and having to run a separate server on a separate port for this particular type of web request can be quite annoying.

There are three useful ways you can look into moving beyond overly simple example code that makes it look as though you have to bring up a new web server for every RPC service you want to make available from a particular site.

First, look into whether you can use the pluggability of WSGI to let you install an RPC service that you have incorporated into a larger web project you are deploying. Implementing both your normal web application and your RPC service as WSGI servers beneath a filter that checks the incoming URL enables you to allow both services to live at the same hostname and port number. It also lets you take advantage of the fact that your WSGI web server might already provide threading and scalability at a level the RPC service itself does not provide natively.

Putting your RPC service at the bottom of a larger WSGI stack can also gives you a way to add authentication if the RPC service itself lacks such a facility. See Chapter 11 for more information about WSGI.

Second, instead of using a dedicated RPC library, you may find that your web framework of choice already knows how to host an XML-RPC, JSON-RPC, or some other flavor of RPC call. This means that you can declare RPC endpoints with the same ease that your web framework lets you define views or RESTful resources. Consult your web framework documentation and do a web search for RPC-friendly third-party plug-ins.

Third, you might want to try sending RPC messages over an alternate transport that does a better job than the protocol's native transport of routing the calls to servers that are ready to handle them. Message queues, which were discussed in Chapter 8, are often an excellent vehicle for RPC calls when you want a whole rack of servers to stay busy sharing the load of incoming requests.

Recovering from Network Errors

Of course, there is one reality of life on the network that RPC services cannot easily hide: the network can be down when you attempt to initiate a call, or it can even go down in the middle of a particular RPC call.

You will find that most RPC mechanisms simply raise an exception if a call is interrupted and does not complete. Note that an error, unfortunately, is no guarantee that the remote end did not process the request—maybe it actually did finish processing it, but then the network went down right as the last packet of the reply was being sent. In this case, your call would have technically occurred, and the data would have been successfully added to the database or written to a file or whatever the RPC call does. However, you will think the call failed and want to try it again—possibly storing the same data twice. Fortunately, there are a few tricks you can use when writing code that delegate some function calls across the network.

First, try to write services that offer idempotent operations that can safely be retried. Although an operation like "remove $10 from my bank account" is inherently unsafe, because retrying it might remove another $10 from your account, an operation like "perform transaction 583812 which removes $10 from my account" is perfectly safe because the server can, by storing the transaction number, determine that your request is actually a repeat and can report success without actually repeating the deduction.

Second, take the advice offered in Chapter 5: instead of littering your code with a try...except everywhere that an RPC call is made, try using try and except to wrap larger pieces of code that have a solid semantic meaning and can more cleanly be reattempted or recovered from. If you guard each and every call with an exception handler, you will have lost most of the benefit of RPC: your code is supposed to be convenient to write and not make you constantly attend to the fact that function calls are actually being forwarded over the network! In cases where you decide that your program should retry a failed call, you might want to try using something like the exponential back-off algorithm for UDP discussed in Chapter 3. This approach lets you avoid hammering an overloaded service and making the situation worse.

Finally, be careful about working around the loss of exception detail across the network. Unless you are using a Python-aware RPC mechanism, you will probably find that what would normally be a familiar and friendly `KeyError` or `ValueError` on the remote side becomes some sort of RPC-specific error whose text or numeric error code you have to inspect in order to have any chance of telling what happened.

Summary

RPC lets you write what look like normal Python function calls, which actually reach across the network and call a function on another server. They do this by serializing the parameters so they can be transmitted; they then do the same with the return value that is sent back.

All RPC mechanisms work pretty much the same way: you set up a network connection and then make calls on the proxy object that you are given in order to invoke code on the remote end. The old XML-RPC protocol is natively supported in the Python Standard Library, while good third-party libraries exist for the sleeker and more modern JSON-RPC.

Both of these mechanisms allow only a handful of data types to pass between the client and server. If you want a much more complete array of the Python data types available, then you should look at the Pyro system, which can link Python programs across the network with extensive support for native Python types. The RPyC system is even more extensive, and it allows actual objects to be passed between systems in such a way that method calls on those objects are forwarded to the system on which the object actually lives.

Looking back over the material in this book, you will be tempted to begin seeing every single chapter as somehow about RPC; that is, about the exchange of information between a client program and a server, mediated by an agreement about what a request will involve and how a response will look. Now that you have learned RPC, you have seen this exchange at its most general, designed not to support any one specific action but to support arbitrary communication. When implementing new services—and especially when you're tempted to use RPC—always consider whether your problem really needs the flexibility of RPC or whether the transaction between your client and server might be reduced to one of the simpler, limited-purpose protocols from earlier in this book. If you select the right protocol for each problem you face, incurring no more complexity than is necessary, you will be well rewarded by networked systems that are simple, reliable, and easy to maintain.

Index

■ X, Y

■ Z

Get the eBook for only $10!

> Now you can take the weightless companion with you anywhere, anytime. Your purchase of this book entitles you to 3 electronic versions for only $10.

This Apress title will prove so indispensible that you'll want to carry it with you everywhere, which is why we are offering the eBook in **3 formats** for only $10 if you have already purchased the print book.

Convenient and fully searchable, the PDF version enables you to easily find and copy code—or perform examples by quickly toggling between instructions and applications. The MOBI format is ideal for your Kindle, while the ePUB can be utilized on a variety of mobile devices.

Go to www.apress.com/promo/tendollars to purchase your companion eBook.

Apress®
THE EXPERT'S VOICE™

Lightning Source UK Ltd.
Milton Keynes UK
UKOW05f0707180716

278535UK00013B/290/P